Global Food Security

Concern, Reality and Remedies

Global Food Security

Concern, Reality and Remedies

Edited by

Dr. Seema Joshi

Mr. Anil Dongre

Dr. Sameer Narkhede

Himalaya Publishing House

MUMBAI • NEW DELHI • NAGPUR • BENGALURU • HYDERABAD • CHENNAI • PUNE • LUCKNOW • AHMEDABAD • ERNAKULAM • BHUBANESWAR • INDORE

First Edition: 2010

Published by : Mrs. Meena Pandey
for **HIMALAYA PUBLISHING HOUSE PVT. LTD.,**
"Ramdoot", Dr. Bhalerao Marg, Girgaon, **Mumbai - 400 004.**
Phones: 2386 01 70/2386 38 63, Fax: 022-2387 71 78
Email: himpub@vsnl.com
Website: www.himpub.com

Branch Offices:

New Delhi : "Pooja Apartments", 4-B, Murari Lal Street, Ansari Road, Darya Ganj, **New Delhi - 110 002.** Phone: 23270392, 23278631 Fax: 011-23256286

Nagpur : Kundanlal Chandak Industrial Estate, Ghat Road, **Nagpur - 440 018.** Phone: 2738731, 3296733 Telefax : 0712-2721215

Bengaluru : No. 16/1 (Old 12/1), 1st Floor, Next to Hotel Highlands, Madhava Nagar, Race Course Road, **Bengaluru - 560 001.** Phone : 22281541, 22385461, Telefax: 080-22286611

Hyderabad : No. 3-4-184, Lingampally, Besides Raghavendra Swamy Matham,Kachiguda, **Hyderabad - 500 027.** Phone: 040-27560041, 27550139, Mobile:- 09848130433 Telefax: 040-27560041

Chennai : No. 85/50, Bazullah Road, T. Nagar, **Chennai - 600 017.** Phone: 044-28344020, 32463737, 42124860

Pune : No. 527, "Laksha" Apartment, 1st Floor, Mehunpura, Shaniwarpeth, (Near Prabhat Theatre), **Pune - 411 030.** Phone: 020-24496323/24496333/32326733

Lucknow : C-43, Sector - C, Ali Gunj, **Lucknow - 226 024.** Phone: 0522-2339329, 4068914

Ahmedabad : No. 114, "SHAIL", 1st Floor, Opp. Madhu Sudan House, C.G.Road, Navrang Pura, **Ahmedabad – 380 009.** Phone: 079-26560126, Mobiles: 09327324149,09314679413

Ernakulam : No. 39/104 A, Lakshmi Apartment, Karikkamuri Cross Rd., Ernakulam, **Cochin – 682011**, Kerala. Phone: 0484-2378012, 2378016, Mob.: 09344199799

Bhubaneswar : 5 Station Square, **Bhubaneswar (Orissa) - 751 001.** Mobile: 9861046007, E-mail:- orissa@himpub.com

Indore : Kesardeep Avenue Extension, 73, Narayan Bagh, Flat No. 302, 3rd Floor, Near Humpty Dumpty School, Narayan Bagh, **Indore (M.P.) 452 007** Mobile: 09301386468

DTP by : HPH Editorial Office, Bhandup (Pushpa)

Printed by : Prabhat Book Binder, Mumbai.

Foreword

It is a great pleasure to know that the Department of Management Studies of this university is going to publish a book based on the papers presented at International Conference on ***"Global Food Security: Concern, Reality and Remedies"***. This international conference is organise by this university in collaboration with CETYS University, Mexico during January 28-29, 2010 which articulated a global vision for eliminating food insecurity.

Being the Chief Patron, I had the opportunity to inaugurate the conference, the theme of which has been concern of the world all over.

The estimate of world food production clearly indicates that the food produced in the world per capita is enough to feed almost twice the population of planet earth. This dismisses the myth that there is not enough food in the world. Today millions of people die every year because of hunger and malnutrition arising out of insufficient food. At the global level, the South Asian region is home to more chronically food insecure people that any other regions in the world and India ranks 94th in the Global Hunger Index of 119 countries. This is probably due to high economic growth rates have failed to improve food security in India leaving the country facing a crisis in its rural economy.

Suppose Food Security can be attained by eradicating the root causes of Food Insecurity, further stringent policy initiative should be implemented in right spirit.

The papers included in this book rightly focus on the present status of global food security, causes of Food insecurity. Some of the papers throw light on the concern to be focused on and remedial measures taken with respect to food security.

I hope that the views and suggestions made by the authors from academics and industries across the world will definitely lead to the attainment of very objective of food security all over the world.

(Dr. K. B. Patil)
Vice-Chancellor

Preface

Food security involves every individual gaining physical, economic, social and environmental access to a balanced diet that includes the necessary macro and micro-nutrients, safe drinking water, sanitation, environmental hygiene, primary health care and education so as to lead a healthy and productive life. The food should originate from efficient and environmentally benign production technologies that conserve and enhance the natural resource base of crops, farm animals, forestry, inland and marine fisheries. According to United Nations Food and Agriculture Organization food security means, every individual should get enough food by maintaining human dignity.

Paradoxically, economic growths in many countries all over the world have failed to improve the food security. Rise in the food prices all over the world is also a matter of concern along with its access and availability. Thus, there is a need to create a Universal Public Distribution System with uniform prices affordable to the poor and the allocation should be based on the number of consumption units in the household.

Considering the figures indicating the chronically food insecure people all over the world, this book intends to focus the issue of 'Global Food Security: Concern, Realities and Remedies'.

The 'concern' deals with the following aspects such as – Food Security: global scenario, Food Security: historical perspective, causes and consequences of food insecurity, role of government, local bodies and NGOs in attaining food security, governance and policy process for food security, developing rural and urban linkage for food security, controlling poverty through food security.

The 'Reality' portray the issues like — food security in developing and developed countries: causes and dimensions, Green revolution and food security, climate change and food security, role of national and international organizations in attaining food security, Impact of technological innovations on food security, role of India and Mexico in global and domestic food security, agricultural development and food security.

Finally, the 'Remedies' are the futuristic in nature, suggesting the measures to be adopted by the policymakers, researchers and professionals. They are – reorientation of economic policies for securing food security, outsourcing of food production, towards a knowledge system for sustainable food security, rehabilitation of waste land and precision farming, water resource management and food security, legal framework for attaining food security, strategic considerations for managing food security, role of finance in maintaining food security. The 'Remedies' could be in the form of 'International Food Security Mission', 'International Food Security Law' and many others instrumental in attaining the mission of global food security.

This book is an outcome of the joint international conference organized by the Department of Management Studies, North Maharashtra University, Jalgaon (MS) India and CETYS University, Baja California, Mexico, CETYS and NMU are partners in various activities for the last couple of years and the cooperation has proved to be one of the most fruitful relationship between the two universities.

The wonderful response from researchers, scholars and industry has helped us to boost our confidence and we look forward to even greater heights. I am highly indebted to the Dr. K. B. Patil, Vice-Chancellor, North Maharashtra University for his continuous support and critique. I gratefully acknowledge the cooperation and support extended by ING. Enrique Blancas, President, CETYS University, Mexico. I also appreciate the support extended by my colleagues, Mr. Anil Dongre and Dr. Sameer Narkhede.Thanks are also due to Mr. K. Surendra of Himalaya Publishing House for nice and timely publication of the book. Last but not the least, thanks to all the team-members from both the universities.

Dr. Seema Joshi

January 2010

List of Contributors

1. **Agrawal Preeti V. & Jain S.D.,** G.H. Raisoni's Institute of Information Technology, Jalgaon, Jain Irrigation Systems Ltd, Jalgaon
2. **Asthana Shaily,** Sinhgad College of Commerce Kondhwa (Bk.), Pune
3. **Azuz-Adeath Isaac,** CETYS-University(Mexico). Engineering School and Master Program in Environment and Sustainable Development. Km 1 Camino Microondas Trinidad S/N, Ensenada, Baja California, Mexico, c.p. 22800
4. **Bendale Shilpa,** Management Department, KCES's COEIT, Jalgaon
5. **Bharambe Shailendra M. and Mahulikar Pramod P.,** School of Chemical Sciences, North Maharashtra University, Jalgaon
6. **Chavan R. R. and Pathak R. C.,** Department of Management Studies, North Maharashtra University, Jalgaon JSPM's Group of Institutions, Wagholi, Pune
7. **Dahad Mamata S. and Chaudhari Anupama P.,** Institute of Management and Research, Jalgaon
8. **Ekhande Kirtikumar,** Shreeyash Institute of Management, Aurangabad
9. **Gadekar Sonali,** MET – Institute of Management Bhujbal Knowledge City, Nashik
10. **Gaikwad Anuradha and Gaikwad Uday,** MBA Unit Shivaji University and Vigyan Prabhodini, Kolhapur
11. **Gharde Sanjay S.,** College of Engineering and Technology, Bambhori (Jalgaon)
12. **Hazra Chinmay, Kundu Debasree and Chaudhari Ambalal,** School of Life Sciences, North Maharashtra University, Jalgaon
13. **Indi R. M. and Dhole Vijay,** Singhad Institute of Business Administration and Research, pune
14. **Jakhete Jyoti Shekhar,** KCE'S Institute of Management and Research, Jalgaon
15. **Jayasankar. K.I and Reddy B. Yuvakumar,** S. S. Maniyar Law College, Jalgaon
16. **Jogdeo Pramod and Mohite Popat N.,**MITCON Institute of Management, Balewadi Research Section and Genereal Management, SIBACA, Lonavala. Pune
17. **Joshi Chandrashekhar V.,**Rohidas Patil Institute of Management Studies, Mumbai
18. **Joshi Seema,** Department of Managament Studies, North Maharashtra University Jalgaon
19. **Kaushik Chandrashekhar Suresh,** IES Management College and Research Centre, Mumbai
20. **Kazi R.R.,** Assistant Registrar Audit, North Maharashtra University, Jalgaon
21. **Khurana Lalit K.,** Research Scholar, School of Management Studies, University of Hyderabad
22. **Saurabh Kumar,** MET's Institute of Management, Adgaon, Nasik
23. **Lad Anuradha Subhashrao,** Department of Extension Education, Marathwada Agricultural University, Parbhani

24. **Mahajan Yogesh D.,** KCES' Institute of Management and Research, Jalgaon
25. **Mohite Bhavna V., Chaudhari Bhushan L. and Chaudhari Girish,** North Maharashtra University, Jalgaon
26. **Nandode Anisha,** Department of Management Studies, North Maharashtra University, Jalgaon
27. **Parate V.R., Thorat S.R. and Dandge K.P.,** North Maharashtra University, Jalgaon
28. **K. Prakash, Patil R.H., Vishwakarma K.S. and Maheshwari V.L.,** Department of Biochemistry, School of Life Sciences, North Maharashatra University, Jalgaon Department of Microbilogy, R.C.Patel College of Arts and Science, Shirpur
29. **Ramteke R. J., Rokade V. M. and Bhoyar C. P.,** Department of Computer Science, North Maharashtra University, Jalgaon; School of Environmental and Earth Sciences, North Maharashtra University, Jalgaon; Department of Geology, S. G. B. Amaravati University, Amaravati
30. **Sabadra Mangala A.,** Head, Department of Commerce and Management, Dhule
31. **Sharma Aasha,** ICFAI National College, Jalgaon
32. **Sonawane A. C., Kulkarni M. N., Thorat S. R.and Parate V. R,** School of Environmental and Earth Sciences, North Maharashtra University, Jalgaon;
33. **Tiwary Pankaj Kumar and Devendra Kumar,** L.N. Mishra College of Business Management, Muzaffarpur (Bihar)
34. **Venezia Scott,** CETYS University, Km 1 Camino Microondas – Trinidad Ensenada, Baja California, Mexico
35. **Wazal Makarand Sachidanand,** Singhad College of Commerce, Kondhawa (Bk), Pune
36. **Zare B.S.,** Shri Shivaji Science and Arts College, Chikhli, Dist. Buldana, Maharashtra (India)

Contents

1

Food Safety Management System: A Strategic Assurance for Food Security – A Case Study of Jain Irrigation Systems Ltd.

Preeti V. Agrawal, S.D.Jain

Introduction

Food control is defined as a mandatory regulatory activity of enforcement by national or local authorities to provide consumer protection and ensure that all foods during production, handling, storage, processing, and distribution are safe, wholesome and fit for human consumption; conform to safety and quality requirements; and are honestly and accurately labeled as prescribed by law.

Consumers expect protection from hazards occurring along the entire food chain, from primary producer through consumer (often described as the ***farm-to-table*** continuum). Protection will only occur if all sectors in the chain operate in an integrated way, and **food control systems** address all stages of this chain.

The Hazards that can make food unsafe are

(a) **Biological Hazards:** Bacteria, Viruses, Parasites, some molds, Poisonous plants, Poisonous mushrooms and seafood that naturally contains toxin.

(b) **Chemical Hazards:** Pesticides, Food additives, Preservative, Cleaning supplies and Toxic metals (Lead, Coper, Brass, Zinc, Antimony, and Cadmium). That can leach into food through cookware equipment or plumbing lines.

(c) **Physical Hazards** : Foreign objects that accidentally contaminates food that include hair, metal staples, broken glass, needles, dirt, wood , nails.

Status of food processing industries in INDIA

(a) Size of food market in India	–	Rs. 8,60,000 Crores
(b) Primarily processed food market	–	Rs. 2,80,000 crore
(c) Value added processed food market	–	Rs. 1,80,000 crore

(d) The Sector attracted a total investment of Rs. 38,531 crores during the 9th plan period

(e) Investment during the 10th plan is estimated at Rs. 62,105 crores

(f) Industry growth rate during the last five years is estimated at 7.14% against GDP of 6.2%

(g) Investment required during next ten years – Rs. 1,50,000 crore

1.2 Status of Fruits and Vegetables Processing Worldwide

- USA - 80 %
- Malaysia - 80 %
- Philippines - 78 %
- Brazil - 70 %
- France - 70 %
- Thailand - 30 %
- **India - 2.2%**

1.3 Level of Processing, Value addition (Sector-wise)

Table: 1

	Organized	Unorganized	Total
Fruits/Vegetables	1.3%	0.8%	2.1%
Milk/milk products	13%	22%	35%

2.0 Needs of Food Safety Management System

Food safety Management system is the key to strategizing consumer confidence, assurance on food safety, global acceptance, market access and reducing costs like insurance premiums, medical litigations and wastages in the entire food chain, ranging from feed producers, primary producers, food manufacturers, transport and storage operators, producers of food processing equipment, packaging materials, cleansing agents, additives, ingredients and pesticide manufacturers.

Food is the major source of human kind's exposure to pathogenic agents, both chemical and biological (viruses, parasites, bacteria), from which no individual in developing and developed countries alike are spared. The importance of food safety stems from, food being a huge disease-burden both in the developing and the developed world, being the primary mode of transmission of disease-causing agents (bacteria, viruses, other germs) and the intricate linkage with development, it not only governs individual and community health, and thereby national productivity, but also promotes export potential and thus, foreign exchange.

Some important considerations in food safety management can be listed as follows

2.1 Health risks posed by microbial pathogens and potentially hazardous chemicals in food, given their detrimental impact on the national economy, are of major concern to all governments. The incidence of food-borne illness is clearly increasing worldwide, particularly so in many industrialized countries during the last few decades, for instance salmonellosis, campylobacteriosis and infections caused by E. coli O157:H7.

2.2 Effective national food control systems are essential to protect the health and safety of domestic consumers. They are also critical in enabling countries to assure the safety and quality of their foods entering international trade and to ensure that imported foods conform to national requirements.

2.3 The new global environment for food trade places considerable obligations on both importing and exporting countries to strengthen their food control systems and to implement and enforce risk-based food control strategies

2.4 Consumers are taking unprecedented Interest in the way food is produced, processed and marketed, and are increasingly calling for their Governments to accept greater responsibility for food safety and consumer protection.

2.5 Food allergy causes an immune system response, causing symptoms that range from uncomfortable to life threatening.

Important Allergen Statistics are:

S.N.	Food Allergen	Percentage of Health Risk and food borne illness
1	Eggs	35%
2	Peanuts	24%
3	Milk	15%
4	Tree Nuts	11%
5	Others	15%

According to the facts, revealed by a study conducted by U.S. Food and Drug Administration in USA nearly 2-2.5 % people (**i.e., 6-7 million Americans**) suffer from food allergy and up to 3 million people suffer from peanut or tree nut allergy and nearly **100-200 people** die each year from food allergy related reactions. Thus, this issue of food related allergic reactions needs very serious and effective management.

This paper unfolds the food safety management at Jain Irrigation Systems Ltd., a global leader in food processing industry, through the case study methodology.

3.0 About Jainis

The founder Chairman of Jain Group of Industries Padmashri **Dr.Bhavarlal Jain,** born in a farmer's family in the tiny village, Vakod, Dist. Jalgaon., began his journey in 1963 with Rs. 7000, a saving of 3 generations. He was involved in trading of agricultural inputs and equipment till 1978. In 1978 he acquired a sick unit for Rs. 30 lacs (3 million) and utilized the unit to make exportable Papain in 1978. Then the company started PVC pipe plant in 1980. With the steady growth and Mr. jain a hardcore farmer pioneered Micro - Irrigation in 1987-88 and ventured into large scale Agro-Food Processing in 1994. Since then the group is toiling to create a world class enterprise with a distinct work culture, i.e., ***"Work is life, life is work"***, **and a unique mission, i.e., "Leave this world better than you found it."**

Group profile

The Jain Group began with trading of agri-inputs in 1963. With sustained efforts to excel, conserve and grow, today, it is a medium sized industrial house with an annual turnover of about Rs.2500 crore. The Group manufactures a diverse range of products: Tissue culture - Banana Plants, Food products (Dehydrated Onions and Vegetables and Fruit Purees, concentrates, clarified juices and frozen products), Extruded and Molded Plastics, Micro Irrigation Systems, Waste management (Bio gas generation, and Vermi compost), solar water heating system and Photovoltaic (Solar Lighting) applications. Jain Irrigation Systems Ltd. has setup a World class state of the art global scale integrated fruit and vegetable processing facilities. Manufacture and supply processed fruit and Vegetable products. The products are well accepted globally due to its excellent quality, food safety assurance system and traceability

Research and Development

The Group has in-house research and development laboratory, which is recognized by the department of Science and Technology since 1981. Its hi-tech agri institute is a recognized R&D center for Ph.D. degree work in Biotechnology by more than 20 leading Universities of Agriculture and Technology. It has been actively engaged in many green field eco-friendly projects like, tissue culture, green houses, waste conversion into renewable energy, etc. Jains are India's only one-stop high-Tech integrated agricultural shop. It's important to note that Jain R&D is certified for ISO: 17025 (NABL) standards.

The application of FSMS **based Hazard Analysis Critical Control Point System (HACCP),** have resulted in taking greater responsibility for and control of food safety risks. Such an integrated approach facilitates improved consumer protection, effectively stimulates the food processing, and promotes domestic and international food trade.

JISL has implemented sustainable food safety programmes by producing products with Traceability of the Product (origin, raw materials), People (social compliance) and Planet(Responsible use of natural resources) by implementing Global food safety standards.

Global Food Safety standards/Benchmarks Implemented at JISL are:

Sr No.	Description	Benchmarks
1	Food Safety Management System.	ISO -22000
2	Environment Management System	ISO: 14001
3	Occupational Health and Safety Assessment Series	OHSAS: 18001
4	British Retail Consortium - Global Food Safety Standard.	BRC
5	Grocery Manufacturers Association-Supplier Assessments for Food Excellence (American Benchmark),	GMA - SAFE
6	SURE - GLOBAL - FAIR, (Germany),	SGF
7	Orthodox Union (America.).	KOSHER

More crops per drop: the catchword of Jain Irrigation Systems Ltd., amplifies the current concern on water scarcity and offers practical solutions. Jain Irrigation targets all its manufacturing and supply processes with a pedantic view to sustain nature and natural resources. The plastic based products save trees, micro irrigation conserves water by limiting its use equating to the actual requirements. Empowering rural small farmers with technology for crop growing, help conserve land, water and energy resources and still resulting in high crop production.

4.0 Major Elements of Food Safety Management System

1. Food Safety Policy,
2. Prerequisite Programmes (PRPs)
3. Hazard Analysis Critical Control Points (HACCP)
4. Environmental Monitoring
5. Finished Product Analysis
6. Traffic Control
7. Preventive Maintenance
8. Food Allergen
9. Food Security System

Various Policies at Jain Irrigation System Ltd., (Food and Agri Park)

4.1 Prerequisite Programmes (PRPs)

PRPs address food safety's basic conditions and activities that are necessary to maintain a hygienic environment throughout the **food chain** suitable for the production, handling and provision of safe **end products** and safe food for human consumption.

4.2 The relationship between the key control mechanisms

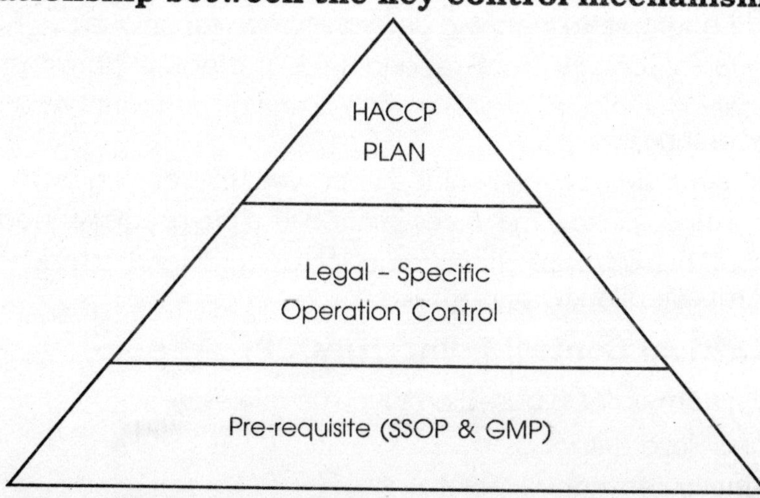

Fig.: 2: Relationship between the key control mechanisms

4.2.1 The PRPs needs depends on the segment of the food chain in which the organization operates and the type of organization, e.g., Good Agricultural Practice (GAP). Good Manufacture Practice (GMP), Good Hygienic Practice (GHP), Good Production Practice (GPP), Good Distribution Practice (GDP) and Good Training Practice (GTP).

4.2.2 The JISL has established, implemented and maintained PRPs to assist in controlling the likelihood of introducing food safety hazards to the product through the work environment, and by controlling biological, chemical and physical contamination of the products, including cross contamination between products, and food safety hazard levels in the product and product processing environment. While establishing PRPs, the JISL utilizes appropriate information, e.g., statutory and regulatory requirements, customer requirements, standard guidelines available.

4.3 The Good Agricultural Practices (GAPs)

The Good Agricultural Practices (GAPs) are designed to reassure about how food is produced on the farm by minimizing detrimental environmental impacts of farming operations, reducing the use of chemical inputs and ensuring a responsible approach to worker's health and safety.

The Salient Features of Global GAP) are

- Food safety should begin on the farm.
- Quality Management System is visible predominantly in Agricultural Production.
- The fruit and Vegetable products should be exportable.

4.4 Good Manufacturing Practices (GMPs) and Good Hygienic Practices,(GHPs)

Good Manufacturing Practices (GMPs) and Good Hygienic Practices,(GHPs) at JISL are ensured by implementing following listed practices:

- The use of appropriate cleaning and sanitization techniques.
- Observation of sanitary practices and use of protective clothings.
- Strict observation of rules of personnel hygiene by personnel involved in handling and processing food.
- Time/Temperature controls in place to prevent microbial growth.
- The use of other sanitary measures controls that are specially needed.

Verification of PRPs is always planned, modified accordingly and necessary records of verifications and modifications are maintained.

4.5 Hazards Critical Control Point (HACCP)

The HACCP system of JISL is based on seven principles:

1. Conduct a Hazard Analysis.
2. Identify the critical control points.
3. Establish critical limits.
4. Establish monitoring requirements.
5. Establish corrective action for deviations from HACCP plan.
6. Establish procedures for verification of the HACCP system.
7. Record keeping systems to document the HACCP system.

Intensified food safety control procedures at JISL is based on HACCP, is applied to identify all known potential hazards, associated with food being processed. The Critical Control Points (CCP) in the processing are identified where controls can be exercised to **prevent, reduce or eliminate** these hazards. A constant vigilance is maintained over the CCPs to prevent any process deviation that would result in loss of control at the CCP. Appropriate corrective actions are taken whenever a CCP is found to be out of control. The suspect food product is prevented from being distributed until its safety and acceptability has been determined.

The moisture level of final products in Onion (De-Hydrated Onion) is kept below 6%. The final product at JISL is monitored regularly for water activity level below 0.6. because the Microbial and Pathogens growth does not occur below water activity (aW) of 0.6.

4.6 Food Allergens

A food allergen is a product or ingredient containing certain proteins that can potentially cause a severe (occasionally fatal) reaction in a food allergic person. In case some food is basic ingredient of the desired product, then, its imperative that they follow the EU and CFR (Code of Federal Regulation) standards along with the specific requirements mentioned by the customers.

4.7 Food Security and Sabotage

Industrial, manufacturing and food security risks that may be faced could include workplace threats and violence, theft and pilferage, counterfeiting, sabotage, terrorist attack, trespassing, activist disruption, vandalism, contamination, etc. JISL has taken special efforts to improve the employee security awareness to deal with the problem which is often lacking or weak in many Industries.

5.0 Continual Improvement of FSMS

Management Reviews are conducted regularly to monitor and improve effectiveness of QMS and FSMS thereby, ensuring compliance to the Quality and Food Safety Policy for enhancing Customer Satisfaction. The major issues discussed during QMS Management Review Meeting are

1. Food Safety Policy/Objectives
2. Resource Adequacy
3. Analysis of result of verification activities,
4. Customer Feedback ,
5. External/Internal Audit Results,
6. Corrective Actions.
7. Supplier development/Evaluation ,
8. Emergency Situation and Withdrawal(If any),
9. Improvements
10. Follow up Action

Conclusion

Thus, with the proactive approach and commitment jains have met the challenges in the food Industries and they have network of satisfied customers worldwide, thereby becoming global leader in food Industry The study also reveals that JISL has taken a proactive stance in initiating climate change mitigation projects or 'captive green projects' like biogas from fruit and vegetable wastes, a forestation, solar lighting and heating, vermi-composting, and usage of electric vehicles that have led to reduction in emissions of carbon dioxide equivalents. The case study also suggests that JISL is committed to produce and supply safe food ingredients to their domestic and international customers, through:

- Procurement and use of raw and other materials as per defined specifications.
- By providing required infrastructure and work environment.
- By maintaining effective communication systems and by compliance to statutory and regulatory requirements and meeting needs and expectations of customers, and most important is by continually improving the food safety.

References

1. BRC,Global standards for Food safety (2008) issue 5, retrieived, Nov 28 2009, www.brcglobalstandards.com.
2. Food Safety Management System - Requirement food chain, ISO - 22000: First edition:2005- 09-01.
3. GMA - SAFE: (.2007) "Supplier Audits for Food Excellence (American):
4. Environmental management systems — Requirements, ISO-14001: Second edition (2004)retrieved from database of EMS
5. Occupational Health and Safety Assessment Series- OHSAS 18001: 2007.
6. General requirements for the competence of testing and calibration laboratories: ISO/ IEC 17025: Second edition: 2005-05-15
7. GLOBALG.A.P. (EUREPGAP February 2009) "Control Points and Compliance Criteria:English Version V.3.0-3.
8. Quality Management Systems - Requirements: ISO- 9001: Fourth edition: 2008-11-15
9. The Global Food Safety Initiative (GFSI Sept.2007)
10. CAC/RCP-1-1969, (2003), Codex Alimentarius Commission - Food Hygiene - Basic Text
11. Allergen auditing and training (2001), retrieved from, AIB International, Nov 29, 2009,www.aibonline.org.
12. Guidance for Industry: Importers and Filers (March 2008)," retrieved from database of Food Security Preventive Measures Guidance Center for Food Safety and Applied Nutrition:
13. S.D.Jain (2007) "A study of water activity in dehydrated onion at JISL" retrieved from Database of JISL.

14. Food Safety Education, retrieved, Dec 5 2009, www. foods afetvsite.com
15. SCOPAS (Sept 2001): A Status Note on Food Safety by TAC Secretariat Food and Agriculture Organization of the United Nations.
16. WHO (2000). Food Safety and Food-borne Illness. WHO Fact Sheet No. 237. Revised September, 2000.
17. Agriculture Technology Notes,World Bank (2000), retrieved from database of Rural Development Department, World Bank.
18. Assuring food safety and quality/guidelines for strengthening national food control Systems - Joint FAO/WHO Publication
19. S.D.Jain (2008) "Quality and Food Safety Standards and Best Practices in Food Processing", retrieved from Database of JISL.

2

Food Security in India

Shaily Asthana

Introduction

The World Food Summit of 1996 defined food security as:

"***When all people at all times have access to sufficient, safe, nutritious food to maintain a healthy and active life***".

Commonly, the concept of food security is defined as including both physical and economic access to food that meets people's dietary needs as well as their food preferences. Food security is built on **three** pillars:

- Food availability: Sufficient quantities of food available on a consistent basis.
- Food access: Having sufficient resources to obtain appropriate foods for a nutritious diet.
- Food use: Appropriate use based on knowledge of basic nutrition and care, as well as adequate water and sanitation.

Food security is a complex sustainable development issue, linked to health through malnutrition, but also to sustainable economic development, environment and trade. There is a great deal of debate around food security with some arguing that:

- There is enough food in the world to feed everyone adequately; the problem is distribution.
- Future food needs can — or cannot — be met by current levels of production.
- National food security is paramount — or no longer necessary because of global trade.
- Globalization may — or may not — lead to the persistence of food insecurity and poverty in rural communities.

Issues such as whether households get enough food, how it is distributed within the household and whether that food fulfils the nutrition needs of all members of the households shows that food security is clearly linked to health. Agriculture remains the largest employment sector in most developing countries and international agriculture agreements are crucial to a country's food security.

The **Food Corporation of India** was setup under the **Food Corporation Act 1964**, in order to fulfil the following objectives of the **Food Policy**:

- Effective price support operations for safeguarding the interests of the farmers.,
- Distribution of food grains throughout the country for public distribution system; and
- Maintaining satisfactory level of operational and buffer stocks of foodgrains to ensure National Food Security.

In its **45** years of service to the nation , FCI has played a significant role in India's success in transforming the crisis management oriented food security into a stable security system.

World Food Summit 1996, says that Food security is when all people at all times have access to enough food that should affordable, safe and healthy, culturally acceptable, meets specific dietary needs, obtained in a dignified manner and produced in ways that are environmentally sound.

It's a well-known fact that families need easy access to food on a regular basis. For families to be food secure, supplies must be available where they live and be accessible to all members of the household, year in and year out. They must be able to grow or afford enough food, in terms of quantity, quality and variety. All family members, especially children, must be free from disease so that their bodies can use the food they eat to grow and thrive. That is why access to clean water, sanitation, and health care is also a part of food security. Poverty, conflict, natural disasters, and outbreaks of disease can all result in food "insecurity." The food security of children is closely linked with the health, nutritional status, education, and economic well-being of their mothers. The rapidly growing epidemic of HIV/AIDS is eroding gains in food security that had been made in the 1970's and 80's, especially in sub-Saharan Africa, where 28 million people are living with HIV/AIDS.

Thus, it could be said that food security happens when all people at all times have enough food that ...

- is affordable, safe and healthy
- is culturally acceptable
- meets specific dietary needs
- is obtained in a dignified manner
- is produced in ways that are environmentally sound and socially just.

The issue of food security, especially in a developing nation like India, raises the twin problems of uncertain food production and unequal food distribution. The impact of unequal food distribution can have adverse effects on the rural and urban population living below the poverty line. Food insecurity is not only economic problem but also problem of non-humanity approach in India. According to the statistical data published by the **'Food Corporation of India'** and the government of India, food grain availability is **229** million tons in **2008-09** which is 230 million tons in previous year. It is happening because, food grain traders are doing speculation practice and selling them at higher prices than fair prices. We may say that, food insecurity is not only natural but also man-made.

Expectations towards Food Security

Commonly, the concept of food security includes both physical and economic access to food that meets people's dietary needs as well as their food preferences. But food security is a complex sustainable development issue, linked not only to health through malnutrition, but also to sustainable economic development, environment, and trade. There is a great deal of debate around food security. If we fail to maintain above, there has been food insecurity.

The Condition of Food Security Across the Globe

Australia

The Australian Government helps developing countries in its region to reduce poverty and address food security by promoting trade liberalisation, peace and stability, good governance, security of land tenure, rural development and agricultural research. Australia also provides emergency food aid to developing countries in need. In **May 2003**, the Australian Government announced a A$1 billion food security pledge for **five** years from **1 July 2003** to **30 June, 2008** for programs and initiatives that enhance the food security of people in the developing world.

Canada

Wealth is significant to food security; wealth by individuals to obtain what is needed, community wealth for adequate infrastructure, and production by food system wealth and distribution. Canada has a very skewed distribution of the benefit arising from financial dimensions of wealth which contributes to food insecurity for many because those who benefit the least are poor whereas, those who benefit the most from wealth is rich.

The Global Agenda for Food Security

- The **World Food Programme (WFP)** attempts to lessen the effects of HIV/AIDS on a community by improving food security and securing the livelihoods of those living with the illness.
- **The International Alliance Against Hunger** aims to unite national governments, the international community, civil society organisations, the private sector and concerned individuals to mobilise the political will, technical expertise and financial resources needed to improve food security.
- The **Special Programme for Food Security (SPFS)** helps governments replicate successful food security practices on a national scale. The SPFS also encourages investment in rural infrastructure, off-farm income generation, urban agriculture and safety nets.

Since 1995, US $770 million from donors and national governments have been invested in FAO-designed food security programmes.

Food security refers to the availability of food and one's access to it. A household is considered food secure when its occupants do not live in hunger or fear of starvation. According to the World Resources Institute, global per capita food production has been increasing substantially for the past several decades.

Worldwide around **852** million people are chronically hungry due to extreme poverty, while up to 2 billion people lack food security intermittently due to varying degrees of poverty (source: FAO, 2003). It is becoming increasingly difficult to maintain food security in a world beset by a confluence of "peak" phenomena, namely peak oil, peak water, peak phosphorus, peak grain and peak fish. More than half of the planet's population, numbering approximately 3.3 billion people, live in urban areas as of **November 2007**.

The most commonly used definition of food security came from the UN's Food and Agriculture Organization (FAO) and the United States Department of Agriculture (USDA):

Food security for a household means access by all members at all times to enough food for an active, healthy life. Food security includes at a minimum:

(1) the ready availability of nutritionally adequate and safe foods, and

(2) an assured ability to acquire acceptable foods in socially acceptable ways (that is, without resorting to emergency food supplies, scavenging, stealing, or other coping strategies). (USDA)(21)

Declining Food Security

Food insecurity has been described as "a condition in which people lack basic food intake to provide them with the energy and nutrients for fully productive lives." (Hunger Task Force (25) Households that are more likely to experience food insecurity are female-headed with children, those with incomes below the poverty line, and those that reside either in principal cities or within rural areas.

One of the major reasons behind food Insecurity is **Global Water Crisis.** The water tables are falling in scores of countries (including Northern China, the US, and India) due to widespread overpumping using powerful diesel and electric pumps. Other countries affected include Pakistan, Afghanistan, and Iran. This will eventually lead to water scarcity and cutbacks in grain harvest which might result into decreasing the standards of the grains. Also intensive farming often leads to a vicious cycle of exhaustion of soil fertility and decline of agricultural yields. Approximately 40% of the world's agricultural land is seriously degraded. In Africa, if current trends of soil degradation continue, the continent might be able to feed just 25% of its population by 2025, according to UNU's Ghana-based Institute for Natural Resources in Africa.

The head of the Food and Agriculture Organisation (FAO), Jacques Diouf, has warned that "The number of people without enough food to eat on a regular basis remains stubbornly high, at over **800** million, and is not falling significantly. Over **60%** of the world's undernourished people live in Asia, and a quarter in Africa. The proportion of people who are hungry, however, is greater in Africa (**33%**) than Asia (**16%**). The latest FAO figures indicate that there are 22 countries, 16 of which are in Africa, in which the undernourishment prevalence rate is over **35%**." In its "The State of Food Insecurity in the World 2003", FAO states that:

'In general, the countries that succeeded in reducing hunger were characterised by more rapid economic growth and specifically more rapid growth in their agricultural sectors. They also exhibited slower population growth, lower levels of HIV and higher ranking in the Human Development Index'.

Food Security in India

INDIA at present finds itself in the midst of a paradoxical situation: endemic mass-hunger coexisting with the mounting food grain stocks. The food grain stocks available with the **Food Corporation of India (FCI)** stand at an alltime high of **62** million tons against an annual requirement of around **20** million tons for ensuring food security. Still, an estimated **200** million people are underfed and **50** million on the brink of starvation, resulting in starvation deaths. The paradox lies in the inherent flaws in the existing policy and implementation bottlenecks.

Supply Side Analysis of Food Insecurity in India

According to the data published by the **Government of India** and the **Food Corporation of India**, total production of foodgrain was **230.78** million tons in **2007-08** and in recent year it is **229.85** million tons. There is just **0.93** million tons of food grain production decreased than last year. Hence question is that, only **0.93** million tons falling production of food grain can create such situations of food insecurity in India ? In the same year population growth is near about hardly **1.10** % and net growth of population may be **0.50** to **0.75 %.** It is not larger growth which may become burden on food supply in India. Because, in the same period:

- fish production is increased from **6.8** to **7.3** million tons;
- fruit production increased from **59563** thousand tons;
- and production of vegetables is increased from **115011** to **125887** thousand million tons.

Apart from the production of foodgrain and supported foods, buffer stock of foodgrain also increased continually since 2007, hence, its not the economic problem. Its altogether a different problem which is rising the Food Insecurity in this country.

Food Security Bill of India

President Pratibha Patil on **June 4, 2009** said that a **National Food Security Act** would be formulated whereby each BPL (Below Poverty Line) family would be entitled by law to get 25 kg of rice or wheat per month at Rs 3 a kg.

If made into a law, the draft **Food Security Bill** would reduce the allocation for a below poverty line (BPL) household (e.g. in the case of Antodaya Anna Yojana) from 35 kg of rice/ wheat per month to 25 kg of rice/wheat per month. This would appear contradictory to many who expected the Bill to be a benign effort of the to ensure food security.

Instead of better implementation of the already existing schemes such as the **Targeted Public Distribution System (TPDS), Antodaya Anna Yojana (AAY), Integrated Child Development Scheme (ICDS), Mid Day Meal Scheme (MDMS)** etc., the Food Security law might make things unduly worse and unnecessarily complicated. A cynical question here would be:

Is the Food Security Bill going to replace all such food related schemes that existed before its enactment?

Secondly, if the Bill is about ensuring food security, how can it leave those who may not fall below the poverty line but are already exposed to food insecurity? It is about nutrition security too. If that is the case, the Food Security Bill has to rethink about the quality of food grains supplied and distributed. The **Food Security Bill** must also aim at providing fortified food grains along with edible oils, salt and essential spices. A balanced diet would ensure both food and nutrition security. The basket of commodities, which would be available to the consumers, should reflect local tastes and preferences and must include locally grown cereals and legumes.

If targeting of BPL households is done under the Food Security Bill, then it might lead to inclusion *(including the non-poor)* and exclusion *(excluding the poor)* errors. It would be wiser to go for universalization (rather than targeting) as was recommended by the Committee on **Long-term Grain Policy** under the chairmanship of **Prof. Abhijit Sen (2000-02)**.

The Sustainability Factor of Food Security in India

For India, it's a million dollar question to ensure sustainable food security for a billion-strong population. "Sustainable food security" means enough food for everyone at present plus the ability to provide enough in future as well. This calls for sound policies and investments in natural resources such as land and water, flora and fauna, forests and biodiversity — the ecological foundations essential for sustainable food security - plus sustainable intensification of crop and animal production. Population pressures and the forces of atmosphere and climate change must also be taken into account.

The M. S. Swaminathan Research Foundation and the World Food Programme have together produced three Atlases — a compendium of facts, statistics, maps and analysis - designed to promote public policy and action to enable a hunger-free India by **15 August 2007**, the 60th anniversary of India's independence. "They will help policy-makers to promote an evergreen revolution in all major farming systems, by enhancing productivity in perpetuity without any ecological or social harm," says Prof. M.S. Swaminathan.

The Food Insecurity Atlas of Rural India revealed that the Punjab-Haryana region, India's breadbasket, could lose its production potential in a few decades if current patterns of groundwater extraction and pollution, soil salinization and rice-wheat monoculture persisted. It was therefore decided to produce an Atlas on Sustainability of Food Security in India to promote ecologically sustainable methods of food production and natural resources management. The third atlas i.e. Atlas of the Sustainability of Food Security in India — was released at the **National Food Security Summit on February 5, 2004**. "Food security has three components," says Prof M S Swaminathan. "The first is food availability, which depends on food production and imports. The second is food access, which depends on purchasing power. The third, food absorption, is a function of safe drinking water, environmental hygiene, primary health care and education."

Challenges Ahead

India's food security policy has a laudable objective to ensure availability of food grains to the common people at an affordable price and it has enabled the poor to have access to food where none existed. The policy has focused essentially on growth in agriculture production (once India used to import food grains) and on support price for procurement and maintenance of rice and wheat stocks. The responsibility for procuring and stocking of food grains lies with the FCI and for distribution with the public distribution system (PDS).

(a) **Minimum support price:** The FCI procures food grains from the farmers at the government announced minimum support price (MSP). The MSP should ideally be at a level where the procurement by FCI and the off-take from it are balanced. However, under continuous pressure from the powerful farmers lobby, the government has been raising the MSP and it has now become higher than what the market offers to the farmers.

(b) **Input subsidies:** Over the years, to keep food grain prices at affordable levels for the poor, the government has been imposing restrictions on free trade in food grains. This has suppressed food grain prices in the local market, where the farmers sell a part of their produce and as compensation, they are provided subsidies on agriculture inputs such as fertilizers, power and water. These subsidies have now reached unsustainable levels and also led to large scale inefficiencies in the use of these scarce inputs. Overuse of fertilizer and water has led to water-logging, salinity, depletion of vital micronutrients in the soil, and reduced fertility. The high subsidies have come at the expense of public investments in the critical agriculture infrastructure, thereby reducing agriculture productivity.

(c) **Issue price:** The people are divided into two categories: below poverty line (BPL) and above poverty line (APL), with the issue price being different for each category. However, this categorisation is imperfect and a number of deserving poor have been excluded from the BPL fold. Moreover, some of the so called APL slip back to BPL, say with failure of even one crop and it is administratively difficult to accommodate such shifts.

Also, the low quality of PDS grains and the poor service at PDS shops have forced many people to switchover to market, which offers better quality grains, allows purchase on credit and ensures flexibility to purchase in small quantities. Also, the high-priced, low-quality Indian rice and wheat find little place in the international market. Recently, two Indian consignments were rejected even by Iraq on quality considerations. The result is bulging stocks with FCI amidst widespread starvation.

Food Insecurity

For the more than 800 million people who do not get enough regular, healthy food, ill health and a shorter life expectancy are real risks. Children, and especially very young children, who suffer from food insecurity will be less developed than children of the same age who have had sufficient food. They will most likely be shorter and weigh less, and be less able physically and intellectually, because of poor nutrition.

Reasons for Food Insecurity

(a) **Poverty:** Poor people lack access to sufficient resources to produce or buy quality food. Poor farmers may have very small farms, use less effective farming techniques, and/or be unable to afford fertilisers and labour-saving equipment, all of which limit food production. Addressing poverty is critical to ensuring that all people have sufficient food.

(b) **Health**: Without sufficient calories and nutrients and good health, the body is also less able to make use of the food that is available. A hungry mother will give birth to an underweight baby, who then faces a future of stunted growth, frequent illness, learning disabilities and reduced resistance to disease. Contaminated food and water can cause illness, nutrient loss and often death in children. The HIV/AIDS pandemic has reduced food production in many affected countries as productive adults become ill or die.

(c) **Water and the environment:** Food production requires massive amounts of water. It takes one cubic metre (1000 litres) of water to produce one kilogram of wheat and 3,000 litres of water to produce one kilogram of rice. Producing sufficient food is directly related to having sufficient water. Irrigation can ensure an adequate and reliable supply of water which increases yields of most crops by **100%** to **400%.** Where water is scarce and the environment fragile, achieving food security may depend on what has been called 'virtual water', that is, importing food from countries with an abundance of water. This may be a more efficient use of a scarce resource.

(d) **Gender equity:** Women play a vital role in providing food and nutrition for their families through their roles as food producers, processors, traders and income earners. Yet women's lower social and economic status limits their access to education, training, land ownership, decision making and credit and consequently their ability to improve their access to and use of food. Food utilisation can be enhanced by improving women's knowledge of nutrition and food safety and the prevention of illnesses. Increasing women's involvement in decision-making and their access to land and credit will in turn improve food security as women invest in fertilisers and better seeds, labour-saving tools, irrigation and land care.

(e) **Population and urbanization:** Population growth increases the demand for food. With most productive land already in use, there is pressure for this land to become more productive. Poor harvests and higher costs lead many poor farmers to migrate to cities to look for work. This increases the cost of all the activities associated with producing and transporting food, and decreases the food security of the poor in cities. In addition, trade imbalances can also prevent poor countries from importing agricultural products that could enhance their food security.

Implemented Measures for Food Security

- **Improving Food Production**

Increasing the amount of food available is necessary to feed the growing population. The Green Revolution of the 1970s and 1980s led to huge increases but further increases in food production depend on better integration of traditional knowledge with research; improving farming practices through training and the use of technology to increase outputs from current land without further loss of productive land.

Economic Growth and Liberalisation

Increasing food production leads to greater availability of food and economic growth in the domestic and/or overseas markets. Generating income can provide access to more and varied foods and provide cash for use in other areas of the economy, such as small enterprise and manufacturing, which in turn helps reduce poverty.

- **Distribution**

While there are sufficient resources in the world to provide food security for all, policy and behavioural changes are necessary to guarantee a fair share for all people, especially the poor. Building on a series of global conferences, in particular the **1992 International Conference** on **Nutrition** and the **1996** and **2002 World Food Summits**, countries have developed national nutrition plans and policies in **nine** major strategic action areas that:

- Include mainstream nutrition goals in development policies and programmes
- Improve household food and nutrition security
- Protect consumers through improved food quality and safety
- Prevent and manage infectious diseases
- Promote breastfeeding
- Care for the socioeconomically deprived and nutritionally vulnerable
- Prevent and control specific micronutrient deficiencies
- Promote appropriate diets and healthy lifestyles
- Assess, analyse and monitor nutrition situations.

Community Food Security

Community food security is a condition in which all community residents obtain a safe, culturally acceptable, nutritionally adequate diet through a sustainable food system that maximizes community self-reliance and social justice

Some of the basic principles of community food security, as defined by the **Community Food Security Coalition** are:

- Low Income Food Needs like the anti-hunger movement.,
- Broad range of problems affecting the food system, community development, and the environment such as increasing poverty and hunger, disappearing farmland

and family farms, inner city supermarket redlining, rural community disintegration, rampant suburban sprawl, and air and water pollution from unsustainable food production and distribution patterns.

- The Role of the Governments/Rulers

As the Nobel Prize-winning economist Amartya Sen has observed that "there is no such thing as an apolitical food problem." While drought and other naturally occurring events may trigger famine conditions, it is government action or inaction that determines its severity, and often even whether or not a famine will occur. The 20th century is full of examples of governments undermining the food security of their own nations — sometimes intentionally. When governments come to power by force or rigged elections, and not by way of fair and open elections, their base of support is often narrow and built upon cronyism and patronage. Under such conditions "The distribution of food within a country is a political issue. Governments with strong tendencies towards kleptocracy can undermine food security even when harvests are good. Thus, comes into the picture the issue of Food Justice which means that no one should live without enough food because of economic constraints or social inequalities is the basic goal. This approach is often referred to as food justice and views food security as a basic human right. The core of the Food Justice movement is the belief that what is lacking is not food, but the political will to fairly distribute food regardless of the recipient's ability to pay.

Food-insecure people are those individuals whose food intake falls below their minimum calorie (energy) requirements, as well as those who exhibit physical symptoms caused by energy and nutrient deficiencies resulting from an inadequate or unbalanced diet or from the body's inability to use food effectively because of infection or disease. hence, it can be said that food security is not just a poverty issue; it is a much larger issue that involves the whole food system and affects every one of us in some way.

Food security happens when...

- Farmers and fishers can earn a fair income for their efforts.
- Food is produced in a way that is safe for people and the environment.
- Local, regional and community food production is supported.

Food insecurity happens whenever food is hard to get, such as when:

- There are no farms or grocery stores nearby.
- Our food travels great distances to get to us.
- There isn't enough money.
- Healthy and safe food is not available.
- Healthy foods cost more than unhealthy foods.
- Our traditional foods are not available or accessible.

SPFS Mission

The aim of the SPFS is to improve food security within poor households through **National Programmes for Food Security (NPFS)** and **Regional Programmes for Food Security (RPFS).** By the end of 2006, 106 countries had engaged in the SPFS and more than half had begun shifting to National Programmes (NPFS), and more are preparing to do so.

Conclusions

In developing countries like India, the root causes of food insecurity include, poverty, corruption, national policies that do not promote equal access to food for all, environmental degradation, barriers to trade, insufficient agricultural development, population growth, low levels of education, social and gender inequality, poor health status, cultural insensitivity, and natural disasters.

Another way to food security is increase in fruit, milk and fish production. We can solve that problem by the increase in inland and sea fish production in India. The policy of mitigating nutritional deficiencies and food security by fisheries is a pragmatic move in India, considering the fact that sea has ample scope for continuous supply of protein rich food. We need to exploit the food from sea to counter the menace of malnutrition. India, with its vast coastline and seas can use science and technology to make full use of fisheries in ensuring food security to its vast populace.

The objectives of the **Public Distribution System — PDS** are good but it was failed to accomplish that objective due to the corruption. PDS is a better way to tackle the problem of food speculation of private traders. If the government will succeed the in the motive of PDS the intensity of food insecurity problem will be reduced in future. However, the cruel reality is that despite this huge food production, a huge buffer stock and an extensive network of PDS, millions of people are food insecure and many even die of starvation. Food Insecurity and tragedy hit different parts of the country every year.

The present food crisis is due to lack of proper distribution and the trading system impeding free flow of food. Even increase in agricultural productivity is also one of the solutions for this problem. This should be based on integrating inputs and outputs — the supply of high yielding varieties of seeds, fertilizers, and irrigation, supported by credit alongside remunerative output prices. A second "green revolution" is essential to stimulate food production in many India.

The problem of food security comes mainly from the slow growth of purchasing power of the people in the rain-fed eco-systems. Efforts must be made to help them by developing drought resistant seeds, cost-effective dry-land farming techniques. A major challenge to food security comes from dietary diversification of the poor.

- Although, we can say that food security problem in India is not serious if we succeed in the proper distribution policy, the problem is that, the government has failed to control and regulate food market in India. This problem becomes serious due to the unfair trade practice by private traders doing in drought situation. At present, **9.4%** poor households (with MPCE < 580/-) were food secure, i.e., were positive deviants while, 51% slum households are food insecure. Addressing urban poor HFI is urgently needed. Almost half of all young children in India are underweight. In this regard, **Different Chapters and Coordination of FIAN India** are active in various fields to defend and promote the human right to feed oneself in the country. The activities and expertise of different FIAN units in India cover a wide range of thematic areas which are crucial to mainstream right to food in the nation.

Suggested Recommendations

(1) There is a need to shift from the existing expensive, inefficient and corruption ridden institutional arrangements to those that will ensure cheap delivery of requisite quality grains in a transparent manner and are self-targeting.

(2) **Futures market and free trade**: To avoid wide fluctuations in prices and prevent distress selling by small farmers, futures market can be encouraged. To start with, all restrictions on food grains regarding inter-State movement, stocking, exports and institutional credit and trade financing should be renounced resulting into free trade.

(3) **Food-for-education programme**: To achieve cent per cent literacy, the food security need can be productively linked to increased enrolment in schools.

(4) **Modified food-for-work scheme/direct subsidies**: With rationalisation of input subsidies and MSP, the Central Government will be left with sufficient funds, which may be given as grants to each State depending on the number of poor

(5) **Community grain storage banks**: The FCI can be gradually dismantled and procurement decentralised through the creation of food grain banks in each block/village of the district, from which people may get subsidised food grains against food coupons. The food coupons can be numbered serially to avoid frauds. If culturally acceptable, the possibility of relatively cheap coarse grains, like bajara and ragi and nutritional grains like millets and pulses meeting the nutritional needs of the people can also be explored.

(6) **Enhancing agriculture productivity**: The focus on accelerated food grains production on a sustainable basis and free trade in grains would help create massive employment and reduce the incidence of poverty in rural areas.

(7) **The Right to Food** : The right to sufficient food is enshrined in the Universal Declaration of Human Rights and in subsequent international law. A rights-based approach to food security would impose obligations on national governments to implement non-discriminatory and non-political strategies to enable their people to feed themselves.

(8) **Another Green Revolution** : The first Green Revolution was launched to ensure food security as there was severe scarcity of food in the country. Hence, with the help of another Green Revolution, Livestock development is another important opportunity to provide gainful self-employment and food security for the poor. A majority of the small farmers in India who do not have good quality land for agriculture, are dependent on livestock for supplementary income.

A five-year transitory period may be allowed while implementing these. Thus, India can achieve food security in the real sense and in a realistic timeframe.

References

1. Keenan, D.P., Olson, C., Hersey, J.C. & Parmer, S.M. 2001. Measures of food insecurity/ security. *J Nutr Edu.*, S49-S58.
2. WHO. 1995. WHO *Expert Committee Report - Comprehensive School Health Education and Promotion.* Geneva, World Health Organization,
3. Perez-Rodrigo, C. & Javier, A. 2001. School-based nutrition education: Lessons Learned and New Perspectives. *Pub Health Nutr.*, 4(1A): 131-9.
4. Connell, C.L., Lofton, K.L., Yadrick, K. & Rehner, T.A. 2005. Children's experiences of food insecurity can assist in understanding its effect on their wellbeing. *J Nutr.*, 135:1683-90.
5. Carrel, A., Manen, A., Garry, C. & Storandt, R. 2005. Effects of nutrition education and exercise in obese children: The Ho-chunk Youth fitness program. *Wisc Med J.*, 104:44-47.
6. Ryan, L., Anderson, J. & Sherman, B.M. 1995. *The effect of nutrition education on improving fruit and vegetable consumption of youth.*
7. Friel, S., Kelleher, C., Campbell, P. & Nolan, G. 1999. Evaluation of the nutrition education program at primary school (NEAPS) programme. *Public Hlth Nutr.*, 2:549-555.
8. Devine, C.M., Olson, C.M. & Frongillo, E.A. 1992. Impact of the nutrition for life program on junior high students in New York State. *J School Health*, 62: 381-5.
9. Kelder, S.H., Perry, C.L., Lytle, L.A. & Klepp, K.L. 1995. Community-wide youth education: Long-term Outcomes of the Minnesota Heart Health Program. *Health Educ Res.*, 10: 119 – 31.
10. Killen, J.D., Telch, M.J., Robinson, T.N., Maccoby, N., Taylor, B. & Farquhar, J.W. 1988. Cardiovascular disease risk reduction for tenth graders: A multiple-factor school-based approach. *J Amer Diet Assoc.*, 260: 1728-33.

3

Climate Change, Food Scarcity, Poverty and Social Inequality in Mexico's Coastal States

Isaac Azuz-Adeath

Mexico General Information

With a territorial surface of 1,900,000 square kilometres and 2,715,012 square kilometres of economic exclusive zone, Mexico is located between the Atlantic and Pacific Oceans and the latitudes 15° to 33° North.

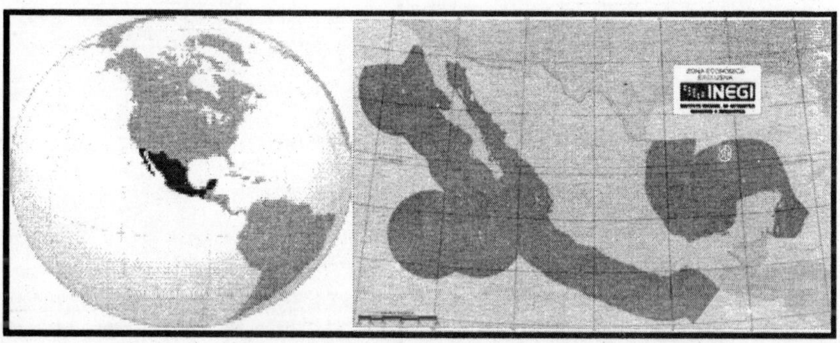

Fig.: 1: Mexico in the world (left) and territorial extension continental and economic exclusive zone (right) (Source of the maps: INEGI).

Mexico possess a clear north/south differentiation in their climatic structure (from semi-arid in the north to sub-tropical in the south), soil and vegetation distribution, altitude variations, geomorphologic characteristics and meteorological conditions (from low rain regimens in the north to cyclonic-dominated in the south), in terms of their biological diversity the country is considered part of the *megadiverse* group (countries with more than 70% of the global biodiversity).

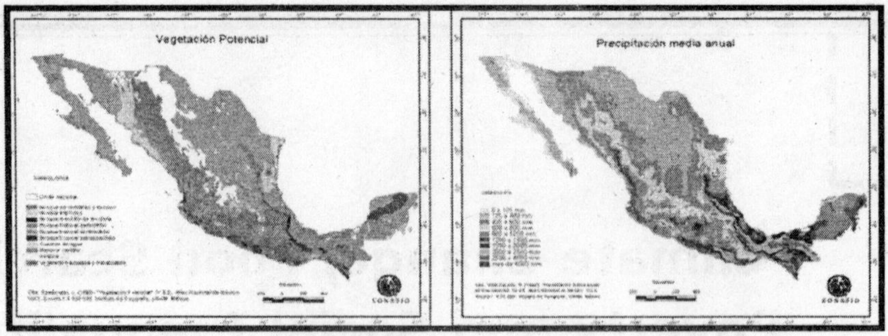

Fig.: 2: Mexico potential vegetation (left) and mean annual precipitation (right) (Source of the maps: CONABIO, 2009).

In 2005 the population of Mexico was 103 millions of inhabitants living in 32 States and 2445 counties.

During the period 2000-2005 the mean national population annual growth rate was 1% and the highest rate was reported in Quintana Roo (coastal state) with around 5%. This exceptional growth rate is associated with the tourism activities, specifically the beach tourism.

In 2005 at national level, the urban population (places with more than 10,000 inhabitants) was 80% and the rural population 20%. Most of the rural population was associated with the economic activities related to agriculture and food production. This process poses a serious challenge to the country to be competitive and to attain the alimentary security (production, distribution, nutrition and technological development).

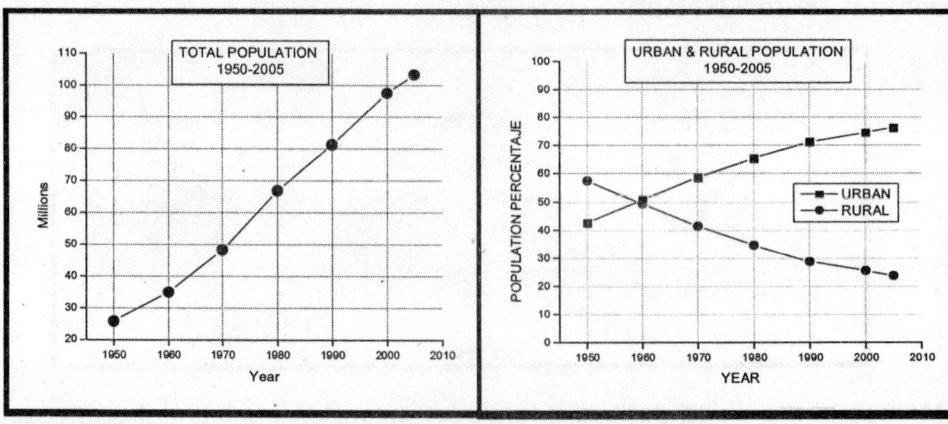

Fig.: 3: Mexico total population 1950-2005 (left) and Urban & Rural population 1950-2005 (right) (Source of the data: INEGI).

The loss of rural population, the changes in societal behavior to more urban-oriented attitudes, the lack of public policies oriented to the production of high added value of agricultural products and the dominant consumer patterns have a profound impact in the agricultural arena.

As a democratic republic, Mexico has 3 government levels: Federal (national level), State (32 states) and Municipalities (county level). Every government level has his owns laws and regulations; in general terms the agricultural and fisheries activities are regulated by federal laws. The State laws establish the local territorial ordinances and the Municipality regulations define the potential use of the soil.

The majority of the rural producers have a communitarian organization in order to develop the agricultural activities. This type of social organization come back from 1910 and actually constrains the process to attain a global food production.

The water availability/scarcity and also the level of technological development in farmer and food production are irregular between different regions of the country, but also between states and counties.

Agriculture Issues

The cultivable territorial surface is only the 10-12% of the country, the central part of Mexico has been traditionally the most important area of harvesting, but actually due to the water scarcity and the inefficient agricultural production technology, a regional crisis is underway.

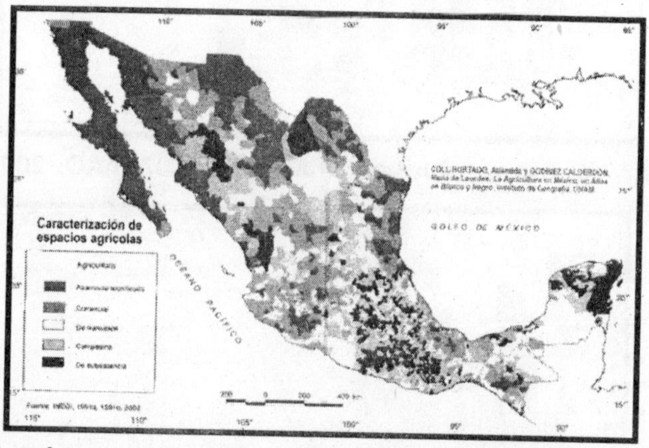

Fig.: 4: Agricultural spaces in Mexico. Box Legend: (a) High technology, (b) commercial, (c) transition, (d) rural people, (e) subsistence. (Source of the map: Coll-Hurtado and Gomez-Calderon, 2004).

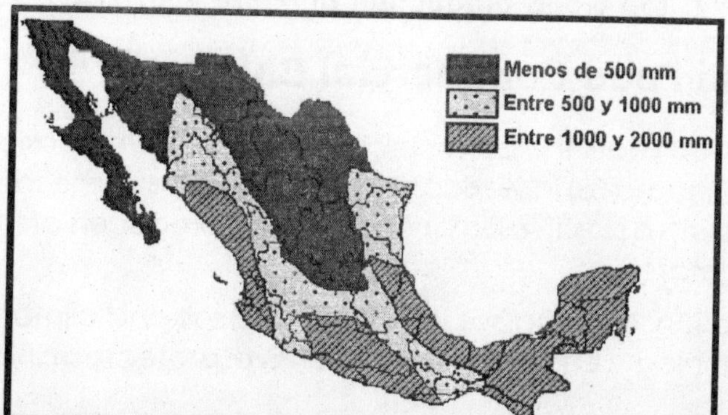

Fig.: 5: Water availability in Mexico. Box Legend: (a) less than 500 mm, (b) between 500 and 1000 mm, (c) between 1000 and 2000 mm. (Source of the map: Ortiz-Rendon *et. al.*, working papers, Atelier 2).

From the above pictures, it is important to note the close correlation between the water scarcity/availability and the use of technology in agriculture.

According to the Food and Agriculture Organization (FAO) the most important products of Mexico by volume are: Sugar Cane and Maize the former is the basic nutritional element of Mexico's population. At international level Mexico is between the second and third place in Maize production

In terms of market price the most important commodities are different kinds of meat (cattle and chicken) and fresh milk and eggs.

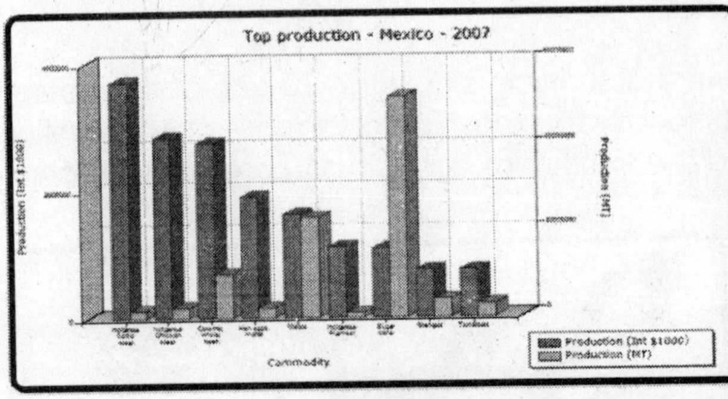

Fig.: 6: Top production of Mexico 2007 (FAO, 2009)

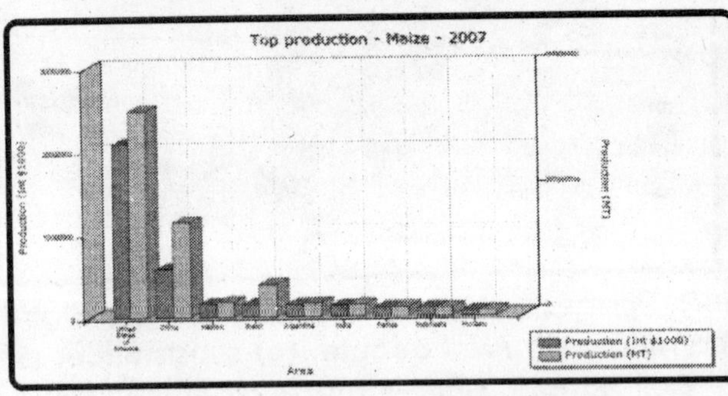

Fig.: 7: Top world production of Maize 2007 (FAO, 2009)

Agricultural and Food Commercial Balance

At least from last 10 years the commercial balance for the basic alimentary products (meat, milk and eggs and maize) in Mexico has been negative. In the same period vegetables, fruits and coffee presents a positive balance, the main producers of these commodities are the Mexican coastal states.

This high production level is associated with the soil and climate conditions but also with the level of technology used in the field (intensive, protected and with irrigate control).

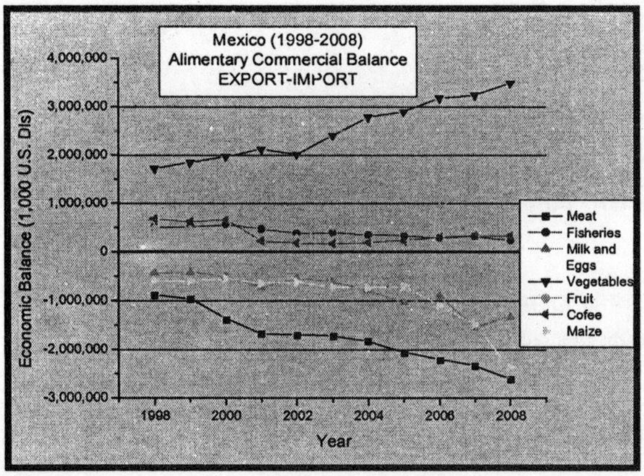

Fig.: 8: Mexicos Alimentary commercial balance (Export-Import) during the period (1998-2009). (Source of the data: INEGI/SAGARPA, 2009).

A collateral problem associated with the production and consumption of maize is the increase of international price of the product due to the demand for bio-fuel generation.

In order to achieve the alimentary security in Mexico the country authorities needs to regulate and manage the cultivated areas of maize for domestic consumption and for exportation.

An extra problem related with the maize is the introduction of alien's genetic modified varieties, which establish a competition with the local maize. The lack of scientific research and technological advances constrains the development possibilities of the Mexican maize farmers. These farmers live usually in the less developed regions of Mexico and work in the agricultural field only to cover their basics necessities.

Alimentary Poverty

If we compare the poverty map (figure 9) with the agricultural spaces in Mexico (figure 4) a close relation can be observed between the technology use and the poverty level, with a marked North/South gradient.

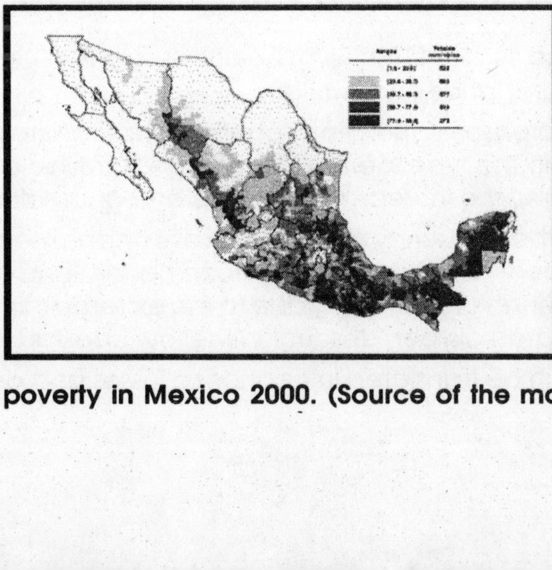

Fig.: 9: Alimentary poverty in Mexico 2000. (Source of the map: CONEVAL, 2009)

The poverty and welfare level in Mexico is measured by the government every 5 years at State, County and town scale.

Officially 3 kinds of poverty exist and can be measured:

- Alimentary poverty (nutritional aspects)
- Economic poverty (salary and employment)
- Capacity poverty (home facilities, commodities and sanitary services)

Also a welfare index is constructed every 5 years using educational, demographic, economics and infrastructure related variables.

The welfare index at county level for the year 2005 is present in the figure 10. This map shows again the North/South gradient, but also a better life conditions in the coastal municipalities.

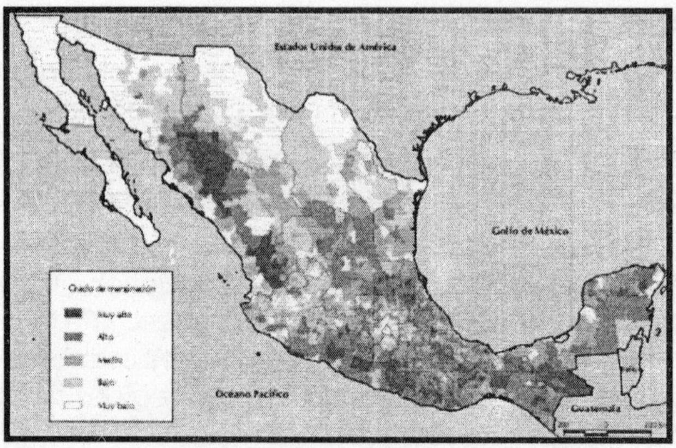

Fig.: 10: Welfare Index at county level for 2005. Box legend translation top/bottom: a) very high; b) high; c) medium; d) low and e) very low. (Source of the map: CONAPO, 2009).

Climatic Change and Food Production In Coastal States

In Mexico the most important effects and impacts of the climatic change in the coastal states will be:

- The accelerated sea level rise with the correspondent impacts in the salinity level of low agricultural lands and aquifers.
- The general increase of the atmospheric temperature with the correspondent direct impacts in the type, periodicity and geographic distribution of alimentary products, but also the increase of plagues and anomalous vegetal diseases.
- The increase in the frequency and intensity of extreme meteorological systems with the correspondent direct impacts by flooding the land fields. Also the losses of fertile soil, sediments and nutrients due to the extreme rain in the upper watershed and the associated oxygen descent in the low coastal lands.

All these impact can be translated in economic losses and poverty increase.

Conclusion and Proposal

In the short and medium term the proposed responses and remedies at national level are:

- Increase the productivity of the coastal states (Commercial Balance +) by means of the implementation of the National Polity for Oceans and Coast.
- Include the Climate Change variable (impacts) in the long term planning and management in the food production arena.
- Increase the technological effort toward the development of intensive food production (sustainable irrigation technology) in the less developed counties.
- Assure the water availability by means of technological development (marine water desalination) and define strategies toward their efficient use.
- Increase the production of regional, traditional and organic products toward their commercialization in the international markets.
- Increase the use of alternative energy (wind, solar, geothermal) and move to a "non-carbon emission society", towards the reduction in the agricultural production cost and environmental impacts.

In the long term we proposed the figure of *Alimentary World Heritage Areas,* with international recognition, international support and technological aid.

Acknowledges

Dr. Seema Joshi, the Organizing Committee of the International Conference on Global Food Security: Concern, Realities and Remedies and North Maharashtra University (India) for their kind support. Dr. Scott Venezia, Director of Academic Relation with India and Ing. Enrique Blancas President of CETYS-University.

References

1. Coll-Hurtado, A. and M. Gomez-Calderon (2004). La Agricultura en México. Un Atlas en Blanco y Negro. Instituto de Geografía de la UNAM.
2. CONABIO (2009). National Commission for the Knowledge and Use of the Biological Diversity (Mexico). (www.conabio.gob.mx)
3. CONAPO (2009). National Council of Population (Mexico). (www.conapo.gob.mx)
4. CONEVAL (2009). National Council for the Evaluation of Social Public Policies (Mexico). (www.coneval.gob.mx)
5. FAO (2009). Food and Agriculture Organization (FAO). Country Statistics. (www.fao.org)
6. INEGI (2009). National Institute of Statistics, Geography and Informatics (Mexico). (www.inegi.org.mx)
7. SAGARPA (2009). Mexico´s Ministry of Food, Fisheries and Agriculture (Mexico). (www.sagarpa.gob.mx)

4

Managing Post-Harvest Losses of Fruits and Vegetables: Strategic Way to Food Security in India

Shilpa Bendale

Introduction

Post-harvest losses of fruits and vegetables are a matter of grave concern for India's agriculture sector. Approximately 20-25% of the horticulture produce goes waste due to improper post-harvest operations which reduces the growers share in the present marketing arrangements. But this is a general phenomenon and it is happening in almost every developing countries and this also used to happen in developed country as well. An additional constraint to improve this situation is that in most developing countries including India, the number of scientists concerned with post-harvest food losses is significantly lower than those involved in production research. In the early days of horticulture in most developed countries, heavy losses occurred in much the same manner as they do today in India. Increasing industrialization in technologically advanced nations gradually brought about improvements in crop handling. Elaborate harvesting equipment replaced the crude harvesting tools. Collection centres were strategically established in major producing areas. Containers were remodelled to add more protection to the produce. Commercial storage plants were installed and grade standards adopted. Engineers and economists became more and more aware of raw material behaviour. Concomitant advances in Refrigeration Technology in the developed countries have made possible establishment of cold chains for the entire post-harvest and handling operations. At the institutional level post-harvest research was initiated. And a number of packaging houses were installed, coupled with the development of intensive training programmes. The improvement of product quality and reduction in post-harvest losses became the main concern of producers, middlemen, marketing specialists and consumers. Today, enormous volumes of quality horticultural crops produced in technologically advanced countries are made available to millions of people through improved post-harvest handling. Thus, historically and by necessity, post-harvest technology is part of the normal development processes in agriculture.

These handling procedures are not fully recognized in less developed countries. With perishable crops like fruits and vegetables, storage, packaging, transport and handling technologies are practically non-existent. Hence, considerable amount of produce are wasted. Post-harvest losses can occur in the field, in packing areas, in storage, during transportation and in the wholesale and retail market. Severe losses occur because of poor facilities, lack of know-how, poor management, market dysfunction or simply the carelessness of farmers. Proper storage conditions, temperature and humidity are needed to lengthen the storage life and maintain quality once the crop has been cooled to the optimum storage temperature.

It is distressing to note that so much time is being devoted to the culture of the plant, so much money spent on irrigation, fertilization and crop protection measures only to be wasted about a week after harvest. It is, therefore important that post-harvest procedures must be given as much attention as production practices the stages from planting until the product reach the consuming public must be a mutual undertaking between the growers and those who handle the products after harvest

Objectives

(1) To study the gap between demand and supply.

(2) To study the causes of post-harvest losses,

(3) To develop post-harvest strategies.

Background to Horticultural Development in India

Horticultural development had not been a priority in India until recent years. In the period 1948-80, the main focus of the country was on cereals. Much planned efforts had not been made for horticultural development, except for some technical support and development efforts for specific commodities. During 1980-92 there was consolidation of institutional support and a planned process for the development of horticulture. It was in the post-1993 period that a focused attention was given to horticulture development through an enhancement of plan allocation and knowledge-based technology. Despite this decade being called a "golden revolution" in horticultural production, the productivity of horticultural crops has increased only marginally from 7.5 tonnes per hectare in 1991-92 to 8.4 tonnes per hectare in 2004-05. The National Horticulture Mission was launched in 2005-06 by the Government of India with a mandate to promote integrated development in horticulture, to help in coordinating, stimulating and sustaining the production and processing of fruits and vegetables and to establish a sound infrastructure in the field of production, processing and marketing with a focus on post-harvest management to reduce losses.

As a result of the huge spurt in horticulture produce in 2005, India has become the second largest producer of fruits and vegetables in the world, next only to China. The Indian horticulture sector is facing severe constrains such as low crop productivity, limited irrigation facilities and underdeveloped infrastructure support like cold storages, markets, roads, transportation facilities, etc. There are heavy post-harvest and handling losses, resulting in low productivity per unit area and high cost of production. However, on the other hand, India's long growing-season, diverse soil and climatic conditions comprising several agro-ecological regions provide ample opportunity to grow a variety of horticulture crops. Thus, efforts are needed in the direction to capitalize on our strengths and remove constrains to meet the goal of moving towards a formidable horticultural growth in India.

Domestic Demand and Supply

According to Engel's law with the economic growth and increase in per capita income, the consumption would shift from the staple food to high value commodities like fruits and vegetables, milk and milk products, fish and eggs. The increase in consumption levels of vegetables and fruits has been quite similar in both the rural and urban areas.

Demand projections are made on the assumptions about population, urbanization, poverty and economic growth. Estimated future domestic demand is mentioned in Table 1.

Table 1: Projected domestic demand of fruits and vegetables in India

Year	Total Demand (million tonnes)		Per Capita Demand (kg)	
	Fruits	Vegetables	Fruits	Vegetables
Base Year	12.37	79.15	12.04	77.07
2010	17.43	103.16	14.78	87.51
2015	21.06	119.12	16.67	94.28
2020	25.47	137.25	18.93	102.00

Note: Scenario of economy growing at 8 per cent per annum
Source: Kumar and Kumar (2003)

Total domestic demand for fruits is expected to increase to 17.43 million tonnes by 2010 and 25.47 million tonnes by 2020. For vegetables, this demand is expected to be 103.16 million tonnes by 2010 and 137.25 million tonnes by 2020. Demand for both fruits and vegetables are expected to rise at the rate of 4-5 per cent per annum in the next 15 years. This huge increase in the demand of fruits and vegetables for domestic consumption is a challenge to be met by the country.

The National Horticulture Mission aims to double the production of fruits and vegetables by 2010. Table 2 projects the future production and supply of fruits and vegetables in India for 2015-16. Based on 1999 as the base year, it is estimated that the production of fruits and vegetables would increase to 66.9 million tonnes and 131 million tonnes respectively by 2010 and almost double by 2015. Due to huge post-harvest losses the actual supply of fruits and vegetables would be 20-25 per cent less than the production. This will help in meeting the domestic demand on the margin leaving no scope for increasing our export potential.

Table 2: Supply of vegetables and fruits in India

Year	Production	Post-harvest losses (per cent of production)	Supply (million tonnes)
Vegetables			
1999-00	83.8	19.0	67.9
2010-11	131.1	19.0	106.2
2015-16	152.5	19.0	123.5
Fruits			
1999-00	44.3	25.0	33.2
2010-11	66.9	25.0	50.2
2015-16	74.9	25.0	56.2

Source: Kumar and Kumar (2003)

The post-harvest losses mentioned in Table 2 of fruits and vegetables at the different stages of farm to fork are -

15% - 20% in Farmers field

15% - 20% in Packaging

30% - 40% in Transportation

30% - 40% in Marketing

Thus, it is required that efforts should be diverted to minimize and remove the supply constraints and make the supply-chain efficient in order to improve the horticultural and agricultural growth rates.

Causes of Post-Harvest Losses

The biological and environmental factors that contribute to post-harvest losses are well understood and many technologies have been developed to reduce these losses, they have not been implemented due to one or more of the following factors.

Biological Causes

Biological (internal) causes of deterioration include respiration rate, rates of compositional changes (associated with colour, texture, flavour, and nutritive value), mechanical injuries, water stress, sprouting and rooting, physiological disorders, and pathological break down. The rate of biological deterioration depends on several environmental (external) factors.

Transportation Facilities

In India and most developing countries, roads are not adequate for proper transport of horticultural crops. Also, transport vehicles and other modes, especially those suited for fresh horticultural perishables, are in short supply.

Transportation losses are mainly due to the following:

- Unsuitable transport containers
- Overloading of mixed fruits and vegetables (in some developing countries people and even animals ride on top of the load)

- Irresponsible driving
- Lack of feeder roads loading to highways or collection centres
- Rough roads
- Heat accumulation or very poor ventilation within the transport vehicles
- Virtual absence of refrigerated and insulated trucks
- Delays in product procurement after harvesting or at collection centres

Storage Facilities

In India, some good storage facilities that were built a few years ago are currently out of order or not functioning properly because of lack of maintenance and unavailability of spare parts. This problem is especially true of public-sector facilities.

Marketing Systems

Growers can produce large quantities of good-quality fruits and vegetables, but, if they do not have a dependable, fast, and equitable means of getting such commodities to the consumer, losses will be extensive. This problem exists in many locations within developing countries. It is emphasized by lack of communication between producers and receivers, and lack of market information.

Government Regulations and Legislations

The degree of governmental controls, especially on wholesale and retail prices of fresh fruits and vegetables, varies from one country to another. In many cases, price controls are counter-productive. Although intended for consumer protection, such regulations encourage fraud and provide no incentive for producing high-quality produce or for post-harvest quality maintenance. Sometimes, the governance has impact on many aspects related to fruits and vegetables. For example, due to sudden rise in railway transportation many wagons loaded with bananas at Savada station were not sent to their destination and being perishable it was total waste.

Unavailability of Needed Tools and Equipment

The harvesting tools are containers, equipment for cleaning, waxing, and packing, and cooling facilities. Most of the tools are neither manufactured locally nor imported in sufficient quantity to meet the demand. Various governmental regulations in some countries do not permit direct importation by producers of their needs.

Lack of Information

The human element in post-harvest handling of horticultural commodities is extremely important. Most handlers involved directly in harvesting, packaging, transporting, and marketing in developing countries have limited or no appreciation for the need for, or how, to maintain quality.

Strategies for Reducing Post Harvest Losses

An evolution of priorities within the post harvest sector from a primarily technical focus geared towards the reduction of losses, to a more holistic approach designed to link on-farm activities to processing, marketing, and distribution. However, the major constraints continue to be high post harvest losses, poor marketing systems, weak research and development capacity, and inadequacies in policies, infrastructure, and information exchange.

The solution to the problems of improper handling of perishable produce in the tropics is rather difficult, owing to the complexity of the problem. It requires the solving of technical problems as well as those of credit, land, transportation and marketing availability. It also requires a change of people's attitudes to proposed solutions and new innovations. Such an approach can only be accomplished over the years, tackling specific problems in a stepwise fashion. There must be concerted efforts by the private and government sectors.

Extension work is needed to show that **post-harvest procedures are as important as production techniques**. It is not enough to produce good quality commodities through variety improvement and proper regulation of soil and climatic factors. The whole process from planting until the harvested products reach the consuming public must be a mutual undertaking between the growers and those who will handle the product after harvest. Post-harvest handling up to the final marketing stage must be considered as a single system. The success of maintaining the harvest-fresh quality of produce demands control each depending upon the previous one. If the initial quality of the product is poor, no post-harvest treatment can improve it, although careful selection and grading may salvage some good quality produce from a mixed-quality sample. Thus, handling procedures from harvesting until the product reaches the consumers are chains of interdependent activities.

The establishment of wholesale markets and cold storage facilities by Governments or other agencies must also meet the general approval of the persons who must use them. Of what use would a modern wholesale market be if the wholesalers would rather use an antiquated one that is more accessible to them? The establishment of a cold storage plant in an area accessible to the users must be accompanied by a sustained information and promotion campaign. Emphasis must be laid on the benefits of the farmer. Realistic rental rates and payments after the sale of product could attract the farmer to use this facility. Above all an essential prerequisite to the taking of a decision to erect a new wholesale market is the need to carry out a sound feasibility study to provide suitable information for the decision-making to use.

The establishment of co-operatives has done much in certain countries but only where the organizations are effectively run and the members are aware of their responsibilities as well as the benefits. The farmers involved in cooperatives have a greater bargaining power and control of the production planning and marketing which may spur them to improve or maintain the quality of their produce. They may also be encouraged to obtain credit.

Technical knowledge of post-harvest handling has been increasing and there is a need to translate this body of knowledge into systems and techniques that the farmer can understand and use. Agricultural extension information must be reliable. The extension worker must have a, good grasp of his job and must know whom to turn to when he cannot solve the problem by himself.

A continuing problem is the **low educational level of farmers in developing countries** and their **skepticism towards new methods** they have never tried or seen before. Farming, especially of fruits and vegetables, is not looked upon as an attractive occupation. Often farming is an occupation of last resort.

Preventing losses through effective cold chains

In the recent report FICCI has pointed out that 30-35% on India's 60million tons of fruits and vegetables get wasted due to lack of adequate facilities. This is due to lack of appropriate post harvest infrastructure like cold chains and infrastructure. Cold Storages help in extending the shelf life and the period of marketing of fruits and vegetables, avoiding gluts, reducing transport bottlenecks during peak period of production and maintenance of quality produce. Cold Storages help the producers to avoid distress sale and realize better prices in the post harvest season. The consumers are assured of constant supply of quality produce at reasonable price.

Supply Chain

Several factors are driving an emphasis on supply chain management. First, the cost and availability of information resources between entities in the supply chain allow easy linkages that eliminate time delays in the network. Second, the level of competition in both domestic and international markets requires organizations to be fast, agile, and flexible. Third, customer expectations and requirements are becoming much more stringent. So to satisfy the consumers, SCM system should operate with the two main objectives ***timeliness* and *quality*.**

For Example the supply chain of **Samridhdhi Brand of Kaushalya Foundation, Patna** is an excellent example of Effective Supply Chain.

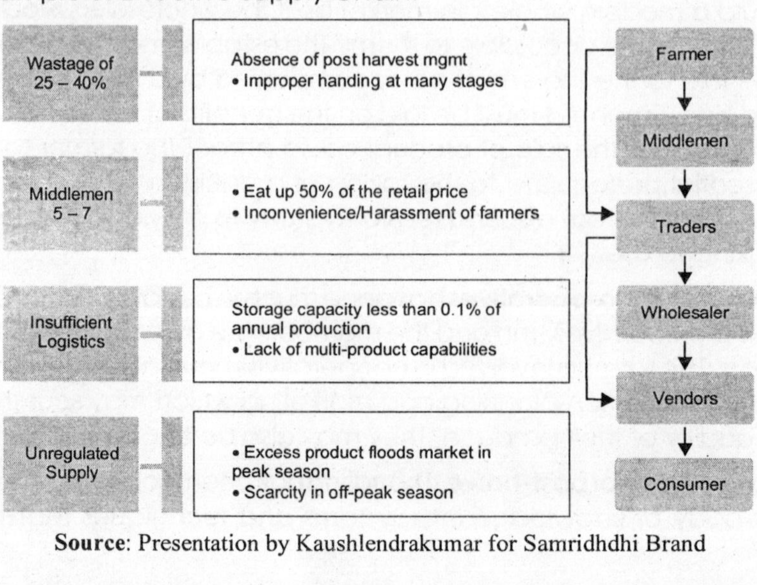

Source: Presentation by Kaushlendrakumar for Samridhdhi Brand

Research and Development

Research and development is said to be the backbone of all the ever-growing industries. In developing countries like India there is a gap between demand and supply due to post-harvest losses, one of the strategies that should be adopted is research and development in order to control the post-harvest losses. Government of India can encourage the FDI and FII to flow in the area of R&D, which would be aimed at controlling the post-harvest losses. Government should promote food-processing industries by providing some incentives. The research activities on the prevention of post-harvest losses, with emphasis placed on the improvement of methods of drying, cooperative sectors and government should promote transportation and storage of the products, quality preservation and evaluation and food processing.

Conclusion

Minimizing post harvest losses of fruits and vegetables is a very effective way of reducing the area needed for production and/or increasing food availability. Solving the post harvest problems of fruits and vegetables will require cooperation and effective communication among all the research, extension, and industry personnel involved. Post -harvest horticulturists need to coordinate their efforts with those of production horticulturists, agricultural marketing economists, engineers, food technologists, and others who may be involved in various aspects of the production and marketing system. In most cases, solutions to existing problems in the post-harvest handling system require use of available information and application of available technologies at the appropriate scale rather than conducting new research, or developing new technologies. Overcoming the gap between demand and supply is essential to achieve the goal of reducing post-harvest food losses.

References

1. Author R.C. Bhutani *"Fruits and Vegetables Preservation"*, ISBN - 8176220809
2. Pankaj Kapoor, M. D. Harrison Malayalam Ltd., *"Food Processing and Agribusiness Transforming India"*, 28-.7-2009
3. A.A. Kader, Department of Pomology, University of California, USA *"Increasing Food Availability by Reducing Post Harvest Losses of Fresh Products"*,
4. Jeremy Smith, *"Specialised Logistics For a Longer Perishable Supply Chain"* November 1, 2005
5. *"Cold Storage and Fruits & Vegetables Programme"*, National Cooperative Development Corpoation
6. Kaushalendrakumar, Samrudhdhi Brand, Kaushalya Foundation, Patna.
7. Business Today, July 2008
8. "Pawar Calls For Private and Public Efforts to Tap Horticulture", One India News.
9. www.postharvest.com.
10. Project Profiles - MP Agros Global AgriSystem Pvt. Ltd.
11. Working Paper Service, Indian School of Business, www.isb.edul

5

Causes of Pesticide Practices in Farming and Remedial Solution to Food Security

Shailendra M. Bharambe, Pramod P. Mahulikar

Introduction

The agriculture sector is a very important part of the Indian economy. The agriculture sector greatly contributes to the overall food needs of the country and provides the domestic industry with agricultural raw materials (Beena Kumari , 2008). Increasing demand of food and fiber in the world has led to greater use of pesticides for production of agricultural crops. It is estimated that without the use of pesticides, approximately 50% of world agricultural production could be lost. Insecticide residues are known to have an impact on microbial populations (Ambrogioni 1987, Zhang 1984). Insecticide residues usually occur in the top 15 cm layer of soil (Harris 1969, Lichtensteln 1962). Soil is an important reservoir for many persistent organic pollutants (POPs) including organochlorine pesticides (OCPs). OCPs have common physical- chemical properties, such as semi volatility, high levels of stability, and hydrophobicity, which are favorable for long range transport and widespread distribution in the environment (Cheng 2008, Zhang 2005). The efficacy and chemical behavior of pesticides in soil depends on many factors such as molecular structure, the nature and extent of adsorption over soil colloids, pH of soil, etc. (Gayatri Verma,2005). A full understanding of the fate of OCPs requires knowledge of their concentrations and distributions in the soil of all major ecological zones (Qui, 2005). Due to their persistence in the environment, most of these pesticides are no longer allowed to be used in many countries (Siriwong, 2008).

The study mainly deals with pesticide-use-practices (PUPs) adopted by farmer and their awareness about the PUPs and contamination occurred due to such practices in cotton growing soils.

Causes of Pesticides

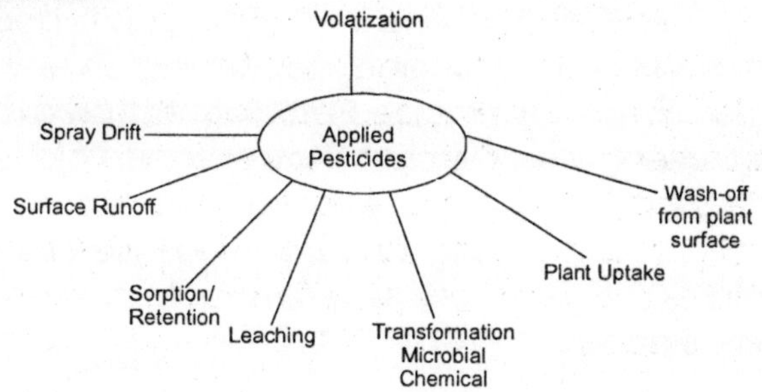

When a pesticide is applied to a crop or soil, it enters ecosystem and immediately begins to be moved from one part of the system to another, degraded *in situ* or moved out of the system into other systems. It is important to determine the relative importance of these processes, because, whereas pesticides that are completely degraded become harmless, those that move to other systems and persist may do some environmental damage.

Soil structure

With a few exceptions, the smaller the particles a soil is composed of, the longer pesticides persist in it. The way in which particle size and structure influences persistence in soil is complex, because structure is also intimately linked with such features as hydrogen ion concentration, organic matter and clay content. One comparatively simple approach was to show that there was a significant correlation between the persistence of pesticide in a range of soils and the available adsorptive surface area, which itself corresponded with a decrease in size of the soil particles.

Organic matter content

The amount of organic matter in soils ranges from less than 1%. There is now much evidence to show that soil organic matter is extremely important in adsorbing pesticides, and many workers have reported strong correlations between the persistence of pesticides in soils and the amount of organic matter in them. Supplementary evidence has been provided by workers who have demonstrated that the uptake of pesticides by plants is inversely related to the amount of organic matter in soil. Most of soil organic matter consists of humic compounds that have not been completely characterized but have a very high cation exchange capacity. The humic compounds have functional groups such as carboxyl, amino and phenolic hydroxyl, which provide sites for hydrogen bonding with pesticide molecules. Together, these characteristics provide a very considerable capacity for pesticide adsorption and increased persistence.

Microbial population of soil:

The soil is a heterogeneous environment in which the microbial population is involved in important cycles of the essential elements (Nannipieri, *et. al.*, 1990., Topp, *et. al.*, 1997). Pesticides reaching the soil may affect non-target organisms, disturbing the local metabolism (Topp, *et, al.*, 1997, Jenkinson, 1976, Kale, *et. al.*, 1989), which is essential for soil fertility, and also for pesticide degradation processes (Kearney, 1985).

Degradation is the process of pesticide breakdown after application. Pesticides are broken down by microbes, chemical reactions, and light or photo-degradation. This process may take anywhere from hours or days to years, depending on environmental conditions and the chemical characteristics of the pesticide. Pesticides that break down quickly generally do not persist in the environment or on the crop. However pesticides that break down too rapidly may only provide short-term control. Microbial breakdown is the breakdown of chemicals by microorganisms such as fungi and bacteria. Microbial breakdown tends to increase when, temperatures are warm, soil pH is favorable, soil moisture and oxygen are adequate, and soil fertility is good

Health problems

Exposure to pesticides both occupationally and environmentally causes a range of human health problems. It is estimated that nearly 10,000 deaths occur annually to use of chemical pesticide worldwide, with about three-fourths of these occurring in developing countries (Horrigan *et.al.,* 2002). At present, India is the largest producer of pesticides in Asia and ranks twelfth in the world for the use of pesticides with an annual production of 90,000 tons (http://www.teri.res.in). Vast majorities of the population in India (56.7 percent) is engaged in agriculture and are therefore exposed to the pesticides used in agriculture (Gupta, 2004, http://planningcommission.nic.in). Pesticides being used in agricultural tracts are released into the environment and come into human contact directly or indirectly. Humans are exposed to pesticides found in environmental media (soil, water, air and food) by different routes of exposure such as inhalation, ingestion and dermal contact. Exposure to pesticides results in acute and chronic health problems. These range from temporary acute effects like irritation of eyes, excessive salivation to chronic diseases like cancer, reproductive and developmental disorders, etc. (Yassi, *et. al.,* 2001)

Case study

In the case study, the cotton growing five tahasils of the Jalgaon district were selected and contamination levels of the pesticide residues were investigated (Bharambe & Mahulikar., 2009). In this study the basic physical and chemical characteristics of the soil were studied and are presented in **Table 1**.

Table- 1: Physical and Chemical Properties of soil

Parameter	Values
pH	7.30 – 7.92
Moisture Content	6.9 % - 19.2 %
Organic carbon	0.58 % – 0.78 %
Bulk Density	1.136 g/cm³ – 1.186 g/cm³
Available Nitrogen	185 Kg/ha. – 282 Kg/ha.
Available Potassium	325 Kg/ha. – 427 Kg/ha.
Available Phosphate	18 Kg/ha. – 29 Kg/ha.

The chromatographic results compared with standards and concentrations of organochlorine pesticide residues were calculated and the results are summarized in **Table 2**. It was found that soil samples contained endosulfan-I ranged from 0.11 μg/ kg (at Bhoras village, Chalisgaon tahasil) to 3.67 μg/kg (at Walziri village of Chalisgaon tahasil), endosulfan-II ranged from 0.14 μg/ kg (at Ozar village, Pachora tahasil) to 5.54 μg/kg (at Walziri village, Chalisgaon tahasil), endosulfan sulfate ranged from 0.12 μg/ kg (at Bhalgaon village, Earondol tahasil) to 4.90 μg/kg (at Khedgaon village, Bhadgaon tahasil), linden ranged from 0.44μg/ kg (at Chorwad village, Bhadgaon tahasil) to 5.80 μg/kg (at Walziri village, Chalisgaon tahasil) and endrin ranged from 0.16 μg / kg (at Bhalgaon village, Earondol tahasil) to 6.12 μg/kg (at Kothli village, Bhadgaon tahasil). The Kothli village had moderately high organic carbon content (0.78%) and the residue of endrin was 6.12 μg/kg. This trend was observed in Walziri, Khedgaon, Deoli and Ranjangaon. This indicates that organic carbon might play an important role in persistence of pesticide residues. In villages like Waghere, Toli, Patonda Walwadi residues were not in proportional to organic carbon content of the soil, indicating that their application and concentrations were reflection of application history and dissipation of pesticides.

In present investigations, among the five tahasils studied, Chalisgaon tahasil was found to be the most contaminated; however, the Earandol tahasil was least contaminated. The increase in concentration of pesticides residues in soil could be harmful to human being as organochlorines are known for their toxicity.

Table 2: Residues of pesticides in Cotton growing soils (μg/Kg)

Name of village	Endosulfan-I	Endosulfan-II	Linden	Endosulfan	Endrin
Bhadgaon tahasil					
Bhadgaon	Nd	Nd	5.58	Nd	2.60
Walwadi	1.40	Nd	2.20	7.7	3.60
Khedgaon	0.79	Nd	1.54	4.9	1.41
Vadji	0.28	0.34	1.47	0.85	0.48
Kothali	3.64	3.99	4.13	3.72	6.12
Anchalgaon	0.36	0.85	0.62	4.55	0.25
Chalisgaon tahasil					
Waghali	0.57	0.56	2.20	0.31	0.78
Patoda	1.55	1.15	2.81	0.20	2.34
Ranjangaon	2.53	4.76	4.37	4.23	2.20
Walziri	3.67	5.54	5.80	4.19	Nd
Deoli	0.67	5.61	2.50	3.63	0.99
Bhoras	0.11	0.27	2.24	0.96	0.40
Earandol tahasil					
Toli	1.45	2.48	3.66	Nd	1.10
Bhalgaon	0.51	0.80	1.27	0.12	0.16
Dharagir	Nd	Nd	1.74	Nd	1.49
Talai	Nd	Nd	3.64	Nd	4.72
Utran	Nd	Nd	3.88	Nd	4.63
Hanumantkhede	0.82	0.94	1.13	Nd	2.62
Pachora tahasil					
Goradkheda	0.52	0.20	2.91	0.62	3.01
Ozar	0.32	0.14	2.12	0.16	0.55

Khedgaon bk	2.04	2.56	3.09	1.45	2.46
Tarkheda	1.51	Nd	1.00	Nd	2.17
Chunchale	2.17	Nd	3.13	Nd	1.66
Ambevadgaon	Nd	Nd	1.41	Nd	1.42
Parola tahasil					
Bodarde	1.36	Nd	1.55	Nd	1.62
Chorwad	0.57	Nd	0.44	Nd	1.47
Bhadarpur	Nd	Nd	0.80	Nd	1.20
Parola	1.12	0.96	.74	Nd	0.98
Waghere	Nd	Nd	4.09	Nd	5.37
Ratnapimpri	nd	Nd	2.60	Nd	4.33

Conclusion

An increased and non-judicious use of different pesticides in last four decades has resulted in increased level of pesticide residues in the soil. To meet the demand of increasing population, in modern agricultural practices, the application of all types of pesticides has resulted in the said problem. Hence, it may be concluded and suggested that proper agricultural practices such as need based application of quantity formulation and integrated crop and pest management could reduce the pesticide contamination in soil and thus, could minimize the associated disadvantages and hazards.

Remedies to pesticides use:

For the improvement in present situation regarding the pesticide use, pest resistant to pesticides, environmental contamination, and health hazard to farmers as well as the consumers from the toxic chemicals, the following recommendations are suggested.

1. Farmers or producers of agro-food products should follow good agriculture practices, which takes account of proper use of certified chemicals within the approved amount or limited dose.
2. The misuse and abuse of such chemicals increases the resultant residue problems in food products as well as environmental pollution. There is need to develop the benchmark standards.
3. Integrated Pest Management, the tool to help farmers to get rid of pesticides, should be implemented to the field level with intensive programs.
4. Pesticide residues is raising a prominent issue on the food safety and environmental pollution. In order to control the resultant residue problem in foods and promotion of food trade in international market, a national pesticide residues monitoring program should be implemented.
5. There should be a coordinating team of public private partnership for close monitoring of appropriate use of pesticides at the field level.
6. A regular training /workshop about the use and safety measures of pesticide should be given to farmers, retailers, distributors and all the pesticide workers. Multimedia awareness activities in local language should be massively conducted.

Use and application considerations for pesticide applications to minimize the adverse effects

- Use right pesticide at right dose at right time against right pest.
- Apply pesticides at the lowest effective level.
- Avoid unnecessary pesticide treatments.
- Use Integrated Pest Management.
- Follow all label instructions.
- Apply proper rates and times as label indicates.
- Calibrate application equipment.
- Apply formulations that minimize drift.
- Use safety equipment when handling.
- Store and dispose of pesticide containers properly.
- Use biological controls when appropriate.
- Alter farming or cropping systems to control pests.
- Use disease and insect resistant crop varieties.

References

1. ***Beena Kumari, V. K. Madan, T. S. Kathpal,*** (2008), Status of insecticide contamination of soil and water in Haryana, India. *Environ Monit Assess* 136:239
2. ***Bharambe S.M. and Mahulikar P. P.,*** (2009) Residues of Organochlorine Pesticides in Banana Growing Soils of Jalgaon District, Bull. Env. Sci. Vol. XXVIII (3rd Issue), pp. 269-273
3. ***Chatwal G. R. Mehea M. C., T. Katyal, M. Satake, M. Katyal, T. Nagahiro*** (1997). *Environmental Analysis:Air, Water and Soil,* 1st Ed, Anmol Publications Pvt. Ltd., New Delhi, p- 157-159.
4. ***Cheng, H. X. S. Fu, Y. H. Liu, D. S. Li, J. H. Zhou, X. J. Xia*** (2008) Organochlorine Pesticides in the Soil in Linfen, China. *Bull Environ Contam Toxicol* **81**:599–603
5. ***Gayatri Verma, A Kumar, Alka Tomar and KK singh*** (2005) Mobility of OP pesticides in soil as affected by physico chemical characteristics of soil. *Pestic Res J* **17** (2): 97-103
6. ***Ghaadiri, H. and Rose C. W.*** (2001). Dogradation of endosulfan in a clay soil from cotton farms of western Queensland. *J Env Management* ***62**: 155-169.*
7. **Gupta P K.** (2004) Pesticide exposure – Indian scene. Toxicology. 198: 83-90.
8. ***Harris, C.R., Sans, W.W.,*** (1969), Vertical distribution of residues of organochlorine insecticides in soils collected from six farms in southwestern Ontario, Proc. Entomol. Soc. Ontario 100: 156.
9. ***Horrigan L,*** Lawrence RS, Walker P. (2002) How sustainable agriculture can address the environmental and human heath harms of industrial agriculture. *Environ Health Prospect.* 110 (5):445-456.
10. http://www.planningcommission.nic.in/plans/planrel/fiveyr/welcome.html
11. http://www.teri.res.in/teriin/news/terivsn/issue31/pesticid.htm>.

12. **Jenkinson, D.S.,** Powlson, D.S., (1976) The effects of biocidal treatment on metabolism insoil. I. Fumigation with chloroform, Soil Biol. Biochem. **8** 167-177.

13. **Kale, S.P.,** Raghu, K., (1989) Relationship between microbial parameters and other14. microbial indices in soil, Bull. Environ. Con. Toxicol. **43** 941-945.

15. **Kearney, P.C., Kellogg, S.,** (1985) Microbial adaptation to pesticides, Pure & Appl. Chem. 57 389-403.

16. **Kundsen D. and G. A. Peterson** (1982) Lithium, sodium and potassium. In A. L. Page (Ed) Methods of soil analysis. *Agronomy monogram No. 9,* Amer Soc of Agron. Inc., Soil Sci Soc of Amer. Inc Publisher, Madison, Wisconsin, USA. p- 225-246.

17. **Lichtenste1n, E.P.,** (1962), Vertical distribution and persistence of insecticidal18. residues in soils as influenced by mode of application and a cover crop, J. Econ.19. Entomol. 55: 215.

20. **Nannipieri, P.** et al., (1990).Ecological significance of the biological activity in soil., Soil Biochemistry, Vol. 6 (BOLLAG, J.-M., STOTZKY, O., Eds.), Marcel Dekker Inc., New York 293-355.

21. **Nelson, D. W. and L. E. Sommers** (1982). Total organic carbon, organic carbon and organic matter. In A. L. Page (Ed) Methods of soil analysis. *Agronomy monogram No. 9,* Amer Soc of Agron. Inc., Soil Sci Soc of Amer. Inc Publisher, Madison, Wisconsin, USA. 539-579.

22. **Qiu X, Zhu T, Yao B, Hu J, Hu S** (2005) Contribution of dicofol to the current DDT pollution in China. *Environ Sci Technol* **39**:4385–4390.

23. **Siriwong, W., K. Thirakhupt, D. Sitticharoenchai, M. Borjan, M. Robson** (2008) Organochlorine pesticide residues in Plankton, Rangsit agricultural area, central Thiland. *Bull Environ Contam Toxicol* **81**:608–612

24. **Subbiah, B. V. and G. L. Asija** (1956). A rapid procedure for the estimation of available nitrogen in soil. *Curr Sci* **25**: 259-260.

25. **Topp, E.,** et al, (1997) .Pesticides: microbial degradation and effects on microorganisms., Modem Soil Microbiology (van ELSAS, J.A., et al., Eds.), Marcel Dekker Inc., NewYork 547-573.

26. **Watanabe F. S. and S. R. Olsen** (1965) Test of ascorbic acid method for determining phosphorus in water and sodium bicarbonate extracts of soil. *Proc Soil Sci Soc Am* **29**: 677

27. www.mahaagri.gov.in/distprofile/Jalgaon.html

28. **Yassi, A,** Kjellstrom. T, Kok.T.K., Gudotli.T.L. (2001)Basic Environmental Health, World Health Organozation. Oxford University Press.

29. **Zhang H, Lu Y, Dawson RW, Shi Y, Wang T** (2005) Classification and Ordination of DDT and HCH in soil samples from the Guanting Reservoir, China. *Chemosphere* **60**:762

30. **Zhang, L.,** (1984), Persistence, degradation and distribution of deltamethrin in an organic soil under laboratory conditions, J. Agric. Food Chem. 32: 1207.

6

The Role of Biotechnology in Sustainable Food Supply to Bestow Food Security

R.R. Chavan, Brig.R.C.Pathak

It is estimated that world population will bite the 8 billion mark in the year 2025 and most of the increase is expected in the developing world. Increasing population worldwide has resulted in competitive survival of human beings on the earth. Except in a few developed nations, availability of food material has become a big challenge. In countries wherein the development of food biotechnology is in its seedling stage, fast developments in the food sector are required. Further improvement of food production is now at the door of genetic engineering and molecular Breeding.

The research explores the current causes of food insecurity, the role of agricultural biotechnology and its implications in various aspects. This paper attempts to review the achievement of biotechnology in ensuring food security and sustainable agriculture. The objective is to examine the facet of agricultural biotechnological advancement in respect of increases in agricultural production and relating such issues with the food insecurity. Accordingly the research is based on a literature review taking into account the most recent and other aspects of the stated topic. Food security and sustainable agriculture have become burning issues in the world as plans are made for a changing global climate and increasing global population. One of the most important environmental challenges facing the developing world is how to meet current food needs without undermining the ability of future generations to meet theirs, thus, agricultural production must be sufficient to feed us now and in future.

Food Security: Concept and Issues

Food security happens when all people at all times have access to enough food that should be affordable, safe and healthy, culturally acceptable, meets specific dietary needs, obtained in a dignified manner and produced in ways that are environmentally sound. The

World Food Summit of 1996 defined food security as existing "when all people at all times have access to sufficient, safe, nutritious food to maintain a healthy and active life". Commonly, the concept of food security is defined as including both physical and economic access to food that meets people's dietary needs as well as their food preferences. But food security is a complex sustainable development issue, linked to health through malnutrition, but also to sustainable economic development, environment, and trade. There is a great deal of debate around food security. If we fail to maintain above there has been food insecurity. Food insecurity exists when all people, at all times, do not have physical and economic access to the sufficient, safe and nutritious food to meet their dietary needs and food preferences for an active and healthy life. Food security has both economic and physical dimensions; the former referring to economic access and the latter to physical availability of food grains in sufficient quantities required for an active and healthy life. The official definition and measurement of income/consumption poverty in India is anchored in a physical norm for food insecurity. Hence, one would expect the estimates of poverty and food insecurity to tally for any given reference year. However, the two sets of estimates could diverge for any other subsequent year for the following methodological reasons (Suryanarayana and Dimtri, 2007): (i) Estimates of poverty are based on monetary measures of consumer expenditure distributions (at current prices) with reference to a base year norm, where only the norm gets adjusted for percentage price changes; and (ii) those for deprivation in physical access to food are made in terms of physical quantities (which respond to changes not only in prices, but also tastes and preferences as well as a host of other variables such as levels of living and infrastructural facilities) with reference to a constant base year physical norm.

Biotechnology: key technology for the new millennium

Biotechnology is a science that deals with the use of microorganisms, plant cells, animal cells, or parts of cells such as enzymes to produce commercial quantities of useful substances. It also deals with the construction of microorganisms, cells, plants, or animals with useful traits by recombinant DNA techniques, tissue culture, embryo transfer, and other methods besides traditional genetic breeding techniques. The biotechnology is a collective term for a group of technologies that use biological matter or processes to generate new and useful products and processes. On the other hand, the potential for altering the genetic structure and characteristics of living organisms, including humans, plants and animals, has resulted in many concerns about safety and ethical implications of the new technologies. Biotechnology applies across a number of fields. Agricultural biotechnology is most crucial for countries and especially for resource-poor farmers whose sole livelihood depends on agriculture. Indeed, worldwide there has been a shift towards greater emphasis on agricultural biotechnology than on pharmaceutical, which dominated the terrain before. So far, most of the safety issues have emerged from agricultural biotechnology, but some cutting-edge developments in medical biotechnology are now presenting the major ethical concerns. By adding genes to conventional crops to help them resist pests, disease, or drought, producers of biotech seed can make crops that use less of an expensive input or crops that produce higher yields. Any one, or several, of these improvements can be tailored to make individual crops more likely to thrive in a particular country's growing conditions, and can potentially allow a wider variety of innovations. A number of economic criteria must be met to unleash the potential of biotechnology. Farmers must be willing to plant biotech varieties, and those varieties must be suited to local conditions. Most of the research in biotechnology thus far has been done by the private sector for temperate climate crops. Some research on the staple crops of developing countries is in progress, but this market has developed more slowly, in part because of concerns related to farmers' ability to purchase the inputs and the lack of protection of intellectual property in developing countries. Some developing-country farmers are already cultivating biotech crops. Developing countries account for about 24 percent of the 44.2 million hectares planted to biotech crops in 2000, although most of that production is in one country- Argentina. As with any technological innovation, growing biotech varieties requires farmers to change their production methods. Farmers will adopt the new varieties if the gains from the higher yields or lower costs of producing biotech varieties outweigh any new costs associated with the technology, like the need to purchase more expensive seeds, to purchase seeds more frequently, or to use more expensive inputs.

Genetically modified crops and food security

The basic argument put forward in favour of genetically modified (GM) crops is that they can provide at least a partial solution to the problem of feeding the world's growing population. Even with improved food distribution and access, this cannot be achieved without dramatic increases in crop production. Converting more land for agricultural use is environmentally unsustainable. Genetic engineering has opened up opportunities for increasing crop yields, reducing crop losses to insects, disease and post-harvest storage problems, and enhancing the nutritional value of some crops. In addition, crops are now being developed to resist abiotic stresses, such as drought and soil salinity. This will allow increased crop production on marginal land and therefore bring possible benefits to poorer rural areas. For example, some of the first commercial releases of GM crops were modified with a gene from a bacterium, *Bacillus thuringiensis* (*Bt*), which codes for a toxin against some crop pests. *Bt* insecticide sprays have been in use for several decades, and are approved for organic farming. However, introducing the *Bt* toxin gene directly into a plant genome raised many concerns about the genetic engineering of crops, and food products derived from them. A very important challenge for developing countries that hope to use biotechnology to address food security objectives is that the new GM crops may not be appropriate to their most urgent needs. Biotechnology firms are unlikely to address these needs unless they are commercially profitable, and this leaves a large gap for the public sector to fill. Bearing in mind that research costs are usually very high, new forms of public-private sector partnerships need to be sought in order that the benefits of biotechnology reach those who need them most. One promising new initiative has been the development of "golden" rice, which has been modified to enhance its production of beta carotene, which is metabolized into vitamin A. This new variety has the potential to address the huge problem of vitamin A deficiency in developing countries, which causes partial or total blindness in around half a million children each year. Consumers in developing countries may also benefit from biotechnology. If domestic food production rises, food prices will decrease, making an adequate diet more affordable. Even if biotech-induced increases in food production occur outside the country, world prices could fall, making food more affordable. Crop varieties can also be altered to provide greater nutrition. Biotechnology can be used to alter conventional crop varieties to enhance their micro-nutrient and protein content. Several research institutes are developing "Golden Rice," which will have a higher Vitamin A and iron content. This development could help to reduce the incidence of diseases like blindness and anemia that are related to vitamin deficiencies. Such varieties might be well received in developing countries. Governments in the developing world will also need to feel confident about using foods produced through biotechnology. Several countries are considering regulations to require labeling of foods produced with biotechnology, and other countries are developing safety regulations for biotechnology. Public agricultural research agencies such as governments, universities, and non-governmental agencies can make biotechnology more accessible for farmers in developing nations, chiefly by targeting innovations to their needs. Some governments, notably that of China, are actively engaged in research. The International Rice Research Institute is working on several varieties of rice, including one that increases yields substantially. The Rockefeller Foundation has been actively involved in developing "Golden Rice" and in training scientists in developing countries. Michigan State University, Scripps College, and Cornell University all have partnerships with Egypt's agricultural research institute to develop genetically engineered varieties of vegetables. Public support can also reduce the cost of seeds for crop varieties developed via biotechnology. Research costs of developing biotech varieties are very high, especially as some of the technology used is proprietary and must be licensed from private companies. It is difficult for low income countries, and even for public institutions, to afford the development costs. The CGIAR centers (Consultative Group on International Agricultural Research) spend $25- $35 million per year on agricultural biotechnology. By comparison, Monsanto's 1998 R&D budget (mostly for agricultural biotechnology) was $1.3 billion. Some public-private partnerships have already begun to facilitate access to biotechnology and the design of new crop varieties for developing countries. The Mexican Government received some technology free of charge from Monsanto. Through Michigan State, the Rockefeller Foundation, and USAID, several U.S. companies are working with the governments of Indonesia, Kenya, and Egypt to develop new crop varieties. How widespread these partnerships are and how many of them will concentrate on varieties relevant to developing nations will affect the usefulness of the biotechnology revolution for developing countries.

Biotechnology and Food Security: Key issues

While a wide range of policies is required to address some of the structural rigidities that undermine prospects of achieving the necessary food security status, biotechnology can enhance agricultural production in the countries. The cluster of techniques that comprise biotechnology can, if effectively harnessed and applied, radically transform farming systems by reducing post-harvest loss and increasing crop resistance to drought. For instance, the application of tissue culture in the production of bananas has increased yields for small-scale farmers in parts of Kenya. Pathogen-free banana planting material can reduce crop loss due to pests. The biotechnology and food security in world debate raises several key issues:

1. How do you transfer biotechnology to countries and strengthen their technological competence to acquire, assimilate, further develop, and effectively apply the technology for enhanced agricultural production?
2. What policy and institutional arrangements should be put in place to make the technology and its products accessible to rural farmers in the counties?

These are complex issues especially considered against the background of the empirically empty rhetoric on biotechnology that is conducted at two extremes. On the one hand there are the pessimists who perceive biotechnology as eroding opportunities to address food insecurity and generating more environmental harm. In this category are environmental lobbies. On the other hand are the optimists who see biotechnology as the panacea for all problems including food insecurity. In this category are biotechnology scientists. No technology by and of itself has internal momentum to create food security for any society or region. It is how the technology is applied and molded by society that determines its usefulness. Indeed, if biotechnology were the panacea for food insecurity problems, we would not be talking about hunger and starvation today in light of the net increases in food production recorded in the world in the last two decades. There are obviously other problems, such as access to the food (Is it affordable? Can it be moved across regions effectively?), equity (at the international and national levels), and distribution of the food globally and nationally, which impact on food security. Such issues impinge on food security but are not strictly speaking biotechnology problems.

1. There is not inherent goodness/badness in any one technology. Most technologies have advantages and disadvantages.
2. The biotechnology revolution is with us and is witnessed by the increase in the acreage of genetically modified crops and the proliferation of genetically modified products and processes. Biotechnology has transformed agricultural and economic systems of countries such as the United States, Canada, and some countries in Latin America and Asia.
3. To deal with biotechnology processes and products requires some level of biotechnology competence. Only those countries that understand genetically modified organisms can effectively monitor and regulate their application. In this regard, African countries such as Egypt and South Africa are poised to leapfrog to higher levels of technological competence and performance as they have invested in sound institutional structures for managing biotechnology.

The Status of Agricultural Biotechnology in the world:

It is noteworthy that most countries have not taken deliberate efforts to understand biotechnology, tap its potential, and use it to address some of their basic agricultural problems. This is so despite evidence that the last two decades have witnessed increased investment in biotechnology research and development (R&D) by a number of countries. Indeed, national agricultural research institutes, public universities, international institutions, and private companies have engaged in some form of agricultural biotechnology.

There are generally three categories of countries in terms of biotechnology R&D capacity and potential in countries:

1. Countries that are generating and commercializing biotechnology products and processes using third-generation techniques of genetic engineering.
2. Countries engaged in third-generation biotechnology R&D, but which have no products or processes yet.
3. Those engaged in second-generation biotechnology.

The actors in agricultural biotechnology R&D in different countries can be distinguished from those in the developed countries where private corporations such as Monsanto are emerging as the main drivers of biotechnology R&D, and consequently own and control biotechnology information. The globalization of the world economy and the emergence of the giant transnational corporations (with economic potential greater than that of a group of developing countries put together) are shaping the development of countries in Africa and elsewhere in the developing world. The concentration of agricultural biotechnology R&D in a handful of companies has implications for access to the technology and products thereof, given the trend toward tighter control of intellectual property promoted by the WTO's agreement on trade-related aspects of intellectual property rights (TRIPS). This concentration and the provisions of TRIPS have resulted in the progressive privatization of biotechnology innovations that have resulted from material provided freely by communities of farmers around the world; this is an issue of great concern today. The main constraints to the capacity of biotechnology to engender food security are limited capacity human, financial, and infrastructural; ill-defined or non-defined institutional arrangements for biotechnology R&D.

Policy Challenges for countries

1. To establish clear priorities in investment in biotechnology. Countries should identify specific areas or technology trajectories in which to invest to meet specific goals and to utilize the available skills and resources optimally.
2. To ensure availability of finances for biotechnology R&D. Current investment in this area is not sufficient. This could be done by forging strategic alliances with the private sector, ensuring that the public good of availing food to all is not compromised by profit motivation.
3. To consider the role of intellectual property rights and their impact on the acquisition, development, and diffusion of biotechnology.

Conclusions

The biotechnology revolution is witnessed by the increase in the acreage of genetically modified crops and the proliferation of genetically modified products and processes. Biotechnology has transformed agricultural and economic systems of various countries. But to deal with biotechnology processes and products requires some level of biotechnology competence. Only those countries that understand genetically modified organisms can effectively monitor and regulate their application. Many observers have suggested that biotechnology has the potential to increase world food output and reduce food insecurity by improving crop yields and reducing crop loss. Taking cognizance of the different applications of Biotechnology in the environment, food and agriculture, health care and the industrial sectors, it is indeed an essential panacea to the pervasive poverty and food security problem.

References

1. Prasad B N, *"Biotechnology In Sustainable Biodiversity & Food Security"*, India Book House Limited
2. Shashi Kumar, *"Biodiversity and Food Security"*, Atlantic Publisher
3. Sujata K. Dass, *"Biotechnology and Food Security"*, Gyan Books
4. Vibha Dhawan, *"Biotechnology for Food and Nutritional Security"*, Teri Press
5. Brian Rappert, *"Biotechnology, Security And The Search For Limits: An Inquiry Into Research And Methods (Series - New Security Challenges)"*, Palgrave Macmillan
6. Julia Wright, *"Sustainable Agriculture And Food Security In An Era Of Oil Scarcity: Lessons From Cuba"*, Earthscan Publications Limited
7. Amitava Mukherjee (2007), Micro-Level Food Insecurity in Contemporary India: Perspectives of the Food Insecure .
8. Bickel, G., Nord, M., Price, C., Hamilton, W. & Cook, J. (2000). *Guide to measuring food security*, revised 2000. Washington, DC, United States Department of Agriculture.
9. Bhalla, G.S.(1994), *"Policies for Food Security in India"*, New Delhi.
10. Jonson, Mascarenhas, Thatte, Chatterji (2002), *"Development Issues of Indian Economy"*, Manan, Prakashan, Mumbai.
11. Radhakrishna , R. (1991) , *"Food and Nutrition: Challenges for Policy"*, Journal of the Indian Society of Agricultural Statistics,
12. Economic Survey of India, 2008-09 (The Government of India)

7

Management of Natural Resource for Food Security

Ms. Mamata S.Dahad, Mrs. Anupama P. Chaudhari

Present Indian Scenario

The **economy of India** is the twelfth largest economy in the world by market exchange rates and the fourth largest by purchasing power parity (PPP). In the 1990s, following economic reform from the socialist-inspired economy of post-independence India, the country began to experience rapid economic growth, as markets opened for international competition and investment. In the 21st century, India is an emerging economic power with vast human and natural resources, and a huge knowledge base. Economists predict that by 2020, India will be among the leading economies of the world.

At the threshold of the twenty-first century, widespread poverty, food insecurity, and environmental degradation cause severe human suffering and threaten to destabilize global, regional, and national economic and ecological conditions. If these trends continue unabated, the world will not be a pleasant place to live for most of humanity. The International Food Policy Research Institute has developed a 2020 Vision of *a* world where every person has economic and physical access to sufficient food to sustain a healthy and productive life, where malnutrition is absent, and where food originates from efficient, effective, and low-cost food and agricultural systems that are compatible with sustainable use and management of natural resources. With foresight and decisive action, we can create the conditions that will permit this vision to be realized by 2020. There are several challenges to assuring food security and sustainable use of natural resources:

(i) Widespread poverty and inadequate human resource development, which inhibit people's capacity to grow and/or purchase the needed food;

(ii) Large increases in developing-country populations, especially in urban areas, which will substantially increase food needs;

(iii) Gross under-investment in agricultural research in developing countries and inadequacies in availability of and access to agricultural inputs-such as water, fertilizer, pesticides, energy, research, and technology, which leads to lagging yield increases in more-favored areas and low and variable yields in less-favored areas;

(iv) Degradation of natural resources—such as soils, forests, marine fisheries, and water—which undermines production capacity;

(v) Inefficient functioning of markets and inadequate infrastructure as well as weakened capacity of developing-country governments to perform their appropriate functions; and

(vi) Insufficient domestic resource mobilization—savings and investment—and declining international assistance, which restrains economic growth and development.

These challenges can be overcome and the 2020 Vision of food security and sustainable use of natural resources realized if all relevant parties—individuals, households, farmers, local communities, civil society, private sector, national governments, and the international community—take appropriate action and change their behavior, priorities, and policies. Priority actions include investing more in poor people, accelerating agricultural productivity, assuring sound management of natural resources, strengthening the capacity of developing-country governments to perform appropriate functions, and expanding and realigning international development assistance. The world's natural resources are capable of supporting the 2020 Vision, if current rates of degradation are reduced and replaced by appropriate technological change and sustainable use of natural resources.

From a nation dependent on food imports to feed its population, India today is not only self-sufficient in grain production, but also has a substantial reserve. The progress made in agriculture during the last four decades has been one of the biggest success stories of independent India.

Despite these impressive gains, India, at present, finds itself in the midst of a paradoxical situation: On the one hand there are record food grain stocks standing at an all-time high and on the other hand, over 200 million of India's population is underfed, and millions are undernourished. The challenge is to bridge this gap.

In a scenario of shrinking land and depleting water resources, the challenge of the new millennium is to increase biological yields to feed the ever-growing population without destroying the ecological foundation.

The following are suggestions towards achieving sustainable agriculture, rural development and food security. They provide a reference for actions to be undertaken by the various stakeholders in this area. Natural resources have to be accessible to the poor, which in the farm sector means secure rights to land, water and genetic resources. For this, there is a need to develop public-private partnerships.

A positive right to life would imply that the State provides to each and every person, adequate food and other basic necessities, and that it ensures a healthy environment, so that people may live and grow in dignity. The most important challenge in the 1980s and 1990s was physical access to food. In this millennium, the challenge is economic and ecological access to food.

A surge in commodity prices has pushed 'food security' up the agenda in policy, business and public debate. Yet the term is used to promote everything from self-sufficiency to social justice.

Natural Resource Management is a discipline in the management of natural resources such as land, water, soil, plants and animals, with a particular focus on how management affects the quality of life for both present and future generations. Natural resource management is interrelated with the concept of sustainable development, a principle that forms a basis for land management and environmental governance throughout the world.

Land, water and forests are the three most important resources for the people living in rural areas. Intensive work is carried out by Gram Vikas in enhancing food security and improving environmental resistance to drought through effective land, water and forest management practices. Communities recognize the fact that sustainability of natural resources will also determine food security and sustainable livelihoods for themselves. Gram Vikas supports village communities in undertaking sustainable management of natural resources through a variety of interventions in promoting community forestry and horticulture, land and water conservation and development.

Atlas of the Sustainability of Food Security in India

How can India ensure sustainable food security for a billion-strong population? "Sustainable food security" means enough food for everyone at present plus the ability to provide enough in future as well.

This calls for sound policies and investments in natural resources such as land and water, flora and fauna, forests and biodiversity — the ecological foundations essential for sustainable food security - plus sustainable intensification of crop and animal production. Population pressures and the forces of atmosphere and climate change must also be taken into account.

"Food security has three components," says Prof M S Swaminathan. "The first is food availability, which depends on food production and imports. The second is food access, which depends on purchasing power. The third, food absorption, is a function of safe drinking water, environmental hygiene, primary health care and education."

The Food Insecurity Atlas of Rural India revealed that the Punjab-Haryana region, India's breadbasket, could lose its production potential in a few decades if current patterns of groundwater extraction and pollution, soil salinization and rice-wheat monoculture persisted. It was therefore decided to produce an Atlas on Sustainability of Food Security in India to promote ecologically sustainable methods of food production and natural resources management.

The Atlas examines the ability of States in India to provide food security at present as well as sustain it in future.

The Atlas concludes with a "Sustainable Food Security Compact," a nine-point action plan for every State and Union Territory. The action points refer to stabilizing population, conserving and enhancing land resources, ensuring water security, conserving and restoring forests with community participation, strengthening biodiversity, improving the atmosphere, managing common property resources, intensifying crop and animal production in a sustainable way, and forming a Coalition for Sustainable Food Security in every State revealing some interesting facts.

In some States like Orissa, Himachal Pradesh, Bihar, Karnataka and Tamil Nadu, Net sown area has been declining. In the process prime agricultural land may shift to non-agricultural uses.

- Land degradation has been fairly high in Nagaland, Sikkim and Himachal Pradesh. In some northeastern State, wasteland accounts for 50 per cent of the total geographical areas.
- Overexploitation of groundwater has reached danger levels in Punjab, Haryana and Tamil Nadu.
- Some States (Madhya Pradesh for example) show high poverty levels at present, yet natural resources are sufficient to sustain agriculture in future. In other states (Punjab and Haryana), livelihood access is good at present, but natural resource endowments for future sustainability are below par.
- In States like Bihar, Uttar Pradesh and Madhya Pradesh, there is an urgent need to diversify livelihoods to non-crop and non- agricultural enterprises.

Every State will have to chalk out its own strategies for sustainable livelihood to move on the path of sustainable food production and sustainable livelihood security.

A State that ranks high in unexploited natural resources such as forests and water, soil fertility (in terms of lower land degradation and greater natural replenishment of soil) and stable crop production, will also rank high in composite index of sustainable food security.

Arunachal Pradesh, Madhya Pradesh and Goa obtain the top three ranks as regards a sustainable food security index. Karnataka, Gujarat and Andhra Pradesh occupy ranks four to six.

"The path towards sustainable development varies from State to State," States with a strong natural resource base may rank high in sustainability but may not be in a position to produce enough food at prosent. Removing pressure on land and water and conserving natural resources for sustainable water supply are essential in TamilNadu; increasing land productivity, diversifying agriculture, improving infrastructure and providing market linkages are essential in Orissa, and to some extent in Bihar and Uttar Pradesh. In states like Bihar and Uttar Pradesh, population stabilization will ultimately hold the key to sustainable food security.

Secure Food Security for All

Food security is a physical, environmental, economic and social issue. It involves not just production, but access; not just output but process; not just technology but policy; not just global balance but also national conditions; not just national figures but household realities; not just rural but urban consumption; and not just quantity of food but also quality.

- The concept of food security should be broadened to make it holistic so as to mean "every individual has the physical, economic and environmental access to a balanced diet that includes the necessary macro and micro nutrients and safe drinking water, sanitation, environmental hygiene, primary health care and education so as to lead a healthy and productive life."
- Issues of food security are part of a bigger whole. Sustainable land and water management must be seen as directly linked to food security. Population growth, environmental sustainability, poverty reduction, agricultural production, distribution, marketing, credit and many other factors also need to be recognized as part of this whole.
- The major challenge is to produce additional food while conserving depleting natural resources. It is also to provide physical, economic and ecological access to food and nutrition security at the household level.
- Food security must focus on a diversified food basket, not food grains alone. Broad-based food security systems are not dependent on two-three species but on over 100 species that are underutilized. This will also prevent locally adapted grains from becoming extinct.
- Nutrition security must be given integrated attention by emphasizing horticulture, animal husbandry, fishery, millets, pulses and several other resources for which India is traditionally known. There is need for investment in science and technology that will promote diversification.
- Food security must not be based on market, but rather on self-reliance and sufficiency. The approach should be one of moving from food security to food sovereignty.
- The elimination of hunger and malnutrition is not just a food problem. It is linked to poverty and population growth. Rising food output is essential but so are the slowing of population growth and maintaining the ecological balance.
- Food banks at grass root levels should be well maintained Promote Awareness and Education Activities National policies and planning should recognize that public awareness can play an important role in establishing a firm basis for sustainable agricultural resource conservation and use. Public awareness should be considered in the development of all national programme activities.
- National strategies should identify objectives and strategies for public awareness, define target audiences, partners and tools for public outreach.
- Governments should recognize and encourage the work of NGOs in raising public awareness.
- Short-term and long-term courses specializing in sustainable agriculture should be run in agricultural universities. A separate curriculum for this subject should be developed for the regular graduate and postgraduate courses also.
- There is generally public apprehension about the possible consequences of agricultural biotechnology. It is important to organize public information programmes and public discussions that would help share relevant work of agricultural and biological scientists with the public.

Ensure Appropriate Application of Research, Science and Technology

- A comprehensive area-specific database of natural resources should be developed and made available for agriculture planning, implementation, research and extension.
- Well-designed information technology packages should be developed, that could help serve as a market information network; weather, pest and disease monitoring system.
- Additional research is necessary to develop drought tolerant, pest and disease-resistant crops, biological pest management, nitrogen fixation, more effective use of locally available organic materials, inter-cropping systems, and perennial crops, including agroforestry.
- Farming systems need to be designed so as to achieve the triple goals of more food, more income and more livelihoods per hectare of land. Such tools include biotechnology, information and communication technology, GIS mapping, space technology, renewable energy technologies (solar, wind, biomass, biogas), and management and marketing technologies.
- The revolution in biotechnology has both promises and problems. Biotechnology should be judiciously used so as to support the mission of environmental protection, poverty reduction and food security. But the adoption of every new technology must be accompanied by a precautionary package. In the case of biotechnology, biosafety and biosurviellance must be considered as important factors.
- Food should originate from efficient and environmentally benign production technologies that conserve and enhance the natural resource base of crop and animal husbandry, forestry, inland and marine fisheries.
- Development of agro-ecology-relevant technologies based on an understanding of local agriculture and resource management practices need to be supported and promoted.
- Chemicals and pesticides banned in developed countries should not be dumped into developing countries in the name of liberalization, globalization and industrialization. Before releasing a new variety, including genetically modified varieties in the market, the following paramoters should be considered for a variety of agro-climatic zones: Impact on soil productivity; hazardous residual effect; health hazards; adverse effects on other crops; adverse effects on other agricultural practices; threat to the indigenous varieties; impact on other professions; and impact on flora and fauna.

Nutrition security must be placed high on the agenda for development plans and programmes at all levels – village, block, district and state. Institutions that will design and monitor locality-specific interventions must be developed.

The way forward on food and nutrition security

The world is facing protracted and especially difficult food and economic crises, and climate change will increasingly provide serious challenges. Hunger is on the rise and the lives and health of millions of people are being compromised. Now more than ever, a global response to the problems facing poor people is needed. This includes new institutional arrangements, for increasing employment, increase in income levels of the poor so that availability and purchasing power increases there by reducing poverty

Fortunately, the G-20 and the UN are calling for a "comprehensive approach" to achieving food security. A truly comprehensive approach for supporting the poor in managing growing food-security risks must include agricultural productivity enhancement, strengthening market and trade opportunities, insurance opportunities, and social-protection opportunities.

Food security risk prevention will not be achieved without accelerated innovation, and therefore at a global level the investments in agricultural research, especially in the Consultative Group on International Agricultural Research (CGIAR), have to increase. This must be complemented by four priorities that need to be addressed now in the context of a comprehensive approach: .

(1) Investing for Nutrition the ancestral way

Industrialisation has led to an increase in consumption of junk foods. The question raised even in developed countries is, "Can junk foods be made nutritious?" The economic costs of malnutrition are very high — several billion dollars a year in terms of lost GDP. Thus, extensive research for making nutrition a reality and in this regard the question really crops up is "How did our ancestors grow up food without the use of artificial fertiliser, any artificial pesticides and were still healthy"? Rerouting our knowledge bag into our ancestral knowledge, using more organic fertilisers, preserving ecology through use of natural pesticide, the productivity of earth and the correlation between various natural resources.

(2) Improving Market Access

Lack of market access for small-scale farmers is one of the biggest barriers to rural development, farmers need reliable price information, contracts enforcement, and other measures to allow them to compete effectively. Government policy to facilitate market access requires strengthening. Increased investment in rural market infrastructure is key, and in this scenario corporate ventures into agri business can be much of help and thus, policies for mutual benefits (farmers & and corporates)can be planned, which help planning and utilisation of natural resources.

(3) Reducing Food Price Volatility

The world's dependability on fossil fuel has led to food price crisis that raged throughout 2008 and still lingers in 2009. Speculative price and the gap between cash and futures prices in commodity markets have risen. These reactions impede the free flow of food to where it is most needed and undermine the flow of price signals to farmers, and impose enormous efficiency losses on the global food system, hitting the poorest countries and people hardest. A demand and supply problem needs to be handled in a delicate manner to ward off the hyper inflation threats looming over the world.

(4) Adapting to Climate Change

Investment for agricultural adaptation to climate change should be increased in order to improve food security under climate change and therefore agriculture and forestry, especially in developing countries should be preserved and utilised for future benefits

(5) Legal Quotas for conversion of agricultural land to non-Agricultural purposes should be made mandatory.

In closing, it is important to remember that the world has achieved great successes in agricultural development that have fed billions of people. Investment in agriculture is accelerating, and it is important that forums such as the World Summit on Food Security help to assure that these investments are done well and contribute to substantially reducing hunger.

Conclusion

Food security is a multifold process.

(a) On the part of Policymakers.

(b) On the part of People

(c) On the part of Traders

It is a responsible process. Due to the decisions taken by the policy makers and the profiteering motive of the traders, the people, are the ones who are affected. Food security is the term which implies the use of natural resources. Thus, intelligent use of these natural resources, in terms of policy and businessmen, we can provide a healthy and fruitful earth for the generations to come.

References

1. Singh, T.(2004).*Resource Conservation And Food Security: An Indian Experience Volume 2*, Concept Publishing Company.
2. http: //www.gramvikas.org/lfs.php. Retreived December18, 2009.
3 http://www.gbpihed.gov.in. Retreived Dece.mber 15, 2009.
4. http://www.ias.ac.in. Retreived December12, 2009.

8

Climate Change and Food Security

Kirtikumar Ekhande

Introduction

The starting of 19th century was the period of industrial revolution. This industrial revolution results in to mechanization. Companies start using machineries for production purpose, which gives them maximum outputs in minimum resources. Excess use of machineries for maximizing profit becomes the base in this competition. This leads to unlimited use of resources as well as wastage of resources. One side industrial revolution gives birth to development; other side it's by product is pollution and environmental degradation.

All this creates its serious effect on environment. The emission of CO_2 increases rapidly with increasing industrialization. These factors not only changes climatic conditions but also create the problems like changes in agricultural production and food supply. Pollution is the most important factor because of which environment changes occurs. Increasing population is the biggest challenge for developing and developed countries. This population contributes more for creating pollution. The pollution level increase resulting into green house effects, global warming, changing climatic conditions, etc.

These changing climatic conditions create food problems like decrease in agricultural production. The small climatic changes are also more sensitive that they damage the whole ecosystem and food chain. Today the food security problem is one of the biggest problems in front of all countries. This becomes priority of nations to protect their food and make it available for all. In this condition we need to see the climatic changes which affect a lot.

Climate Change

First of all let us see what climate change is. As per definition climate change refers to a change in the state of the climate that can be identified using statistical tests. Some of the climatic changes which are proved on the basis of tests are like....

1. Cold days and cold nights have been less frequent over most land areas while hot days and hot nights have become more frequent.
2. Heat waves have become more frequent.
3. The frequency of heavy precipitation events has increased over most areas.
4. Incidence of extreme high sea level has increased at a broad range of sites worldwide since 1975.
5. Increased intense tropical cyclone activity in some regions.
6. Enlargement and increased numbers of glacial lakes.
7. Increased ground instability in ice regions and rock avalanches in mountain regions.
8. Changes in some Arctic and Antarctic ecosystems including those in sea-ice biomes.

All these are the climatic changes, which affects entire food chain. The availability of food becomes critical. Let's see **some of the facts** related to climate change that affects food system.

1. 1^0C change in temperature increases 0.18 – 0.38 sea levels. This decreases availability of land for food production.
2. 1.5 – 2.5^{0}C increase in temperature damages 20-30% of plants.
3. Temperature increase of up to 1 to 3^{0}C results in crop productivity decrease.

Globally, climatic conditions creating their effect on food production system. It is a **continuous chain** which results in to environmental degradation. The increasing population which is technologically advanced creates pollution that leads to climate change, this further results in less food production. Less availability of food means less distribution of food, it creates deaths of human beings. Whereas the other individuals will contribute to total population, in this way the circle completes and each and every time it affects the environment and creates food problems.

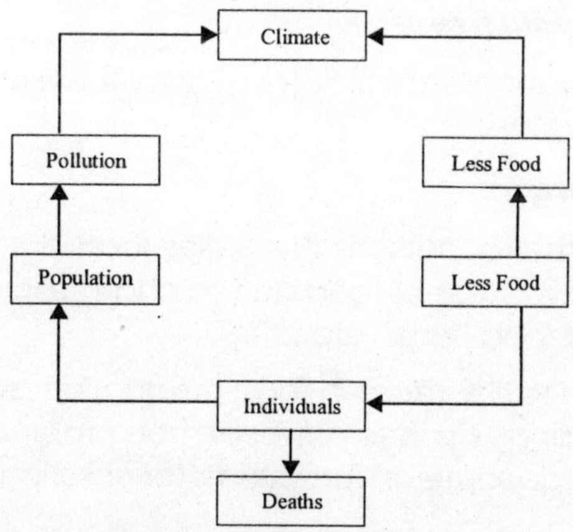

Technology/Industrialization

The food problems created by climate change situation are like....

Food Problems

1. Decrease Yield

The increase in temperature of earth surface increases the temperature in environment and results in decrease in total production of food grain, vegetables and fruits. The increased temperature of earth surface affects the plant and reduces their production capacity. It creates serious problem of decrease in total yield in some regions.

2. Increased insect outbreaks

Changes in occurrence of seasons like delay in winter season creates favorable environment for insects. The crop damages because of insect outbreaks, at the same time the quality of food decreases. Food goes waste. This also leads to increasing use of insecticides.

3. Damage to crop and failure

The irregularity of monsoon damages the crop, result is crop failure. Due to unavailability of water crop may not grow properly. Whereas in some areas the heavy rainfall creates flood situation and damages the crop.

4. Increased livestock deaths

Increased heat in the environment affects the perishable food. The storage of these types of food items becomes a problem. It reduces the freshness as well as quality of food and increases the wastage of food.

5. Wind throws of trees

Climate change also increases number of cyclones in some regions. These cyclones damage the entire crop in that region. The crop goes waste and no production is the result of it. In India during rainy seasons the damages of crop due to wind thrown is more.

6. Increased danger of wildfire

In summer season the heat increase creates wildfire. This wildfire damages the crop and makes land unproductive.

7. Food Distribution System

Due to changing weather conditions the entire food distribution system and supply chain system affected, like wastage of food due to change in atmospheric temperature, delay in supply, handling of food items, etc...

All these problems lead to decrease in food production as well as availability of total food and food security. Dealing with these types of food problems we need to adopt some strategies. We have to change some of our systems for ensuring food security. Some of the strategies are like.......

Strategies to Come out

1. Adjustment of planting dates and Variety

   Changes in planting date could be the strategy when we are dealing with changes in occurrence of seasons. The seasonal changes are their because of climate change, so we need to match the period and change our planting which facilitates us a good results. Also we need to try different variety of plants which can survive in this changing environment.
2. Crop relocation:-

   When we understand that temperature in some regions increasing constantly, we should change the place for crop and utilize other suitable place. It may be option that plantation should be according to crop. Like production of rice in area where rainfall is more.
3. Construction of warehouses in large manner:-

   The wastage of food because of wheather and change in temperature is more so we need to build up large numbers of warehouses where we can store food and protect it from environmental changes. As well we can store them for long period.
4. Making food distribution system more efficient and reducing wastage
5. Reducing the use of chemicals and pesticide (organic farming) it will reduce the chances of environmental pollution.
6. Gandhian Philosophy: -

   The Philosophy of Mahatma Gandhi is proper use of natural resources which we need to implement. Limited use of resources can help us in controlling environmental degradation.
7. Environmental Education at all levels.

These are some of the strategies which we need to adopt for food security. We cannot stop the climatic changes but we can control the environmental pollution. The environmental changes are so sensitive that can creates harm to human society. So you and I can change the world it just that just we need to start somewhere.

Reference

1. Chatwal, C., & Sharma, H. (2005). *A Text Book of Environmental Studies,* Mumbai: Himalaya Publishing House.
2. Behara, H.P., & Khan, M.S. (2009). *Environmental Management,* Mumbai: Himalaya Publishing House.
3. Intergovernmental Panel on Climate Change. (2007), Climate Change 2007: *Synthesis Report, Cambridge:* Cambridge University Press.
4. www.ipcc.ch/
5. www.worldbank.org
6. www.wamis.org
7. www.envfor.nic.in

9

Causes and Consequences of Food Insecurity

Sonali Gadekar, Ajit Gaikwad

"Earth provides enough to satisfy everyman's need, but not everyman's greed."

- Mahatma Gandhi

Introduction

Indian Economy is nourished by the lifeline of Agriculture sector. The performance of this sector influences the growth of Indian Economy. Agriculture sector including allied activities has accounted for 17.8 % of GDP in 2007-08 as compared to 21.7 % in 03-04. The declining share of this most important sector is serious matter to worry as it has direct linkage to food security scenario.

India's first wheat imports in six years marked a reversal in the march toward "food independence" that the country began in the 1970s. To M. S. Swaminathan, one of the agronomists credited with sparking the so-called Green Revolution, the return of grain imports should be seen as "a wake-up call" for a country that has in recent years taken its ability to feed its people for granted.

The growth rate of grain production has fallen from 1.5 percent before 1995 to 1 percent today, due to a combination of bad management, unpredictable weather and a growing water shortage. Meanwhile, the growth rate for all crops has fallen to 1.25 percent a year, the lowest level since India gained independence in 1947, says Ramesh Chand, acting director of India's National Centre for Agricultural Economics and Policy Research.

We will shape laws for our food freedom. This is our food sovereignty. This is our *Anna Swaraj.*

Meaning of Food Security

Food security exists when all people, at all times, have physical, social and economic access to sufficient, safe and nutritious food which meets their dietary needs and food preferences for an active and healthy life.

This indicates that food security has four key elements: availability, access, utilization and stability.

Elements of food security

The important four main elements of food security identified by FAO are as under :

- **Food availability** – The availability of sufficient quantities of food of appropriate quality, supplied through domestic production or imports, including food aid.
- **Food access** – Access by Individuals to adequate resources - entitlements — for acquiring appropriate foods for a nutritious diet. Entitlements are defined as the set of all commodity bundles over which a person can establish command, given the legal, political, economic and social arrangements of the community in which s/he lives, including traditional rights such as access to common resources.
- **Utilization** – Utilization of food through adequate diet, clean water, sanitation and health care to reach a state of nutritional well-being where all physiological needs are met.
- **Stability** – To be food secure, a population, household or individual must have access to adequate food at all times. They should not risk losing access as a consequence of sudden shocks, such as economic or climatic crises, or cyclical events such as agricultural seasons. Stability is, thus, needed in both availability and access.

Achieving food security under a changing climate requires substantial increases in food production on the one hand, as well as improved access to adequate and nutritious food and capacities to cope with the risks posed by climate change on the other hand.

Existing Challenges to Food Security

In the last fifty years the world population has more than doubled: from 3 billion to 6.7 billion people. Over one billion of them are undernourished – an unacceptable situation and a big challenge to global efforts to end hunger and poverty. In the next forty years, world population will increase by another 50 percent, reaching more than 9 billion by 2050. meeting the demand of such a large population will put enormous additional pressure on food production systems. Regardless of climate change, demand for food will increase, while resources needed for its production, such as land, water and petrol-based fertilizers – are becoming scarcer and scarcer.

Objectives

1. This paper intends to study the various causes of Food Insecurity and its subsequent consequences.
2. To identify the remedial measures and suggest the action plan to combat the serious threat of Food Insecurity.

Causes of Food Insecurity

Global Food Insecurity is the result of various factors such as,

- Loss of agricultural land due to rampant urbanization,
- Neglect on less investment in agriculture,
- Climate change and Global Warming,
- Declining bio diversity,
- Increase in population,
- Decreasing crop land,
- Continuous crop loss due to natural disasters,
- Underinvestment in Agricultural Innovation,
- Poverty,
- Export restrictions,
- Land degradation and
- Expanding deserts, etc.

Other causes which can be enlisted are as follows

1. **High Energy Prices** : Increasing cost of oil, fuel, fertilizers and electricity results in turn in higher cost of production of food grains and agri-commodities.
2. **Poor Harvest** : Poor harvest due to global warming and climate change and extreme unexpected weather conditions as well as irregular monsoon has wide impact on Food Security.
3. **Rise in Demand** : Imbalance in the forces of demand and supply due to rapidly increasing population results in continuous rise in demand for food.
4. **Bio Fuels** : More and more tendency to shift the use of land under cultivation for growing the produce for bio fuels rather than food crops or vegetables results in serious threat to food security.
5. **Export Ban in few Countries** : Export restriction by few countries like India, China, (in order to feed its own countrymen sufficiently) have restricted the supplies on world market.
6. **Forgotten in International Politics** : In world politics much of the priority and attention was on issues like Terrorism, Pollution, Global warming instead of Sustainable Agricultural and Farm Management.

7. **Skyrocketing Prices** : The input costs per hectare and the output generated has no matching due to costly transportation and warehousing facilities. The costs of seeds , tools , fertilizers, equipments are required to be monitored.
8. **Less Production – Less Productivity** : War- hit refugees cannot work on their fields which results in low productivity across the world.
9. **Waste land and soil degradation** : Organic farming and excess use of modern fertilizers and chemicals affects the land fertility and soil quality which results in lower productivity.
10. **Slow pace of progress** : Slow efforts or progress in reducing local or regional level food insecurity makes the situation more grim at national or international level.
11. **Financial Market Impact** : Speculation and assets bubble in commodities market, Use of Futures contracts and Fluctuation in dollar value also has its own impact on food security.

Global Causes Local Consequences

Consequences of Food Insecurity : Serious consequences which may result from the threat of Global Food Insecurity can be listed as,

- High and ever rising food prices,
- Hunger (923 million people in the world go hungry everyday out of which 907 live in developing countries and emerging economies.)
- Malnutrition,
- High risk of illness and less resistance power due to undernourishment,
- Cutting the budgets of food consumption.
- Food riots and its spread worries about the peace and stability around the world.
- Shift in preferring low price-cheap quality food due to weak economic and physical access to food in developing countries.
- Organic farming or super farming leaves the land unfertile and creates an ecological imbalance.

Other Consequences

1. Major threat to Food Security

Climate change will act as a multiplier of existing threats to food security: it will make natural disasters more frequent and intense, land and water more scarce and difficult to access, and increases in productivity even harder to achieve. The implications for people who are poor and already food insecure and malnourished are immense.

Climate change will affect all four dimensions of food security: availability, accessibility, stability, and utilization. it will reduce food availability, because it negatively affects the basic elements of food production – soil, water and biodiversity. Rural communities face increased risks including recurrent crop failure, loss of livestock and reduced availability of fisheries and forest products.

Changing temperatures and weather patterns, furthermore, create conditions for the emergence of new pests and diseases that affect animals, trees and crops which has direct effects on the quality and quantity of yields as well as the availability and price of **food, feed and fiber.**

2. Shortage of Food and Water :

Decreasing availability of water and food will also increase sanitation and health problems and increase the risk of diseases and malnutrition. Competition over increasingly scarce resources will also increase the risk of conflicts, displacement and migration, which in turn will again increase the risk of food insecurity.

In tropical and sub-tropical regions, especially in seasonally dry areas, crop and animal productivity may decrease significantly due to temperature increases of 2 to 3°c.

By 2020, global warming effects and climate change could cause, for example:

- significant decreases in crop yields in some rain-fed systems;
- declines of 40 to 90 percent of grassland productivity in semi-arid and arid regions;
- high levels of desertification and soil salinisation(salt percentage in soil) in some areas in Asia, sub-Sahara Africa and Latin America's coastal parts; and
- increasing water stress, particularly in irrigated production systems.

Threat to Food Availability

Reduced food availability due to decreasing yields as a result of climate change has additional direct implications for food accessibility: as food becomes scarce, prices go up and food becomes unaffordable, i.e., inaccessible, for a growing part of the population. The food price rise that peaked in 2008 clearly demonstrated how major fluctuations in global food markets can have far-reaching implications for food security and emergency relief needs. At the same time, the food price rise led to a dramatic increase in the global total of undernourished people by more than 20% to over a billion in July 2009.

3. Impact on Domestic crop:

Sinha and Swaminathan (1991) – showed that an increase of 2_{0C} in temperature could decrease the rice yield by about 0.75 ton/ha in the high yield areas; and a 0.5_{0C} increase in winter temperature would reduce wheat yield by 0.45 ton/ha

Saseendran *et. al.,* (2000) – showed that for every one degree rise in temperature the decline in rice yield would be about 6%.

Model to achieve Food Security : (proposed by the researcher)

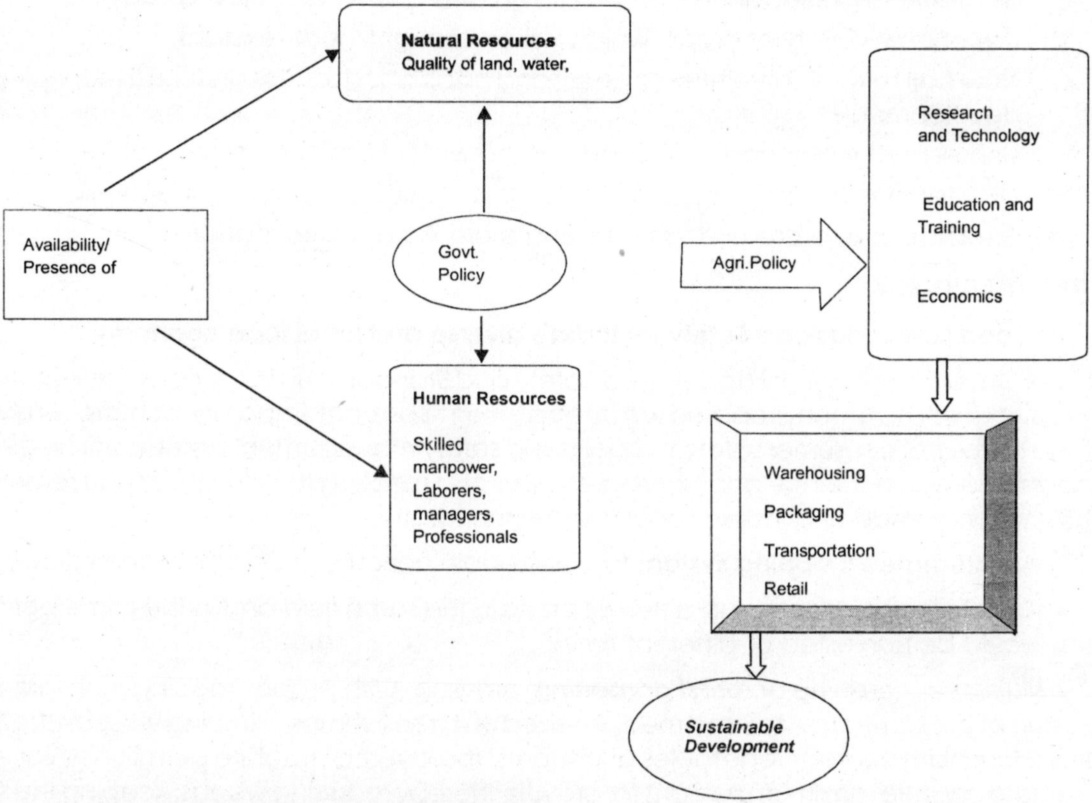

Measures to Tackle the Problem

1. Building food Reserves: One of the important measure to tackle the problem of food security is to build and manage the Food Reserve which will take care of low cost but diet rich food.
2. Appropriate attention to be paid for conservation of common property, bio diversity resources and rehabilitation of waste lands.
3. Launching and managing of food based interventions like Public Distribution System should be effectively undertaken.
4. Enriching the land, conservation and generating fertile soil, regenerating natural soil fauna, conserving natural resources, harnessing surface water, conserving indigenous seeds and other practices related to sustainable farming should be followed by each state.
5. Contract farming and Regulated farm management.
6. Adjustment to food consumption patterns by maintaining dietary quality and diversity.
7. Preserving and enhancing plant and animal genetic resources.
8. Effective Water Management and Waste Land Management.

9. Shifting to adoptable cropping patterns like the one type of Rice Quality named **as "Satthi" in India** which can be grown and cultivated in **just 60 days**.
10. Use of new variety of crops which will be drought/heat resistant.
11. New Agricultural Universities to be set and established for research and technology development.
12. Unused rain water and untapped sun off water form hills can be conserved.
13. Disaster recovery management programs can be set and run effectively.
14. Establishing and promoting more and more Agro based industries .

Other Measures

1. Food Laws and Food Safety for India's diverse and local food economy

The Government has drafted a Food Safety and Standards Bill 2005, as an "Integrated Food Law" which has been prepared with the intention to be contemporary, comprehensive, and ensure better consumer safety through food safety management systems and settling standards based on science and transparency as also meeting the dynamic requirements of international trade and Indian Food Trade and Industry.

2. An integrated cropping system for sustainable agriculture combines the following:

• ***Multiple cropping:*** growing different crops in the same field and in the same period which would be harvested at different times.

• ***Multilayer cropping or forest gardening:*** growing, with proper spacing in the same area and at the same time, tall and medium-sized fruit trees, shrubs, climbing vines and leafy plants, along with cereals, vegetables and tubers; the layered structure permits the variety of plants to capture maximum sunlight for growth, thereby reducing weeds, keeping the soil healthy and effectively expanding the cultivable area.

• ***Mixed cropping:*** traditional farming system growing a diversity of crops, to extend the harvesting period and help alleviate seasonal food shortages, thus, stabilizing household food access.

In view of the emerging global situation of reduced food availability and a worldwide rise in food prices, a meeting of the Agriculture Ministers of the SAARC member states was held in New Delhi, India in November 2008, to evolve and implement people-centered short to medium term regional strategy and collaborative projects that would, among others, lead to:

- Increase in food production;
- Investment in agriculture and agro-based industries;
- Agriculture research and prevention of soil health degradation;
- Development and sharing of agricultural technologies;
- Sharing of best practices in procurement and distribution; and
- Management of the climatic and disease-related risks in agriculture.

Conclusion

For India, a 2002 study which used 19 indicators ranked Jharkhand and Bihar the most food insecure states – followed by Madhya Pradesh, Chhattisgarh, Gujarat, Uttar Pradesh, Orissa, Rajasthan and Uttaranchal. The challenge of achieving food security for all people is not distant dream if the national and global policy makers undertake planned and focused efforts. The Indian vision is not only to produce the food for its growing population or to export in offshore market but also to fully exploit the comparative and competitive advantages it posseses like, - agro climatic variety, scientific capabilities, low labour cost, abundance of natural resources so as to become a low cost- high profit producer for the world economy to contribute significantly in global food security.

"The air, the water and the soil are not a gift from our parents , they are loan from our children"

- (Old Indian Proverb)

References

1. Dr. N. Chattopadhay, Climate Change and Food Security in India, International symposium on Climate Change and Food Security in South Asia, at Dhaka, Bangladesh.
2. Grebmer K.V., The Challenge of Hunger, by Concern Worldwide Oct. 2008
3. Dr. Muhammad Hanif,General Report on Agriculture Perspective and Policy, Ministry of Food, Agricultural and Livestock, Islamabad
4. Bhairviya N, Rise in Food Prices, online paper at www.Google.com
5. Dr. Gupta S. P., Report on Agricultural Policy – Vision 2020, Indian Agricultural Research Institute, New Delhi
6. Report on Sustainable Agricultural and Food Security in Asia and The Pacific, United Nations, Economical and social Commission for Asia and Pacific at google.com
7. Gulati Ashok, Indian Agricultural and Rural Development, a paper prepared at International Food Policy Research Institute.
8. www.ifpri.org
9. www.foodandwaterwatch.org
10. http://media.ft.com

10

Experiment to Achieve Self Reliance in Food Production — A Case of Small Farmer in India

Anuradha Gaikwad, Udai Gaikwad

Introduction

India has a population of 1.14 with total land mass of 3,287,263 square kilometre. Out of these 1,69,739 thousand hectares is arable land. That means more than 50 % of land available in India can be brought under cultivation. The net availability of food grains in India has increased from 394.9 grams per day in 1951 to 439.3 grams per day in 2007. The share of agriculture in GDP has been around 30 % of total. The total production of food grains in India has increased from 50.82 in 1950-51 to 227 million tons in 2007 – 08. At the same time inputs into agriculture have also increased with time. The consumption of fertilizers increased from 60.64 lakhs tons in 1981-82 to 216.51 in 2006-07. The area brought under cultivation has increased due to better irrigation facilities and increasingly two or three crops are taken per year. In fact after the implementation of policy of the green revolution facilitated this and India became changed from a starving nation to one of the world's leading agriculture nation. Double-cropping was a primary feature of the Green Revolution. Instead of one crop season per year, the decision was made to have two crop seasons per year. This was basically possible due to availability of irrigation from water stored in dams. However the policy of Green Revolution is not without its problems. First of all it comes with usage of additional fertilizers which are essential for the growth of high yielding varieties of seeds used and water that came from big dams. All of this led to a host of other environmental and social problems.

"The Green Revolution has been a failure. It has led to reduced genetic diversity, increased vulnerability to pests, soil erosion, water shortages, reduced soil fertility, micronutrient deficiencies, soil contamination, reduced availability of nutritious food crops for the local population, the displacement of vast numbers of small farmers from their land, rural impoverishment and increased tensions and conflicts. The beneficiaries have been the agrochemical industry, large petrochemical companies, and manufacturers of agricultural machinery, dam builders and large landowners. The "miracle" seeds of the Green Revolution have become mechanisms for breeding new pests and creating new diseases". (Shiva 1991)

The problem

So in spite of all the technological innovations, we as a country today seriously face the problem of food security. One major reason for increasing needs of food is of course the growing population of the country. Coupled with this are the socio-political policies of the country, the forces of free market, the tendency to take cash crops instead of food crops (since they yield better profit margins), the trend of using food crops like maize for production of biofuels and the changing climate and uncertainty of rainfall.

One of the major features of Indian agriculture is size of land which the farmer owns. 1 out of 18, 06,523 hectares of land under cultivation 47, 673 hectare is landholding below I hectare and it accounts for 65 % of the total land. Obviously this group of farmers suffers from all the problems of agriculture like lack of enough capital investment for inputs into agriculture (like better seeds, fertilizers and water). About 60 % of the farmers in the country fall in this category. If Food Security is defined as availability of food in the market, access to food through adequate purchasing power, and absorption of food in the body then these farmers can hardly make their ends meet. If we look at indebtedness amongst farmers the need is to rethink of means of making these farmers self reliant and self sufficient so that they come out of shackles of poverty.

Table 1: Indebtedness of Farmer Households

Indebtedness of Farmer Households (all-India) in Different Classes of Land Possessed						
< 0.01	Estimated Number of Farmer Households (in Lakhs)	% to Total in each Class	Land Possessed Estimated Number of indebted Farmer Households (in Lakhs)	% to Total in each Class	% of In-debted Farmer Households to Total	Average Outstanding Loan Amount(Rs)
0.01-0.04	12.59	1.40	5.71	1.3	1.3	6121
0.04-1.00	292.87	32.80	130.11	30.0	30.0	6545
1.01-2.00	283.61	31.70	129.21	29.8	29.8	8623
2.01-4.00	160.60	18.00	81.92	18.8	18.8	13762
> 10.00	93.50	10.50	54.41	12.5	12.5	23456
All	42.58	4.80	27.73	6.4	6.4	42532
	7.75	0.80	5.15	1.2	1.2	76232
	893.50	100.00	434.24	100.0	100.0	12585

Source: Report No. 498(59/33/1), Situation Assessment Survey of Farmers: Indebtedness of Farmer Households, National Sample Survey 59th Round (January-December 2003)

The table given below shows distribution of operational holdings for India. This table makes it clear that one of the factors responsible for low productivity in agriculture is the size of its land holdings.

Table 2: Land Holdings in India

Category of Holdings	Number of Operational Holdings(in thousands)		Area operated(in thousand hectares)		Av. Size of Operational Holdings(in hectares)	
	1995-96	2000-01*	1995-96	2000-01*	1995-96	2000-01*
Marginal Less than 1 hectare	71179 (61.6)	75408 (62.3)	28121 (17.2)	29814 (18.7)	0.40	0.40
Small 1.0- 2.0 hectares	21643 (18.7)	22695 (19.0)	30722 (18.8)	32139 (20.2)	1.42	1.42
Semi-Medium2.0-4.0 hectares	14261 (12.3)	14021 (11.8)	38953 (23.8)	38193 (24.0)	2.73	2.72
Medium 4.0-10 hectares	7092 (6.1)	6577 (5.5)	41398 (25.3)	38217 (24.0)	5.84	5.81
Large More than 10 hectares	1404 (1.2)	1230 (1.0)	24163 (14.8)	21072 (13.2)	17.21	17.12
Total	115580 (100.00)	119231 (100.00)	163357 (100.00)	159436 (100.00)	1.41	1.33

Note: Figures in parentheses indicate the percentage of respective column total. Excluding Jharkhand

Source: Agricultural Census Division, Ministry of Agriculture, New Delhi.

Possible Solution

The answer to increasing the production of food can be found in one of the following three ways:

1. By use of genetically modified crops
2. Use of agricultural technology
3. Turning towards organic farming and looking for alternative means of increasing production of food. (Purandare, 2009)

The first two options are based on the currently dominant model within capitalist agriculture, i.e., the Input –Output model. The Input-Output Model, however, has a tendency to over-simplify factors that can affect output. It also has a tendency to externalize costs. For instance, it may deliver cheap food (defined as food Accounting for a reduced proportion of household expenditure) but it has an unfortunate tendency to disguise or add to the environmental health bill. The use of pesticides has grown immensely world-wide under the tutelage of the Input-Output currently the dominant model within capitalist agriculture. This Model in general assumes that humans are in control of all important variables. (Walter-Towes & Lang 2000). Even today as proponents of GM food support this technology a variety of issues are overlooked. For instance this technology will be controlled by market forces and would not be a viable option for the small and marginal farmer. Also the effect of introduction of such crops into environment and in the human system has not yet been documented. The ecological behaviour of the transgenic gene in the host genome cannot be predicted. For, e.g., Petunia do not have unstable colouring but genetically engineered petunias change their colour unpredictably due to `gene silencing. (Shiva 1999)

Thus, the option that is viable, achievable, would not harm environment have to be thought out along the lines of sustainability. "Sustainable food security can to be defined as physical economic social and ecological access to balanced diet and safe drinking water so as to enable every individual to lead a productive and healthy life in perpetuity.' (S Swaminathan 2001)

Achieving sustainable food security will require more than improving farm productivity and profitability while minimizing environmental impacts. The 'concept is broader than sustainable agriculture: it fuses the goals of household food security and sustainable agriculture. (Speth 1993). A number of experiments in agriculture in order to achieve self reliance have been tried out in practice. These experiments work on the concept of self reliance as given by Gandhi in his concept of 'Sarvodaya'. He resented a situation of gross economic inequality in which a few roll in riches and the masses do not get even enough to eat. Being self reliant and self governing was the key to the poor man's Swaraj.

.........every village's first concern will be to grow its own food crops and cotton for its cloth. It should have a reserve for its cattle, recreation and playgrounds for adults and children. Then if, their is more land available it will grow useful money crops, thus, excluding ganja, tobacco, opium and its like (Sinha 1976).

Approach by Shri S A Dhabolkar

Mr S A Dhabolkar was a well kmown mathematician turned into experimental farmer cultivator. His experiments and his theory are well articulated in his book plenty for all. His basic assumption in obtaining high yields from fields is based on maximum harvesting of solar energy from the sun and on using natural organic farming. He has come up with a new system of farming called as 'Natueco Culture'.

Natueco Culture

This is a new concept of farming based on scientific inquiries and experiments. It is based on understanding the principles and concepts of nature and then applying them to farming. Major features of Natueco Culture are:-

1. Harvesting the sun.
2. Recycling process.
3. Establishing proper energy pool and energy chain as food chain.

Principles of Natueco Culture

The process of Natueco Culture is based on the following principles:

1. Establishment of canopy index at the earliest so that plant will be capable of taking full advantage of sunlight it has to harvest.
2. Only mature leaves of the plant are capable of doing optimum harvesting of the sun.
3. In order to achieve optimum photosynthesis there should be matching storage organ growth in plants at the time when optimum photosynthesis is taking place.

In order to get good yields from the soil Mr. Dhabolkar gives the concept of use of 'Nursery Soils'. This term is used for soil that contains well composed organic parts and mineral parts in equal volume. Based on his work he has given an equation for the self reliance of a house of five people including children and grand parents. The land required to sustain a family of five with basic food needs can be obtained from 10 gunthas or 10,000 sq. ft. (one tenth of a hectare) of land. The details of use of land are given below:

Table 3: Agriculture for Consumption

Land	Purpose
1000 sq ft	To build house
1000 sq ft	For fruit trees
1000 sq ft	For grains
1000 sq ft	For sprouts
1000 sq ft	Workshop and godown
1000 sq ft	For vegetables
1000 sq ft	For goats and chicken
1000 sq ft	For cotton, jute and fibre.
1000 sq ft	For fuel and firewood.
500 sq ft	For spices
500 sq ft	For oilseeds

As a result of these experiments farmers in Nandurbar, Jaipur, Panvel, Khudawadi, Solapur and Satara have started this type of farming. The yields obtained by some farmers are given below:

Table 4: Record yields using Natueco Culture

Crop	Approx record yields per sq ft
1. Fruit Plants : Grapes, Bananas, Mango	500 gms
2. Starch Crops : Potatoes, Elephant foot	1000 gms
3. Grain Crops: Millets, Rice	125 gms
4. Watery Vegetables : Cucumber, Water Melons	2000 gms
5. Nuts: Groundnuts, Oil seeds, Sunflower.	60 gms
6. Pulses : Pigeon pea, etc	50 gms

Dhabolkar : Plenty for All

Conclusion

To conclude I think we need to understand the limitations of the present system of agriculture and the forces that dominate perusal of these systems. All problems of poverty and mankind especially the problem of food security cannot be solved by market forces.

Lessons may have to be learnt from alternative systems about the development and maintenance of local, sustainable food system projects – those that attempt to integrate the environmental, economic, and social health of their food systems in particular places. Public participation, new partnerships, and a commitment to social, economic, and environmental justice principles are very much essential if we have to solve the problem of food security. Basically each and every system has its own carrying capacity. Human beings have tried to enhance the carrying capacity of agricultural ecosystems by the use of technology which were effective in the short term but cannot possibly give us long term sustainable results. Hence the effort has to be to implement such experiments in the governmental policies thereby making this knowledge available to the common farmer. An approach of understanding the scenario at micro level is, thus, essential to solve the problem of Food Security.

References:

1. Agricultural Census Division, Ministry of Agriculture, New Delhi
2. Prof Dhabolkar S A, 1998, Plenty For All Prayog Pariwar Methodology : Mehta publishing House.
3. Feenstra Gail, 2002, Internet-Creating space for sustainable food systems: Lessons from the field, Agriculture and Human Values, *Vol* 19, 99–106, Sprigerlink database
4. Dr. Patil J F: 2004 Food Security and Agricultural Policy, Sangli, Shri Arun Laad.
5. Purendare Chandrashekhar, 2009, Food Rights: A World Perspective, Andolan Dec 2009,
6. Shiva Vandana : !999, Stolen Harvest The Hijacking of the Global Food Supply, Cambridge South End Press, Dec2009 from Google books.
7. Shiva Vandana March-April 1991,Internet, The Green Revolution in Punjab, The Ecologist, Vol. 21, No. 2, Dec 2009, retrived from Liviung Heritage database.
8. Sinha Radha 1076, Food and Poverty – Need for New Ideology , New Delhi, Ambika Publications, 83.
9. Speth James Gustave ,1993, Internet,Towards Sustainable Food Security (Administrator United Nations Development Programme), World Bank document.
10. Swaminathan M. S; 25 OCTOBER 2001, Internet,Food security and sustainable development. Current Science, VOL. 81, NO. 8, 948-954
11. Waltner-Toews David and Lang Tim 2000,Internet-A new conceptual base for food and agricultural policy: the emerging model of links between agriculture, food, health, environment and society; Global Change & Human Health, VOL 1, NO. 2 ,116-130, Sringerlink database.

11

Information Technology: A Means for Attaining Global Food Security

Sanjay S.Gharde

Introduction

Food security and hunger are global concerns. Hunger is having various views such as increased susceptibility to disease, shortfalls in nutritional status, loss of energy, disability, and death due to starvation or infectious diseases. Information Technology interaction, policy, the availability of natural resources, economic development, culture and ecological factors are major areas to look into to deal with these consequences of hunger.

Food security exists when all people at all times have physical or economic access to sufficient safe and nutritious food to meet their dietary needs and food preferences for an active and healthy life. Food security depends more on socio-economic conditions than on agroclimatic ones, and on access to food rather than the production or physical availability of food (Killmann, 2008). Besides this production and availability of food, Information Technology emphasize on to the quality, dietary and nutritious food at the time of producing. Recently, food riots have taken place in many countries across the globe. It is becoming increasingly difficult to maintain food security. Information technology provides helping hands to reduce the difficulties in attaining food security (http://en.wikipedia.org/wiki/food_security, 2009).

Information Technology (IT) stands out as a means to reduce their potential negative effects on affordability of food. The large number of projects is being carried out across the world and almost every project is implemented by using information technology. This paper discusses such technologies and its applications that are useful to attain the food security (Gurstein, Rural Development and Food Security A Community Informatics based conceptual Framework, 2001).

Hunger Measures

Food security and hunger are correlated with each other. So, to provide food security, it is necessary to measure the hunger. GHI and ISHI are two hunger indices to measure the hunger.

Global Hunger Index (GHI): The Global Hunger Index (GHI) is a tool for calculating hunger and malnutrition. The average of PUN, i.e., proportion of the population that is undernourished (in %), CUW, i.e., prevalence of underweight children under five (in %) and CM, i.e., proportion of children dying before the age of five (in %) is GHI (Klaus Van Grebmer, October 2009) (Global Hunger Index, 2009). So, we can formulate GHI as follows:

(PUN + CUW + CM)/3

The India State Hunger Index (ISHI): The India State Hunger Index is based on the same underlying variables as the GHI (Purnima Menon, October 14, 2008).

Techniques Implemented for Achieving Food Security

Ecommerce

E-Commerce enables peoples to access global market information and open up new regional and global markets that fetch better prices and increase farmers' earnings. For example, if farmer wants information about fertilizer or crops, he can access information instantaneously for 24 hours/day or 7 days/week through e-commerce (Gurstein, E-commerce and Community Economic Development: Enemy or Aally?, 2000).

The countries that are facing the problems of Food Insecurity not because of insufficient food production but because of insufficient information about crop production, utilization of fertilizers, climate, nutritional foods, and awareness about various food policies of research carried out by researchers, planners, policy makers, development workers. Thus, e-mail and Internet could be used to transmit information to the inaccessible areas which save time, cost and distance (Munyua, 2000).

World Wide Web

It enables people to access information on millions of other computers. For scattering the information required for quality food and quality crops, Internet enables the remotest village to access regular and reliable information from the web. Along with the internet, World Wide Web used with different media combinations through radio, television, video cassettes, audio cassettes, video conferencing, computer programs due to which food security based information spread more rapidly among people (Munyua, 2000).

Internet Radio

Internet Radio is a conventional radio connected with Internet. For example, Internet Radio in Sri Lanka (http://www7.itu.int/itudfg7/About/Means_Methods.html, 2009) enables users to access programs related with agriculture and nutritional food on the web at any convenient time, and send feedback through e-mail or chat. Broadcasters can disseminate the latest information promptly such as weather forecasting, crop selection based on seasons and environmental conditions, advanced methodologies to produce nutritional food (Munyua, 2000).

Community Informatics (CI)

It is well known fact that Farmers in the countries like Nigeria, Bangladesh and other such developing nation are not aware about the recent happening in the field of agriculture, thus, Community Informatics is an approach that provide a set of resources and tools pertaining to economic development, cultural affairs, civic activism, community based health and environmental initiatives to the communities and individuals living in society which is supplementary to the food security (Gurstein, Rural development and food security: A "community informatics" based conceptual framework for FAO, 2000).

Telecentres

Telecentres is being used in developing countries for the purpose of communication in rural areas. These Telecentres translate the required information in retrievable, understandable form for farmers and consumers. It provide the information which include crop, weather or market information like current prices, futures, shipping information; availability of local production support services like fertilizers, livestock inspection services; weather or crop advisories and so on. Important role of Telecentres is to create and maintain index web sites and search engines that meet the objective of food security in the respective regions. For example, a technologically trained professional translate the needs of people for better and quality food production into the appropriate Internet search criteria then interpret and translate the returned information putting useable form by people (Gurstein, Rural Development and Food Security A Community Informatics based conceptual Framework, 2001).

Information Technology in worldwide projects

Food Security Portal

Portal provides current, country-specific information about developments in the world food system. It publishes the recent food security news so that global hunger spots can be identified. It provides latest information on undernourishment, poverty, consumption, stocks, and many more which depict the overall scenario of the food security in a given country. Such information make authenticated and analyzed by using food crisis reports and analytical models, and publish using simulations, indicators, and other statistical tools.

Harvest Choice

Harvest Choice program is IFPRI's main climate-change activities where food and water security are major area of research. Research focuses on investment choices to increase crop productivity. Harvest Choice launched a new website with collection of expanding data, knowledge products, and interactive query tools regarding crop production, productivity, and market-sheds in Sub-Saharan Africa (Garnaut, 2008-2009).

Internet-based project: The Internet-based project (1994-97) called as "Comunicación para el Desarrollo en América Latina", shares information and skills related to food security and agriculture with small farmers in Latin America by developing national communication systems. The project proved very successful and soon spread throughout the region and beyond to China, Mali, Indonesia and the Republic of Korea.

FIDAMERICA

FIDAMERICA works for eradicating the poverty from rural communities and improving their quality of life. It is one of the necessary steps to attain food security. The system uses ICTs to access agricultural, market and technical information. It offers facilities for knowledge and information exchange through electronic conferencing, e-mail, databases and web sites.

Electronic Delivery of Agricultural Information

In Uganda, the National Agricultural Research Organization (NARO) and CAB International (CABI) are implementing a project titled "*Electronic Delivery of Agricultural Information to Rural Communities in Uganda*". The project improve access to agricultural information by rural communities through use of selected traditional media and modern ICTs such as radio, video, television, print media, e-mail, CD-ROMs and Internet to increase agricultural production.

NARKIS

The project, National Agricultural and Rural Knowledge and Information System (NARKIS) assess user needs and facilitate agricultural information flows and knowledge building. The implemented programs include the building and management of an agricultural Web portal, packaging of multi-media publications, rural networking and ICT deployment and support services. These activities are useful for making awareness about recent trends in agriculture and hence helpful to get nutritional and quality food to people.

FARMNets

In Latin America, FARMNets is farmer information networks which is meant for enhancing food security. It involves agricultural producers and farmer associations, extension services and NGOs in Chile and Mexico. Essential information on weather, markets, inputs, prices and credit are exchanged through the electronic network using Internet to farmer organizations, co-operatives and local government.

FITS

The Farmers' Information & Technology Service (FITS-Techno-Pinoy) is a web-based information service in the Philippines. FITS contribute to the empowerment of farmers, processors and traders. Also, it provides information and technology services that facilitate decision-making for agriculture by rural communities.

Also, following projects which are based on information technology are carried out worldwide: The Agricultural Science and Technology Indicators (ASTI), Biosafety Systems, Pedagogia Audiovisual, Audiovisial pedagogy, Rural Radio Support Program, Potato Extension & Training Information System (PETIS), Virtual Extension-Research Communication Network (VERCON), Mango Information Network (MIN).

Information Technology in Indian Projects (Vijayaditya, November 3, 2005)

Agriculture Online

The Vision 2020 document of the Central Department of Agriculture and Cooperation (DAC) envisages that "the tools of IT will provide networking of Agriculture Sector not only in the country but also globally and the Centre and State Government Departments will have reservoir of databases"; and will also bring farmers, researchers, scientists and administrators together by establishing "Agriculture Online" through exchange of ideas and information. This project will be beneficial for advancement in agriculture sector which will result in better food quality, crop production, climate change and awareness in rural people for nutritional food. Hence, food security can be achieved by adopting this project nationwide. Many ICT Projects provide relevant agricultural information. These include: AGRISNET, AGMARKNET, ARISNET, SeedNET, CoopNet, HORTNET, FERTNET, VISTARNET, PPIN, APHNET, FISHNET, LISNET, AFPINET, ARINET, NDMNET, Weather NET.

Weather Watch Monitoring System

Directorate of Wheat Development collects the information (Weather Watch Report) on the availability of various inputs like fertilizers, pesticides, seeds, irrigation, power, diesel, etc., along with information on crop condition and irrigated area under Wheat, Barley and other crops from all the states, on a weekly basis. This information provides for better food production.

Agricultural Census and Input Survey

This project serves as the interface between agriculture sector in the Indian economy, Department of Agriculture and Cooperation, Ministry of Agriculture, Government of India. Also, it collects and maintains agricultural statistics regularly and makes it accessible on a timely basis to planners and policy makers for decision making regarding harvesting, better food quality and proportion of fertilizers for different crops (http://agcensus.nic.in, 2009).

Biofertilizer Informatics Online

Biofertilizer Informatics Online is a web-based Online Monitoring Information System developed by NIC for faster and reliable information dissemination across Biofertilizer Production Units, Ministry of Agriculture and farming community. Biofertilizer Informatics Online includes: Food Quality Standards, Food Quality Control, Farmer Interaction (FAQs) Databank and Cooperation (DAC), Production Units, Marketing and Sales, R&D activities, Ministry of Agriculture, Government of India.

Computerized Registration of Pesticides (CROP)

CROP simplifies the registration process, brings transparency in the working, improves decision-making process in selection of pesticides for specific crop, eliminates time delay in the delivery of certificates to customers, provides and disseminates information through the portal (http://www.cibrc.nic.in, 2009) to government, pesticides industry and farming communities. The Government of India has enforced the Insecticides Act (1968) and their rules framed in 1971 for the registration of pesticides to regulate safe and judicious use of pesticides in the country. Definitely, this government policy is additional strength for food security in India.

Food Network (Food.NET)

This connects all the agencies involved in procurement, distribution and management of food grains. The agencies involved include HAFED, HSAMB, FCI, HWC, HAIC, Confed, Food and Supplies, and Agriculture department. A web-enabled application has been developed to monitor daily procurement Data and Storage Information System and to monitor and manage the food procurement, lifting and storage activities. The e-Food.Net project has been implemented in Haryana. It provides a better platform for disseminating information among people for better food production.

MAHAFOOD

This is an e-governance project based on web technology for monitoring of allotment and lifting of food grains in Maharashtra for effective decision making in food security under various schemes with the help of progressive and summarized information.

Besides the above project, VISTARNET and Integrated Foodgrains Management Information System are also the projects which implements information technology for attaining food security.

Conclusion

Attainment of Food security is to be realized by disseminating information and making awareness among the peoples across the globe. Governments and NGOs of various countries are being taken initiatives. ICT, IFPRI, NIC- India are doing well to provide information for food security. So, information technology plays a vital role to achieve the objective of food security. Also, GHI and ISHI provide the measure for hunger due to which the various organizations are capable to deal with the food security.

Bibliography

1. Garnaut, R. (2008-2009). *2008-2009 Annual Report.* IFPRI.
2. *Global Hunger Index.* (2009, December). Retrieved December 2009, from www.wikipedia.org: http://en.wikipedia.org/wiki/Global_Hunger_Index
3. Gurstein, M. (2000). E-commerce and Community economic development: Enemy or Aally? *Shaping the Network Society: the Future of the Public Sphere in Cyberspace.* Seattle WA: DIAC.

4. Gurstein, M. (2001). Rural Development and Food Security A Community Informatics based conceptual Framework. *Proceeding of the 34th Hawaii Internaional Conference System Sciences* . IEEE.

5. Gurstein, M. (2000). Rural development and food security:A "community informatics" based conceptual framework for FAO. *The role of information and communication technologies in rural development and food security.* Sustainable Development.

6. *http://agcensus.nic.in.* (2009). Retrieved 2009, from www.nic.in: http://agcensus.nic.in

7. *http://en.wikipedia.org/wiki/food_security.* (2009, December). Retrieved December 2009, from www.wikipedia.org: http://en.wikipedia.org/wiki/food_security

8. *http://www.cibrc.nic.in.* (2009). Retrieved 2009, from www.nic.in: http://www.cibrc.nic.in

9. *http://www7.itu.int/itudfg7/About/Means_Methods.html.* (2009). Retrieved 2009, from www.itu.int: http://www7.itu.int/itudfg7/About/Means_Methods.html

10. Killmann, W. (2008). *Climate Chnage and Food Security A Framework Document.* Rome: Food and Agriculture Organization of United Nations.

11. Klaus Van Grebmer, B. N.-L. (October 2009). *2009 Global Hunger Index The Challenge and Hunger: Focus on Financial Crisis and Gender Inequality.* Bonn, Washington D.C., Dublin: Welt Hunger Hilfe, IFPRI, Concern Worldwide.

12. Munyua, H. (2000). Information and Communication Technologies for rural development and food security:Lessons from field experiences in developing countries. *The role of information and communication technologies in rural development and food security.* Sustainable Development Department.

13. Purnima Menon, A. D. (October 14, 2008). *India State Hunger Index: Comparisons of Hunger Across States.*

14. Vijayaditya, N. (November 3, 2005). Good Governance Through ICT. *National Informatics Center* , 27-37.

12

Biosurfactants: An Economical and Eco-friendly Sustainable Tool for Global Food Security

Chinmay Hazra, Debasree Kundu, Ambalal Chaudhari

Introduction

Food: An Index of Development

Food is an integral component of sustainable health and economy of the world. It provides a livelihood for the majority of rural people living in villages. For mankind, it may be a lifestyle/a festival/a tradition and is by far, the largest industry on this planet. Each country's economic growth and prosperity depends on an annual rich harvest of crops, a principal source of food and feed.

2.0 Food Security and Crisis: Tragedy of the Commons

2.1 Global Population and Food Scenario: The Rude Awakening

The world's population is anticipated to increase to 7.7 billion in 2020 and is expected to double by 2050 (Onsando and Wambugu, 2009). The bearing capacity of this planet is of 200 million people (Lovelock, 2009) to 650 million (Gorshkov *et. al.*, 2000), i.e., 1.3 planets in terms of resources (WWF, 2008).

Estimated global food demands for cereals, meats, roots and tubers will be 41, 63, and 40%, respectively upto 2020. The average world price for rice, wheat, maize and soybeans is elevated by 217, 136, 125 and 107%, respectively. Such steep increase of agricultural commodities imposes great hardship on the poor strata, whose 50–70% of income is spent on food.

Further, the last vestiges of undernourished people in developing countries may loom large due to (i) increase in their number to 923 million in 2007 (von Braun, 2009), (ii) rise in chronic hunger to one billion population, (iii) death of 25,000 people per day from malnutrition, and (iv) elevated 15.2 Global Hunger Index (GHI) score (Onsando and Wambugu, 2009).

2.2 Population and Food: Pan India Scenario

India is home to 1.1 billion people. Out of these, an estimated (i) 340 million people reside in urban areas (Office of Registrar General and Census Commissioner of India, 2006), (ii) one-third of India's urban population (100 million) live in extreme poverty (Ministry of Health and Family Welfare, 2000), in slums and squatters, (iii) 54.2% poor urban children under 5 years of age stunted due to chronic undernutrition, (iv) 38.5% of poor urban women of reproductive age suffer from acute undernutrition, (body mass index < 18.5 kg/m^2) (Urban Health Resource Center, 2008) and (v) 29% of India's urban poor bears yellow cards, and has subsidized access to food under Targeted Public Distribution System (PDS) (Press Information Bureau, Government of India, 2007).

In the last decade, the trend in growth of staples like rice, wheat and total food grains has reached to stagnancy and annual per capita availability of food grains declined to 160.4 kg per annum in 2007. Thereby, per capita net food grains availability has steeply fallen by 12% (22.2 kg) from 1991 to 2007. It is reflected from decline in agriculture's share of GDP from 36.4% in 1982-83 to 18.5% in 2006-07. This is an alarming situation for a country where agriculture provides a livelihood to over 600 million people and employment for 52% of the workforce.

3.0 Plant Pathogens, Agro-Terrorism and Crop Biosecurity

The last few decades have been characterized by the emergence of new infectious diseases and re-emergence of old infectious ones as another white scourge over the current crisis (Wilcox and Ellis, 2006). Crop biosecurity, defined as 'protecting a state from invasive plant pathogens' (Brasier, 2008) has become a subject of widespread concern, capitalized on emerging plant diseases and its regulations and quarantine measures. Besides, agro-terrorism as warfare has been deemed 'low-tech, high impact' (Wheelis *et. al.*, 2002). It is estimated that 10% of global food production is lost to plant diseases. About fourteen potential food crops are vulnerable to attack by 143 species of zoosporic plant pathogens. In addition, there are less intensively grown plants to fulfil nutritional requirements in restricted areas of the globe. All are subjected to disease by viruses, bacteria, Oomycetes, fungi, nematodes, and parasitic plants, both in the field and post-harvest.

The painful impact of these plant pathogens can be recollected from the following examples: (i) total extinction of Irish population in Europe due to potato blight by *Phytophthora infestans* (1840s), (ii) infection to rice caused by *Cochliobolus miyabeanus* in Great Bengal Famine (1943) which eliminated 2 million people owing to their sole dependence on rice, (iii) the southern corn leaf blight epidemic (1970–1971) in USA by *Cochliobolus heterostrophus* demonstrated the risk for dependence of a large proportion of the population on a few crop(s).

4.0 Food Preservation: A Closer Look at an Emerging Crisis

Many food products are perishable by nature and hence, require imparting better shelf-life and protection from spoilage during their storage and distribution system. The process of food preservation safe-guards mankind against notorious food spoilage microorganisms. In summary, the development of food preservation processes has mainly been driven by (i) the need for extended safe shelf-life, (ii) protection from spoilage during their preparation, storage and distribution and (iii) continuous fight against microorganisms spoiling the food or making it unsafe.

5.0 Survey of Existing Methods to Monitor Bio-control and Food Preservation

5.1 Agricultural Bio-Control of Plant Pathogens: Meeting The Challenge

Several remedial approaches to plant diseases based on (i) exclusion of the pathogen through plant quarantine, (ii) judicious use of pesticides, (iii) exclusion, elimination or reduction of the pathogen's inoculums with Integrated Pest Management (IPM) and Integrated Plant Nutrition System (IPNS), (iv) intercropping and rotation, (v) exploiting the gene pool of the plants through breeding, (vi) combating virulence of pathogens, (vii) post-harvest protection, and (viii) improving plant performance through biotech inputs and present day biotechnology have been envisaged. However, several surmounted hurdles, for example, (i) technical problems in the mass production of microbes, (ii) formulation into products with a long shelf-life, (iii) expensive and time-consuming registration procedure, and (iv) possibility of plant-associated bacteria, especially of the rhizosphere origin, play an emerging role as opportunistic human pathogens, need to be addressed before innovative biocontrol studies can be transformed to practical strategies.

5.2 Food Preservation: A Biopreservative Approach

Food-borne pathogens (FBP) have represented major concern among food industries aiming to safe-guard the end-users. Apart from food preservation techniques, such as (i) heating, (ii) refrigeration, and (iii) addition of antimicrobial compounds, the food industry amends newer replacement for food preservation simply due to (i) the increased consumer demand for acceptable, nutritious, natural and easy-to-handle food products, (ii) adverse changes in organoleptic characteristics and loss of nutrients and (iii) failure of existing methods to assure the quality and safety of all perishable foods. Against this background, and relying on improved understanding and knowledge of the complexity of microbial interactions, recent approaches are increasingly directed towards possibilities offered through biological preservation.

6.0 Central Dogma of the Proposed Biotech Approaches

6.1 Biosurfactants as Biopesticides: Emerging Trends in Agricultural Bio-control

The unequivocal tirade against consistent, intensive and injudicious use, misuse, and abuse of pesticides has led agriculture to envision a new eco-friendly approach to combat insect pests by exploring naturally occurring products, thereby calling for scientific community to viable alternatives and unveiling the potential of microbial surfactants as biopesticides.

Microbial biosurfactants are amphiphilic heterogeneous extracellular metabolites, secreted by microorganisms, which reduce the surface and interfacial tension, thereby promoting better wetting, spreading, foaming and detergency traits. The U.S Environment Protection Agency (2004) recently approved a biofungicide formulation (Zonix^{TM}) containing 8.5% rhamnolipids (a glycolipidic anionic biosurfactant) for controlling (i) *Phytophthora infestans* (late blight of potato), (ii) *Plasmopara viticola* (downy mildew of grape), (iii) *Phytium aphanidermatum, Phytophthora capsici* and (iv) *Plasmopara lactucae-radicis* on a variety of crops (tubers, vegetables, citrus fruits, ornamental plants, trees, shrubs, bedding plants and turf grasses) through spray, fogging, drenching, chemigation and hydroponics (Kulkarni *et. al.*, 2007). Furhermore, they inhibit spore germination of *Colletotrichum orbiculare* and mycelial growth of *Phytophthora capsici* on pepper and cucumber. Mechanism of their action sequentially involved (i) intercalation, (ii) disruption of the zoospore plasma membrane through surfactant action, (iii) destruction of permeability, (iv) loss of motility, and finally (v) rapid lysis of zoospores. Similarly, Abalos *et. al.* (2001) observed rhamnolipids for growth inhibition against Gram positive, Gram negative bacteria and filamentous fungi. They exhibited antifungal properties against *Aspergillus niger, Gliocadium virens* (at 16 $\mu g.ml^{-1}$), *Chaetonium globusum, Penicillium chrysogenum, Aureobasidium pullulans* (32 $\mu g.ml^{-1}$), whereas the growth of *Botrytis cinerea* or *Rhizotocnia solani* was inhibited (at 18 $\mu g.ml^{-1}$). The spectrum of activity widened when Benincasa *et. al.*, (2004) observed that rhamnolipid-like compounds are active against *Penicillium, Alternaria, G. virens* and *C. globosum* at 32 mgL^{-1}. Rhamnolipids also controlled tobacco mosaic virus (TMV), Potato Virus-X disease (Haferburg *et. al.*, 1987) and growth of harmful bloom algae such as *Heterosigma akashivo* and *Protocentrum dentatum* at 0.4 to 10.0 mgL^{-1}. Effective control of spidermites in naturally infested tomato plants and lemon trees was achieved within fifteen minutes of application using 0.1% and 1.5% rhamnolipids, respectively (Awada *et. al.*, 2007). Further, rhamnolipids, in combination with sesame oil as adjuvant, showed 100% killing effect against grasshoppers, even at 100 times dilution. In addition, stimulatory effects of rhamnolipids have also been investigated on composting mixture of rice straw and bran. Recently, Awada *et. al.*, (2007) investigated the combined action of rhamnolipid-phosphite formulation and found that neither rhamnolipid (5%) nor phosphite (8%) alone was very effective against the powdery mildew at the concentrations used; however, combination of both reduced the infection down to 76-100%. It is believed that the rhamnolipid enhances the activity and mode of action of phosphate through (i) membrane disturbance and (ii) penetrating the fungus protective layers. In addition, due to the powerful micro-emulsifying and penetrating activity of the biosurfactants, especially in combination with sesame/cottonseed oil, an imaginative approach has been their use as non-selective herbicides to control weed pests of certain cereal crops. Preliminary tests further revealed anti-nematode activity of rhamnolipids (0.75%) to the tune of 93% against potato, tomato, and sugar beet nematode pests. To underpin the synergistic role of lipopeptide biosurfactants and phenazines from *Pseudomonas* sp. as antagonists against *Verticillium* (*V. dalhiae* and *V. longisporum*) microslerotia, Debode *et. al.*, (2007) hypothesized that (i) lipopeptides disrupts the storage lipids of *Verticillium* microslerotia via membrane permebilization, an absolute necessity for germination and (ii) phenazines diffuse across and insert into the membrane of *Verticillium* and act as reducing agent, resulting in the generation of superoxide radicals and hydrogen peroxide. It has been assumed that biosurfactants migrate to the surface of the microsclerotia and form a thin film, thereby (i) acting as a carrier molecules for phenazines, (ii) enhancing the possibility of encountering the target cell and concentrating the antibiotics at the place of action, and (iii) facilitating the access of phenazines into the cell. Recent investigations also showed that rhamnolipids had (i) slight stimulatory effect on the microbial population, including bacteria, actinomycetes and fungi, (ii) 15% higher xylanase activity as compared to control, (iii) stimulated higher water soluble carbon (WSC) in the substrates and (iv) superior performance than Tween 80, a non-ionic chemical surfactant.

With the shrinking availability of agricultural land and recent rethinking by the Govt. of India, it is presumed that only degraded/culturable/fallow/waste land will be available to mitigate the sky-rocketing demand of food supply. The nature and acreage of such land available in India is summarized in **Table 1**. It indicated that vast soil tracks are terribly deficient, at least in organic carbon, nitrogen and phosphorous and rich in residual quantity of solubilized pesticides and heavy metals. This reality has necessitated the application of biotensioactives, while devising experimental protocols for captive and agro-forestry to rejuvenate the wastelands.

In an ongoing research effort, we have recently screened a potential biosurfactant-producing *Pseudomonas* sp. with various high-throughput screening methods and de-oiled seed cakes and biodiesel co-product stream as cheaper substrates (Ghosh, 2009). Partially-purified glycolipid biosurfactant, identified as rhamnolipids, were further examined for (i) anti-fungal and anti-bacterial activity (unpublished data) in a bid to explore its possible efficacy in combating pre- and post-emergence damping-off staple cereals and spices (**Table 2**), and (ii) heavy metal and pesticide (insecticide and fungicide) sequestration ability, particularly of lead (Pb), cadmium (Cd) and *p*-nitrophenol to investigate its potential in accruing these pollutants from agricultural lands (**Table 3 and 4**). The results showed a Minimum Inhibitory Concentration (MIC) of 100 μgmL^{-1} against *Fusarium oxysporium,* while 64 μgmL^{-1} were found effective against *Bacillus subtilis*. Further, 1% (w/v) rhamnolipids was found to remove 90% of *p*-nitrophenol (100 ppm), 40 and 50% of lead (Pb) and cadmium (Cd), respectively (unpublished data; Ghosh, 2009). These findings are of critical interest in light of the facts that Indian agricultural scenario still experiencing the problem of residual pesticides and heavy metals in crop lands effecting (i) low yield, (ii) persistence non-point pollution, and (iii) economical burden on the farmers.

6.2 Biosurfactants as Biopreservative

Surface colonization of pathogenic microbes in food processing plants leads to (i) food spoilage, and (ii) numerous disastrous outbreaks of food-borne diseases. However, in most of the cases, traditional cleaning operations are insufficient to achieve satisfactory decontamination, contributing to un-hygiene and malnutrition. To address these problems, biosurfactants have come to play an important role by (i) markedly reducing the pathogenic microbial bio-burden on pre-conditioned materials and thus, delaying or discouraging the subsequent development of biofilms and (ii) prolonging shelf-life of food service products.

Recent investigations suggested significant reduction of adhered cells of food-borne pathogens, for example, *Listeria monocytogens, Salmonella Enteritidis,* and *Enterobacter sakazakii* (from 7.9 to 5.7 log CFU cm^{-2}) by the pre-treatment of stainless steel and polypropylene surfaces with surfactin and rhamnolipids (Nitschke *et al.*, 2009). Further, in an interesting experiment, Meylheuc *et al.* (2006) reported biosurfactant-enhanced bactericidal activity of sodium hypochlorite (NaOCl) and peracetic acid/hydrogen peroxide (PAH) against *Listeria monocytogens* LO28. By reducing the number of pathogens adhering to stainless steel and polytetrafluoroethylene (PTFE), pre-conditioning with biosurfactant reduced the level of contamination of both surfaces and thus favored the microbicidal activities of the disinfectants tested.

7.0 Biosurfactants as Biopesticides and Biopreservatives: Market Forecasts and Future Prospects

In 2004, the global market for biocontrol was valued at about $588 million (Berg, 2009). This was divided into 43.5% of sales in North American Free Trade Agreement countries (including Mexico), 20.7% in Europe, 12.2% in Asia, 11.2% in Oceania, 8.3% in Latin America (excluding Mexico), and 3.9% in Africa. The current annual growth rate of 9-10% in biopesticide sales is expected to stabilize at about 5%. Microbial surfactants have gradually begun to enjoy a conceivable market, with a potential to capture 10% of the total surfactant market by 2010, with sales of US $200 million in USA alone. Assuming the cost of biosurfactants to be Rs. 50-150/kg and the harvest cycle of plant between 6-8 years, total input is reduced to a paltry sum of about 5-10% of the fertilizer and conventional biopesticides cost by the incorporation of biosurfactants.

8.0 Concluding Remarks

In the current perspective of food and energy crisis and increasing environmental pollution, it is imperative to bring down the use of chemicals and live biologics directly in agro-forestry systems and promote the bio-rationale approach of biotensioactives. There appears to be an erroneous impression that they are not as economical as chemical counterparts. However, from the large body of available empirical data, this assumption does not stand even cursory scruting, since pilot scale production using cheaper sources will make it cost-competitive. This observation also unequivocally point out to the ground realty that success of biotensioactives would be enhanced by complementary inputs either through soil conditioners or inoculants. Intensive agro-productivity with these approaches has the potential for quantum jump in higher food productions, however, quantification of its cost effectiveness remains to be determined.

Table 1: Area available for agro-productivity and reforestation (Goyal *et. al.*, 2001)

Land area	Million ha
Forest land	66.9
Wasteland	20.4
Culturable wasteland	15.6
Fallow land	29.6
Total	132.5

Table 2: Anti-fungal and anti-bacterial spectra of rhamnolipids, a microbial biosurfactant

Microorganism	Minimum Inhibitory Concentration(μgmL^{-1})^{a,b}
Fungi and oomycete	
Aspergillus niger NCIM 16404	> 500
Fusarium oxysporum NCIM 1008	100
Rhizopus microsporus	> 500
Saccharomyces cerevisiae	30
Bacteria	
Bacillus subtilis	64
Escherichia coli NCIM 8069	> 500

[a]: The lowest concentration of rhamnolipids required for complete inhibition of microbial growth; [b]: >100 and >500 indicates that growth of the microorganisms was not completely inhibited at 100 and 500 ìgmL^{-1}, respectively.

Table 3: Exploring the role of rhamnolipid (an anionic glycolipid biotensioactive) in solubilization of *p*-nitrophenol (PNP). Data are means of the results from at least three individual experiments

Treatment Time (min)	Residual *p*-nitrophenol (ppm)		
	Triton X-100 (1% w/v)	Rhamnolipid (1% w/v)	Control(without surfactant)
0	97.22	98.05	99
3	90	72.02	91
6	76.22	64.78	80
9	78.2	58.21	79
12	70.02	32.12	75
15	69.21	21.25	71
18	54.32	16.95	68
21	54.22	10.65	59

Rhamnolipid-assisted heavy metal sequestration *in vitro*. Data are means of the results from at least three individual experiments

Salt solution	Initial salt concentration (ppm)	Filtrate containing salt (%)	Chelated cation (%)
		Rhamnolipid (1% w/v)	
Pb	5	60	40
Cd	5	50	50

References

1. Abalos, A., Pinazo, A., Infante, M.R., Casals, M., Garcia, F., and Manresa, A. 2001. Physico-chemical and antimicrobial properties of new rhamnolipids produced by *Pseudomonas aeruginosa* AT10 from soybean oil refinery wastes. *Langmuir.* 17:1367-1371.
2. Adak, G.K., Long, S.M., and O'Brien, S.J. 2002. Trends in indigenous food-borne disease and deaths, England and Wales: 1992 to 2000. *Gut.* 51:832-841.
3. Awada, S.M., Spendlove, R.S., and Awada, M. 2007. Microbial biosurfactants as agents for controlling pests. European Patent Application EP1750738.
4. Berg, G. 2009. Plant-microbe interactions promoting plant growth and health: perspectives for controlled use of microorganisms in agriculture. *Appl Microbiol Biotechnol.* 84:11-18.
5. Benincasa, M., Abalos, A., Oliveira, I., and Manresa, M.A. 2004. Chemical structure, surface properties and biological activities of the biosurfactant produced by *P. aeruginosa* LBI from soapstock. *Anton van Leeuwenhoek.* 85: 1-4.
6. Brasier, C.M 2008. The biosecurity threat to the UK and global environment from international trade in plants. *Plant Pathol.* 57:792-808.
7. Debode, J., De Maeyer, K., Perneel, M., Pannecoucque, J., De Backer, G., and Höfte, M. 2007. Biosurfactants are involved in the biological control of *Verticillium* microsclerotia by *Pseudomonas* sp. *J Appl Microbiol.* 103: 1184-1196.
8. Ghosh, P. 2009. Biotechnological studies on production of microbial surfactant using cost-effective substrate. M. Phil. Thesis. North Maharashtra University, Jalgaon.
9. Goyal, D., Sharma, R.K., Ramamurthy, V., and Kothari, R.M. 2001. An integrated biotech approach for the sustainable improvement in agro-forestry systems. In: *Innovative Approaches in Microbiology*, pp. 367-377. Maheshwari, D.K. and Dubey, R.K. Eds., BSMP Singh, Dehradun, India.
10. Gorshkov, V.G., Gorshkov, V.V., and Makarieva, A.M. 2000. Biotic regulation of the environment. Springer Praxis Publishing, Chichester, UK.
11. Haferburg, D., Hommel, R., Kleber, H.P., Klug, S., Schuster, G., and Zschiegner, H.J. 1987. Anti-phytovirale aktivitat vonn rhamnolipid aus *P. aeruginosa. Acta Biotechnol.* 7: 353-356.
12. Kulkarni, M., Chaudhari, R., and Chaudhari, A. 2007. Novel tensio-active microbial compounds for biocontrol applications. In: *General Concepts in Integrated Pest and Disease Management.* pp. 61-70. Ciancio, A., and Mukherji, K.G. Eds., Springer Publishers, The Netherlands.
13. Lovelock, J. 2009. The vanishing face of Gaia. Basic Books, New York, USA

14. Meylheuc, T., Methorier, C., Renault, M., Herry, J.M., Pradier, C.M., and Bellon-Fontaine, M.N. 2006. Adsorption on stainless steel surface of biosurfactants produced by Gram –ve and Gram +ve bacteria: Consequence of the bioadhesive behaviour of *Listeria monocytogens. Colloids Surfactant B: Biointerfaces*. 52: 128-137.
15. Ministry of Health and Family Welfare. 2000. National Population Policy. Ministry of Health and Family Welfare, Government of India, New Delhi (http//www.populationcommission.nic.in/npp_intro.htm).
16. Nitschke, M., Arujo, L.V., Costa, S.G., Pires, R.C., Zeraik, A.E., Fernandes, A.C., Freire, D.M., and Conteiro, J. 2009. Surfactin reduces the adhesion of food-borne pathogenic bacteria to solid surfaces. *Lett Appl Microbiol*. 49: 241-247.
17. Office of the Registrar General and Census Commissioner of India. 2006. Population Projections for India and the States 2001-26. Office of the Registrar General and Census Commissioner, New Delhi.
18. Onsando, J.M., and Wambugu, F. 2009. The role of plant pathology and biotechnology in food security in Africa. In: *The Role of Plant Pathology in Food Safety and Food Security*, Plant Pathology in 21st Century, vol. 3, pp. 77-86. Strange, R.N. and. Gullino, M.LEds., Springer Publishers, The Netherlands.
19. Press Information Bureau, Government of India. 2007. Public distribution system and other sources of household consumption, 2004–05. New Delhi: Press Information Bureau, Government of India, New Delhi (http://www.mospi.gov.in/press_note_510-Final.htm).
20. Urban Health Resource Center. 2008. Health of the Urban Poor in India. Key results from the re-analysis of NFHS-3, 2005–06 data by wealth index quartiles (Wall chart). Urban Health Resource Center, New Delhi (http://www.uhrc.in/downloads/wall-chart.pdf).
21. USEPA. 2004. Rhamnolipid biosurfactant (110029). Fact Sheet. 2005. http://www.epa.gov/oppbppd1/biopesticides/ingredients/factsheets_110029.htm.
22. von Braun, J. 2009. Addressing the food crisis: governance, market functioning, and investment in public goods. *Food Sec*. 1:9-15.
23. Wheelis, M., Casagrande, R., and Madden, L.V. 2002. Biological attack on agriculture: low-tech, high-impact bioterrorism. *Biosci*. 52:569-576.
24. Wilcox, B.A., and Ellis, B. 2006. Forests and emerging infectious diseases of humans. *Unasylva*. 224:11-18.
25. WWF. 2008. Living planet report 2008. World Wide Fund for Nature, Gland, Switzerland.

13

Global Food Security: Indian Economy Perspective

Prof. R.M.Indi, Prof. Vijay Dhole

Global Hunger Statistics

The latest report released by United Nations World Food Program reveals some of the key facts and figures about the hunger.

- An estimated 1.02 billion (15% of the estimated world population of 6.8 billion) will not get enough food this year. The number of undernourished people in the world increased by 75 million in 2007 and 40 million in 2008. 907 million people in developing countries alone are suffering from severe hunger.
- Over 500 million people in the Asian, African and Latin American countries are living in absolute poverty. 65% of the world's population, suffering from starvation lives in only seven countries: China, India, Pakistan, Bangladesh, Indonesia, Congo and Ethiopia.
- More than 60% of chronically hungry people are women.
- After every 3.6 seconds there is one death out of hunger.
- 66 million children go to school hungry every day.
- Six million children die of hunger every year which is equal to 17,000 deaths per day.
- Half of all children under five years of age in South Asia and one third of those in Sub-Saharan Africa are malnourished and this has resulted in more than half of all child deaths worldwide.
- The World Health Organization estimates that one third of the world is well-fed, one-third is under-fed and one-third is starving.
- Nearly one in four people, 1.3 billion- a majority of humanity – live on less than $ 1 per day while the world's 358 billionaires have assets exceeding the combined annual incomes of countries with 45% of the world's population.

- The assets of the world's three richest men are more than the combined GNP of all the least developed countries in the world.
- 3 billion people in the world today struggle to survive on $2 per day.

The most recent estimate, released on October 14, 2009 by FAO, says that 1.02 billion people are undernourished, a sizeable increase from its 2006 estimate of 854 million people. The increase has been due to following reasons.

(1) Neglect of agriculture relevant to very poor people by governments and international agencies.
(2) The current worldwide economic crisis.
(3) The significant increase of food prices in the last few years of new millennium.

Apart from the above reasons following factors are also responsible for poor agricultural yields compounding the situation of global food security.

These factors are,

- Climate change
- Global Warming
- Salinity of lands under cultivation.
- Fragmented land holdings.
- Deforestation
- Natural Calamities like cyclones, floods etc.

The following chart shows the region-wise distribution of the figures.

Sr.No.	Part of the Continent	Hungry peoplein Millions
1	Near East and North America	42
2	Latin America and Caribbean	53
3	Sub Saharan Africa	265
4	Asia and the Pacific	642
5	Developed Countries	15

Indian Scenario

Agriculture has always been the backbone of the Indian economy and despite industrialization, it still occupying a position of pride making it the single largest private sector generating mass employment.

The following table shows the production of food grains in India over the last decade.

(Million tones)

Crop	1998-1999	1999-2000	2000-2001	2001-2002	2002-2003	2003-2004	2004-2005	2005-2006	2006-2007	2007-2008
Rice	86.1	89.7	85	93.3	71.8	88.5	85.3	91.8	93.3	95.7
Wheat	71.3	76.4	69.7	72.8	65..8	72.2	72.0	69.4	75.8	76.8
Coarse Cerals	31.3	30.3	31.1	33.4	26.1	37.6	33.9	34.7	33.9	39.7
Pulses	14.9	13.4	11.1	13.4	11.1	14.9	13.4	13.4	14.2	15.2
TOTAL	203.6	209.8	196.8	212.9	174.8	213.2	204.6	209.2	217.3	227.3

Source: Department of Food & Public Distribution GOI

The table shows rising foodgrain stocks making India self-sufficient in foodgrains production. Despite rising stocks of foodgrains, the share of agriculture in the composition of GDP is constantly declining. In 1950-51 it was around 55% and there is a sharp decline to 19% in 2008-09. However, the population dependent on agriculture has shown only steady decline; from 70% in 1951 to average 57% during the tenth five year plan period 2002-07. Interesting demographics within the agricultural population shows that the % of cultivators declined from 50% to 32% and that of agricultural labourers, in fact increased from 20% to 27% over the said period. The sectoral growth of agriculture averaged modest 2.3% annually against 7-8% per annum for the entire economy over the last decade.

India at present finds itself in the midst of a paradoxical situation: endemic mass hunger coexisting with the mounting foodgrain stocks. The lopsided nature of economic growth of recent years continues to put more money in the hands of about 30% of the country's 200 million families; while the majority, still dependent on agriculture and related activities for livelihood, have limited financial capacity to be able to afford even those minimum levels of basic food that nutritionists recommend. The widening income disparity is a serious cause of concern. To be sure, despite rising output, per capita availability of foodgrains has actually declined in the last ten years- from 500 gm per day in 1999 to 400 gm per day currently. An estimated 200 million people are underfed and 50 million on the brink of starvation. India ranks 94th in the global hunger index of 119 countries.

From the above discussion, it is clear that, the problem of food insecurity in India is not related to the availability of the foodgrains but more related to the distribution of available resources fairly that will dictate food security. At the world level, the estimates of the World Resources Institute show that over a period 1961-2005 the growth in food production has been always greater than population growth. The FAO also in its latest report has expressed cautious optimism that global food production would rise 70% by 2050 to meet the needs of the projected 40% rise in the world population from today's 6.8 billion to 9.1 billion. As such, the crux of the food insecurity scare in India lies not in the production of foodgrains but more concerned with its equitable distribution.

Economic Policy Measures In India To Ensure Food Security:

India's food security policy has a laudable objective to ensure availability of foodgrains to the common people at an affordable price and it has enabled the poor to have an access to food where none existed. The policy has focused essentially on growth in agriculture production and on support price for procurement and maintenance of rice and wheat stocks. The responsibility of procurement and stocking lies with the Food Corporation of India (FCI) and for distribution with the Public Distribution System (PDS).

Minimum Support Price (MSP)

The FCI procures foodgrains from farmers at the government announced MSP. The government has been raising the MSP, under the continuous pressure from the powerful farmers lobby and it has now become higher than what the market offers to the farmers. The FCI is also under pressure to procure beyond its procurement target and storage capacity. Thus MSP has become more of a procurement price rather than support price. The quality norms in the procured grains are not strictly observed as well. The rich farmers and traders have cornered most of the benefits. The small farmers who lack access to FCI are sidelined from procurement process, resort to distress selling in which they fail to recover the cost of their produce. This makes the agriculture as unviable profession.

The MSP, thus, needs to be standardized and adhere to the prices as recommended by CACP (Commission on Agricultural Costs & Prices). The access to small farmers' co-operatives to FCI will provide the justice to these farmers.

Input Subsidies

In order to keep the foodgrain prices at affordable levels, government providing subsidies on agriculture inputs such as fertilizers, power and water. On the other hand, government has been imposing restrictions on free trade in foodgrains which suppress the prices in the market. These subsidies have reached to the level of 25% of gross revenue receipts (more than Rs. 1lakh cr during 2008-09) of the government and thus, become unsustainable. The tenth five year plan estimates the food subsidy bill alone is more than 5% of the total government expenditure. Subsidies also lead to large scale inefficiencies in the use of these inputs. Overuse of fertilizer and water has led to waterlogging, salinity, depletion of vital micronutrients in the soil and reduced fertility. The high subsidies have come at the expense of public investments in the critical agriculture infrastructure, thereby reducing agriculture productivity.

Thus, the policy of input subsidies is required to design so as to target only the small and marginal farmers in order to improve their productivity and yields. The subsidies should directly reach the ultimate beneficiaries and not the intermediaries. More importantly, the pending infrastructure projects like the irrigation projects which have suffered from time and cost over-runs, need major investments.

Issue Price

The entire population of the country is divided into two categories : Below Poverty Line (BPL) and Above Poverty Line (APL), with differential issue prices. However, this categorization is imperfect and the numbers of deserving poor have been excluded from BPL data. In its latest report by an expert group of PM's economic advisory council putting the incidence of poverty in India at 37% of population. In its report it is stated that as much as 41.8% of the rural population and 25.7% of the urban population is below poverty line. Official estimates of poverty released by the Planning Commission in 2007 stated that the incidence of poverty in India came down from 35.97% in 1993-94 to 27.34% in 2004-05. The chairman of the expert group Mr. Suresh Tendulkar was of the opinion that, the estimates are 'not comparable' as the former is based on a new basket of goods.

To reduce the fiscal deficit, the government has sought to curtail the food subsidy bill by raising the issue price of foodgrains and linking it to the economic cost at which FCI supplies stocks to PDS. The economic cost comprises the cost of procurement (MSP), warehousing cost, transportation and administration cost which go high on account of artificially inflated MSP and operational inefficiencies of the FCI. This has pushed the issue price to BPL category beyond their purchasing power and for APL category some times higher than the market rates. It is therefore required to have a consensus about the definition of poverty line, unanimity in deciding the basket of goods and services. Operational efficiencies in terms of the supply chain management on part of FCI can bring the issue prices to their logical levels.

Public Distribution System (PDS)

The main purpose of PDS in India was to act as a price support programme for the consumer during the periods of food shortage of 1960s. It acted as an instrument of price stabilization and became a countervailing force against private traders, who were interested to exploit the situation of scarcity to acquire more and more profits. The basic was to provide essential commodities such as rice, wheat, sugar, edible oil and kerosene at subsidized rates. Since the mid-1980s, the coverage of the PDS was extended to rural areas. Thus, it acquired the status of a welfare programme. The basic question is whether PDS purchases are able to effectively help the poor. Radhakrishna *et. al.*, have studied this problem on the basis of 43nd NSS round, 1986-87. Their study brought many disquieting facts such as –

- The virtual exclusion of backward states such as Bihar, UP from PDS network.
- In states like Kerala and Andhra Pradesh generally poor purchased less while the non-poor purchased more. In this sense, the PDS was regressive.
- The monthly per capita purchase was meagre 0.9 kg in rural areas and 1.3 kg in urban areas.
- The coverage and food subsidies at state level do not guarantee a better service for BPL families.

PDS, thus, has remained an expensive and largely untargeted programme. Thus the basic question is, how to improve the efficacy of PDS in cost effectively transferring food to the poor. It is necessarily required to reform the PDS and it may be made more efficient.

The present system can be replaced by a system of food credit cards. The scheme of decentralized procurement by adhering to the prices recommended by CACP needs to be encouraged and more states should be brought under its fold. Similarly, the operation of PDS could be decentralized with the states taking their own decisions regarding issue prices and quantum of foodgrains to be supplied. The foodgrains subsidy could be distributed among the states in proportion of their revenue earnings. The Essential Commodities Act should be amended to make it an emergency provision for a limited period for specific commodities. All restrictions on inter-state movement of foodgrains should be removed. Octroi and all sorts of taxes/ levies on food articles should be eliminated. The ban on future trading in all agricultural commodities be lifted. To encourage the private sector to play an enhanced role in the distribution system, 26% FDI should be allowed in food retailing and 100% FDI in insurance for agriculture.

Warehousing Facilities

During the procurement season FCI faces acute storage problem due to lack of adequate infrastructural facilities of warehouses. It has to hire the warehouses by paying high rentals.

In order create the infrastructure the FCI can gradually decentralize procurement and create community grain storage banks in each block/village of the district, from which people may get subsidized foodgrains against food coupons/credit cards. The food coupons can be numbered serially to avoid frauds. The grain storage facilities can be created within two years under the existing rural development schemes and the initial lot of grains can come from the existing FCI stocks. The community can be authorized to manage food banks. This can solve the perennial problem of warehousing in the procurement season of FCI. The decentralized management will improve the delivery of entitlements, reduce handling and transportation costs and eliminate corruption, thereby bringing down the issue price substantially.

Irrigation Potential

Progressive agriculture will demand among other things (i.e. Favourable institutional and organizational structure), improvement in inputs and methods irrigation, better seeds, better manures and fertilizers. Irrigation infrastructure is absolutely essential, where rainfall is scanty, uncertain and concentrated in a short period of the year. Irrigation facilitates growing multiple crops in a year. During 60 years of independence government has spent about Rs. 2,31,400 cr (at 1996-97 prices) on major, medium and minor irrigation works. As a result, the country's irrigation potential has increased from 23 million hectares in 1950-51 to 102.8 million hectares at the end of tenth five year plan (2002 - 07). Following table shows the irrigation potential created and utilized during the period.

Million hectares

Source	Potential Created	Potential Utilised	% utilisation
Major and Medium Irrigation	42.4	34.4	81
Minor Irrigation	60.4	52.8	87
Total	**102.8**	**87.2**	**88**

Source: Planning Commission - Eleventh Five Year Plan Vol.III

Unfortunately, the gap between irrigation potential created over the years has been widening which is obvious from the figures in the table. The following are some of the important factors for under-utilization and the necessary steps to remove them :

- Indian farmers, by and large lack the necessary knowledge to optimize irrigation use. They are not aware of the appropriate agronomic practices including suitable varieties of short-maturing crops, appropriate crop rotations, etc. It is necessary to provide better extension services suitably linked with research organizations, and adapted to multi-cropping practices.
- Even major and medium irrigation works have not been properly maintained. Minor irrigation works, particularly tanks and open wells, have been largely neglected. To remove this important defect, it is necessary to undertake extensive rehabilitation, renovation and modernization of existing irrigation system

Social Sector Schemes

Government is running certain social sector schemes like food-for-work, mid-day-meal, and food-for education to provide purchasing power to the poor. The schemes are, however, not successful, since central government is required to meet only the foodgrain component and the cash strapped states are expected to meet the cash component which is almost 50% of the total expenditure. In many states the schemes have even failed to take-off.

With rationalization of input subsidies and MSP, the central government will be left with sufficient funds under the scheme, which may be given to states in the form of grants depending on the BPL population of the states. The state governments will in turn distribute the grants to the beneficiaries through NGOs.

Proposed Food Security Act: A Prospective Legal Framework

By definition, food security involves every individual gaining physical, economic, social and environmental access to a balanced diet that includes the necessary macro and micro-nutrients, safe drinking water, sanitation, environmental hygiene, primary health care and education so as to lead a healthy and productive life. In view of this the Government of India has prepared the draft of the 'National Food Security Act' to be presented before parliament. According to the provisions of the act, the most vulnerable sections of society will have a legally enforceable right to food that guarantees their nutritional requirements. Thus, every BPL family living in rural and urban areas will be entitled, by law, to 25 kg of rice or wheat per month at Rs.3 per kg. Such a legal responsibility will be a great challenge to the government.

Prof. M.S.Swaminathan, Chairman of the M.S.Swaminathan Research Foundation and MP has echoed optimism about the proposed legislation. He says, 'The successful implementation of National Rural Employment Guarantee Act (NREGA) and Right to Information Act (RTI) indicates that the climate is conducive for a far-reaching, rights-based legislation to eliminate hunger and deprivation." Supreme Court rulings reinforce the view that the right to food is basic to achieving the right to life enshrined in Article 21 of the constitution. In developing the proposed legislation concurrent attention to the following aspects is required –

Food availability

This is a function of domestic production of foodgrains or where absolutely essential, the imports.

Food Access

This is a function of livelihood opportunities and purchasing power.

Food Absorption

The utilization of food in the body will depend on non-food factors such as safe drinking water, environmental hygiene and primary healthcare.

The emergence of food security as a key policy topic reverses almost 30 years of neglect, during which time the share of official development aid devoted to agriculture plunged from 17% in 1980 to 3.8% in 2006. Food security used to be the issue of discussion of agriculture and development officials, but the food crisis of 2007-08 has elevated the issue to the highest level of government. Since 2007 there had been food related riots in more than 60 countries.

Conclusion

"Food Security is not just about food. But it is all about security - economic security, environmental security, even national security." - Hillary Clinton, US Secretary of State.

References

1. Business Line -The issue 2/11/2009
2. Business Line Chennai -2/11/2009.
3. Global Hunger Forces Itself to the Top of Political Agenda.-Author- Zaviar Bias Financial Times London -1/11/2009
4. Indian Economy -Edition 2009- Publisher S. Chand and Company
5. India 2009 -Compiled by Research- Reference and Training Division, Ministry of Information and Broadcasting Government of India.
6. The Many Roads to Food Security - Author - Allan Beattie 023/11/2009
7. The Hindu Business-Issue 10/01/2002- Article 'Food security in India" Authored by Prashant Goyal
8. Web References-www.friendsofwfp.org.
9. Web References-www.wfp.org/hunger/stae
10. Web Reference=http//:en.wiipedia.org

14

Role of Food Processing Industry for Food Security in India (With Special Reference to Haldiram's Food)

Jyoti Shekhar Jakhete

Introduction

The food industry in India is high with attempts at value-addition to make food more nutritious and healthy. Ready-to-eat food packs are gaining popularity even in small towns. This has been fuelled by growing urbanisation, large disposable incomes, change in people's lifestyles as well as consumption patterns. The new wave in food industry is not only about multinational companies arriving here attracted by the prospective size of the market, it is also about traditional Indian food and spices making a mark in the world market. Looking at the rapid rate at which the shelf space of the global food market is being gobbled up by Indian food processors, it is only a matter of time that the whole world relishes the taste of India. Ironically the Indian food processing industry began its journey with a variety of products of western origin that were marketed primarily to cater to the urban middle class. For example bread, butter, cheese, jam, biscuits, noodles, hamburgers, pizzas and pastas, soft drinks, carbonated beverages, chocolates, ice-cream, etc., which have their origin in the west. Now ready-to-eat/cook Indian food items, dairy products, marine and meat products and also agri food products are going in reverse gear to foreign countries. The Indian food sector, however, has not yet realised its potential and there is scope for further value creation by modernising the sector. With better technologies, quality standards and hygiene in production, India can become the food factory of the world. (Food processing industry is yet to realise its full potential, 2009)(Food & Beverage News Nov-16-30)

1.1 India's strengths in Food processing: Favourable Factor conditions

India's Food Processing industry is one of the largest industries in the country – it is ranked fifth in terms of production, consumption, export and expected growth. The Indian food industry is estimated to be worth over US$ 200 billion and is expected to grow to US$ 310 billion by 2015. India is one of the world's major food producers but accounts for only 1.7 per cent (valued at US$ 7.5 billion) of world trade in this sector – this share is slated to increase to 3 per cent (US$ 20 billion) by 2015.

The Indian food processing industry is estimated at US$ 70 billion. It contributed 6.3 per cent to India's GDP in 2003 and had a share of 6 per cent in the total industrial production. The industry employs 1.6 million workers directly. Food processing is a large sector that covers activities such as agriculture, horticulture, plantation, animal husbandry and fisheries. It also includes other industries that use agriculture inputs for manufacturing of edible products. The Ministry of Food Processing, Government of India has defined the following segments within the Food Processing industry:

- Dairy, fruits & vegetable processing
- Grain processing
- Meat & poultry processing
- Consumer foods including packaged foods, beverages and packaged drinking water.

Out of the country's total agriculture and food produce, only 2 per cent is processed. The highest share of processed food is in the Dairy sector, where 37 per cent of the total produce is processed, of which 15 per cent is processed by the organised sector.

Primary food processing (packaged fruit and vegetables, milk, milled flour and rice, tea, spices, etc.) constitutes around 60 per cent of processed foods. It has a highly fragmented structure that includes thousands of rice-mills and hullers, flour mills, pulse mills and oil-seed mills, several thousands of bakeries, traditional food units and fruits, vegetable and spice processing units in unorganised sector. In comparison, the organised sector is relatively small, with around 516 flour mills, 568 fish processing units, 5,293 fruit and vegetable processing units, 171 meat processing units and numerous dairy processing units at state and district levels. (www.investmentcommission.in)

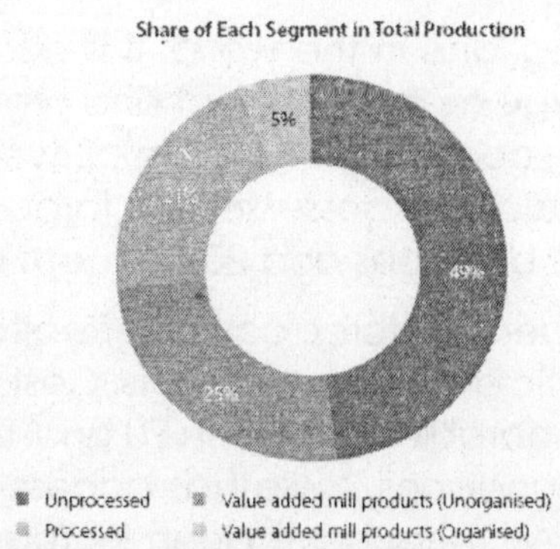

The market for dairy products is expected to grow at 15-20 per cent over the next three years. Ghee is the most widely marketed and branded product with a nation-wide penetration of 24.1 per cent. It is estimated to be growing at a rate of 8 per cent per annum •

Consumer Foods Including Packaged Foods, Beverages and Packaged Drinking Water

Packaged foods segment in India registered a growth of 8 per cent in 2005-06. Noodles/ Vermicelli is the fastest growing category in this segment with a CAGR at 15 per cent. The market for branded noodles is estimated at 230 million servings per year. The Soups market is still small and nascent in India and is approximately US$ 14 million in value. The market for culinary products is estimated at US$ 475,000 and estimated to grow at 18 to 20 per cent per annum. Products like Tomato Ketchup and Jams currently have low penetration levels, but are growing rapidly. Ketchups, for example, have a penetration of just 3 per cent in India; however this category is estimated to be growing at 20 per cent per annum.

Beverages

The beverages market primarily consists of non-alcoholic beverages which can be broadly classified into carbonated drinks, non-carbonated drinks and hot beverages.

Staples – Bread, Wheat Flour, Salt and Sugar

Bread is slowly coming to be a staple product consumed by people of all economic classes in India. Total bread production in the country in 2004-05 was estimated at 2.7 million tons, growing at 7.5 per cent. About 55 per cent of bread production comes from the organised sector.

India has access to several natural resources that provides it a competitive advantage in the food processing sector. Due to its diverse agro-climatic conditions, it has a wide-ranging and larger raw material base suitable for food processing industries. Presently a very small percentage of these are processed into value added products. semi-processed and ready to eat packaged food segment is relatively new and evolving.

India is the second largest producer of wheat in the world with an output of more than 70 million tonnes. Branded 'atta' (wheat flour) is an important item in this

1.2 India's Competitive Edge in Food Processing

India has the largest irrigated land in the world. It is also world's largest producer of milk, tea and pulses. India has large marine product and processing potential with varied fish resources along the 8,041 km coastline, 28,000 km of rivers and millions of hectares of reservoirs and brackish water. India also possesses the largest livestock population in the world with 50 per cent of world's buffaloes and 20 per cent of cattle.

India's comparatively cheaper workforce can be effectively utilised to set up large low cost production bases for domestic and export markets. Cost of production in India is lower by about 40 per cent over a comparable location in EU and 10-15 per cent over a location in UK. Along with these factor conditions, India has access to significant investments to facilitate food processing industry. There have been increasing investments not only by domestic firms and Indian government, but also foreign direct investment.

India's Competitive Edge in Food Processing

	India	Global Rank	Share in Global Production
Arable Land (million hectares)	161	2	-
Irrigated Land (million hectares)	55	1	-
Cost Line (km)	8041	19	-
Major Food Crops (MT)	35	3	4%
Fruits (M)	47	2	10%
Vegetables (MT)	82	2	10%
Rice/Paddy (MT)	132	2	22%
Wheat (MT)	65	2	12%
Milk (MT)	88	1	16%
Sugarcare (MT)	289	2	21%
Pulses (MT)	12	1	21%
Tea (MT)	0.88	1	28%
Edible Oildseed (MT)	25	3	7%
Cattle (million)	226	1	20%

Source: Cygnus report, India Food Processing Sector, 2005

1. Research Question

This research work attempts to study a typical Indian family run FMCG business,its inception,its aspirants,the challenges faced in the context of food security and the possible roadways to map the future.

2.1 Empirical Context

Haldiram's Profile

Sweet and Salt are as diametrically opposite to each other as North pole and South Pole but they perform wonders when used on the taste buds, this delicate use of both the tastes in Mithais (Sweetmeat) and Namkeens (Salty Snacks) has made Haldiram's undisputed leader of the sweet industry. Haldiram's synonymous with sweetmeat as Cadbury is to Chocolates. By default Haldiram's can be termed as "Taste of Tradition".

From a humble beginning in Bikaner in 1937 Haldiram's have grown phenomenally and are today an internationally renowned sweet manufacturer with chain of restaurants and has also started Indian fast food restaurants and amusement parks. It is the flag bearer of the traditional Indian sweet, Haldiram's was started by Shri Gangabisanji Agrawal alias Haldiram, who is the grandfather of Shri Shivkisan Agrawal, the man responsible for the successes and fame of Haldiram's he has made the brand a household name in India. Haldiram's products inherits the matchless quality, zero impurity and world class packaging, efficient distribution network are the hallmark of each and every Haldiram's product and to top it up the trump card of reasonable prices and efficient marketing strategy and the key to success. Headquartered at Nagpur (M.S.) India.

The management at Haldiram's is quality conscious no doubt. Shri Shivkisan Agrawal always believes in superior input superior output. It has regional offices at Mumbai, Bengalury and Chennai. It is a member of the SFA (Snacks Food Associations of America) & ESA (European Snacks Food Association). The company has won prestigious International Food award from TROFEO International Alimentocian of Barcelona Spain in 1999. The company has ISO:9001-2000 certification and HACCP certification by Det Norske Veritas of Netherlands.The coveted Coca-Cola Golden Spoon Awards 2009 -given in recognition of excellence in food retailing in India. Haldiram's bagged the most admired food & beverages retailer of the year in the Quick Service Restaurant (QSR)Indian origin this year. (Agrawal, 2009)

3 Critical Role in the context of Food Security for Manufacturers in this Sector

The Indian food processing industry's growth potential cannot be disputed; however, it requires certain competencies and success factors to fructify this potential.

These include addressing the current gaps in the value chain as well as leveraging on the various advantages the country provides. Manufacturers in the sector need to be aware of these factors and build the required capabilities in their business to ensure Food Security. Some of the key factors are discussed below:

3.1 Integrated Supply chain and Scale of Operations

While India ranks second in production of fruits and vegetables, nearly 20 to 25 per cent of this production is lost in spoilage in various stages of harvesting.

The key issues are poor quality of seeds, planting material and lack of technology in improving yield. Ensuring good quality produce entails investments in technology and ability to sustain a long gestation period for the harvest. Good quality production also results in better quality of processed fruits. Hence there is a need to establish backward linkages with the farmers with the help of arrangements such as contract farming to improve the quality of the produce. Scale is a key factor in the processing industry. Nearly 90 per cent of the food processing units are small in scale and hence are unable to exploit the advantages of economies of scale. This is also true with land holdings.

3.2 Processing Technology

Most of the processing in India is currently manual. There is limited use of technology like pre-cooling facilities for vegetables, controlled atmospheric storage and irradiation facilities. This technology is important for extended storage of fruits and vegetables in making them conducive for further processing. Bringing in modern technology is an area that existing as well as new investors in the sector can focus on, this will make a clear difference in both process efficiencies as well as quality of the end product.

3.3 Increasing Penetration in Domestic Market

Most of the processing units are export oriented and hence their penetration levels in the domestic market are low. For example, Penetration of processed fruits and vegetables overall is at 10 per cent. The relative share of branded milk products especially ghee is still low at 2 per cent. Penetration of culinary products is still 13.3 per cent and is largely tilted towards metros Consumption of packaged biscuits for Indian consumers is still low at 0.48 per cent while that for Americans is 4 per cent However, there is increasing acceptance of these products amongst the urban population. India has a large untapped customer base and even a small footprint in the domestic market would enable the player to gain significant volumes.

Acceptance in the domestic market and hence higher penetration is driven by the following factors:

3.4 Competitive Pricing

Consumers of processed foods are extremely price sensitive even a small change in pricing can have significant impact on consumption. For instance, the launch of PET bottles, new price points and package sizes in non-carbonated drinks (such as Coca Cola) has increased in-home consumption from 30 per cent in 2002 to 80 per cent in 2003. Competitive pricing also enables penetration in the rural markets.

3.5 Brand competitiveness

Share of branded products in purchases of Indian consumers has increased by 25 per cent to 35 per cent. This is especially true for urban consumers. Branded products like Basmati rice and KFC's chicken have been very successful implying that there is a good demand for hygienic branded products at reasonable prices.

3.6 Product Innovation

Certain processed food categories such as snack foods are impulse purchase products where consumers look for novelty and new flavors and hence these categories lack brand loyalties. Visibility through attractive packaging boosts consumption.

Increasing time constraints amongst the working middle class has boosted consumption of products like instant soups, noodles and ready-to-make products. Innovation in packaging and product usage is an important success factor for processed foods.

2 Role of " Haldiram" in the context of Food Security

India, more than in any other country in the world, has a colourful and diverse range of food and tastes to offer. While Indians are great lovers of food, their second love without a doubt, is the love for 'Traditional Indian sweets. India is a country of sweet and Haldiram is offering hundreds of milk product by processing milk such as branded ghee, Rasgulla (spongy cheese balls, dipped in sugar syrup), Gulabjamun, Rasmalai not only in India but in other counties too. Fast food has not become global because of the characteristics of the product like Rajkachauri, as one have to have ten different kinds of inputs to add to make a rajkachauri. For example, curd and then two or three different types of spices.There is also a couple of ingredients which don't have a long shelf life. The other reason could be the fact that none of the Indian companies have invested into packaging in order to increase the shelf life of the product. In contrast to western products like burgers, pizzas, chips, etc., are available in western markets in a frozen form and have a good shelf life. There is no problem for western countries to send their products from America to India. They package it, freeze it and send it across due to frozen technology and frozen supply chain.

A major problem in the context of food security they face in day to day working in food industry is that the customer's in India prefer everything fresh, they are not very much interested in packaged food even today, apart from Namkeens. Like the perishable sweets, if you keep a box packaged like you packaged it yesterday and it says shelf life of 20 days, he will again question that I want it fresh, give me fresh sweets, and pack it in front of me. So, that is a challenge, which is driving Haldiram's to develop improved packaging.

In America, one can easily get frozen samosas or frozen parathas that technology is already implemented there but in India since the infrastructure is not so good for frozen products, the whole cold chain is apparently missing or incomplete. Due to this lot of packaged food expired before it reaches to end consumer and this is really a role which is played by food processing Industry for security of packaged Foods.

Conclusions

India has access to several natural resources that provides competitive advantage in the food processing sector. Due to its diverse agro-climatic conditions, it has wide-ranging and larger raw material base suitable for food processing industries. Presently a very small percentage of this is being processed into value added products.

India's cheaper workforce can be effectively utilised to set up large low cost production bases for domestic and export markets. Along with these conditions, India has access to significant investments to facilitate food processing industry. Efforts should be made to harness these resources for fostering economic growth and attaining Food Security in India.

References

1. Agrawal, s. s. (2009, June 28). profile of Haldiram. (Jyoti, Interviewer)
2. Food processing industry is yet to realise its full potential. (2009, Nov). *Food & Bevarage News*.
3. Prabhakar, G. P. (2008). Haldiram's: India's Entrepreneurial Answer to the McDonald's and the Pizza Huts. *International Journal of Business and Management*, *3* (5), 95-99.
4. *www.investmentcommission.in*. (n.d.). Retrieved october 2008-09, from food & agro products.
5. Food Processing Market & Opportunities IBEF(Indian Brand Equity foundation), retrieved from www.ibef.in.
6. www.haldiramusa.com.

15

Global Food Crisis is Food Security Human Right Perspective

Jayasankar K.I, B.Yuvakumar Reddy

Introduction

The human right to food has its contemporary origin within the U.N. Universal Human Rights framework. The main reference point is located within the Universal Declaration of Human Rights. In spite, of this much of Asia and Africa are today beset with hunger. With more than 200 million children, women and men go to bed now partially hungry. According to the report of UN Food and Agricultural Organization almost, a billion people go hungry each day, after food prices pushed 40 million more vulnerable people around the world into the ranks of the undernourished. Around 963 million people, which constitute 14% of the world's population, were reported to be starving in 2008, with a rise of 40 million people from last year. In the global hunger index of the recent report by the Food and Agricultural Organization, India ranks 66th among 88 countries India is declared by the Food & Agricultural Organization (FAO) of the UN as a low-income food deficit country. 350 people in India face hunger, the largest number of hungry people worldwide. Many thinkers believed that the right to food is a political problem which will be solved by itself and that the law may not be enough to secure this right. Fundamental rights cannot be effectively enforced and become illusionary unless there is adequate budget to back them up. Courts have responded on this issue by saying that budgets are not justitiable and courts cannot get into this area. This is a seriously questionable proposition, for if fundamental rights are to be a reality and the courts undoubtedly have jurisdiction to enforce these basic human rights without which a man cannot survive and if basic rights such as food ,education, health and housing are flouted because the state chooses not to make enough money available, then are courts to remain silent?

Food prices have reached record heights over the last 12 months, with prices for basics commodities such as corn and rice hitting historic levels. There have been food riots in countries across the world where food prices have hit the poor and vulnerable. Twenty four people were killed in riots in Cameroon, while in Haiti, protests at food prices forced the Prime Minister to resign in the year 2007 itself. The World Bank has warned that the rising cost of food could lead to political destabilization in 33 countries worldwide. The sudden price hikes, which follow years of falling prices for agricultural produce, are a result of rising demand combined with supply shortages. US and European demand for crops for biofuels is competing with the demand for animal feed crops to produce meat for western consumption and increasing demand in emerging economies.

Poor harvests in countries hit by drought (a likely result of climate change) have also affected supplies, while rising oil prices have pushed up fertilizer and transport costs. Escalating speculation on global commodity markets has aggravated the situation - with ever rising prices fuelling further commodity price rises.

The global food crisis in 2008-09 made the World once again aware that investment in agriculture matters. In view of the long period of food surpluses and depressed food prices, many policy decision makers concluded that hunger is just a distribution problem. As a consequence, public funding for further crop improvements was cut back worldwide over the past two decades, while the private sector continued to invest primarily in the improvement of high value cash crops designed for large-scale and capital intensive farms. A global food security strategy for the 21st century must end this divergence of public and private sector activities and create more incentives to invest in tailor-made technologies that facilitate the economic empowerment of the rural poor and enable a more sustainable use of natural resources. This paper explores the various aspects of the food crisis and the problem of food security which we are facing in the global level from the human rights point of view.

Definition and Legal Foundation

The Human Right to adequate Food has been realized when every man, women and child, alone or in community with others, has physical and economic access at all times to adequate food or means for its procurement This human right is enshrined in the International Covenant on Economic, Social and Cultural Rights of 1966. Article 25 of the Universal Declaration of Human Rights also contains a statement to this effect. After the adoption of the Universal Declaration of Human Rights and the ratification of the ESC Covenant, a further milestone was reached in 1999 with the publication of General Comment No. 12.In 2004, the member states of the FAO Council adopted the Voluntary Guidelines on the Right to Food. In concrete terms the Guidelines contain recommendations on 20 thematic areas, from access to resources such as land and water to school feeding programmes and social protection.

The human right to adequate food is explicitly recognized as part of the broader human right to an adequate standard of living. While the focus here is on food, we have much to learn from the work that has emerged on health, education, housing, and other issues relating to an adequate standard of living. The Right to Food stipulates that every person must have access to adequate nourishment. This is unconditional; the Right to Food is not linked to work or other prior conditions. Furthermore, the Right to Food also implies access to the resources necessary to be able to feed oneself. To ensure immediate access to essential foodstuffs, it is imperative that social programmes exist to which each person has legally enforceable access. If essential foodstuffs are not distributed free of charge, every person must be guaranteed an appropriate level of income

Individuals and organizations working to end hunger and malnutrition sometimes use the slogan" food first". The concept expresses their feelings that the food issue should be given high priority. However, it should be recognized that food and nutrition constitute just one of the dimensions of adequate livelihood, and it would be inappropriate to argue that nutrition is more important than, say, housing or education. All aspects of livelihood are interrelated, and should be kept in balance Human rights are mainly about upholding human dignity, not about meeting physiological needs. Dignity does not come from being fed. It comes from providing for oneself. In any well structured society, the objective is to move toward conditions under which all people can provide for themselves. One of the major critiques of humanitarian assistance programs has been that "Aid processes treat lives to be saved as bare life, not as lives with a political voice". The human rights approach responds directly to this concern. One can assure that people are treated like dignified human beings, rather than like animals on a feedlot, by making sure that they have some say in how they are being treated. This is why, in a human rights system, the people must have some institutionalized remedies available to them that they can call upon if they feel they are not being treated properly. There must be some meaningful action they can take if they feel their rights are not being acknowledged.

Food in International Human Rights Law

Historically, national and international responses to problems of malnutrition have been based on compassion and the recognition that reducing malnutrition can be of considerable benefit to the society as a whole. These responses have ranged from small local feeding programs to large scale international act ions involving the United Nations Children's Fund, the World Bank, the World Food Program, and many nongovernmental organizations. Now, however, there is increasing recognition that adequate food is a human right, and thus, there is a legal *obligation* to assure that all people get adequate food. The articulation of the human right to adequate food in modern international human rights law arises in the context of the broader human right to an adequate standard of living.

In the *International Covenant on Civil and Political Rights,* which came into force in 1976, article 1, paragraph 2 says, "In no case may a people be deprived of its own means of subsistence." In addition, article 6 says, "Every human being has the inherent right to life". This clearly implies the right to adequate food and other necessities for sustaining life. The human right to adequate food was affirmed explicitly in international agreements.

The human right to adequate food has been reaffirmed at the international level in many different settings. It is well accepted that the basic rights are those rights which are necessary for the enjoyment of all other rights. In these terms, there can be no question that the human right to adequate food is a basic right. The foundations for the human right to adequate food lie in the *Universal Declaration of Human Rights* and the binding international human rights instruments in which it is explicitly mentioned, primarily the *International Covenant on Economic, Social and Cultural Rights* and the *Convention on the Rights of the Child*. Other binding international human rights agreements such as the *Convention on the Elimination of All Forms of Discrimination Against Women* contribute to the articulation of relevant rights. The Food and Agriculture Organization of the United Nations has identified a large number of authoritative international instruments that address the human right to adequate food.On reviewing the hunger data, Philip Alston and Katarina Tomaševski observed that "these statistics make hunger by far the most flagrant and widespread of all serious human rights abuses." Alston added that "the right to food has been endorsed more often and with greater unanimity and urgency than most other human rights, while at the same time being violated more comprehensively and systematically than probably any other right." There is no need to propose the human right to adequate food; it is already well established in international law. The task now is to assure the universal recognition and realization of that right.

Food Crisis and Food Security-Global Level

In 2008, agricultural commodity prices on world markets reached their highest levels in 30 years. In some cases, the nominal prices set new records. In the year from March 2007 to March 2008, the price of rice rose 74 percent on world markets. Most of that happened in a six-week period early in 2008. The price of wheat, another food staple, rose 130 percent during the same period. From 2005, agricultural commodity prices started to climb, defying decades of an established trend: namely, that commodity prices were volatile but steadily falling, interrupted by short-lived, supply-related, price spikes. Initially, most developing country governments were not too alarmed. Many of them had pursued policies of trade liberalization and were party to trade agreements that locked other countries into open trade as well. They believed that global supply would be adequate to meet demand, so that if they were to face a domestic shortfall they could get the food they needed on world markets. Officials expected that an adequate global supply would also correct climbing prices, ensuring that any price spike would taper off before causing undue harm. This sanguine attitude was misplaced. By late 2007, grain prices were reaching record levels and a number of governments were starting to panic. Food riots broke out, ultimately affecting close to 40 countries. A debate on causes began. Media coverage of food prices became commonplace, in rich and poor countries alike. Suddenly every international agency and most heads of state were talking about the food crisis.

The crisis was an accident waiting to happen. The confluence of factors that led to dramatic price rises starting in 2007 highlights long-standing failures of public policies in relation to agricultural production and food security around the world. Rather than some overwhelming act of nature—described by too many commentators as a "silent tsunami"—the food price crisis is largely human made. Supply shortfalls are cyclical, and have been happening since agriculture began: the weather is not reliable, nor was it in the days before climate change started to make itself felt. But much of the food price crisis is the result of poor policy choices. These included the abolition of public stockholding, the failure to invest in appropriate agriculture and infrastructure that supports local food production, and the failure to protect ecosystems and natural resources. It has also included policy choices that have encouraged a gradual global trend towards a more homogenous diet, modeled on the eating patterns established in rich countries.. These choices have led governments to ignore biological diversity and the human knowledge associated with cultivating and collecting a broad range of crops and foods. The authors believe that if governments aim to resolve the crisis by focusing on reducing prices back to pre-2005 levels, not only will they have missed a vital opportunity to strengthen food security and agriculture but they will also quickly find themselves back in crisis, as the underlying problems with global food and agriculture make themselves increasingly apparent. These problems were explored in the report of the EcoFair.

Food Insecurity and Food Prices

Today, it is estimated that 854 million people are in a state of food insecurity in the world. Sixty percent of these persons live in Sub-Saharan Africa or in South Asia. 25 million live in transition countries, and 9 million in the developed North. In addition, 2 billion persons suffer from under-nutrition and malnutrition, due to micronutrient deficiencies in vitamins and minerals. According to the World Health Organization, deficiencies of iron, vitamin A, and zinc rank among the top ten leading causes of death through disease in developing countries. Iron deficiency affects an estimated1.7 billion people worldwide, half of whom suffer from iron deficiency anaemia. Vitamin A deficiency affects 254 million preschool children in 118 countries, and still is a leading cause of child blindness across developing countries. Iodine deficiency affects 780 million people worldwide and is the greatest single cause of brain damage and mental retardation, particularly in the first weeks and months of life. Zinc deficiency contributes to growth failure and weakened immunity in young children; it results in some 800,000 child deaths per year. According to some estimates, each year, 5.6million of children of five years or less die as a direct or indirect result of malnutrition. This is an intolerable situation, because it is an preventable one.

Last year record numbers of the world's poor experienced hunger, this at a time of record harvests and record profits for the world's major agrifood corporations. The contradiction of increasing hunger in the midst of wealth and abundance sparked "food riots," not seen for many decades. Protests in Mexico, Morocco, Mauritania, Senegal, Indonesia, Burkina Faso, Cameroon, Yemen, Egypt, Haiti, and twenty other coun-tries were sparked by skyrocketing food prices. In June 2008, the World Bank re-ported that global food prices had risen 83 percent over the last three years and the FAO cited a 45 percent increase in their world food price index in just nine months. While commodity prices have since fallen due to the world economic downturn and speculators lessening their bets on commodities, food prices remain high and are not expected to return to pre-crisis levels.

The widespread food protests were not simply crazed "riots" by hungry masses. Rather, they were angry demonstrations against high food prices in countries that formerly had food surpluses, and where government and industry were unresponsive to people's plight. In some cases, starving people were just trying to access food from trucks or stores. Alarmed by the specter of growing social unrest, the World Bank announced that without massive, immediate injections of food aid, 100 million people in the South would join the swelling ranks of the word's hungry. These shrill warnings immediately revived Malthusian mantras within the agrifood industry and unleashed a flurry of heroic industrial promises for new genetically engineered high-yielding, "climate-ready," and "bio-fortified" seeds. The World Bank called for a "New Deal" for Agriculture and trotted out a portfolio of $1.2 billion in emergency loans. The FAO appealed (unsuccessfully) to OECD governments to finance a $30 billion a year revival of developing country agriculture. *Über*-philanthropist Bill Gates invited multinational corporations to follow him into a new era of "creative capitalism," promising that his new alliance for a Green Revolution in Africa (GRA) would provide four million poor farmers with new seeds and fertilizers.

But with record grain harvests in 2007, according to the FAO, there was more than enough food in the world to feed everyone in 2008—at least 1.5 times current demand. In fact, over the last twenty years, food production has risen steadily at over 2.0 percent a year, while the rate of population growth has dropped to 1.14 percent a year. Globally, population is not outstripping food supply. Over 90 percent of the world's hungry are simply too poor to buy enough food. High food prices are a problem because nearly three billion people—half of the world's population—are poor and near-poor. Around half of the people in the developing world earn less than two dollars a day. Nearly 20 percent are "extremely poor" earning less than one dollar a day. Many of those officially classified as poor are subsistence farmers who have limited access to land and water and cannot compete in global mar-kets. In addition, the diversion of large quantities of grains and oil crops for the growing industrial feedlots in the emerging economies, as well as the diversion of land and water for "green" agro fuels has put significant pressure on markets for many basic foods.

Unsurprisingly, the food crisis has provided the world's major agrifood monopolies with windfall profits. In the last quarter of 2007 as the world food crisis was breaking, Archer Daniels Midland's earnings jumped 42 percent, Monsanto's by 45 percent, and Cargill's by 86 percent. Cargill's subsidiary, Mosaic Fertilizer, saw profits rise by 1,200 percent.

Colonization of National Food System

The steady concentration of profits and market power in the in-dustrial North mirrors the loss of food producing capacity and the growth of hunger in the global South. Despite the oft-cited productiv-ity gains of the Green Revolution, and despite decades of develop-ment campaigns—most recently, the elusive Millennium Development Goals—per capita hunger is rising and the number of desperately hungry people on the planet has grown steadily from 700 million in 1986 to 800 million in 1998.Today, the number stands at over 1 bil-lion. Fifty years ago, the developing countries had yearly agricultural trade surpluses of $1 billion. After decades of capitalist development and the global expansion of the industrial agrifood complex, the southern food *deficit* has ballooned to $11 billion a year. The cereal import bill for low-income food-deficit countries is now over $38 bil-lion and the FAO predicts it will grow to $50 billion by 2030.8 This shift from food self-sufficiency to food dependency has been accom-plished by colonizing national food systems and destroying peasant agriculture.

We produce enough food for all. At the heart of the problem of hunger and malnutrition, there is the problem of the lack of purchasing power for those in need. As noted by president

Lula da Silva, the world food crisis 'is, above all, a crisis of opportunities and distribution'. Famines are characterized as sudden and exceptional crises – a break from the normal state of affairs, associated with, for example, by the failure of certain harvests, by conflicts, or by speculation on food commodities, combined with inappropriate public action. We have learned however, from economist Amartya K. Sen's study of famines, that these are not caused by a drop in food availability : they are caused by a sudden shift in the entitlement set of certain segments of the population, who become vulnerable because they cannot work, or because the value of the services or goods they offer on the market has fallen.

Causes of the current crisis

The current crisis is the result of a number of pressures all coming to bear at the same time. The causes are certainly complex. Whilst it is possible to list some here, there are also national or local causes that have further complicated the issue.

Increased demand: Figures suggest that the global supply of food hasn't decreased however population growth and greater affluence in some regions, such as India and China has certainly led to an increase in demand. Not only are people eating more, but they are also eating more meat and processed food which requires more inputs.

The price of oil: The price for a barrel of oil has risen from $65 in May 2007 to $135 a year later. With fuel needed to provide fertilizers, drive machinery and transport food this has had a dramatic effect on the overall price of food.

Speculation: Sparked by fears about the security of investments made in the US housing market, a wave of concern has spread across many Western investors causing them to invest in items that they see as relatively safe. This has included basic food commodities and the increase in demand has contributed to the increasing prices.

Bio-fuel: Europe and the US have increased incentives for growing bio-fuels (either through subsidies or quotas). Whilst this has reduced the price of fuel in some regions it has meant that less food has been produced than would have otherwise been the case.

Falling subsidies: Another long-term trend has been the reduction in developed countries' agricultural subsidies. Although the global supply of food has not decreased, the reduction in subsidies has resulted in some increase in prices for net food importing countries.

National factors: Actions by some governments and traders have exacerbated the rises and caused panic buying and hoarding, pushing prices up even higher in local markets.

Solutions

First of all it should be remembered that millions of people have been living with a food crisis for along time. Two years ago the Food and Agriculture organization was reporting that forty countries faced food emergencies and required external assistance.

The recent crisis only underlines the fact that more needs to be done to tackle poverty and the availability of food. Some increase in food prices is probably inevitable, and where it reduces wasteful consumption, it could also be welcomed. If higher prices were also a result of better quality food produced in amore environmentally sustainable manner and fairer prices for producers who were previously receiving very low prices then it could even be considered a good thing. However there is little evidence to suggest this is the case. The current food crisis is more to do with speculation, increased pressure on resources and alack of international planning and foresight.

Food aid: The people hit hardest by food price rises are those living on the razor's edge of poverty. According to the WFP people in rich countries spend 10-20 percent of their income on food. In many poor countries people spend 60 percent, sometimes even 80percent, of their budget on food. In the short term governments have a moral obligation to ensure that the poorest do not go without food due to the rapid increases in price.

Speculation: Aggressive global and national efforts are needed to clamp down on speculation that artificially drives up prices to benefit market traders with no meaningful long-term commitment to stable food prices.

Support food production in developing countries: For many years agricultural development in developing countries has been a relatively neglected area. The latest crisis has shown that this can leave people in many of the world's poorest countries especially vulnerable to changes in international trade. Increased food production in developing countries not only helps raise incomes but also increases food security.

Bio fuels: With the rising cost of oil subsidies for bio-fuels are no longer necessary or worthwhile. A thorough investigation should ascertain the impact that the increased production is having on food production and climate change.

Adapt to climate change: The need to adapt to climate change requires all countries to reduce their use of oil and seek renewable sources of energy. This should be done in an equitable way so that people in rich and poor countries benefit and the poorest are not-exposed to negative impacts.

Conclusion

The current crisis is unlike any food emergency the world has faced in the past. It is caused by a web of interconnected forces involving agriculture, energy, climate change, trade, and new market demands from emerging markets. And it carries grave implications for economic growth and development, international security, and social progress in developing countries decision makers who serve leaders of national governments need information and analytical tools in order to assess the risks and opportunities that their country and its citizens face from the current and future global food crises, to determine how they might respond to those risks and opportunities, and to monitor both the impact of a food crisis and the effects of governments' policy responses.

Although the implications of a global food crisis differ across countries and population groups, there are relatively well-defined sets of information and analyses that governments can employ to manage such crises in their respective countries. As such, economies of scale can be captured at the international level through joint action to collect data on food crises and on their national, household-, and individual-level effects; to build capacity in the analysis needed to guide policy formulation and program design; and to evaluate the effectiveness of those policy responses. Similarly, there are a relatively small number of types of policy responses that governments might take in the face of these crises.

Here too there is scope for international action—the lessons learned from effective and failed policy responses by national leaders can be shared to aid countries considering similar policies. The global initiative is needed to provide reliable, appropriate information and decision-support tools to enable national policymakers to respond quickly to changes in world food prices and thereby, in recognition of the gains that can be realized through joint action across countries and institutions to address the crisis.

References:

1. Article 25, Universal Declaration of Human Rights, 1948, "Everyone has the right to a standard of living adequate for the health and well-being of himself and his family, including food." It provided a reference point for human rights legislation that followed but is not itself a binding international legal instrument.
2. Hunger report-state of food insecurity in the world, Chronicle, feb. 2009, vol xix no.8
3. *Ibid*
4. *Ibid*
5. Wroughton, Lesley. "Global response needed on food crisis – Zoeilick," Alertnet, April 2, 2008. Accessed April 12, 2008
6. General Comment No.12 of the United Nations Committee on Economic, Social and Cultural Rights
7. Eide, Asbjørn, "The Right to an Adequate Standard of Living Including the Right to Food", in Eide, Asbjørn; Krause, Catarina; and Rosas, Allan, eds., *Economic, Social and Cultural Rights: A Textbook.* (Dordrecht, Netherlands: Martinus Nijhoff, 1995), pp. 89-105
8. Edkins, Jenny. *Whose Hunger? Concepts of Famine, Practices of Aid.*(Minneapolis: University of Minnesota Press, 2000 p. xvi
9. In the *International Covenant on Economic, Social and Cultural Rights* (which came into force in 1976), article 11 says that "The States Parties to the present Covenant recognize the right of everyone to an adequate standard of living for himself and his family, including adequate food, clothing, and housing . . ." and also recognizes "the fundamental right of everyone to be free from hunger . . . "In the *Convention on the Rights of the Child* (which came into force in 1990), two articles address the issue of nutrition. Article 24 says that "States Parties recognize the right of the child to the enjoyment of the highest attainable standard of health . . . (paragraph 1)" and shall take appropriate measures "to combat disease and malnutrition . . . . through the provision of adequate nutritious foods, clean drinking water, and health care (paragraph 2c)." Article 24 also says that States Parties shall take appropriate measures . . . "To ensure that all segments of society, in particular parents and children, are informed, have access to education and are supported in the use of basic knowledge of child health and nutrition (and) the advantages of breastfeeding . . . ."Article 27 says in paragraph 3 that States Parties "shall in case of need provide material assistance and support programmes, particularly with regard to nutrition, clothing, and housing."Even if the human right to adequate food had not been stated directly, it would be strongly implied in other provisions such as those asserting the right to life and health, or the *Conventionon the Rights of the Child*'s requirement (in article

24, paragraph 2a) that States Parties shall "take appropriate measures to diminish infant and child mortality".

10. (FAO 1999). Food and Agriculture Organization of the United Nations. *Extracts from International and Regional Instruments and Declarations, and other Authoritative Texts Addressing the Right to Food.* (Rome: FAO Legislative Study 69,1999).http://www.fao.org/Legal/Rtf/legst68.pdf
11. Alston, Philip and Tomaševski, Katarina, eds., *The Right to Food* (Dordrecht, Netherlands: Martinus Nijhoff, 1984, pp. 7, 9
12. Daniel G. De La Torre Ugarte and Sophia Murphy The Global Food Crisis: Creating an Opportunity for Fairerand More Sustainable Food and Agriculture Systems Worldwide,Ecofair Trade Dialogue Discussion Paper, No. 11 / October 2008
13. *Ibid.*
14. Trade Dialogue'sresponse to the World Bank's *World Development Report 2008* (Murphy & Santarius, 2007).
15. S. Wiggins, and S. Levy, *Rising Food Prices: A Global Crisis* (London: Overseas Development Institute, 2008).
16. World Bank,"Rising Food Prices,"http://siteresources.worldbank.org/NEWS/Resources/risingfoodprices_backgroundnote_apr08.pdf
17. ibid
18. *Global Monitoring Report 2008* (World Bank, Washington, D.C., 2008).
19. E. Holt-Giménez, R. Patel, and A. Shattuck, *Food Rebellions* (Oakland: Food First/Fahamu, 2009).
20. G. Lean, "Rising Prices Threaten Millions with Starvation, Despite Bumper Crops," *The Independent* (2008)
21. F. M. Lappé, J. Collins, and P. Rosset, *World Hunger* (New York: Food First, 1998).
22. FAO, "The State of Agricultural Commodity Markets 2004," ftp://ftp.fao.org/docrep/fao/007/y5419e/y5419e00.pdf.
23. O. De Schutter, "Promotion and protection of all human rights, civil, political, economic, social and cultural rights, including the right to development" (New York: Human Rights Council, United Nations, 2008)
24. See Human Rights Council Resolution 7/14, 27 March 2008, para. 3.
25. Speech from President Lula da Silva, conference of the Food and Agriculture Organization (FAO) held in Brasilia, 16April 2008.
26. A. K. Sen, *Poverty and Famines,* Oxford Univ. Press, 1981.
27. http://news.bbc.co.uk/1/hi/business/7414093.stm
28. http://www.fao.org/newsroom/en/news/2006/1000416/index.html
29. World Food Programme.
30. http://www.wfp.org/english/?ModuleID=137&Key=2797
31. Pressure on air freighted food is one example of how poor people may be unfairly targeted in the effort to reduce fuel use. In fact other production factors often have a greater impact on CO2 emissions

16

Agricultural Development and Food Security

Pramod Jogdeo, Popat N.Mohite

Introduction

After the Independence and the ensuing communal violence, India leapt from agricultural feudalism under colonial rule into industrial democracy, and is now becoming an information technology giant. All these social changes bring cultural challenges or opportunities for value developments. Now Indians take pride in having a white collar job, would like to work in a Firm than on a Farm, would like to stay in cities deserting villages where their ancestors stayed and made their livelihood on agriculture. But in the process they fail to realize that "Jeevan Ke Bas Teen Nishan-Roti, Kapda aur Makan" is the reality of life.

Indian Constitution entering the 61st year of its existence accepts every citizen the right to the availability of food, clothing and shelter as the fundamental right. Unfortunately even after sixty years of independence, we are still facing the problems of inadequate access lo food, malnutrition and poor health of the exploding population. This adversely affects the future of India because especially children are exposed to this harsh reality. A man can do away with clothing and shelter requirements, or bring down his other needs but bare food requirements cannot be dispensed with. It is said that "Bhuke Pet Bhajan na Hoi!" which means that on an empty stomach no one can think or cannot be like hoarding, black-marketing, criminal tendencies and other anti-social activities which lead to poverty, mal-nutrition and health hazards. World's poorest households spend 60% -100% of their incomes on food. The World Food Program (WFP) says that 100 million people will be added to those below the hunger threshold, taking the global total to almost one billion and creating a new class of urban poor unable to afford sufficient food. Hunger is a cause as well as a consequence of poverty which could be fought by food security.

What is food security?

Food security is the condition in which everyone has access to sufficient and affordable food; it can relate to a single household or to the global population. But if the food supply or availability is obstructed by scarcity, high prices, inaccessibility, etc., it will create food insecurity.

Causes of Food Insecurity

(1) Developing countries neglected development of agricultural/sustainability of environment

(2) Lack of investment in rural economies which account for about 75% of world hunger.

(3) Cheap imports from rich countries

(4) Trade barriers

(5) Farmers hold uncertain land tenure, lack capital, fluctuating prices, un-favorable weather

(6) Meat production impedes the goal of global food security because 7 kg of grain is required to produce 1 kg of beef.

(7) Violent conflict between individual/society/country invariably leads to extreme food insecurity.

(8) Collapse of economies such as North Korea, Zimbabwe has aggravated food insecurity.

(9) US remain the largest food donor country but it causes delay and high prices. It donates surplus grain from US stocks rather than in cash, and insists that the chain of delivery to the recipient country must be handled entirely by US contractors.

Agenda of United Nations

United Nations gave a serious thought to the food problem and decided the Millennium Development Goals (MDG). If efforts are made to comply with these goals, it will help improve position on food front. The Agenda of United Nations fixes goals for the following:

(1) Food Security

(2) Climate Change

(3) Health and Education

(4) Human Rights

(5) Conflict

(6) Politics

Indian Position

In India, neglect and mis-management of the rural economy are the contributory factors for depleting food stock which actually determines the fate of the Government. With India's status as an emerging global superpower, Government need to give serious thought to the economic reality of food shortage generally and agronomy in particular.

India cannot go by the narrow economic data drawn from its booming middle class of 50 million people, staying in Metros and urban centers, because it is not representative. It represents less than 5% of the total population, as such. it is not real. Real India lives in rural pockets. The reality is that hundreds of millions of people face daily struggle for essentials in urban and rural areas. Some contributory factors for deteriorating food situation are:

(1) Regional disparities. Bihar, Orissa, Uttar Pradesh, Madhya Pradesh and Rajasthan are some States where there is severe concentration of population and poverty.

(2) India preferred "Poverty headcount Ratio" based on the basket of essential food and non-food items valued separately for each State, and for urban and rural environment. On the basis of these criteria, 37.5% of the population was below the poverty line on the MDG baseline year 1990. Fortunately by 2005 it has fallen to 22%, but further improvement is very much required.

(3) Contribution of agriculture and allied sectors in GDP, at present, is only about 4.9% (2007-08).

(4) Galloping oil prices. Last serious world food crisis of the early 1970s coincided with the oil price shocks of that period.

(5) Action of speculative rich country traders in commodities

(6) Many countries have resorted to stockpiling food and blocking exports in order to keep down domestic prices.

Why Food Security is important

The dramatic rise in world food prices has forced hunger to the top of the humanitarian agenda. Current alarm about prices and shortages of food aid, climate change has made it worse. India is one of the many hunger countries at risk. To overcome these difficulties food security is important. So far India ignored this for which we have to pay a heavy price by way of:

(1) Ten million hunger-related deaths every year, half of them are children

(2) The recent escalation of world food prices has transformed food insecurity from a difficult development problem into an emergency.

(3) To meet with 'minimum dietary energy requirement' for each person as stipulated by the UN Food and Agriculture Organization (FAO).

(4) Majority of child mortality is attributed to malnutrition.

(5) As rightly said by UN Secretary-General Ban Ki Moon "high food prices threaten to undo the gains achieved so far in fighting hunger and malnutrition". Food security will help to control food prices.

Agricultural Development

Socialistic pattern of Government prompted industrial development, but overlooked developing Agriculture sector. We have seen industrial revolution, IT revolution, but have not cared to bring in Agricultural revolution which is the real need of India. Dr. Swaminathan did some pioneering work and introduced high yielding varieties of grains. Dr. Varghese Kurien helped to develop dairy sector and brought in white-revolution. But this is not sufficient.

We need to have long-term concrete plans for agriculture. Agriculture should be developed as an industry, and for every agriculturist it should be a viable proposition. To match with the changed economic and social conditions, agricultural sector needs revolution in respect of the following:

(a) Use of alternative seed varieties.

(b) Improved soil management.

(c) Maintenance of water management systems and reforestation.

(d) Integrated land and water resources management

(e) Protect and maintain fertility of land, resorting to organic farming and reducing use of non-organic fertilizers.

(f) Water management

(g) Avoid use of food items for Bio-fuel. One tank of Bio-fuel such as ethanol for a Sports Utility Vehicle consumes corn that could feed a man for a year, as such food items need to be used with care. Otherwise bio-fuel targets could create 600 million additional hungry people by 2025.

(h) Promotion of bio-fuels has been cited as a breach of the right to sufficient food enshrined in the Universal Declaration of Human Rights and other international treaty commitments.

(i) Food crisis need to be addressed as human rights emergency and freeze need be imposed on new investment in converting food into fuel.

Present position in India

In an agricultural economy like India some special efforts need to be taken to exploit our agricultural potential. Exploding population, illiteracy and poverty are the hurdles in our efforts to improve the food position in India. But it must be remembered that though increased population brings with it a stomach to feed, the opportunity is that, it also provides two hands to work, which if properly employed will help us overcome the problems of increasing population and poverty. With the rise in the World population and erosion of resources, the pressure on the unit area of land to produce more food grains has been mounting. The domestic food grain production has been believed to rise to 320 million tons by 2011-12, which is possible only through higher productivity by using improved farming practices, expansion of irrigation, better seeds and extensive and balanced use of fertilizers. The Punjab Government has asked banks to open zero balance accounts for farmers to facilitate payment of the paddy bonus to them, such liberal and inclusive credit policy should be followed by other States and banking industry.

It is not only the production, but food storage and security is more important. Following facts are worth noting:

(1) Declining food productivity and escalating food prices is the main cause of concern.

(2) Almost half of all young children in India, particularly in rural and remote areas are underweight.

(3) Over 1 lac farmers committed suicide during the last decade with the burden of crippling debts for expensive seeds and chemicals.

(4) Government's Public Food Distribution System (PDS) reaches to less than 100 million people and is impaired by corruption at District level.

(5) Lack of investment in Infrastructure, lack of irrigation, poor control over industrialization has contributed to collapse of ground water levels and cultivable land has been reduced.

(6) Neglect towards development of rural economy is the main cause of food problems. Even after 60 years of Independence, nearly 2.20 lac villages lack electricity, many remote areas are not connected with roads and access to factors of development.

(7) Yield of wheat falling and rice production is static this issue should be addressed on top priority.

(8) Mandi on mobile for live commodity updates in Uttar Pradesh – It updates current prices and day-to-day arrivals of 108 commodities to different mandies in UP. Such facilities should be extended to all other states and more commodities included.

(9) Government purchased 3.52 lakh tonnes of pulses from the global market to meet domestic demand. The public sector agencies like MMTC, STC and PEC and cooperative major NAFED are doing these purchases, but it is lacking proper canalizing and distribution.

(10) Regulations of the World Trade Organization (WTO) which force Indian farmers to compete on an uneven playing field have been a key factor in the food crisis.

Strengthening Retail Agriculture

For India, which prides itself of an agrarian economy, mother nature has always been merciful and showered its land with rainfall that is the lifeline of our nation. It requires man's acumen to reshape nature's abundance to his advantage. Government has lot of role to play in providing infrastructure and inputs such as water, electricity, seeds and fertilizers. Organizations like Rashtriya Chemicals and Fertilizers Ltd., are in the business of reshaping the destiny of India's Agrarian Economy. RCF understands the true philosophy by reaching out to millions of farmers and peasants in as many as five States. It is the only company in the Agricultural business that reaches its produce to such a wide base across the country from a single point production unit. RCF does not stop at producing and marketing fertilizers alone; it keeps in constant touch with the farmers. The welfare of the farmer has always been RCF's business. ITC Choupal has also done good work. Many more such corporate should come forward.

Farm Literacy

It includes increasing literacy and educating farmers to take rational decision. Farmer friendly schemes like training programs through two of its farmers training institutes, free soil analysis, modern farming methods and distribution of product literature detailing proper cropping methods are being constantly supplied to farmers all over the country. Village adoptions, providing drinking water and sanitation to the backward areas of the state have been an ongoing process. ITC which speaks of enduring value has contributed significantly in the growth of agriculture. Apart from food processing value chain based agricultural growth, one of the most powerful means of bringing about transformational change in rural India lies in the relatively untapped agro-forestry sector. ITC has also helped to develop allied areas across the entire wood-based value chain.

Causes peculiar to India

(1) Uncontrolled population growth

(2) Lack of infrastructure such as roads, ports, transport facilities, warehousing facilities, cold storages, efficient local markets and standards of governance

(3) Undeveloped food processing industry

(4) Dominance of middlemen in marketing of agricultural products

(5) Fragmented holding of farmers

(6) Inability to use advanced agricultural technology/mechanized agricultural operations due to small land holding, poverty of farmers,

(7) Underdeveloped technology.

(8) Lack of research in agriculture.

(9) Lack of resources/funding by Commercial Banks - 20% industry gets 80% of bank finance, whereas 80% agriculture comprising economy gets only 7% of financial outlay.

(10) Excessive dependence on nature-vagaries of monsoon

(11) Apathy of politicians. Illiterate, poor villagers are only vote banks for the politicians and not the power house to develop agriculture.

(12) Lack of realization of the fact that food should be subject to the same market forces as manufactured goods with minimum state involvement.

(13) Inability to restore the priority for food security over trade volume-which could be called as "food sovereignty"

(14) Inadequate provision of subsidized inputs and credit for encouraging sustainability of small farms.

(15) Absence of proper Public Distribution Schemes (PDS)

(16) High food prices are deterrent to the poor rather than availability.

(17) Conversion of agricultural land to non-agricultural use.

(18) Regulations of the World Trade Organization (WTO) which forces Indian farmers to compete on an uneven playing field in the matter of subsidy have been a key factor in the food crisis.

To overcome these problems

Having considered various problems and difficulties let us see how we can overcome it. The rule to be applied is "diagnose if you want to digest" Food scarcity and security should be given top priority on national agenda. Make villages attractive and agriculture remunerative. It is a strong mental block to consider agriculture as a non-viable proposal; if that block could be removed the things might improve. The "obstruction is in the brain than in the grain" It is not within the reach of an individual or a particular institution, but should be addressed at Government, individual and economy level as shown below:

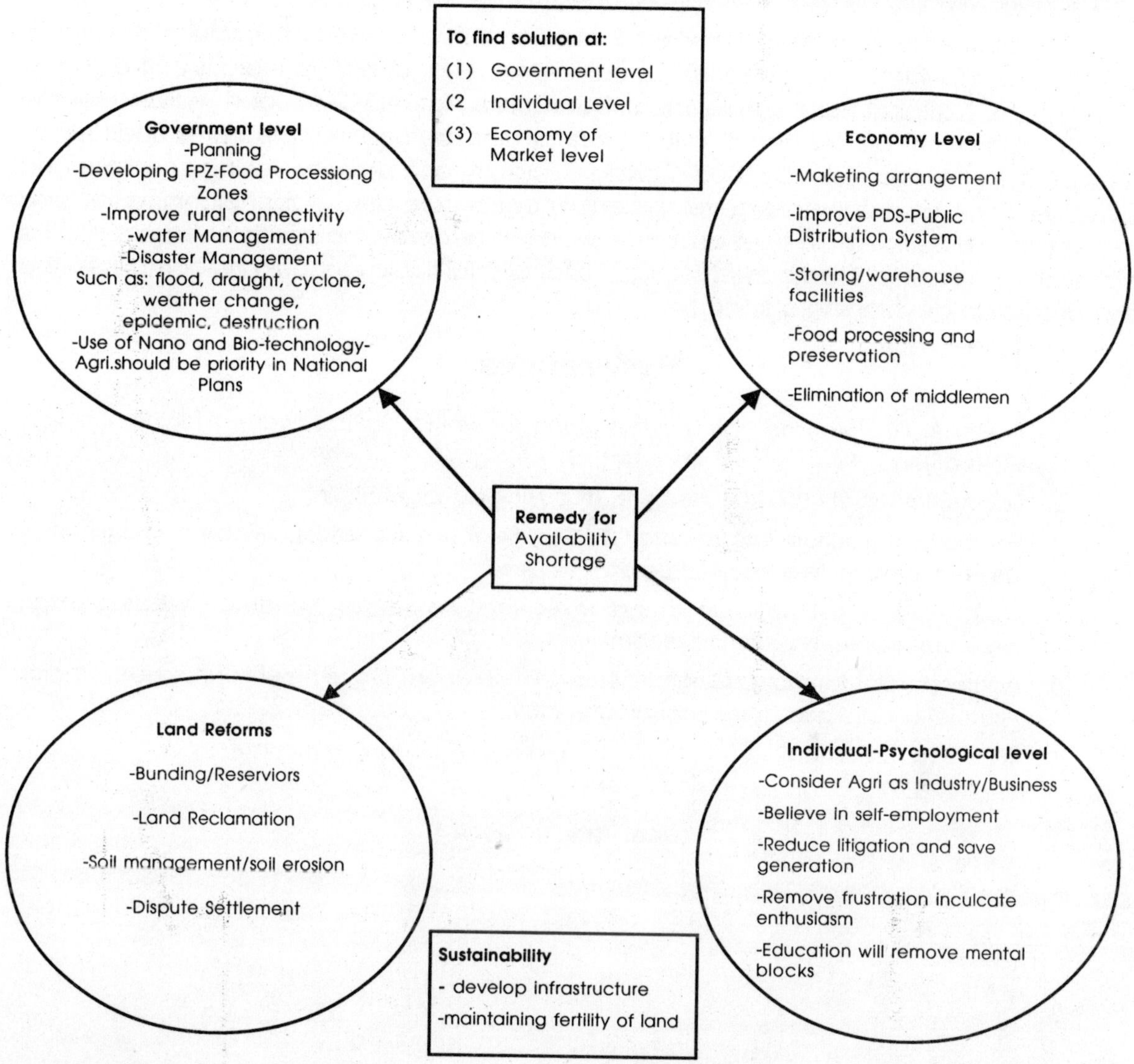

Conclusion

The advances in crop yields since 1970s has helped "green revolution", but at the cost of significant degradation of soil quality, severe depletion of water resources, loss of environment, etc.. The organic farming will help us to have sustainable development. Genetically modified (GM) crops sound like the panacea to food insecurity because it offers high yield, lower chemical inputs and higher nutritional value. But this may give rise to conflicts of interests between the local stakeholders such as farmers, consumers and governments and global shareholders who control the intellectual property rights of GM. A proper blend of all these measures is required to be arrived so that every poor is assured of a 'square meal every day' which is his fundamental right.

China prides itself on food sufficiency, feeding 20% of the world's population with 7% of the land, of which only about 10% is cultivable. As against this, India is in the grip of scarcity. The National Rural Employment Guarantee Act (NREGA), loan waiver scheme amounting to write off the debts of 40 million farmers are onetime measures and help to remove the effects caused by food shortage, scarcity and poverty. Taking concrete and effective steps for sustainable development of agriculture and proper planning for food security should be the main agenda if India wants to become food sufficient. India has the capacity to become "food basket" of the world. Wishful thinking should be complimented by consciously developing agronomy.

References

1. *Indian Agriculture and Agri-business Management,*Dr. Smita Diwase, Kridhi Publication, First edition.
2. Economic Survety 2007-08, website: http://indiabudget.nic.in
3. Food and Agriculture Organisation (FAO) ," Selected indicators of Food and agriculture Development in Asia-Pacific Region",
4. India Agro Industry, Guide to Indian Agriculture Sector, Indiamart Website http:/ www.agriculture-industry-india.com
5. Address by Dr. Manmohan Singh, Finance Minister(then), Government of India to the Indian Association of Agricultural Economists, 2004.
6. IIBF Vision, a publication of Institute of Banking and Finance,Mumbai

17

Food Insecurity with Focus on India

Chandrashekhar V.Joshi

Introduction

Rapid increases in food prices in 2007 and the first half of 2008 attracted serious policy attention. During the course of 2008, the United Nations organized an inter-agency High-Level Taskforce on the Global Food Security Crisis and issued a Comprehensive Framework for Action. Over 40 heads of state and government attended a High-Level Conference on World Food Security sponsored by the Food and Agriculture Organization (FAO) of the United Nations, and focused mainly on how to address the price increases. Donors pledged more than US $12 billion to assist low-income, food-importing countries in coping with the effects of soaring prices.

The speeches, declarations, plans and pledges all duly noted the vulnerability of poor urban dwellers that rely primarily on market purchases for their food, which account for the bulk of their expenditures. Yet most policy prescriptions focused on addressing constraints to rural based food production. In addition to strengthening of social protection schemes, the declarations called for increased investment in smallholder agriculture, attention to macroeconomic and trade measures, and the development or rebuilding of national and regional food stocks. While action in these last three areas potentially contributes in the longer term to greater urban food security, policymakers and analysts nevertheless paid less attention to efforts that would have a direct impact on preventing urban hunger.

The disproportionate attention that policy solutions to the food price crisis give to rural dwellers is probably misplaced. Although in developing countries rural poverty is often deeper and more widespread than urban poverty, rural dwellers are often net producers of food, frequently of the very staples whose prices are rising (IIED & UNFPA, 2009).

What is Food Security?

Food security, regardless of location, depends first on having food available in the markets. The ability of the household to access that food depends on household income, as well as food prices. Households can also acquire food through their own production or by receiving it from others, say neighbours or government or NGO programmes. Individual food security depends on the distribution of food within the household. Sufficient food may exist on a per capita basis at the household level, but some individuals, such as boys or those who work outside the home, may get preference in allocations. Determinants of food security include community, household and individual paradigms.

In towns and cities, food is likely to be available in the market, even if not affordable. And that distinction is the source of the paradox. Urban dwellers have to purchase almost all their food as well as other goods and services, including housing, transportation, healthcare and education.

Food security in the cities thus, depends to a large extent on individual household circumstances as the household operates within this 'purchasing environment'. The question becomes whether the relatively higher income compared to rural dwellers can compensate for what may be higher food prices and demands to spend remaining income on other needs, as well as the much lower capacity to buffer food price shocks by actually growing or raising the food the family needs.

Studies by the International Food Policy Research Institute (IFPRI, 2002) and others show the extent of the vulnerability of urban poor people. Using data from 20 developing countries, IFPRI found that the budget share devoted to food in extremely poor urban households ranged from 48 per cent in Guatemala to 74 per cent in Tajikistan; in 18 of the 20 countries households allocated more than half their budgets to food (Ahmed *et. al.*, 2007). Redwood (2008) found that low income residents of Dar es Salaam, Tanzania, devoted 85 per cent of their income to food, while those in Bangkok, Thailand and Kinshasa in the Democratic Republic of Congo spent 60 per cent. In contrast, low-income city residents in the United States spend around 12 per cent.

Most food is purchased in, Ghana, urban households (without regard to income class) purchase 92 per cent of their food (FAO, 2008). Other data show that urban residents of Egypt purchase about 95 per cent (97 per cent in major metropolitan areas). Residents of Lima in Peru purchase 91 per cent and people in other urban areas of the country purchase 88 per cent (Garrett, 2002). Not surprisingly, urban poor people are overwhelmingly net buyers of staple foods.

According to the FAO (2008), more than 97 per cent of poor urban households are net purchasers. In Guatemala the figure is 98 per cent; in Malawi 99 per cent; and in Vietnam full 100 per cent.

Nutritional status in town and countryside results from the interaction of food, health and care. So the determinants of nutritional status go beyond income alone. For instance, women in the cities are more likely to work outside the home than their rural sisters, and this may mean that they have less time and more difficulty in caring for their children. These constraints can lead to sub-optimal child feeding practices, as urban women tend to end breastfeeding two to three months earlier than rural women. This often leaves their children poorly nourished and lacking immunity to disease (Ruel, 2000).

In low-income neighbourhoods, people frequently live in crowded conditions, with poor-quality housing, poor or non-existent garbage collection, unsafe drinking water and non-functional or nonexistent sewage systems. In the urban areas of low and middle-income countries, between 25 and 50 per cent of the population lack access to clean drinking water and safe sanitation (UNESCO, 2006). Urban poor people often do not have physical access to healthcare, and even when they do, they may not be able to afford it (USAID, 2004).

Food Insecurity in India

India is a country of its people, being the world's largest democracy. Indians have had freedom of speech, religion, and the press ever since their constitution was adopted on January 26, 1950. Within this democracy people still live everyday being food insecure. "Food insecurity exists when all people, at all times, do not have physical and economic access to sufficient, safe and nutritious food to meet their dietary needs and food preferences for an active and healthy life." Poverty easily coexists with food insecurity and is the main cause of hunger and malnutrition. Poverty exists when there is lack of income, productive malnutrition, illiteracy, inadequate housing, unsafe environment, social discrimination, and many more factors. More than 850 million people all over the world live everyday as being food insecure. One in seven people live with a problem that can be fixed. "Malnutrition not only denies people their right to health; it also has serious economic implications. Malnourished children are less able to concentrate in school, and malnourished adults are less able to work effectively thus, undermining productivity and economic growth." Although urbanization is increasing, the poor are still mainly in the rural areas. An estimated 7.3 million people move into the rapidly growing urban areas of India every year. Though the number of middle class citizens is growing, there is an extreme gap between the rich and poor. Around 35 percent of the population is living below the poverty line. The growing population is over straining natural resources. For example, water and electricity in the cities has not been able to keep up with the number of people moving in. The back-up of low cost housing being built has also led to many people having to live in the slums, having up to ten people in a one room shack. The governmental policies that relate only to a country's internal affairs are known as domestic policies. Though India's overall economy and trade relations are improving, the poor people are still struggling to survive. Food and nutritional security can be improved through developments in domestic policies (Chakravarty, 2006).

Almost 1.1 billion people live in India, a population that is growing rapidly. India's population has tripled in size since the beginning of the twentieth century. It occupies 2.4 percent of the world's land, and contributes to 15 percent of the world's population. Almost half of India's land is covered with farms. Part of the reason India's population is growing so rapidly is because family is very important to the Indian people. Indian tradition is to have many children because the parents will most likely rely on the children to support them when they are older, though often some children will die from disease, malnutrition, or accidents before they reach adulthood. Almost 40 percent of Indians are younger than 15 years of age. Also population growth is increasing because the mortality rate is decreasing due to better healthcare. The better healthcare may include better access to facilities, and more doctors. Only fifteen percent of people suffer from no healthcare, but with India's population being so large, fifteen percent is over 150 million. There are still only 48 doctors for every 100,000 people. Though not everyone has healthcare, it has drastically improved, causing the fatality rate to decrease. Most households include all generations of a family from great-grandparents to a new-born baby. When a daughter gets married she will move into the household of her husband, and when a son is married his wife will move into his household with his parents and grandparents. Most couples tend to have an average of three children. Indians' diets are based around a staple grain, such as rice or wheat, served with vegetables and yogurt. 93 percent of daily intake of food in India consists of vegetable products and only 7 percent consists of animal products. Vegetables eaten are those that are currently in season. The most commonly eaten meat is fish, while lamb, goat, beef, chicken, shark, lobster, and shrimp are also occasionally eaten too. Animal products are not a staple part of the Indian diet because they require refrigeration, and over 80 percent of Indians are Hindu, and the Hindu culture does not allow them to consume beef. Food is usually bought the same day it is eaten. Although most Indians are vegetarians, animals are very important to farmers. They not only provide milk, they also serve as their work force for ploughing land and hauling crops.

Food insecurity in India is also impacted by the economy. The economy is an important part in increasing growth from poverty and malnutrition. India's economy is slowly increasing due to many factors. India has become a part of the global economy; they contribute engineers, scientists, and computer specialists that help to improve the well-being of the world. In 1991, laws allowing foreign companies to build factories and invest in India were passed. Outsourcing from other countries in India has resulted in new jobs for the people of India. Companies such as IBM have not only provided jobs for Indians, they have also brought technology to the country. Since 1992 IBM has a regional headquarters in Bengaluru and offices in fourteen other cities. They also help children in India become modernized with technology. One of IBM's goals, known as the IBM Kid Smart Early Learning Program, is teach children with technology from their first years of being educated so the children become more likely to succeed in a technologically advanced world. The majority IBM's programs are directed for the disadvantaged sections of society. India is great prospect in being a well prospering country in the future, and has a powerful economy within itself. The growing population is a social, economic and environmental problem. The government borrowing has kept interest rates high and tariffs are still very high too, with non-agriculture items which average 20 percent. Most of the people who are migrating to the urban, industrial areas of India have no skills to work in urban areas and have only one skill which has to do with agriculture. The main reason rural farmers move to urban areas is because their crops have failed too often to make their farms profitable.

The Millennium Development Goal's also known as MDGs, were adopted in September of 2000 at the United Nations Millennium Summit. The MDGs place human development at the centre of social and economic progress, and emphasizes the value of global partnerships for development. One of the goals was to strengthen fair trade, which included three main points. The three main points consisted of: industrialized countries should improve access to their markets, developing countries should do their part to reduce trade restrictions, and wealthy countries should provide more assistance to connect poor farmers to markets. The MDG agenda for reducing hunger and malnutrition included: strengthening governance of food and agriculture system at the global, country, and local levels, improving public investment for agriculture and rural growth, taking targeted steps to improve nutrition and health, and creating an effective global system for preventing and minimizing disasters. The goals set by the MDG were meant to be achieved by 2015, but the process is slow moving. "India is on its way to achieve the millennium development goals adopted by the United Nations in September 2000 and funds will not stand in its way", the Indian government said on February 14, 2006. A specific target in India is to promote gender equality. Although India is a nation where men and women are supposed to live freely in most cases women obtain worse jobs than men. For example, a family may be forced to move into an urban area because a drought caused their crops to fail. The mother of the family will not only have her traditional job of taking care of the family but they will also have to learn a new skill in order for the family to make enough money to afford to live in an urban area. The mother, most likely never had a formal education. This would be the situation without the MDG"s in place. With the MDG's in place, the mother and the rest of the family will have had a formal education earlier in their life and would be more adapted to have a job in an urban area because of threat of livlilihood.

India is suffering from a double whammy. On top of the impact of the global recession, now there is worsening drought situation in 2009. As of now, according to the Finance Minister, Mr Pranab Mukherjee, the cumulative deficiency in the South-West monsoons is around 26 per cent. Already, nearly half of the country has been officially declared as drought-affected. Even if the September 2009 rains make up for some of the deficiency, the Kharif sowing season is over and the sown crops have dried up in the parched fields.

However, there are a few redeeming factors. First, nearly 70 per cent of wheat production and 30 per cent of rice production come from the irrigated areas in Punjab and Haryana. This production would be largely unaffected by the bad monsoons. Second, at present the total food grains stocks are more than 50 million tonnes, which is 15 per cent higher than last year. These are substantially above the mandated buffer stock requirements (Source: Alok Ray, 2009, at www.environmentalportal.org.in accessed on December 19, 2009).

Hence, the Government can afford to offload from these stocks to smooth-out the shortfall in food grains production. Third, the foreign exchange reserves are at $270 billion, which again is a lot more than the precautionary needs of the economy. So, food grains can now be imported freely, as needed.

But then, the international price of rice has started to move up in anticipation of increased imports by India in the coming months, despite good crops in Thailand and other rice-producing countries. Along with the rise in the price of rice (by 16 per cent over the period April 4 to August 8, 2009) the price of pulses and vegetables has also gone up by 18 and 40 per cent respectively. So, even if the total supply of food grains in the market can be maintained by imports and offloading of buffer stocks, the prices of food items will move up, leading to a significant rise in the inflation rate.

The official inflation rate which is currently negative (mainly because of the fall in petroleum prices compared with the same period last year) refers to year-on-year WPI, which gives a much lower weightage to food prices (16 per cent) than the CPI for agricultural labourers, rural labourers and industrial workers where the weightage of food items is above 60 per cent. Inevitably, the WPI will be higher and the CPI would be even higher in the coming months as a result of the further spurt in food prices, possibly accompanied by a hardening of oil prices if the global recession comes to an end, leading to a rise in energy demand. The CPI for agricultural and rural labourers in July was already near 13 per cent.

However, the changing composition of GDP may come to the rescue. Currently, agriculture accounts for less than 20 per cent of GDP. Even a minus 2 per cent growth in agriculture would cause a less than 0.5 per cent fall in the overall growth rate of GDP. Of course, the GDP growth rate would be otherwise lower (between 5 and 6 per cent, according to various projections by the International Monetary Fund, UNCTAD, Reserve Bank India and the Ministry of Finance), because of the continuing fall in exports for the last 11 months, the impact on demand for manufactured goods due to the fall in rural incomes consequent to the drought and the slowdown in investment expenditure.

Though the rise in prices of food grains, pulses, oilseeds and vegetables would partially offset the fall in income due to decline in output for some farmers, the marginal farmers and landless labour who are the net buyers of food would be the hardest hit for two reasons — they will have to buy food at higher prices while suffering a loss of jobs and income. Already, there are reports of suicide cases from indebted farmers facing a crop failure as well as cattle deaths due to shortage of fodder. Such cases would mount in the months to come. All these are offshoots of hidden food insecurity in India till the year 2009.

Relief Measures

In addition to offloading from Food Corporation of India stocks and liberal imports, the Government will have to reschedule existing loans, provide additional crop loans and possibly loan waivers. More food subsidies, especially for BPL families, and additional subsidies on seeds, cattle fodder and diesel (for running pump sets) would inevitably form components of the relief package. The National Rural Employment Guarantee (NREG) schemes will have to be pursued more vigorously to provide jobs.

The success of these programmes in alleviating the distress of the people will, of course, depend on the effectiveness of the implementation machinery at the State, district and local levels. Along with such short-term measures, the Government should resort to long-term measures to reduce the severity of the impact of any future drought situation.

Public investment in rural small irrigation projects to store and conserve rainwater has been much below what is needed. Indiscriminate drawing of water from deep wells, with the use of heavily subsidised electricity and diesel to run pump sets, has dangerously reduced the water table.

De-clogging and de-silting of canals and ponds should receive the highest priority. Most disturbing is the fact that a high percentage of funds allocated for rural infrastructure projects remain unspent in many areas for want of proper planning and identification of projects at the local levels. This is particularly the case in many remote areas which incidentally are the poorest regions. .

The emergency relief measures will surely add to the Government's budgetary deficits, which have already reached alarming levels as a result of the stimulus packages to moderate the effects of global recession. But the additional fiscal risks will have to be taken as no Democratic Government can afford to ignore so much of human misery.

One only hopes that the current crisis will underline the urgent need to adopt long-term measures, and the policy-makers would not go back to the business-as-usual attitude once the current emergency situation recedes.

The issue of food security, especially in a developing nation like India, raises the twin problems of uncertain food production and unequal food distribution. The impact of unequal food distribution can have adverse effects on the rural and urban population living below the poverty line. Food insecurity is not only economic problem but also problem of non-humanity approach in India. There availability of the food grains is enough to satisfy their needs. According to the statistical data published by the 'Food Corporation of India' and the government of India food-grain availability is 229 million tonnes in 2008-09 which is 230 million tonnes in previous year. While it is happening because, food-grain traders are doing speculation practice and sealing them in high prices than fair prices. Food insecurity is not only natural but also manmade.

India is second largest country in the world in the manner of population. It is most important considerable plus point of the India, because it involvs large human capital. Even we all Indian are thinking that, we will become super power in the world. But when we look at the basic problems of the Indian peoples, we know that the Indian common man is facing lots of problems today. Recently most of Indian peoples are struggling with the bread and butter due to the continuously increasing prices of food-grains, vegetables, pulses and other cereals.

Food security happens when all people at all times have access to enough food that should be affordable, safe and healthy, culturally acceptable, meets specific dietary needs, obtained in a dignified manner and produced in ways that are environmentally sound. The World Food Summit of 1996 defined food security as existing "when all people at all times have access to sufficient, safe, nutritious food to maintain a healthy and active life". Commonly, the concept of food security is defined as including both physical and economic access to food that meets people's dietary needs as well as their food preferences. But food security is a complex sustainable development issue, linked to health through malnutrition, but also to sustainable economic development, environment, and trade. There is a great deal of debate around food security. If we fail to maintain above there has been food insecurity. Food insecurity exists when all people, at all times, do not have physical and economic access to the sufficient, safe and nutritious food to meet their dietary needs and food preferences for an active and healthy life.

According to the data published by the government of India and the Food Corporation of India, total production of foodgrain was 230.78 million tonnes in 2007-08 and in recent year it is 229.85 million tonnes. There is just 0.93 million tonnes of foodgrain production decrease than last year. Hence question is that, only 0.93 million tonnes falling production of foodgrain can create such situations of food insecurity in India? When we looked at the statistics relating to the major foodgrain production. We found that, rice production has increased from 96.69 to 99.37 million tonnes in 2007-08 to 2008-09, wheat production is decreased from 78.57 to 77.63 million tonnes, production of coarse cereals decreased from 40.76 to 38.67 million tonnes, cereals production decreased from 216.02 to 215.67 million tonnes and production of pulses is near about stable it changed from 14.76 to 14.18 million tonnes in the same year.

In the same year population growth is near about 1.10 percent and net growth of population may be 0.50 to 0.75 percent. It is not larger growth which may become burden on food supply in India. Because, in the same period fish production increased from 6.8 to 7.3 million tonnes, fruit production increased from 59,563 thousand tonnes and production of vegetables increased from 1,15,011to 1,25,887 thousand million tonnes. Apart from the production of foodgrains and supported food buffer stock, of foodgrains also increase continually since 2007. In year 2006-07 buffer stock of wheat were 54.28 million tonnes and 119.77 million tonnes of rice stock. In year 2007-08 stock of wheat were 77.12 million tonnes and 114.75 million tonnes of rice and in year 2009 stock of wheat is increased to 182.12 million tonnes and stock of rice is increased to 175.76 million tonnes. There has been net growth in the major foodgrain production in India. So we can conclude that, it is not an economic problem it may be another type.

Supply side analysis of the food market shows that, there is no change in foodgrains production in India. But recently all Indians are facing a problem of low availability of foodgrains in the market and its higher prices. It is questionable, because generally trend of rising price can be found when production of particular goods is decreases. But unfortunately production of foodgrain is near about stable while prices are rising rapidly in India. It is happening in the retail market due to the speculative practice of the traders. According to the supply department the government of India and the government of Maharashtra most traders are keeping illegal stock of foodgrains and pulses. They are doing for profit motive only. Hence, we can say that it is not only natural problem but also manmade. In other words we can say that "Hunger created by nature but supported by traders".

It may be possible to make food security in India in good manner, if we the proper planning of foodgrain production and fair practices in food market. There is need of strong control over the food market in India. In developing countries like India, the root causes of food insecurity include, poverty, corruption, national policies that do not promote equal access to food for all, environmental degradation, barriers to trade, insufficient agricultural development, population growth, low levels of education, social and gender inequality, poor health status, cultural insensitivity, and natural disasters. If the government concentrate the problem specific it is possible by the existing majors, but there is need of implementation of that in proper manner and accurately. Public distribution system is very good way to overcome the problem of speculation by the private traders.

Another way to food security is increase in fruit, milk and fish production, Fish is not only a vital food it is also a source of livelihood for millions of people around the globe. We can solve that problem by the increase in inland and sea fish production in India. The policy of mitigating nutritional deficiencies and food security by fisheries is a pragmatic move in India, considering the fact that sea has ample scope for continuous supply of protein rich food. We need to exploit the food from sea to counter the menace of malnutrition. India, with its vast coastline and seas can use science and technology to make full use of fisheries in ensuring food security to its vast populace.

The objectives of the Public Distribution System-PDS are good but it was failed to accomplish that objective due to the corruption. PDS is better way to tackle the problem of food speculation of private traders. If the government will succeed in PDS the intensity of food insecurity problem will be reduced in future. However, the cruel reality is that despite this huge food production, a huge buffer stock and an extensive network of PDS, millions of people are food insecure and many even die of starvation. Food Insecurity and tragedy hit different parts of the country every year.

The present food crisis is due to lack of proper distribution and the trading system impeding free flow of food. Even increase in agricultural productivity is also one of the solution for this problem. This should be based on integrating inputs and outputs—the supply of high yielding varieties of seeds, fertilizers, and irrigation, supported by credit alongside remunerative output prices. A second "green revolution" is essential to stimulate food production in India. It is crucial to ensure that farm and trade policies of developed countries do not artificially reduce the prices of their foodgrains. This makes it virtually impossible for farmers from developing countries to compete both in their own domestic markets, due to cheap food imports, and also in the international market.

The problem of food security comes mainly from the slow growth of purchasing power of the people in the rain-fed eco-systems. Efforts must be made to help them by developing drought resistant seeds, cost-effective dry-land farming techniques. A major challenge to food security comes from dietary diversification of the poor. If cereal pricing is left to the market forces, government playing the facilitating role, land will be released from rice and wheat cultivation to meet the growing demand for non-cereal crops such as oilseeds, fruits and vegetables in accordance with diet diversification. At the movement the problem is the problem of distribution of existing comfortable level of supply. However with increasing population combined with low agricultural productivity. Therefore we should strive to increase productivity and re-correct the distribution problems.

Although, we can say that food security problem in India is not serious if we succeed in the proper distribution policy. But the problem is that, the government has failed to control and regulate food market in India. This problem becomes serious due to the unfair trade practices by private traders during drought situation. The problem of hunger is due to poor economic accessibility. It is result of poor implementation of policy measures.

Conclusion

Short-term shocks, such as rising prices and natural disasters, are a fact of life, both in the North and South and in towns and countryside alike. It is important to have good monitoring and information systems in place, so that governments and civil society know when and where to deploy response measures quickly. The engagement of potential beneficiaries in monitoring activities and management of programmes can help assure their effectiveness. Preparedness for the next crisis will also reduce the likelihood that governments, in the heat of crisis and with an eye on quelling potential or actual urban unrest, take *ad hoc,* quick-fix measures that may have unintended negative side effects. Such measures include export embargoes or untargeted and unsustainable food price subsidies.

Developing countries face difficult macro economic choices as a result of high food and fuel prices. Inflation has been rising throughout the world, with food price inflation generally outpacing that for other goods and services, especially in developing countries (where food tends to account for a much larger share of the consumption basket).

Management of inflation presents difficult policy trade-offs with important implications for food security. Raising interest rates will help to reduce inflationary pressures but tend to reduce investment and cause the exchange rate to appreciate, with adverse effects on exports, growth and employment. This may reduce the incomes of the poor and, hence, their access to food. On the other hand, continued rapid price increases will erode the value of real wages and the purchasing power of wage earners, with adverse effects on food security.

Attempts by governments to shield consumers from rising food prices through general subsidies or the establishment of safety nets are costly and cause budgetary constraints for low-income countries. If domestic prices rise in line with world prices, procuring food domestically for resale to targeted groups will entail increased budgetary outlays. Restricting exports in order to maintain domestic consumption will result in lost export revenue and foreign exchange earnings. Some countries may be able to finance budget deficits for a limited period, but others with rudimentary financial systems may need substantial external assistance to deal with macro economic imbalances.

Higher food prices present governments with difficult trade-offs.They can: (i) reduce subsidies and risk an immediate deterioration in food security; (ii) reduce investment in public goods, such as health, education and infrastructure, and risk slowing the pace of longer-term growth and development; or (iii) do neither and risk substantial macro economic imbalances that also threaten long-term growth and welfare.

References

1. Ahmed, A.U., R.V. Hill, L.C. Smith, D.M. Wiesmann and T. Frankenberger (2007), "*The world's most deprived: Characteristics and causes of extreme poverty and hunger*", 2020 Vision for Food, Agriculture, and the Environment Discussion Paper No. 43, International Food Policy Research Institute, Washington, DC, 2007.
2. Catholic Relief Services (2009), "*The Causes of the Global Food Crisis*", as reported on Internet at address http://crs.org/public-policy/food-crisis-causes.cfm, on December 01, 2009
3. Chakravarty, Sujoy (2006), "*Food Insecurity in India: Causes and Dimensions.*" 11 Apr 2005. Indian Institute of Management Ahmedabad, Research and Publication Department, 22 Jun 2006
4. FAO (2008), "Soaring food prices: Facts, perspectives, impacts, and actions required", Information Paper prepared for the High-Level Conference on World Food Security: The Challenges of Climate Change and Bioenergy, Rome, 3–5 June 2008, FAO, Rome, 2008
5. Garrett, J. (2002), "*Livelihoods in the city: Challenges and options for the urban poor*" in Towards Eliminating Urban Poverty, Seminar Series, USAID, Washington, DC, pp.29–38, 2002
6. International Food Policy Research Institute (IFPRI) (2002) "*Living in the city: Challenges and options for the urban poor*", IFPRI Issue Brief No. 9, IFPRI, Washington, DC, 2002.
7. James Lamont (2009), "India raids food hoarders as prices soar", Financial Times, Mumbai, December 01, 2009
8. Redwood, M. (2008), "*Urban agriculture and changing food markets*", Draft Paper Prepared for the International Governance Reponses to the Food Crisis Workshop, Centre for International Governance Innovation, University of Waterloo, Waterloo, Ontario, Canada, 4-5 December 2008
9. Ruel, M.T. (2000), "*Urbanization in Latin America: Constraints and opportunities for child feeding and care*", Food and Nutrition Bulletin 21:12–24, International Food Policy Research Institute, Washington, DC, 2000
10. UNESCO (2006), United Nations Economic, Social, and Cultural Organization, "*Water: A shared responsibility*", The United Nations world water development report, Berghahn Books, New York, 2006
11. USAID (2004), US Agency for International Development, "Improving the health of the urban poor: Learning from USAID experience", Unpublished paper, Available at www.ehproject.org/PDF/Strategic_papers/SR12-UH%20ImproveHealth.pdf (accessed 19 December 2009).

18

Food Security Through Family Owned 'Small Farm'

Seema Joshi

Introduction

The concept of food and food security has local, national, international, and global dimensions. Similarly it has several social, economic and political implications. These dimensions and implications are interwoven, making the food security problem severe. Today there are one billion people deprived of food and it is expected that by 2050, there will be 9 billion people deprived of food. To cope with the demand for food, the food production should increase by 50% by 2030 and it should be increased by 70% in the year 2050. According to United Nation's Food and Agriculture Organization food security means, every human being should get enough food by maintaining the human dignity.

Thus, the task of attaining food security is very challenging. The researcher intends to focus on the concept of farm management which would be instrumental in attaining food security.

1.2 Farm management:

According to Encyclopedia Britannica, Farm Management is making and implementing the decisions involved in organization and operating a farm for maximum production and profit. Farm management deals with the organization and operation of a farm with the objective of maximizing profits from the farm business on a continuing basis.

The term farm management has been defined by international Farm Management Association as 'Farm management is the collective term for various management strategies and methods that are employed to keep a farm productive and profitable.'

The need for farm management arises because individual farmer needs to adjust his farm organization from year to year to keep abreast of changes in methods, price, variability and resources available to him. Therefore, farm management is a science which deals with the analysis of the farming resources, alternative choices and opportunities within the farm work of resource restriction, social and personal constraints of farming business. This complex information is integrated and synthesized to increase profitability of the farming business, the ultimate aim being to raise the standard of living of the farming community. This does not mean that farm management deals exclusively with the maximization of income, in fact, it takes into account the goals and objectives of individual farmer other than income maximization. Thus, this discipline deals with people or organizers and decision makers in respect of farms and agricultural production.

However, the term/the process of the farm management is often associated with large commercial farms although many of the same methods can be utilized with equal success on a family owned, even small and medium size farms

2. Objectives of the study:

2.1. To suggest how various management principles can be applied for managing small farms.

2.2 To suggest the theory and practical courses which could be taught to farmers in order to bring them in the mainstream of farming.

2.3 To suggest any other ways and means by which farming can be managed more effectively and efficiently so as to increase productivity or profitability.

3. Research Methodology:

The research paper is conceptual in nature. In order to develop basic insight regarding the concept; the researcher has made use of secondary data. The researcher has refered to books, journals, articles in magazines and newspaper in addition to visits to various websites.

The researcher's earlier study in the area of agricultural marketing and researcher's own experience in farming has led to the conceptualization of this research.

4. Plan of Action:

4.1 Application of management tools and techniques in farming –

Basically management is the process of achieving organizational goal by engaging in the four major functions of planning, organizing, leading and controlling.

4.1.1 Planning-

Planning is the management function that involves setting goals and deciding how best to achieve them. Unfortunately, in case of farming goals cannot be decided in advance as agriculture depends on wishes and whims of nature. But still, setting goals become imperative as goals facilitates controlling and goals lead to increased motivation.

Agricultural production either results into over production or under production, affecting the price mechanism .Therefore crop patterns within a particular geographical region must be decided in advance. e.g., the state of Punjab can specialize in production of wheat or basmati rice only.

As farming to a large extent depends on natural and climatic conditions, farmers must keep ready their contingency plan in case of any emergency. Planning should also have a time dimensions. Farmer must have their short, medium and long term plans ready.

An important ingredient of the planning is decision making. The basic decision any farmer needs to take are in the following areas-

- What to produce?
- How much to produce and what is the most profitable level of the production?
- What should be the size of an individual enterprise which, in turn, will determine the best overall size of the farm business?
- What method of production should be used?
- What and where to market?

The decision which the farmer makes, should be informed and should not be based on intuition or mere past experience. Knowledge is the key to decision making.

4.1.2 Organizing:

Organizing is the process of arranging and allocating work, authority and resources among an organization's members so that they can achieve the organization's goals. The challenges faced by farmer while organizing are

A. Small farmers may face the problems in securing resources like finance and labour. Labour shortage can be dealt with by making use of alternative technologies, but then, it should be cost effective.

B. **Division of work** – Farmers should divide the total work load into tasks that can logically and comfortably be performed either by individuals or by groups. This saves labour and cost; avoids duplication and leads to specialization.

C. **Preparing work schedules** – As most activities in farming depends on the performance of prior or earlier activity; work schedules cannot be exactly prepared and adhered to.

D. **Need for coordination** – As various activities are performed at farms either simultaneously or one after another, securing coordination becomes difficult. A well thought out information system is likely to help in securing coordination.

E. **Use of slack resources** – A slack resource is a cushion of resources that facilitates adaptation to internal and external pressures, as well as initiation of changes. Sometimes farming comes to a standstill because of non availability of resources. In that case, it is better to have readily available slack resources.

4.1.3 Leading:

The task of leading will be very negligible while managing small or medium farms. However, leading involves directing, influencing and motivating employees to perform essential tasks.

One of the important aspects of leading is communication and negotiation. If the farmer will adapt to business communication practices, he will be able to market his product well and can negotiate the price and other terms and conditions of sales as well.

Usually, farming requires hiring labour. The labour will be motivated to work hard only if the farmer will set an example before labour. Because ultimately, management is not only getting the work done through and from others.

4.1.4 Controlling:

Controlling is the process of ensuring that actual activities conform to planned activities. For designing control system, it is imperative to first of all identify key performance areas and then identifying strategic control points.

In case of farming using control for production purposes is almost impossible as production is mostly governed and affected by natural and climatic conditions. However financial controls must be used to maintain economic viability of farming. Budgeting and auditing are the integral part of financial controls.

Apart from the above mentioned four management functions, farmer is expected to perform some business functions as well. They are –production management, marketing management, finance management and personnel management.

4.2 Introduction of management related courses in agricultural studies:

It is essential to popularize various farm management principles and techniques among farming community. While popularizing these techniques what is important is to blend the conventional knowledge with latest technology. Numbers of agricultural colleges and schools must increase. Even the basic farming technology can be popularized through ITIs. One move is under consideration of the governmental authorities, that is, to teach agriculture or farming in conventional schools.

There are many courses incorporated in the curriculum of agricultural schools and colleges but the researcher is of the opinion that intensive training and guidance is essential in some areas. These areas are-

(1) Laws governing farming and farmers-

e.g., APMC Act, Laws relating to land holding, inheritance

(2) Art of communication and negotiation-

With respect to written communication, farmer must learn to write project reports, which are required by various funding agencies. They must be able to handle all the paper work required in farming. Art of negotiation will help the farmer in securing better, other terms and conditions.

(3) Logistics and supply chain management-

As agricultural production is perishable in nature, it requires fast moving and modern logistics.

(4) Food processing and preservation-

Due to the perishable nature of farm produce, farmers should develop vertical integration.

(5) Retailing-

Through organized retailing of farm produce collectively, farmers will be able to improve their collective bargaining power and profitably.

(6) Information regarding infrastructural set up provide by governmental and non-governmental agencies working at the national and international level.

(7) Bookkeeping and accountancy-

Maintaining, preparing cash book or receipt payment account, income and expenditure account, balance sheet to determine actual surplus or deficit resulting from agriculture.

(8) Agricultural economics-

How to match demand, supply and how to make agriculture an economically viable activity.

(9) Agricultural marketing-

Agricultural production is seasonal in nature and consumption is throughout the year. This leads to the problem of marketing. Therefore knowledge of fundamentals of marketing is essential. Farmers should be made aware of the various schemes and assistance provided by government and other relevant bodies.

4.3 Other measures:

The researcher has included here some other measures required to be taken for betterment of small and medium farmers.

4.3.1 Popularizing farm management principles and techniques-

This can be done with help of Gramsevak and Anganwadi teachers. They can either deliver lectures or demonstrate to the farmers. If there is a shortage of such services, it can be also done with help of a C.D.

The farmers who are literate can get such knowledge through books, hand outs, but those who are illiterate, TV and Radio programs should be arranged. Such a program should preferably be in local language, telecasted/broadcasted at a suitable time. On the contrary special Radio and TV channel should be created.

In some states the concept of **e- choupal** has become popular and many farmers have benefited. But this should become a regular feature for providing useful information to the farmers. Such information is also now made available with the help of mobiles. This could be the most affordable methods for providing information to the farmers.

4.3.2 Advertising campaign for improving status of farming community in the society-

Usually in our society, the farming community do not enjoy a status. It is not considered a good occupation. Nobody enters into this occupation by choice, but by some compulsion. The state of affairs must be changed. Farmers should feel proud of being a farmer. The society must realize the importance of farming as an occupation.

For reducing the dropout rate of students from schools, the government introduce a campaign with the punch line 'School Chale Hum'. On the same ground such campaign should be introduced to improve the status of the farming community in the society.

4.3.3 Developing substitute for conventional food-

Agricultural mix has been undergoing a silent and steady shift away from grains. With rising income, this change is driven by consumer's tastes and preferences. Quantity of wheat, rice and cereals consumed is reducing. What goes up in Indian consumer's thali is fruits, vegetable, livestock (dairy, eggs, meat and fish) the so called high value agriculture. It is this changing complexion of the thali, which will drive the change in the field of the farmers. Call it 'from plate to plough revolution' in a demand driven system.

Small and medium farmer must take note of such change in consumption pattern. They should develop more non-conventional substitutes, which are demanded by the market.

Conclusion

Even in the era of technological advancement, agricultural production cannot be improved only with the help of technology. Technology has its own limitation, Moreover some technologies cannot be implemented without proper support systems. Genetically modified food and organic farming are in its infancy and is carried out on an experimental level only. In such a situation, in a country like India, where most of the land holdings are marginal, small and medium, making farming an economically viable occupation becomes challenging.

With the help of the measures suggested by the researcher, farm management can become a panacea for attaining the food security. Farmer should no longer remain mere cultivator but should become a farm manager.

References:

Books:

1. Kent D Olson (2004) *"Farm Management;Principles and Strategies"*, Wiley Blackwell publishers.
2. Andrew Boss, George Pond (2008) *'Modern Farm Management Principles and Practice'* Daya Publishing House.
3. Stoner, Freeman ,Gilbert *'Management'* (2000) Prentice Hall.
4. Kathryn Bartol and David Martin *'Management'* Mc Graw Hill Publication, 2nd edition.

Magazines:

- Business Today, Dec. 2009. India Today Group.
- 'Andolan' Shashvat Vikasasathi, Dec. 2009.

19

Green Revolution and Food Security: Criticisms, Impacts, Problems and Risks

Chandrashekhar Suresh Kaushik

Green Revolution

Green Revolution refers to the process of transformation of agriculture. It is due to Mr. Norman Ernest Borlaug who was an American agronomist and an humanitarian that the word "Green Revolution" came into picture.

During the mid 20th century, Borlaug developed semi dwarf, high yield, and disease resistant wheat varieties. Borlaug led the introduction of these high yielding varieties combined with modern agricultural production techniques to Mexico, Pakistan and India. As a result, Mexico became a net exporter of wheat by 1963. Between 1965 and 1970, wheat yields nearly doubled in Pakistan and India, greatly improving the food security in those nations. These collective increases in yield have been labeled the Green Revolution and Borlaug is often credited with saving over a billion people worldwide from starvation. This great personality recently expired on September 12, 2009.

In 1943, Mexico imported half its wheat, but by 1956, the Green Revolution had made Mexico self-sufficient; by 1964, Mexico exported half a million tons of wheat.[1] The associated transformation has continued as the result of programs of agricultural research, extension, and infrastructural development.

The Green Revolution allowed food production to keep pace with worldwide population growth. The Green Revolution has had major social and ecological impacts.

Indian success of Green Revolution:

In 1961 India was on the brink of mass famine[2]. With the experience of agricultural development begun in Mexico in 1943 judged as a success, Borlaug was invited to India. Despite bureaucratic hurdles indian government collaborated to import wheat seeds. Punjab was selected by the Indian government to try the new crops because of its reliable water supply and a history of agricultural success.

India began its own Green Revolution program of plant breeding, irrigation development, and financing of agrochemicals. India soon adopted IR8 - a semi-dwarf rice variety that could produce more grains of rice per plant when grown with certain fertilizers and irrigation. In 1968, Indian agronomist S.K. De Datta published his findings that IR8 rice yielded about 5 tons per hectare with no fertilizer, and almost 10 tons per hectare under optimal conditions. This was 10 times the yield of traditional rice. IR8 was a success throughout Asia, and dubbed the "Miracle Rice".

1960s, rice yields in India were about two tons per hectare; by the mid-1990s, they had risen to six tons per hectare. In the 1970s, rice cost about $550 a ton; in 2001, it cost under $200 a ton. India became one of the world's most successful rice producers, and is now a major rice exporter, shipping nearly 4.5 million tons in 2006.

Green Revolution and Agriculture Production

Technologies

The projects within the Green Revolution spread technologies which included pesticides, irrigation projects, synthetic nitrogen fertilizer and improved crop varieties developed through the conventional, science-based methods. The novel technological development of the Green Revolution was the production of novel wheat cultivars, maize, wheat, and rice that are generally referred to as high yielding varieties.

Production increases

Cereal production more than doubled in developing nations between the years 1961 - 1985. Yields of rice, maize, and wheat increased steadily during that period. The production increases can be attributed roughly equally to irrigation, fertilizer, and seed development, at least in the case of Asian rice.

While agricultural output increased as a result of the Green Revolution, the energy input to produce a crop has increased faster, so that the ratio of crops produced to energy input has decreased over time. Green Revolution techniques also rely heavily on chemical fertilizers, pesticides and herbicides, some of which must be developed from fossil fuels, making agriculture increasingly reliant on petroleum products.

Criticisms on Green Revolution

Quality of diet

Some have challenged the value of the increased food production of Green Revolution agriculture. One agriculturist Mr. Miguel A. Alfieri, writes that the comparison between traditional systems of agriculture and Green Revolution agriculture has been unfair, because Green Revolution agriculture produces monocultures of cereal grains, while traditional agriculture usually incorporates polycultures. These monoculture crops are often used for export, feed for animals, or conversion into biofuel.

According to Dr Emile Frison, Green Revolution has also led to a change in dietary habits, as less people are affected by hunger and die from starvation, but many are affected by malnutrition such as iron or vitamin-A deficiencies. High-yield rice, introduced since 1964 to poverty-ridden Asian countries, (such as the Philippines), was found to have inferior flavour and be more glutinous and less savory than their native varieties. This caused its price to be lower than the average market value. The introduction of pesticides to rice production poisoned and killed off fish and weedy green vegetables that traditionally coexisted in rice paddies. These were nutritious food sources for Filipino farmers prior to the introduction of pesticides.

Political impacts of Green Revolution

There is significant evidence that the Green Revolution weakened socialist movements in many nations. In countries such as India, Mexico, and the Philippines, technological solutions were sought as an alternative to expanding agrarian reform initiatives, the latter of which were often linked to socialist politics.

Globalization

In the most basic sense, the Green Revolution was a product of globalization as evidenced in the creation of international agricultural research centers that shared information, and with transnational funding from groups like the Rockefeller Foundation and Ford Foundation. Additionally, the inputs required in Green Revolution agriculture created new markets for seed and chemical corporations, many of which were based in the United States.

Environmental impacts of Green Revolution

Pesticides

Green Revolution agriculture relies on extensive use of pesticides, which are necessary to limit the high levels of pest damage that inevitably occur in monocropping - the practice of producing or growing one single crop over a wide area.

Water

Likewise, rivers are drying up at an alarming rate. Famous lifelines such as the Nile and Ganges along with countless other rivers are sharing in the same fate. Also the water quality is being compromised. In the Aral Sea, water salinization has wiped out all native fish, leaving an economy even more dependent on the agricultural model that originated the problem.

Biodiversity

There are varying opinions about the effect of the Green Revolution on wild biodiversity. One hypothesis speculates that by increasing production per unit of land area, agriculture will not need to expand into new, uncultivated areas to feed a growing human population. A counter-hypothesis speculates that biodiversity was sacrificed because traditional systems of agriculture that were displaced sometimes incorporated practices to preserve wild biodiversity, and because the Green Revolution expanded agricultural development into new areas where it was once unprofitable or too arid.

Food security

When it comes to Food Security there are two universal definitions of food security come from the UN's Food and Agriculture Organization (FAO) and the United States Department of Agriculture (USDA):

- Food security exists when all people, at all times, have physical and economic access to sufficient, safe and nutritious food to meet their dietary needs and food preferences for an active and healthy life. (FAO)
- Food security for a household means access by all members at all times to enough food for an active, healthy life. Food security includes at a minimum (1) the ready availability of nutritionally adequate and safe foods, and (2) an assured ability to acquire acceptable foods in socially acceptable ways (that is, without resorting to emergency food supplies, scavenging, stealing, or other coping strategies). (USDA)

Growth in food production has been greater than population growth.

Food security refers to the availability of food and one's access to it. A household is considered food secure when its occupants do not live in hunger or fear of starvation. According to the World Resources Institute, global per capita food production has been increasing substantially for the past several decades.

Worldwide around 852 million people are chronically hungry due to extreme poverty, while up to 2 billion people lack food security intermittently due to varying degrees of poverty (source: FAO, 2003). Six million children die of hunger every year - 17,000 every day.[20] As of late 2007, increased farming for use in biofuels, world oil prices, global population growth, climate change, loss of agricultural land to residential and industrial development, and growing consumer demand in China and India have pushed up the price of grain. Food riots have recently taken place in many countries across the world.

It is becoming increasingly difficult to maintain food security in a world. More than half of the globe's population, numbering approximately 3.3 billion people, lives in urban areas as of November 2007. Any disruption to farm supplies may precipitate a uniquely urban food crisis in a relatively short time. The ongoing global credit crisis has affected farm credits, despite a boom in commodity prices. Food security is a complex topic, standing at the intersection of many disciplines.

In developing countries, often 70% or more of the population lives in rural areas. In that context, agricultural development among smallholder farmers and landless people provides a livelihood for people allowing them the opportunity to stay in their communities. In many areas of the world, land ownership is not available, thus, people who want or need to farm to make a living have little incentive to improve the land.

A direct relationship exists between food consumption levels and poverty. Families with the financial resources to escape extreme poverty rarely suffer from chronic hunger;

while poor families not only suffer the most from chronic hunger, but are also the segment of the population most at risk during food shortages and famines.

Problems in food security

Global water crisis

Water deficits, which are already spurring heavy grain imports in numerous smaller countries, may soon do the same in larger countries, such as China or India. The water tables are falling in scores of countries (including Northern China, the US, and India) due to widespread overpumping using powerful diesel and electric pumps. Other countries affected include Pakistan, Afghanistan and Iran. This will eventually lead to water scarcity and cutbacks in grain harvest. Even with the overpumping of its aquifers, China is developing a grain deficit. When this happens, it will almost certainly drive grain prices upward. Most of the 3 billion people projected to be added worldwide by mid-century will be born in countries already experiencing water shortages. After China and India, there is a second tier of smaller countries with large water deficits— Afghanistan, Algeria, Egypt, Iran, Mexico and Pakistan. Four of these already import a large share of their grain. Only Pakistan remains self-sufficient. But with a population expanding by 4 million a year, it will also likely soon turn to the world market for grain.

Land degradation

Intensive farming often leads to a vicious cycle of exhaustion of soil fertility and decline of agricultural yields. Approximately 40% of the world's agricultural land is seriously degraded. In Africa, if current trends of soil degradation continue the continent might be able to feed just 25% of its population by 2025, according to UNU's Ghana-based Institute for Natural Resources in Africa.

Land deals

Rich governments and corporations are buying up the rights to millions of hectares of agricultural land in developing countries in an effort to secure their own long-term food supplies. The head of the Food and Agriculture Organization (FAO), Jacques Diouf, has warned that the controversial rise in land deals could create a form of "neocolonialism", with poor states producing food for the rich at the expense of their own hungry people. The South Korean firm Daewoo Logistics has secured a large piece of farmland in Madagascar to grow maize and crops for biofuels. Libya has secured 250,000 hectares of Ukrainian farmland, and China has begun to explore land deals in Southeast Asia.

Climate change

According to a UN climate report, the Himalayan glaciers that are the principal dry-season water sources of Asia's biggest rivers – Ganges, Indus, Brahmaputra, Yangtze, Mekong, Salween and Yellow could disappear by 2035 as temperatures rise. Approximately 2.4 billion people live in the drainage basin of the Himalayan rivers. India, China, Pakistan, Afghanistan, Bangladesh, Nepal, and Myanmar could experience floods followed by severe droughts in coming decades. In India alone, the Ganges provides water for drinking and farming for more than 500 million people.

Economic approaches on Food Security

There are many economic approaches advocated to improve food security in developing countries. Three typical approaches are listed below. The first is typical of what is advocated by most governments and international agencies. The other two are more common to Non Governmental Organizations (NGO's).

Westernized view

Conventional thinking in westernized countries is that maximizing the farmers profit is the surest way of maximizing agricultural production; the higher a farmer's profit, the greater the effort that will be forthcoming, and the greater the risk the farmer is willing to take. An increased profit also increases the farmer's incentive to engage in double cropping, soil improvement programs, and expanding usable area.

Food justice

An alternative view takes a collective approach to achieve food security. It notes that globally enough food is produced to feed the entire world population at a level adequate to ensure that everyone can be free of hunger and fear of starvation. That no one should live without enough food because of economic constraints or social inequalities is the basic goal. This approach is often referred to as food justice and views food security as a basic human right.

Food sovereignty

A third approach is known as food sovereignty; though it overlaps with food justice on several points, the two are not identical. It views the business practices of multinational corporations as a form of neocolonialism. Under this view subsistence farmers are left to cultivate only lands that are so marginal in terms of productivity as to be of no interest to the multinational corporations. Many communities calling for food sovereignty are protesting the imposition of Western technologies on to their indigenous systems and agency. Those who hold a "food sovereignty" position oppose allowing low-cost subsidized food from industrialized nations into developing countries, what is referred to as "import dumping".

Risks to food security

Fossil fuel dependence

Between 1950 and 1984, as the Green Revolution transformed agriculture around the globe, world grain production increased by 250%. The energy for the Green Revolution was provided by fossil fuels in the form of fertilizers (natural gas), pesticides (oil), and hydrocarbon fueled irrigation.

Price setting

On April 30, 2008 Thailand announces the project of the creation of the Organization of Rice Exporting Countries (OREC) with the potential to develop into a price-fixing cartel for rice.

Treating food the same as other internationally traded commodities

Food is not a commodity like others. We should go back to a policy of maximum food self-sufficiency. It is crazy for us to think we can develop countries around the world without increasing their ability to feed themselves.

– Former US President Bill Clinton, *Speech at United Nations World Food Day, October 16, 2008*

Conclusion

The effects of the Green Revolution on global food security are difficult to understand because of the complexities involved in food systems.

The world population has grown by about four billion since the beginning of the Green Revolution and many believe that, without the Revolution, there would have been greater famine and malnutrition. The production increases fostered by the Green Revolution are widely credited with having helped to avoid widespread famine, and for feeding billions of people.

"The number of people without enough food to eat on a regular basis remains stubbornly high, at over 800 million, and is not falling significantly. Over 60% of the world's undernourished people live in Asia, and a quarter in Africa. The proportion of people who are hungry, however, is greater in Africa (33%) than Asia (16%). The latest FAO figures indicate that there are 22 countries, 16 of which are in Africa, in which the undernourishment prevalence rate is over 35%."

As such, according to FAO, addressing agriculture and population growth is vital to achieving food security. Other organizations and people too have come to this conclusion and advocate improvements in agriculture, and population control.

Unites States Agency for International Development (USAID) proposes several key steps to increasing agricultural productivity which is in turn key to increasing rural income and reducing food insecurity. They include:

- Boosting agricultural science and technology. Current agricultural yields are insufficient to feed the growing populations. Eventually, the rising agricultural productivity drives economic growth.
- Securing property rights and access to finance.
- Enhancing human capital through education and improved health.
- Conflict prevention and resolution mechanisms and democracy and governance based on principles of accountability and transparency in public institutions and the rule of law are basic to reducing vulnerable members of society.

The UN Millennium Development Goals are one of the initiatives aimed at achieving food security in the world. In its list of goals, the first Millennium Development Goal states that the UN "is to eradicate extreme hunger and poverty", and that "agricultural productivity is likely to play a key role in this if it is to be reached on time".

References

1. www.rand.org/pubs/occasional_papers/2007/RAND_OP179.pdf
2. http://news.nationalgeographic.com/news/2001/06/0621_bamboo.html
3. http://www.cgiar.org/newsroom/releases/news.asp?idnews=532
4. De Datta SK, Tauro AC, Balaoing SN (1 November 1968). "Effect of plant type and nitrogen level on growth characteristics and grain yield of indica rice in the tropics". *Agron. J.* 60 (6): 643–7. http://agron.scijournals.org/cgi/content/abstract/60/6/643.
5. Barta, Patrick (July 28, 2007), "Feeding Billions, A Grain at a Time", *The Wall Street Journal*: A1, http://online.wsj.com/article/SB118556810848880619.html
6. http://online.wsj.com/article/SB118556810848880619.html
7. http://www.inwent.org/ez/articles/070224/index.en.shtml
8. Conway, 1997 chpt. 4.
9. Why Our Food is So Dependent on Oil
10. Fuel costs, drought influence price increase
11. The end of India's green revolution?
12. Kindall, Henery W & Pimentel, David (May 1994). "Constraints on the Expansion of the Global Food Supply". *Ambio.* **23** (3). http://dieoff.org/page36.htm. (2)
13. Spitz, 1987
14. Technology Review: Green Revolutionary
15. Altieri 1995.
16. Chapman, Graham P. (2002). "The Green Revolution." The Companion to Development Studies. London: Arnold. (pp.155-159).
17. Ross 1998. Chpt. 5.
18. Agriculture and Food—Agricultural Production Indices: Food production per capita index, World Resources Institute
19. http://edition.cnn.com/2009/WORLD/europe/11/17/italy.food.summit/
20. Amid strong farm economy, some worry about increased debt, Associated Press, April 20, 2008
21. Rich countries launch great land grab to safeguard food supply, The Guardian, November 22, 2008
22. http://www.energybulletin.net/281.html, Eating Fossil Fuels. EnergyBulletin.net
23. Australia | April 30, 2008 | Mekong nations to form rice price-fixing cartel
24. http://www.sfgate.com/cgi-bin/article.cgi?f=/n/a/2008/10/23/international/i142025D32.DTL

20

Root Causes of Food Insecurity and its Remedial Measures

R. R. Kazi

Food shortages causing food crisis was previously considered as a regional matter to be dealt with by the respective regional governments. However, it has become a global issue requiring various international agencies to tackle with it. Despite considerable resolutions passed to this effect by the international agencies, the problem of hunger and poverty which the ultimate effect of food crisis has not been effectively tackled with. In general parlance the major factor affecting this issue is being considered as the increase in population. However, in the light of some studies showing stagnation or declining trend in the fertility rate, shrinking of families, changes in lifestyles and other relevant factors, the population factor no longer appears to be a major cause for food crisis.

In this context it is worthwhile to take note of the report of The Special Food Programme for Food Security which has revealed that, "While the world population has more than doubled in less than 50 years to over 6 billion people, average per capita food consumption has risen from about 2350 to 2800 kcal per day. The world agriculture has been highly successful in increasing average food availability per person by about 20%. The Global food supplies are ample to meet essential needs, yet over 800 million people are chronically undernourished. Global food supplies are ample to meet everyone's essential needs. Governments at present try to achieve to halve the number of undernourished persons by 2015, so instead eradicate all (World Food Summit), they have new goals. This suggests that the size of interventions is too small or the wrong measures are being used. " (1) According to J. Chandler "The world produces enough food to feed everyone. However, there are countries, regions within countries, villages within regions, households within villages and individuals within households that are not able to meet their food needs. Food security is a complex, multifaceted issue that can only be fully addressed through the active cooperation of all actors. Food security is caused by two major problems. The primary obstacle to food security is poverty; people living in poverty are faced with food insecurity. The second obstacle is; Access to food. Despite the world produces enough food to feed the whole world population, there are disparities in access to food and in nutritional well-being. Vulnerable groups are the most affected. These groups include: children, single parent women, elderly people, refugees, homeless persons and unemployed people.

- Over 800 million human beings do not have enough to eat in a world that produces enough food to feed every man, woman and child.
- At the World Food Summit in Rome, in 1996, 187 nations endorse the Summit's goal to eradicate hunger and to reduce the number of undernourished people by half, no later than 2015

An article published in the Economist has recalled that, "In 1974 Henry Kissinger, then America's secretary of state, told the first world food conference in Rome that no child would go to bed hungry within ten years. Just over 35 years later, in the week of another United Nations food summit in Rome, 1 billion people will go to bed hungry." This shows the failure of the policy makers at national and international levels to eradicate the hunger and poverty around which the problem of food crisis is encircled. The article has further clarified that, "This failure may soon get worse. None of the underlying agricultural problems which produced a spike in the food prices in 2007-08 and increased the number of hungry people has gone away."

This shows that the brainstorming discussions and powerful resolutions resolved at the so-called apex bodies have not been successfully implemented as desired. At this point it is pertinent to quote Raghav Gaiha and Vani S. Kulkarni who have opined that, "Crises precipitate summits and summits usually spew a bunch of banalities." In support of their claim they have cited that, "2009 witnessed several summits - the G-8, a few G-20s with different levels of government representation and just concluded World Summit on Food Security, convened by the Food and Agriculture Organisation of the United Nations (FAO) in Rome." In their opinion, "The motivation for it stems from the devastation caused by the financial crisis. While estimates of hunger and poverty attributable to the global slowdown vary, with the World Bank and FAO competing with each other in producing inflated estimates, there is legitimate concern that the progress achieved so far in MDG-1 of halving poverty by 2015 has suffered a serious setback." They have quoted on the authority of a document prepared by FAO for the World Summit, which asserts that the number of poor and hungry is likely to go up by 105 million in 2009."

According to the article published in the Economist, as referred to above, "Between now and 2050 the world's population will rise by a third, but demand for agricultural goods will rise by demand for agricultural goods will rise by 70% and demand for meat will double." The article considers "these increases in a sense good news in they are a result of rising wealth in poor and middle-income countries." "But," the article warns that, "they will have to happen without farmers clearing large amounts of new land (there is some scope for expansion but not much) or using up lots more water (in parts of the world, water supplies are stretched to their limit or beyond)." "Moreover," the article states, "they will take place while farmers also wrestle with the consequences of climate change, which, on balance, will do more harm than good to farmland round the world." However, the article warns that, "Boosting world food production without gobbling up land and water will also require technology to play a large role in the next 40 years than it has in the past 40, when people have been more or less living off the gains off the Green Revolution."

In view of these and other perspectives, an eandeavour has been in this paper to find various factors, which directly or indirectly aggravate the gravity of food crisis. One of the most explicit factors affecting food production is the adoption of policies implementing alternative sources of energy in the form of biofuels. Biofuels production has become an important player in the global food system as it diverts resources and crop output from food (agricultural) to non-food (non-agricultural) uses. As a result, the linkages between energy and food systems have strengthened, with important implications for food security in developing countries and the welfare of the poor. Surprisingly, this phencmenon has taken place as an effect of environmental awareness which is the outcome of the propagation of global warming. Thus, the remedy for one problem becomes cause of giving birth to another problem.

The Effect of Biofuel Production On Food Security

Due to increased demand for energy, the governments of under-developed and developing countries are proving lands for production of bio-fuel-generating species by the multinational corporations. The acquisition of farmland called land-grabbing, from the world's poor by rich countries and international corporations is accelerating at an alarming rate. Whereas in most of the cases the land is being used for biofuel products, in some cases the countries having less cultivable lands and the countries which are unable to product sufficient food products from the land at their disposals are also searching lands in the poor countries. Some of the world's largest food, financial and car companies have invested in land. To some analysts this may cause civil unrest in due course of time. Apart from this, the factors like commodity exchange, introduction of genetically modified products by some multinational corporations, are some factors which adversely affect the process and quantum of food products.

More and more land is being provided for cultivating the biofuel generating species. Whereas renewable energy sources like wind, hydro, solar are non polluting energy sources, the biofuel generated from sugarcane is also less polluting as compared to conventional gasoline but biofuels derived from corn, soyabean and other sources could not be considered environment-friendly. On the one hand they decrease the food cultivable land on the other hand they adversely affect the climate.

"Indeed the current global warming has made people more environment conscious and governments more serious towards alternate fuels. But has it really benefited us the way it was suppose to? While renewable energy sources like wind, hydro, solar are really great non polluting energy sources, the same cannot be said about biofuels. While biofuel generated from sugarcane is indeed less polluting as compared to conventional gasoline, the same cannot be said about biofuels derived from corn, soyabean and other sources. If all environmental effects of biofuel production from corn is considered it's probably more polluting than traditional gasoline. This is after one considers deforestation done to grow corn, the fertilizers consumed, water consumed and all. The initial hypothesis that biofuels will drastically cut environmental pollution was based on the assumption that no deforestation would be done for biofuels and that the corn needed would probably be grown on non cultivable land lots. Apart from the environment crisis, this new found fantasy of politicos around the world has led to drastic increase in biofuels production throughout the world. Investment in biofuels has increased from $5 billion in 1995 to $ 38 billion in 2005 and is expected to top $100 billion by 2010. Now, that's huge greater than the GDP of most countries and 1/14 of expected Indian GDP in 2010. If was to be done on non cultivable land, it would have been great but looking at the huge profits to be made in biofuel farming, large tracts of forest land and cultivated land is being directed towards biofuel production. The amount of corn required to produce enough biofuel to fill one SUV tank is sufficient to feed one person for a year. US produced 7 billion gallons (26.5 l) of biofuel in 2007 and is targeting a production of about 60 billion gallon by 2030. Rice price has increased from $360 per metric ton in late 2007 to about $760 as on March 2008, a whopping 110% increase in a span of about 4-5 months. I have never heard of such a ROI ever in my life. High corn prices have sparked riots in Mexico city, skyrocketing flour prices have destabilized Pakistan, high inflation threatens to bring Indian government down, also food shortage in under-developed countries like Senegal have led to violence killing many. Although last tracts of farmland have been transferred towards producing biofuels, it doesn't justify the huge increase in food prices. Only a small part of price rise can be justified as due to biofuels. The current scale of biofuel production is still small to make any significant dent in food production. But the projected biofuel production by different countries does raise an alarm as such a huge biofuel production has the potential to drastically curtail food production leading to acute food shortage throughout the world. Developed countries will anyways have surplus production but it is the developing and under-developed countries that will bear the brunt."

According to a report published by the United Nations, "The global rush to switch from oil to energy derived from plants will drive deforestation, push small farmers off the land and lead to serious food shortages and increased poverty unless carefully managed, says the most comprehensive survey yet completed of energy crops." The report in question which is compiled by all 30 of the world organisation's agencies, points to crops like palm oil, maize, sugar cane, soya and jatropha. Rich countries want to see these extensively grown for fuel as a way to reduce their own climate changing emissions. Their production could help stabilise the price of oil, open up new markets and lead to higher commodity prices for the poor."

As such, biofuels production has become an important player in the global food system as it diverts resources and crop output from food (agricultural) to non-food (non-agricultural) uses. As a result, the linkages between energy and food systems have strengthened, with important implications for food security in developing countries and the welfare of the poor.

In this regard, J. Chandler has reported that, "A surging demand for agrofuels (biofuel produced from ethanol and sugarcane, as well as biodiesel) and access to new sources of raw materials for manufacturing goods is also driving land purchases.

The demand for agrofuels has increased rapidly over the past several years as oil-dependent countries establish ambitious targets for agrofuel production and for incorporating biodiesel and bioethanol with traditional transport fuels." To cite an example, the U.S.

Renewable Fuel Standard aims to increase ethanol use by 3.5 billion gallons between 2005 and 2012, and the 27-nation bloc European Union aims to increase the proportion of biofuels used in land transport to 10 percent by 2020."

The report further states that, "With these and other impetuses, the use and production of biofuels has skyrocketed over the past several years, such that the quantity of U.S. corn used to produce ethanol increased by 53 million metric tons between 2002 and 2007. It now accounts for 30 percent of the total global growth in wheat and feed grains use."

In addition to biofuels, the use of grain for making alcohol is also an issue which has adversely affected the food insecurity.

Incidentally, Panos and K.S. Jayaraman have reported the case of Government of India giving clearance for the Canadian transnational Seagram to turn coarse grains - the poor person's staple - into whisky, a rich man's drink, is worrying agricultural and social scientists alike. Vandana Shiva, president of the Research Foundation for Science, Technology and Ecology has alleged that, "Seagram is actually trying to steal food from the poor." She has further cautioned that, "Diverting coarse grains for whisky-making will have a serious impact on India's food security," she says.

A lot is being said and written about food shortage in various parts of the globe. Varied reasons have been cited for this crisis depending upon one's intuition and ideology. As a matter of fact, the growth of population is logically related with the food security but despite fast growth in world population during the last 50 years, some studies have now shown the sign of either stagnated or diminishing trend in some countries. In the light of these studies and in the light of some other non-population-related factors affecting the food security, the population factor's impact on food security could not be considered as the major cause.

Global Food Crisis: The Outcome of Multiple Factors

In Manila, health experts and some lawmakers have been blaming the rising population growth, but former Catholic Bishops' Conference of the Philippines president Archbishop Oscar Cruz has argued that, the problem is related to what he called a "crisis of management" on the part of the government.

Fertility is falling and families are shrinking in places— such as Brazil, Indonesia, and even parts of India—that people think of as teeming with children. As our briefing shows, the fertility rate of half the world is now 2.1 or less—the magic number that is consistent with a stable population and is usually called "the replacement rate of fertility". Sometime between 2020 and 2050 the world's fertility rate will fall below the global replacement rate.

S. Philip Morgan, a professor at Duke University who studies fertility rates, is predicting a 5 to 10 percent decline this year in the total fertility rate, which is the number of babies born to a woman in her lifetime. The rate has hovered between 2 and 2. (Herald Online, SC — Lifestyles)

Population shrinkage is killing many nations Oct 15, 2009. The fertility rate (average births per woman) must be greater than 2. 1 to replace those who die. (Fredericksburg.com, VA) He expects the fertility rate to start to drop next year. "Usually people become more risk averse and tend to put off birth until they are more sure about their future," he said.

Land Grabbing By Rich Countries Affecting Food Production

"The acquisition of farmland from the world's poor by rich countries and international corporations is accelerating at an alarming rate, with an area half the size of Europe's farmland targeted in the last six months, reports from UN officials and agriculture experts say. De Schutter said that, "Some of the world's largest food, financial and car companies have invested in land." In this context, Devinder Sharma, analyst with the Forum for Biotechnology and Food Security in India, has predicted civil unrest."

In this connection, J. Chandler has observed that, "Throughout history, corporate agribusiness has been known to establish itself in developing countries with the effect of either driving independent farmers off their land or turning farmers into plantation workers.

"No matter how convincing the claim that these massive international acquisitions will bring much-needed agricultural investment to poor countries, evidence shows there is simply no place for the small farmer in the vast majority of these land grab situations that will only increase monoculture-based, export-oriented agriculture, further jeopardizing international food security".

Anuradha Mittal, Executive Director of the Oakland Institute and co-author of the report says: "Our report dismantles the myth of the 'win-win' argument that has been offered to quell concerns around this trend. A myopic focus on potential benefits, such as increased investment in agriculture in poor countries, is sidelining the issue of food security for the world's poor and land reform from the forefront of the debate."

The Great Land Grab critically examines the role of the private sector in agricultural development and exposes implications of private sector control over food resources. The report concludes that those who promote the benefits of private sector growth in agriculture fail to recognize that acquisition of crucial food-producing lands by foreign private entities poses a threat to rural economies and livelihoods, land reform agendas, and other efforts aimed at making access to food more equitable.

His fear of unrest is based on the fact which Lorenzo Cotula has pointed in his posting at IIED in which he has stated that, "When in 2008 the government of Madagascar agreed a deal with Korean Daewoo Logistics for the company to access 1.3 million hectares of agricultural and to grow maize and palm oil for export, protests, political crisis and ultimately the fall of the government and the cancellation of the deal followed. Madagascar's citizens were not consulted." In his opinion, the 'land grab' phenomenon is a key issue of democracy and sustainable development.

According to De Schutter "Outsourcing food production will ensure food security for investing countries but would leave behind a trail of hunger, starvation and food scarcities for local populations," he said. "The environmental tab of highly intensive farming - devastated soils, dry aquifer, and ruined ecology from chemical infestation - will be left for the host country to pick up."

Worldwide demand for food is expected to grow steadily over the next 40 years, but 25 percent of the world's food production may be lost to 'environmental breakdowns' by 2050 unless urgent action is taken.

In the opinion of De Schutter, "Increased investment may bring benefits such as GDP growth and improved government revenues, and may create opportunities for economic development and livelihood improvement. But they may result in local people losing access to the resources on which they depend for their food security – particularly as some key recipient countries are themselves faced with food security challenges", said the authors. According to a US-based thinktank, the International Food Policy Research Institute, nearly $20bn to $30bn a year is being spent by rich countries on land in developing countries."

Mike Soron in his post has informed that, "Nearly $20 to $30 billion a year is being spent by our so-called "rich" countries to acquire agriculture land in poorer regions." Reports from UN officials and agriculture experts reveal that, "Roughly 20 million hectares of farmland, about half the size of all arable land in Europe, has been sold or prepared to be sold in the last six months. Ten million hectares were acquired last year. The reports also reveal that, acquisition of farmland from the world's poor by rich countries and international corporations is accelerating at an alarming rate, with an area half the size of Europe's farmland targeted in the last six months".

"This flood of land grabs by emerging nations, mostly of land under local customary land tenure, is eerily reminiscent of past and ongoing European and U.S. colonial practices," states Dr. Glen Barry, Ecological Internet's President, who is a practicing Political Ecologist and hold a Ph.D. in Land Resources. "We are witnessing the intensification of social turmoil caused by climate change, land and water scarcity, and over-population and inequitable consumption. Until these root causes of global ecosystem collapse are addressed, there is no chance of achieving equitable and just global ecological sustainability."

The Impact of Climate Change Remedies on African Land

A new study by FSE Director Rosamond Naylor and David Battisti from the University of Washington estimates that rising temperatures will create food shortages for half the world's population by 2100. "Australian farmers have cut rice production by as much as 97% in the last 5 years. Australia from being the largest rice exporter has today become just self sufficient in rice. Global warming has led to acute droughts in many parts of Australia forcing farmers to switch from water intensive crops like rice to not so water intensive crops like Grapes for wine production. The effects of global warming are increasingly being felt in more and more countries and have the potential to paralyze the World food production. The current Australian crisis may have a cascade effect and other countries may follow suit."

As per a briefing by The African Biodiversity Network, Biofuelwatch and the Gaia Foundation, a new technology called "Biochar" is being promoted as a major "geo-engineering" solution to global climate change, as well as a means of improving soils and addressing poverty. But the brief warns that, this technology raises serious scientific and social concerns as Africa is a particular target for biochar, largely due to the commonly held perception that there is abundant land available waiting for development. Africa is already experiencing massive land grabbing. Indigenous communities, forests, water resources and food production are already impacted by large-scale land grabs for agrofuels (biofuels) production and foreign agricultural investment. This has exacerbated evictions, food insecurity and land conflicts at a time when the continent is already suffering from the impacts of climate change.

Encashment Of Food Crisis For Introducing GM Products

Besides biofules, land-grabbing, commodity exchanges, introduction of genetically modified products are some factors which adversely affect the process and quantum of food products leading to aggravation of food crisis which, if left unattended, may cause civil unrest.

According to Kim, "A multinational company like Monsanto has got the opportunity to infuse hitherto objectionable or debatable genetically modified foods in the face of food shortages. According to Kim, global investors are seeing the plight of millions to get enough to eat as a cash cow. He has informs that, Monsanto has pledged that they would double yields of corn, soybeans and cotton by the year 2030. They would magically create seed that would require 30 percent of both land and water to grow. This announcement coincided nicely with the United Nations summit in Rome to discuss global food shortages. Whereas many countries in Europe and Asia have sanctions against genetically modified foods; leading to sanctions on US imported agriculture. Monsanto may be using the global food crisis to it's advantage trying to garner approval for foods that at any other time are shunned by the global community. He has cited as reference The Future of Food, a documentary about genetically modified foods which explains the business and science behind these foods. He has further stated that Monsanto isn't the only company cashing in on the food crisis. While much of Wall Street is in the pooper, agriculture stocks are through the roof. Investment firms and private investors are investing heavily in crops, land for farming and farm technologies."

As reported by Mike Mande, "Tanzania farmers in key arable areas face eviction by multinational corporations out to cultivate agrofuel products. More than 5,000 rice farmers from various parts of the country could be affected. This will trigger an environmental and humanitarian crisis as displaced villagers are left without land to grow food crops. A new report made available to The East African last week by an international environmental group warns that Tanzania's water sources, so critical to food production, will also be diverted to fuel production, increasing conflicts over access to water. The report was compiled by a local environmental group, the Environmental, Human Rights Care and Gender Organisation (Envirocare) Tanzania, and an international organisation, the Impact of Jatropha Trade in Tanzania. It says the government has few qualms about evicting farmers from their only means of livelihood, even if this sparks civil conflict. According to the report, the government ants to fast-track agrofuel initiatives and switch vast areas of land to sugarcane, palm oil and jatropha production, pushing out locals to poorer lands."

The Effects of IMF and World Bank Policies on Agro Product

According to Koeing, Dolores, and Tiemen, Diarra, "Structural adjustment programs do little to help the agricultural sector of developing nations. Due to the conditions of SAPs, one of which is to devalue a nation's currency, a developing nation's agricultural exports become more competitive due to their devalued currency. Essentially a country is able to export more goods out due to other country's ability and demand to purchase the previous country's agricultural good. However, the nation also loses purchasing power which may not be able to be compensated by the increase in demand for its export goods. Ultimately, the agricultural sector of a developing nation will suffer and decline."

The example of this degradation is, as Tiemen and Koeing reveal, Western Mali during the 1980's. Firstly, the privatization of the agricultural sector increased the inequality of food distribution and inequality wealth in general as some farmers adapted to privatization and flourished and others fell behind. Secondly, in stead of "mining",(using a plot of land until it was depleted of nutrients then moving to a different plot of land allowing the first to replenish), the land like farmers did before structural adjustment, farmers were introduced to fertalizers that left the land nutrient barren and unusable.

"Despite the growth in the GDP, structural adjustment does not appear of much help to the agricultural sector. In theory, devaluation, by lowering the relative price of farm commodities on the international market, should make a country's agricultural exports more competitive. However, it is by no means certain that increased exports compensate for the loss of purchasing power of a cheaper currency."

From whatever has been stated in the foregoing paragraphs, it can be concluded that, so many factors have directly or indirectly affected the food security.

Suggestions

The article published in Economist mentions that, "Despite a global recession and the largest grain harvest on record in 2008, food prices are heading up again." The article states that, "the food-price spike of 2007-08 shocked governments out of their quarter-century of neglect....The food-price trauma of 2007-08 is persuading some countries to say that they need to divert part of their wealth to subsidize food so they can be self-sufficient and avoid future crises. But the demands of feeding 9 billion people in 2050 tell a different story: farming needs to be as efficient as possible. That requires markets and trade. Investing in agriculture is boon; rejecting agricultural markets would be a disaster."

In this context, the article suggests some short term remedies like investment in the productive capacity of agriculture and improvement in the operation of food markets. Although they have acknowledged that the government has taken care of first suggestion still little has been done with regard to the other. It states that, "farming is far and away the single most important economic activity in most poor places." Due to this reason, "some of the new splurge of public money is going on safety-net programmes for poor farmers, which are justified on anti-poverty grounds: three-quarters of the world's poorest live in rural areas. However, the article also points out "a danger inherent in all this government activity: the temptation of self-reliance." It states that, self-reliance in itself is not bad but the problem is that the new rhetoric of self-sufficiency coincides with a growing distrust of markets and trade as grain importers no longer trust world markets to supply their needs.

The article clarifies that; the money will pay dividends in the long run only if it improves farmers' access to market. With regard to the operation of markets it has pointed out that, "distrust of markets and reaction against farm trade are growing." In view of this, they have warned that, "Unless government restrain those impulses, they will undermine the gains from rising investment."

Lack of reliable markets is the biggest barrier to rural development, since without them farmers have little incentive to grow more." Therefore, the article suggests that, "the increase in rural road-building is welcome, as are measures to improve the operations of local markets by spreading price information and building grain stores." It also suggests the measures for correction of the markets, it states that, "temporarily subsidizing better seeds and fertilizers in places where local markets are failing to provide them: this is an example of correcting market failure."

In this connection an example of the positive contribution of technology providing information to the villagers is cited. It is the story of extension of technological services in remote areas. The Indian Express has published a story of a village named Loni in Maharashtra state of India, which belongs to that part of the world that isn't wired to the internet where the 'World Wide Web' sounds like a boastful misnomer. It's for places like Loni that Rose Shuman, a social entrepreneur and CEO of a California-based non-profit venture Open Mind, thought up the idea of a Question Box. The Question Box works much like an internet search engine. It's small, metallic box with a cellphone inside. A farmer in Loni who wants to find out, say, the price of tuwar dal in the market would press the green button on the unit and his call would be connected to an operator. The operator looks up a database or uses the internet to find the answer to the question and relays the answer back to the farmer, who hears it over a speaker to the box. The Boxes have the potential to bridge the technological divide in far-flung places without millions of dollars in investment or extensive computer training. In Uganda, Shuman is working with the Grameen Foundation. There, she replaced the Boxes with Grameen's 40 operators who work with cellphones. So when the locals needed information, they would go to Question Box workers who would dial the call centre and ask the question for them. And because Internet charges in Uganda are prohibitive, the people who handle the call looked up a database instead of searching on the Net like in India.

This type of development may prove to be a boon for the people of underdeveloped and poor nations. In the light of utility of this small and cheap instrument right from knowing market price to providing help for performing homework and checking of availability of tickets, it has indirectly connected the hitherto non-connected villagers with the world at large. The feedback from the farmers stating that, "Earlier, traders would cheat us by buying our crops at lower prices. But now before leaving, we ask the Box for the market price. We also ask about tractors, tillers and so on. Why, just a week ago, when a storm hit our village, we were prepared for it." These are the words of Mr. Ajay Kalbhor, the box is installed outside his grocery shop.

Taking into consideration the usefulness of this instrument, the governments may take decisions to make use of it.

According to J. Chandler, suggests the following measures to solve the problem:

- Educate policy makers about Food Security, share the knowledge between the different governmental organizations and institutions.
- Full engagement of governments and civil society institutions, where members combine forces to work jointly on an interdisciplinary basis to undertake very practical actions towards eradicating hunger.

- Research by monitoring and evaluation system/programme, to find the cause of problems within regions, so there will be fitting solutions on "small" scale.
- Legal Environment and Supportive policy which addresses issues about the right to food access to land water resources and exchange rate, subsidies and decentralization.
- Try to eradicate corruption to minimize the risk of waste, to have observers on the right critical places and Invest into long term self-sufficiency projects and durability.

References

1. Resource: The Food and Agriculture Organization of the United Nations (FAO), the special programme for food security.
2. J. Chandler, Development: Land Grab No 'Win-Win' For The Poor, IDN-In Depth News Service, Toronto http://podium.iwmi.org accessed: 15th December 23, 2009.
3. How to feed the world, published in Indian Express, p. 13, dated November 24th 2009 citing reference of The Economist.
4. Raghav Gaiha and Vani S. Kulkarni, The quest for food security, Indian Express, OP-ED p. 11, dated November 21st 2009)
5. Indian Express, p. 13, op cit.
6. http://thebigdady.blogspot.com/2008/04/food-crisis-myth-and-reality.html, Linkages with Food System Analysis
7. Global rush to energy crops threatens to bring food shortages and increase poverty, says UN, http://www.guardian.co.uk/world/2007/may/09/foodanddrink.renewableenergy. accessed: December 15, 2009
8. J. Chandler, op cit.
9. Panos and K.S. Jayaraman, India: Plans To Turn Grains Into Whisky Worry IndianScientists, http://www.sunsonline.org/trade/process/followup/1999/01120699.htm., accessed: 15th December, 2009
10. http://www.cbcpnews.com/?q=node/2087
11. Congrats to the World on Having Fewer Kids, EconomistMom.com
12. Another sign of difficult economic times: People are putting off having babies Oct 18, 2009
13. (Sydney Morning Herald — Australia) Global bust halts baby boom Apr 5, 2009 http://news.surfwax.com/economics/files/Fertility_Rate.html. Global Food and Natural Resources, International Food Policy Research Institute (IFPRI),
14. Land-grabbing-food-environment, http://www.guardian.co.uk/environment/2009/jul/03, Center for Contemporary Studies & Research, Posted by CCSR.
15. J. Chandler, op cit.
16. *Lorenzo Cotula,* Land grab 'in the public interest': an issue of democracy and sustainable development, IIED, 29 October 2009

17. De Schutter, Land-grabbing-food-environment, http://www.guardian.co.uk/environment/2009/jul/03, Center For Contemporary Studies & Research, Posted by CCSR.
18. Food Crisis Under the Spotlight ipsnews.net 2/19/2009, http://earthblipsdailyradar.com
19. De Schutter, Land-grabbing-food-environment, http://www.guardian.co.uk/environment/2009/jul/03, Center For Contemporary Studies & Research, Posted by CCSR.
20. Mike Soron, Global land grab 2009: consequences loom, www.newresilient.com, July 9th, 2009
21. Malaysia's global oil palm rainforest land grab just the beginning of larger land and water scarcity issues, By Earth's Newsdesk, a project of Ecological Internet (EI) CONTACT: Dr. Glen Barry, glenbarry@ecologicalinternet.org, Published: 13 May 2009
22. "Historical Warnings of Future Food Insecurity with Unprecedented Seasonal Heat", published in the Jan. 9 edition of the journal *Science*.
23. http://thebigdady.blogspot.com/2008/04/food-crisis-myth-and-reality.html
24. Biochar, Land Grabbing: the impacts on Africa
25. Kim, "Oh, Wall Street you're so corny", http://www.thegreatamericanfoodfight.com/2008/06/oh-wall-street-youre-so-corny.html, , Friday, June 06, 2008
26. Mike Mande, Rice farmers may be evicted by new biofuel companies, The East African, 09.9.28, http://www.theeastafrican.co.ke/news/-/2558/663988/-/qyclh8z/-/index.html, Posted Monday, September 28 2009
27. Koeing, Dolores, and Tiemen, Diarra. 1998. The environmental effects of policy change in the west African Savannah: resettlement, structural adjustment and conservation. "The journal of political ecology 5(1): 23-52
28. Greenberg, James B. 1997. A Political Ecology of Structural-Adjustment Policies: The Case of the Dominican Republic. Culture & Agriculture 19 (3):85-93. www.wikipedia.com, accessed as on 16th December 2009
29. Indian Express, p. 13, dated November 24th 2009 op cit.
30. Uma Vishnu & Pranav Kulkarni, Google in a box? Just an out-of -the-box idea, Indian Express, November 22nd 2009.
31. J. Chandler, op cit.

21

Food or Fuel? Need for De-conflicting Food and Energy Security

Lalit K. Khurana

Introduction

Food and energy constitute the major problems that the world is facing at the moment. While food is basic human need for survival, energy plays a vital role in socio-economic development and raising standards of human beings. Both are of great importance and also have a number of dimensions that go beyond just production and availability. For an instance, the question of food security is not mere a question of availability but also an issue of nutritional security. And the question of energy security is not just more generation but sustainability and pollution to be controlled. Although, appreciable efforts by many a country and technological developments in these areas have allayed many apprehensions but issues still remain due to ever expanding population and economy each year. This is correspondingly causing increases in demand of food and energy as well. There are concerns that these increasing demands have to be met keeping in view the sustainable development in the economy and raising living conditions of mankind.

Very recently, we have been witnessing fast and dramatic rise in food prices in India and world over. Food prices in India rose at the fastest pace in 11 years **(Bloomberg 2009)**. India's primary articles index, with a 22.02 percent weight in the wholesale-price inflation basket, comprising mainly of food items, rose 13.9 percent in the week ended November 28, 2009. From a year earlier, this is the highest since December 1998. This caused central bank's concern for need to use monetary policy to stabilize inflation expectations. In fact, the problem needs disaggregation from the overarching head of rising food prices in much larger perspective. There are many contributing factors to the phenomenon of rising food prices and one amongst them is increasing use of bio-fuels to meet energy requirement. The direct and indirect linkages between food and energy security are well known. But in the current scenario, they are becoming more pronounced and worrying. Food and energy issues are being debated as a global challenge which calls for more positive progress. This paper attempts to explore an interface of food and energy security from the perspective of increasing use of bio-fuels for ever increasing energy requirement and proposes arguments for mitigating the effect. The paper is organized in four sections. *Section I* is background of the theme and *Section II* is conceptual discussion of food and energy security. *Section III* discusses food price rise and its linkages with energy. *Section IV* concludes the theme.

I. Food and Energy security

Ensuring food and energy security have become issues of great importance for many developing countries. In the country like India this is more particular. India has large population to feed and simultaneously energy demand is increasing due to expanding economy. Some reports highlight that one-fourth of population is estimated to be absolutely poor and one-half of all children are malnourished. Taking stock of developing countries, almost 800 million people in the developing world do not have enough to eat and another 34 million people in the industrialized countries and countries in transition also suffer from chronic food insecurity.

According to FAO (1999), if all the world's undernourished people were gathered together, the population of the continent of the hungry would dwarf that of every other continent except Asia. The hunger of these people is not a transitory condition. It is chronic. It is debilitating. Sometimes it is deadly and blights the lives of all who are affected and undermines. The studies indicate that developing countries spend 50% or more of their income on food. Therefore, any price increase for food is likely to result in increase in hunger and malnutrition. Any policy should not exacerbate problem of food security.

Energy security is a broad umbrella that covers many concerns. The perspective may vary depending upon a country's position in value chain. In earlier periods, oil was used as major source for energy and traditional elements of energy security included its continued supply and geopolitics. From the major crisis of oil in 1970's when the OPEC oil embargo and the Iranian revolution threatened to cause price increases, since then energy security is viewed in different way. In recent years, natural gas and other sources are becoming important in the energy mix. Biofuel development gained the attention of researchers in recent years owing to the rate of depletion of fossil fuels. **(Yee Kang & Bhatia S. 2008)**.The term biofuel is referred to as solid, liquid, or gaseous fuels that are predominantly produced from biorenewable or combustible renewable feedstocks **(Demirbas, 2007a)**. A variety of liquid fuels can be produced from renewable resources and these are ethanol, methanol, biodiesel, etc. Liquid biofuels are primarily used to fuel transportation vehicles, but they are also applicable to fuel engines or fuel cells for electricity generation. *Figure 1 a & b* give an overview of biofuel production from feedstock.

Fig.: 1 (a): An overview of biofuel feedstock and production route

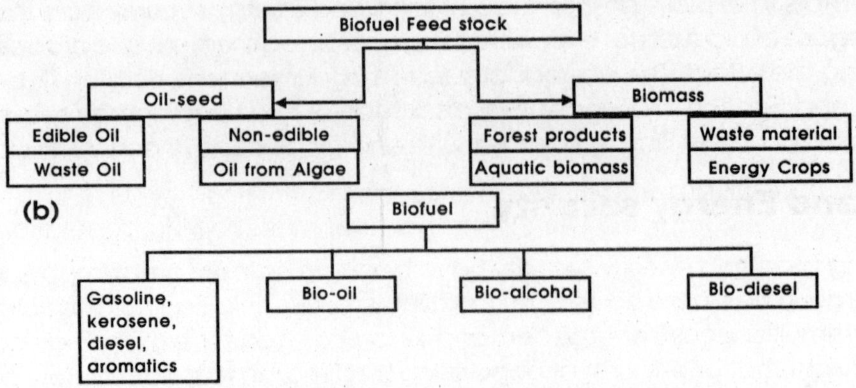

35(2010) 111-119 Yee Kang & Bhatia S.(2008).

The resultant products of the processing of biomass materials are generally referred to as 'biofuel'.

In the various forms of energy, electricity energy constitutes major part in the energy mix. Apart from hydro, solar, nuclear power generation, power can be produced using different kinds of raw materials like coal, gas, biofuel. In India, coal continues to play a vital role as a ***raw material for power generation.*** Soaring fuel prices and an increase in energy demand are making power generation from biomass more economical and competitive than ever before. In Europe, currently only 8.5% of the energy consumed comes from renewable sources. In the U.S., ethanol is currently made almost entirely from corn. Bio power generation is expected to play a vital role in achieving the 20% share of renewable energies by 2020 and it is being viewed as an industry with huge growth potential. But there are serious concerns about the impacts of biofuels production in countries that are facing high levels of food insecurity. The demand for biofuels from wealthy countries could impair food production in these countries.

II. Food vs. Energy

The growth in the use of biofuels for energy production is indicating profound impact on food prices in recent years. A study finds the following patterns that characterize primary energy consumption in both industrialized and developing countries:

- Per capita primary energy consumption per year in developing countries averages less than 30 gigajoules, compared to about 380 gigajoules for the United States plus Canada.
- Fossil fuels represent 81% of primary energy consumption in industrialized countries and 70% in developing countries where three quarters of the world population lives.
- Biomass represents 4% of primary energy consumption in industrialized countries

and is the most widely used form of energy elsewhere. (Traditional biomass represents about 90% of total energy consumption in some least developed countries.)

- In the developing world, biomass tends to be used very inefficiently, with serious environmental and health consequences.
- Energy growth was about 1.5% in OECD countries in the pre-period 1987-1997 and 4.5% in developing countries. The increase in global energy demand in the next 15 to 20 years will be largely from developing countries as they strive to meet the basic needs of and improve living standard of or their growing populations.

While the above facts remain, our thinking about how to expand supplies of energy is deeply troubled by issue of food security and environment security and equity implications as well. On one side, about two billion people lack access to affordable modern energy. This limits their choices and opportunities and leads to wide disparities. On other side, almost two thirds of the people in the world face problems of food insecurity. Around the world there have been several debates on America's overly aggressive food-to-fuel policy that has also played the current crisis of rising food prices. Many experts view that U.S. biofuel policy may result in more global hunger in the context of expanding renewable energy use in the U.S. Corn-based ethanol and started getting attention to replace fossil fuels. Corn-

Fig.: 2 : U.S.Corn Usage 2006

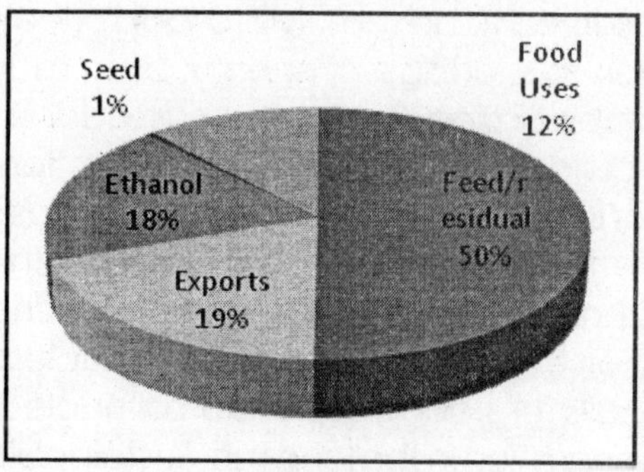

Table 1 : Percentage of Corn Exports to 10 most undernourished countries

	Undernourished population (%)	U.S. corn exports received (%)
Eritrea	75	0.0
Rep. of Congo	74	0.0
Burundi	66	0.006
Comoros	60	0.0
Tajikistan	56	0.0
Sierra Leone	51	0.0
Liberia	50	0.0004
Zimbabwe	47	0.0
Ethiopia	46	0.0
Haiti	46	0.0
Zambia	46	0.0
Total percentage of U.S. corn exports		0.0064

based ethanol production other biofuels such as soybean-based biodiesel attracted much attention in the US Policy.

Shifting corn usage from food and animal feed to fuel for gas-guzzling automobiles looks like a step backwards for combating hunger (IATP, USA). Focus on biofuel alternative fuel has also diverted attention on reducing demand for fuels and efficient use of inputs. Encouragement of production from food crops to biofuels crops leads to debate and further investigation of "food versus fuel" conundrum in a larger context. Environmentalists, international groups and some countries are becoming increasingly wary of biofuels which could accelerate global warming. By encouraging deforestation to increase arable land can contribute heavily to hike in commodity prices.

It needs to be understood well how U.S. corn is actually used. Domestic corn production provides a negligible contribution to the diet of hungry people in U.S. Furthermore, a chronic oversupply of corn for the past ten years has resulted in below-cost prices for corn farmers in the U.S. and throughout the world. This reduced the income of farmers and wreaked havoc on rural communities. Corn is used to meet the ever increasing demand for liquid fuel. But this corn could be used to feed undernourished people, many other parts of the world. How can we justify risking the future food security of growing global population is a big question in the context of production of corn for ethanol. It is claimed that Biofuel contributes 2-3% rise in food prices. There is need to de-conflict ***fuel*** and ***food*** security objectives. As the biofuels market develops around the world, important concerns about access to food are expected to become much more acute. Industry experts predict that by 2015, ***U.S. biofuel production*** will be over 16 billion gallons. Roughly 10-20% of energy production will be from use of biofuels which could become a serious contributor to problem of food security

Conclusion

The relationship between biofuels and access to food is complicated and it is clear that ripple effects of bio fuel need to be understood. There is need to meet the challenge of combating food and energy insecurity. The food situation needs to be analyzed and redefined with the leverage of biofuel. Energy input of biofuel is observed to be sensitive to food prices. While many thinkers strongly believe bio fuel as a solution to shortage of energy, but it may lead to food crisis and overall the resultants could be disappointing. Strategies must address both the issues and its dimensions together in order to build a better framework for action. It is suggested that actions are needed in the direction of improving efficiency of energy use to help reduce its impact on food security. Many more effective steps could be taken in this direction such as accelerating development of new technology and deployment of existing technologies worldwide can be an important step. For example, expansion of nuclear power can satisfactorily resolve the issue. But this also calls for stalling expansion of nuclear weapons as it gets linked to adequate nuclear power generation in the long run. Sustainable biofuels can increase energy security and reduce greenhouse gas emissions and would not heavily affect on food prices.

References

1. Goldemberg,J. et.al. (2001) *Energy for the New Millennium,* Ambio, Vol. 30, No. 6 (Sept 2001), pp. 330-337
2. Tweeten, L. (1999), The Economics of Global Food Security, *Review of Agricultural Economics,* Vol. 21, No. 2 (Autumn - Winter, 1999), pp. 473- 488
3. Press Summary FAO 1999
4. Diwan P., Sarkar A N (2009) *Energy Security,* Pentagon Energy Press, New Delhi
5. Dev S M et. al., (2003) Towards a Food Secure India, IHD & CESS
6. Shafi M, Aziz A (1989) *Food Systems of the World,* Rawat Publications Jaipur
7. IEA Energy Technology Essentials 2007
8. http://www.fao.org
9. http://www.indiaenews.com
10. http://www.bloomberg.com/
11. http://www.tradechakra.com/indian-economy/infrastructure/power.html
12. http://www.greenpowerconferences.com/
13. http://www.iatp.org/iatp/publications.cfm

22

Indian Agriculture's Role in World Food Production and World Food Crisis is: Causes, Trends and Solutions

Saurabh Kumar, Mr. Jaffar Khan

Introduction

India is one of the fastest growing economies of the world and is currently the focus of a great deal of international attention. It is the seventh largest country in the world in terms of its geographical size. Today it has a population of nearly 1.1 billion which makes it the second most populous nation in the world. With current population growth by 2025 India may even have caught up with China according to the UN.

India has a large and diverse agriculture and is one of the world's leading producers. It is also a major consumer, with an expanding population tc feed. For this reason and because of its agricultural and trade policy, its presence on the world market has been modest in relation to the size of its agriculture.

India is still a big unknown. While it has been a small net agricultural exporter overall since 1990, in recent years there have been many changes in its agriculture and trade policies and significant changes in its net trade position for many individual products.

The leading forecasting institutions expect that India will play a bigger role in world markets in future. In a number of markets it is expected to consolidate its position among the world's leading importers (vegetable oils) and exporters (rice). Given the size of Indian agriculture, changes in its balance sheets for key commodities have a potentially large impact on world markets.

Economic developments

India is the third largest economy in Asia after Japan and China, as measured in terms of its Gross Domestic Product (GDP) and it is continuing to grow rapidly.

The Indian economy has seen high growth rates of more than 8% since 2003. In 2005 and 2006 GDP grew at a rate of over 9%. Globally India's growth is surpassed only by that of China. This is expected to continue with growth just under 7% by 2015. Graph 1 compares GDP growth in India, China and Brazil, where growth has been much slower.

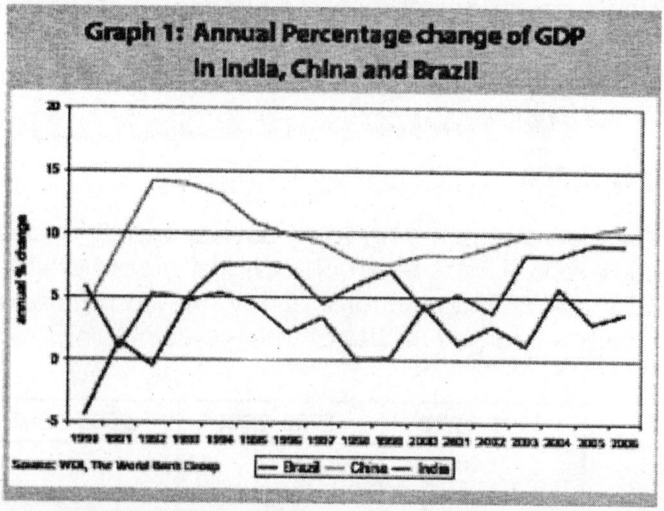

Graph 1: Annual Percentage change of GDP in India, China and Brazil

High growth rates have significantly reduced poverty in India. However it's GDP per head is still very low (estimated at US$ 820 in 2006), so it remains classified by the World Bank as a low income country. The World Development Report 2008 states that over one third of the population of India was living below the poverty line in 2004-2005, managing on less than $1 a day.

Cereals are the staple food in India, providing over half the calories consumed, while pulses are the main protein supplement in the diet. Rising incomes and the influence of globalization have contributed to changes in the diet with a slight decrease in cereals consumption and an increase in pulses, edibleoils, fruits and vegetables, milk and meat, which is growing from a low base. In the case of edible oils, the fall in prices after the liberalization of imports further stimulated consumption. However although diets are diversifying, India still lags behind Brazil and China in terms of daily calorie intake per capita. Table 1: Food consumption –

Daily calories per capita

Agriculture plays an important, though declining role in the economy. Its share in overall GDP fell from 30% in the early nineties, to below 17.5% in 2006 (graph 2). This is high compared to China and Brazil, at 12% and 5% respectively. Over this period the share of industry has stayed relatively constant, reaching nearly 28% in 2006.

Meanwhile the services sector has grown rapidly (accounting for about 65% of total GDP growth from 2000-2005), to almost 55% of GDP in 2006. The World Bank predicts that the shift towards the service sector will continue at the expense of agriculture, whose share could decline by 30% by 2030.

Despite India's economic development, over 70% of the population still lives in rural areas. Agriculture is the key employer with around 60% of the labour force, down from 70% in the early nineties. This compares with 44% in China (2002) and 21 % in Brazil (2004).

The decline in agriculture in the labour force has not kept pace with its decline in the economy. This stickiness has been attributed to low labor mobility and slow grow thin productivity in agriculture. In India agricultural value added per worker has grown by only 15% in real terms from 1990 to 2004. By comparison productivity in China rose by over 60% and more than doubled in Brazil.

Agriculture Structure

India's agricultural area is vast with total arable and permanent cropland of 170 million hectares in 2003-2005. It has the second largest arable area in the world after the United States. OECD in its 2007 agricultural policy monitoring report notes that Indian agriculture is dominated by a large number of small scale holdings that are predominantly owner occupied.

	1990-1992	1998-2000	2003-2005
Brazil	2860	3001	3223
China	2696	2917	2957
India	2396	2463	2512

The average size of holding in the late nineties was about 1.4 hectares and continues to decline, as farms are usually divided on inheritance. Out of India's 116 million farmers, around 60% have less than 1 hectare and together they farm 17% of the land.

Graph 2: Main economic sectors share of Indian GDP

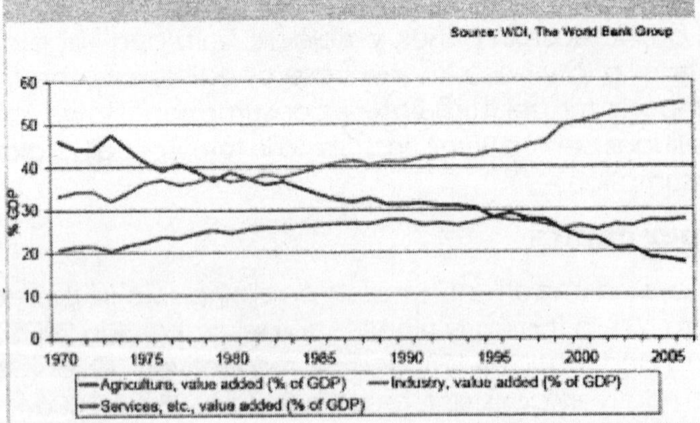

The share of medium to large farms (above 4 hectares) is very small at just over 7% of all holdings, but these farms account for around 40% of the land. The implication is that many of the very small farms are subsistence holdings, with low investment and little productivity growth.

Agricultural Policy

Indian agriculture policy is aimed essentially at improv-ing food self sufficiency and alleviating hunger through food distribution. Aside from investing in agricultural infrastructure, the government supports agriculture through measures including minimum support prices (MSP) for the major agricultural crops, farm input subsidies and preferential credit schemes.

Under the price support policy, MSPs are set annually for basic staples to protect producers from sharp price falls, to stabilise prices and to ensure adequate food stocks for public distribution. In the past guaranteed prices have been below the prevailing market prices, according to the International Food Policy Research Institute (IFPRI) in 2007.

At the same time subsidies on farm inputs including fertilisers, electrical power and irrigation water have led to inefficient use of inputs and indirectly subsidise income. IFPRI concluded that "support for agriculture (from 1985-2002) has been largely counter cyclical to world prices".

OECD appears to reach a similar conclusion. Its 2007 monitoring report points out that the level of agricultural support (covering transfers from taxpayers and consumers) for India "would appear to be slightly below the OECD average but considerably higher than that of the emerging economies reviewed by the OECD". Furthermore the instruments of support used are "the least efficient and the most trade distortive forms of support".

Key Agricultural Sectors

India is among the world's leading producers of paddy rice, wheat, buffalo milk, cow milk and sugar cane. It is either the world leader or the second largest producer in eight out of its top ten products. Some of these are widely traded while others are more specialist products.

Table 2 shows the composition of production by value for 2003-2005, when paddy rice was the top sector, followed by buffalo milk and wheat. India is now the largest milk producer in the world and the second largest producer of paddy rice, sugar cane, wheat, cow milk, groundnuts and certain fresh vegetables. But it is also a leading consumer. So although it exports these products the quantities will vary depending on the size of the crop and demand.

Table 2: Top 10 sectors of India & world rank

Commodity	Rank India	World Rank 2005	ProductionAvg 2003-2005	
			Billion $	Million T
Paddy rice	1	2	27.5	129.2
Buffalo milk	2	1	25.2	50.5
Wheat	3	2	10.9	69.7
Cow milk	4	2	10.0	37.5
Fresh vegetables	5	2	6.6	34.9
Sugar cane	6	2	5.2	250.0

Potatoes	7	3	3.6	25.0
Groundnuts	8	2	3.4	7.1
Pimento	9	1	3.3	1.1
Buffalo meat	10	9	3.1	1.5

Thus India is a net exporter of agricultural food products with a small surplus of just under $4 billion. Between 1993-1995 and 2003-2005, exports nearly doubled while imports grew almost threefold. The value of exports grew from $4 to $7.7 billion while imports rose from $1.8 to $5.2 billion (graph 3) within a decade.

The balance of agricultural trade has always been in surplus though there were sharp fluctuations during the nineties. Since 2000 both imports and exports have grown steadily.

India's Main Export Partners

India is diversifying its export markets (graph 4). The EU remains its top market, accounting for 16% of the value of export sales in 2003-2005, although this is a decline from 21% a decade ago.

Graph 3: Structure of Indian agricultural trade (million $)

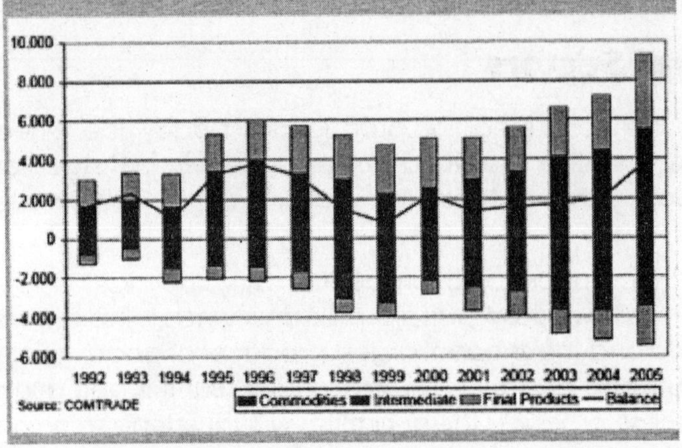

ASEAN is in 2nd place with 14%, although its share has also fallen. This trend may be reversed however as India is negotiating Free Trade agreements with the EU and with ASEAN. Meanwhile trade with neighboring Bangladesh and China (currently 7.5%) is growing fast. The US market share has remained steady at 10% and also that of Saudi Arabia.

Graph 4: Indian agri-food exports by destination (million $)

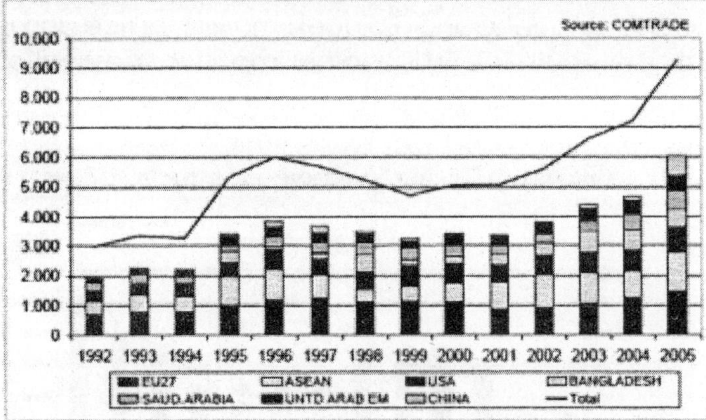

As regards the composition of agricultural exports (shown in graph 3), commodities represent around one third, intermediate products over one quarter and final products account for the remaining 40% of total agricultural exports. The biggest growth was in the export of commodities which increased by 134% from 1993-1995 to 2003-2005.

The single biggest export is milled rice, accounting for 16 % of the value of exports in 2003-2005 (see graph 5).

Graph 5: India - top 10 agricultural exports Average 2003-2005 (million $)

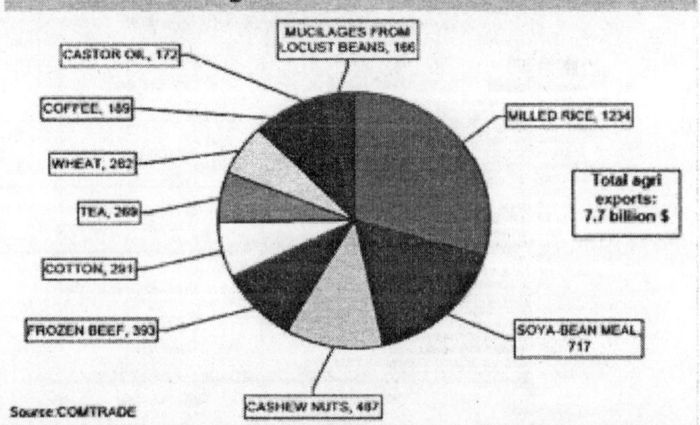

Two other commodities, cotton and wheat, are also within the top 10 exports. Soyabean meal, an intermediate product, is the second most important export with 9% of sales. However 6 out of the top 10 are final products, including cashew nuts, beef, coffee and tea which together represent around 14% of the value of exports.

In the nineties the value of exports fluctuated considerably (graph 6). This reflects big swings both in the price and the volume of rice exports, the latter depending on the balance between production and consumption. Despite those fluctuations, since 1999 India's exports have grown steadily. In addition to rice, beef (buffalo meat) and soyabean meal exports are also expanding. Graph 7 shows the destination of the top 5 exports and concentration in key markets. Saudi Arabia is the single biggest market for rice and is also a big market for buffalo beef and cashew nuts. The EU is another important destination for rice and cashew nuts.

Graph 6: India - top 10 agricultural exports (million $)

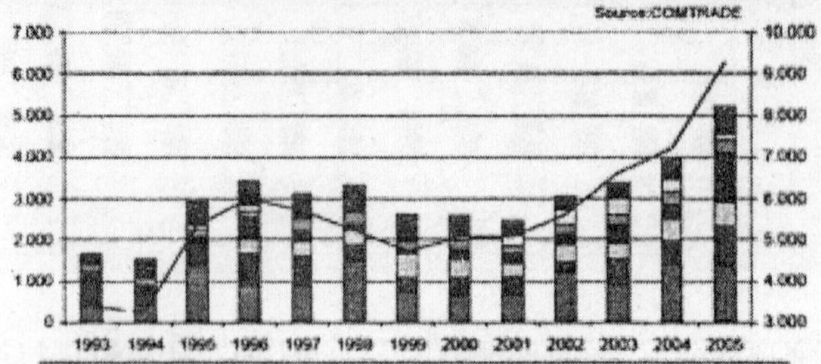

The cotton market is also heavily concentrated on a few key neighbouring countries, which absorb 83% of exports. China, Bangladesh, Pakistan and ASEAN are important markets for soyabean meal and buffalo beef.

Graph 7: India - top 5 exports and destination Average 2003-2005 (million $)

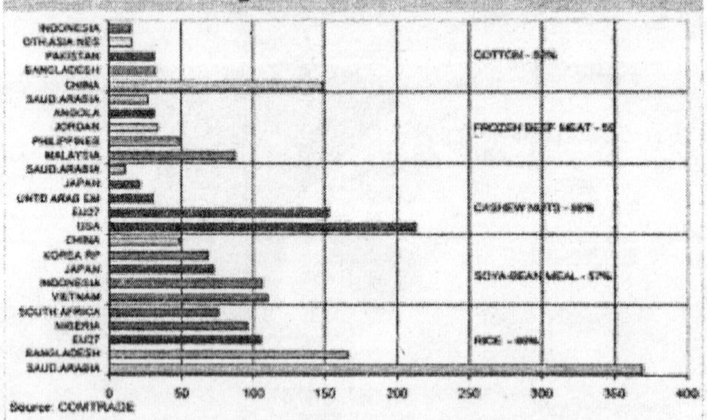

A closer look at India's imports

ASEAN is by far the biggest supplier of agricultural products to India, accounting for a massive 40% of its imports in 2003-2005 (graph 8). Argentina and Brazil rank 2nd and 3rd respectively while the EU only has 4% market share (down from 7% a decade ago), ranked at number six in 2003-2005.

Graph 8: India agri-food imports by origin (million $)

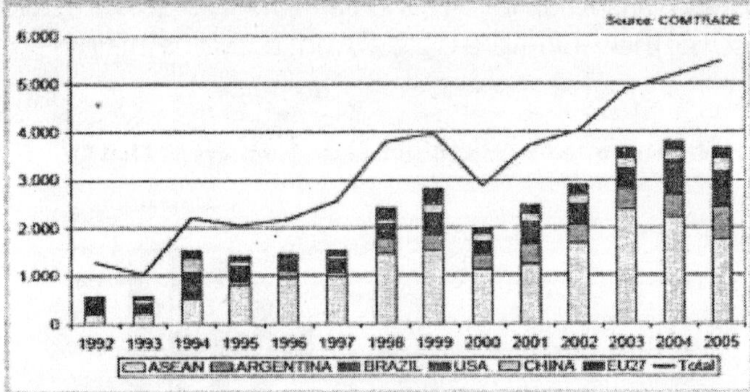

While this is roughly equivalent to the share of imports from China and the United States, it is far below the share enjoyed by Mercosur (supplying about 17% of imports) and ASEAN countries. Over the past decade ASEAN and Argentina have both substantially increased their market share at the expense of the US, the EU, Brazil and China. Together the top six suppliers now account for over 70% of imports.

India's agricultural imports are focused mainly on intermediate products (referring back to graph 3). These account for 56% of imports; final products are 31%, while the share of commodities is just 13%. The biggest growth has been in intermediate products which increased nearly fourfold over the period.

This reflects the importance of vegetable oils in Indian imports (graph 9). Palm oil is by far the biggest import at 29% of the total. Together with soyabean oils, they represent over 40% of imports. Protein rich peas are also within the top 5. The increase in imports of these foodstuffs is driven by population growth. While cashew nuts and cotton are among the top exports, they also appear in the top 10 imports. Cashew nuts are imported for further processing as are silk and cotton, which are used in the Indian textile industry.

Graph 9: India - top 10 agricultural imports
Average 2003-2005 (million $)

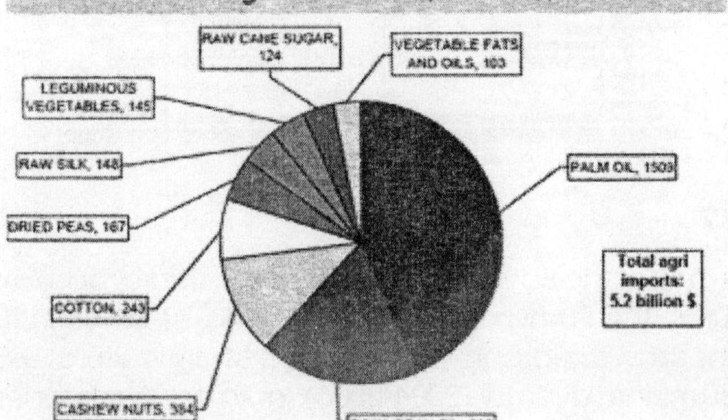

The evolution of imports is shown in graph 10. In particular the growth in imports of vegetable oils has been dramatic with an increase of over 800% between 1993-1995 and 2003-2005, with soyabean oil and other oils and fats taking a growing share of an expanding market. The phasing out of the multi-fibre agreement explains the increase in cotton imports.

Graph 10: India - top 10 agricultural imports (million $)

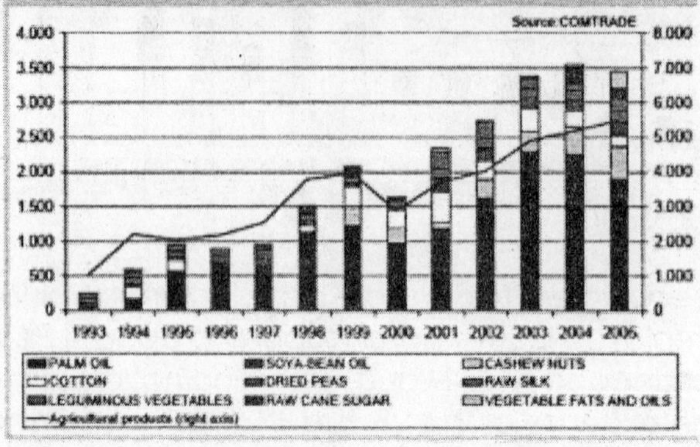

Given the importance of vegetable oil imports, it is not surprising that India depends on a few key suppliers (graph 11). Palm oil is supplied essentially by 2 ASEAN trading partners, with over 72 % of India's palm oil imports coming from Indonesia and 27 % from Malaysia. This concentration is almost perfectly mirrored in the soyabean oil market, with Argentina supplying 72 % and Brazil around 24 %.

Graph 11: India - top 5 imports and origin
Average 2003-2005 (million $)

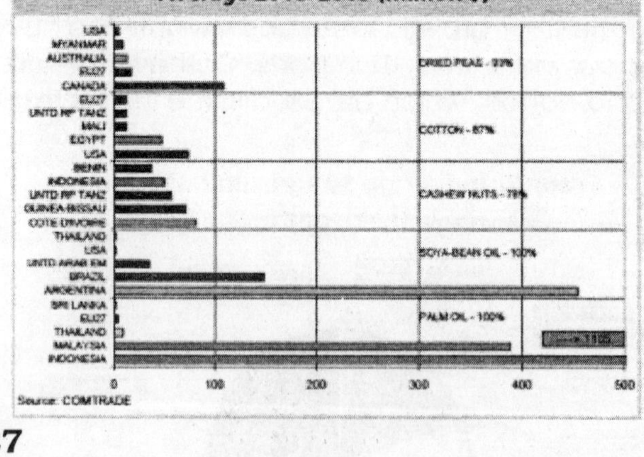

Trade with EU-27

In this section we look at the EU's declared trade with India, based on the EU's COMEXT data expressed in euros. The EU has a deficit of around • 1 billion in its trade in agri-food products with India, as shown in graph 12. The value of agricultural exports from the EU to India is only about • 250 million (average 2004-2006). India accounts for less than 0.5% percent of the EU's total agricultural exports. Meanwhile the EU imports • 1.3 billion worth of agri-food products from India, equivalent to 2% of the EU's global agri-food imports.

Graph 12: EU-27 structure of agricultural trade with India (million €)

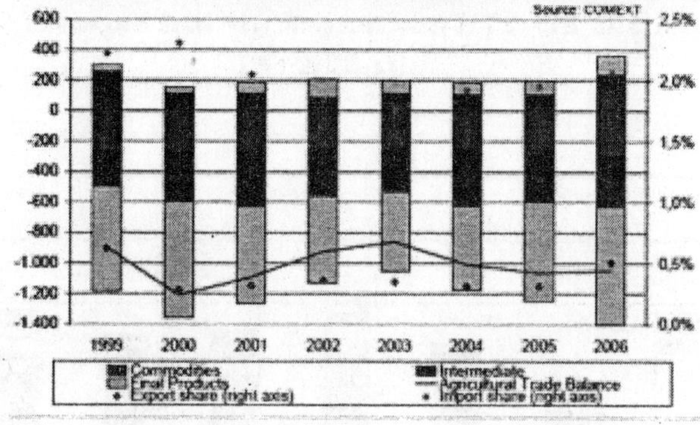

This is just half the value of the EU's imports from China. India ranks as the 12th most important EU supplier.

The breakdown of the EU's exports to India is shown in graph 13. In 2004-2006 wheat was the EU's top agricultural export to India, valued at •40 million and accounting for 16% of exports. Scotch whisky exports were worth •32 million, around 13% of exports. Exports of raw wool and hides for further processing in the Indian textile industry were valued at •18 and •14 million respectively. Dried peas were •11 million. Other specialised products are exported to India, such as vegetable seeds (•6 million), wine and olive oil both valued at around •4 million.

Graph 13: EU-27 main agricultural exports to India Average 2004-2006 (million €)

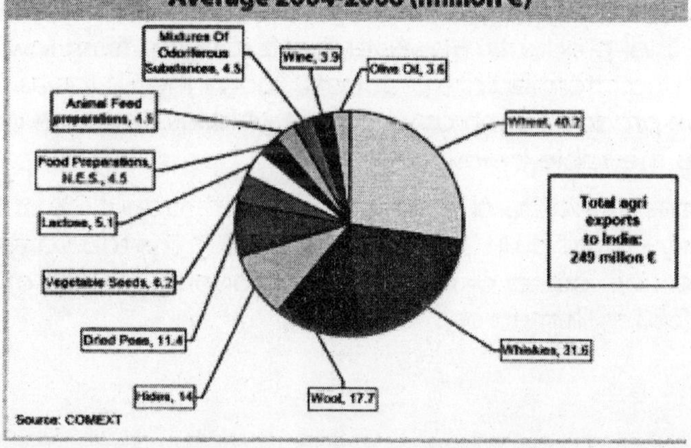

India is an intermittent importer of EU wheat (graph 14). Having been a small net exporter of wheat since 1999/00, India became a net importer in 2006/07. The EU's wheat exports were worth •120 million in 2006, equivalent to one third of the value of exports.

Exports of whiskies have grown fourfold from 1999 to 2006 and now account for 10% of export sales. Dried peas accounted for 6% of exports in 2006 but have fluctuated over the period.

Graph 14 Evolution of EU- 27's main agricultural exports to India

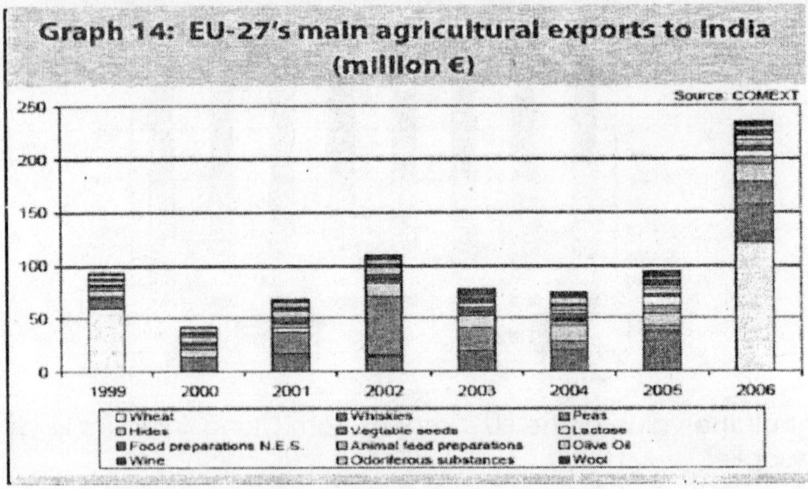

The current average bound tariff for agriculture is 117.2 % according to the WTO's 2007 Trade Policy Report for India.

There is often a significant difference between bound and applied tariffs. The current average applied tariff is 40.8% according to the WTO. Applied tariffs are subject to frequent adjustment, depending on domestic supply. For example the wheat tariff was reduced in 2006 as India needed imports to compensate for its poor harvest. Therefore the EU was able to export wheat at zero tariff that year. Meanwhile EU exports of dairy products are currently very low mainly due to high Indian tariffs.

The profile of applied tariffs shows a degree of tariff escalation with the highest tariffs of 150% applied to final products. However tariffs ranging from low or zero to 100% also apply to some final and intermediate products. Today the EU faces tariffs of 100-150 % on exports of high value products such as wine and whiskies. The tariff profile for a number of products is shown in the table below.

Turning to imports, agricultural products represent about 7% of total EU imports from India, reaching nearly • 1.3 billion in 2004-2006 (graph 15). The top 5 are specialised products: cashew nuts, coffee, rice, castor oil and tea and account for 43% of the value of the EU's imports from India (550 million euros).

Table 3: India's Tariff Structure for selected products (2006)

Product	Avg. Bound (%)	Avg. Applied (%)
Animal products	105.0	33.0
Dairy	65.0	35.0
Fruit, vegetables	100.9	31.5
Coffee, tea	133.1	56.3
Cereals	119.4	37.3
Fats and oils	168.9	52.5
Sugars	124.7	48.4
Beverages	127.5	68.9
Cotton	110.0	17.0

Some of these products already enter the EU market duty free (basmati rice) or with a low tariff (5% for oils). Overall 97% of imports from India enter duty free or with a tariff lower than 30%.

Graph 15: EU-27 main agricultural imports from India Average 2004-2006 (million €)

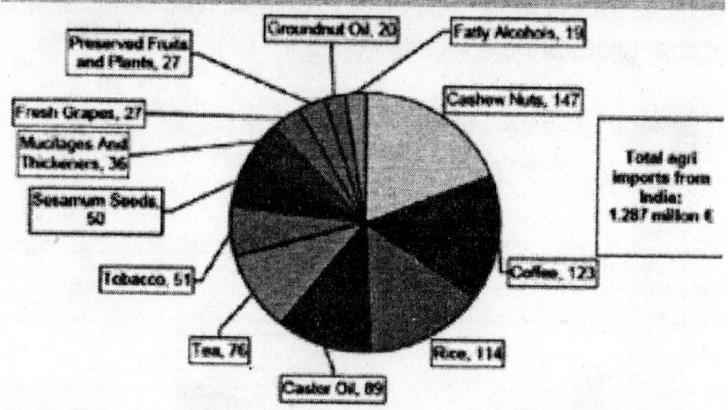

Source:COMEXT

The trend in agricultural imports from India is shown in graph 16. Total imports were valued at • 1.4 billion in 2006, up from just over • 1 billion in 2003. Coffee was the top import in 2006 but its value has fluctuated considerably since 1990. The value of tea imports has declined over the period by over 20%.

Outlook for agriculture and trade

OECD and FAPRI (Food and Agricultural Policy Research Institute) both expect India to play a bigger role in world markets in future. It is likely to remain a small net exporter overall. India is forecast to consolidate its position among the world's leading exporters of rice (its top export), though the volume of exports has been erratic since the mid nineties (depending on the size of the crop and on domestic consumption).

Graph 16: Evolution of EU-27 main agricultural imports from India (million €)

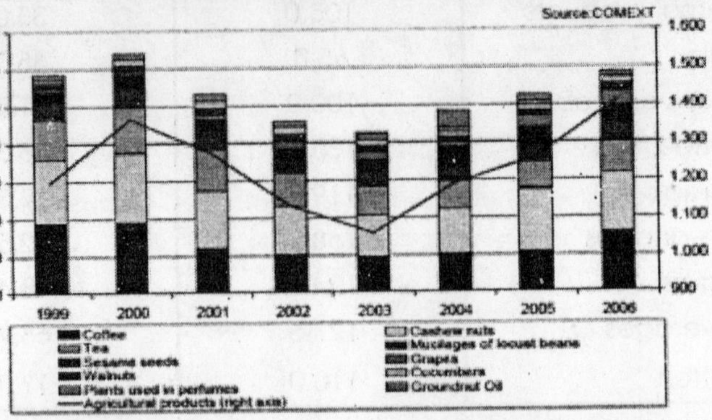

Currently it is the second largest rice producer after China and the third largest net-exporter after Thailand and Vietnam.

FAPRI expects it to increase its world market share from 16% to 20% by 2015 as area and yields increase and per capita consumption declines. OECD meanwhile takes a more conservative view of production prospects and therefore of export potential. FAPRI's and OECD's projections for the global rice trade (graph 17).

Graph 17: Evolution of World Rice Trade ('000 t) Average 2014/15 to 2016/17

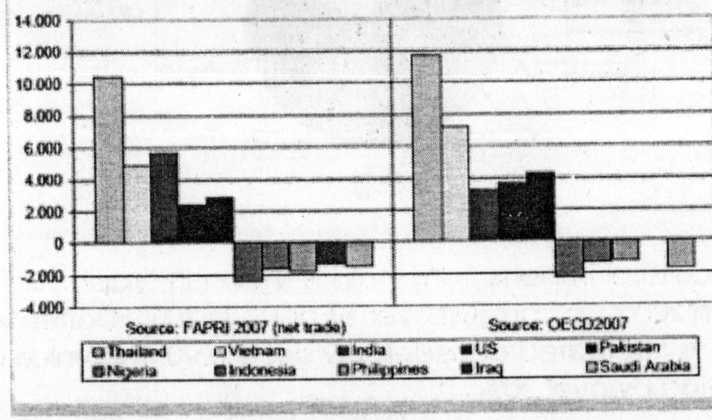

For sugar a big change is expected with India forecast to switch from being a net importer to a net exporter (over 2 million tonnes).

Its world market share is expected to rise from 4% to 6% over the coming decade, thanks to robust growth in production (second only to Brazil's) and a slowdown in consumption growth. For soya meal India's world market position is relatively stable and it is expected to stay at about 6% world market share (FAPRI).

Indian buffalo beef exports are projected to grow as production rises faster than demand, with world market share for beef stable at around 11%. On the dairy side, net exports of butter and SMP will also grow. For butter although there is a strong increase in production, this is in response to surging demand growth, so India remains a small net exporter. On the other hand it becomes a significant net exporter of SMP, with its share of world trade rising from 4% to 6%.

Turning to imports, in 2006/07 India became a net importer of wheat having been a net exporter for the 5 years previously. However it is not expected to be a big net exporter in the coming decade. For dairy there may be opportunities for EU in the future. If an EU-Indian FTA is agreed, then, given changing consumer habits, India is a potential market for EU exports of high quality processed milk products.

Last but not least, India is projected to remain a leading vegetable oils importer, absorbing one quarter of world soyabean oil imports and 14% of palm oil imports. Although the share does not increase much over the projection period, this masks an increase in imports from 5 million tonnes to 6-8 million tonnes by 2016/17, given the expansion in world trade in vegetable oils. Indian consumption of vegetable oils has grown faster than production since the mid-nineties and the trend is expected to continue. Combined with the recent hike in prices, this could lead to a doubling of India's vegetable oil import bill in 10 years.

Conclusions

Agriculture occupies a prominent position in Indian policy-making not only because of its contribution to GDP but also because of the large proportion of the population that is dependent on the sector for its livelihood.

The growth in population and wealth has stimulated demand to the extent that domestic production has not always been able to keep up and there is increasing speculation that the Indian economy may be overheating leading to inflation. The downside of the increased import demand and the current commodity boom is that India's food import bill will rise sharply.

However it is clear that India's agricultural sector has made huge strides in developing its potential. The green revolution massively increased the production of vital food grains and introduced technological innovations into agriculture. This progress is manifested in India's net trade position. Where once India had to depend on imports to feed its people, since 1990 it is a net exporter of agri-food products. Its agriculture is large and diverse and its sheer size means that even slight changes in its trade have significant effects on world agricultural markets.

How India will develop is still a big unknown, with the picture changing rapidly. Questions have arisen about India's capacity to compete in global markets under the current farm structure and farm policy. As the service economy grows, the share of agriculture will diminish, which may also have implications for India's stance on trade and agriculture policy in the future.

References

1. Evenson, R.E.; Pray, C. and M.W. Rosegrant. (1999), Agricultural Research and productivity Growth in India. Research Report No 109. International Food Policy Research Institute, Washington, D.C
2. Fan, S., Hazell, P.B.R. and S. Thorat. (1999), Linkages between Government Spending, Growth, and Poverty in Rural India. Research Report No 110. International Food Policy Research Institute, Washington, D.C.
3. Gulati, Ashok, Ruth Meinzen-Dick, and K.V. Raju (2005) *Institutional Reforms in Indian Irrigation,* Sage Publication.
4. Kumar, Praduman and Surabhi Mittal (2006). "Agricultural Productivity Trends in India: Sustainability Issues" *Agricultural Economic Research Review.* Volume 19, Pp 71- 88.
5. Kumar, Praduman and Surabhi Mittal (2003). Crop Diversification in India: Analysis by State and Farm Size Group. Agricultural Situation in India, Special Number,August, 2003. Directorate of Economics and Statistics, Ministry of Agriculture, Government of India. Pp 273-280.
6. Kumar, Praduman. and Mark W. Rosegrant (1994): Productivity and Sources of Growth for Rice in India, *Economic and Political Weekly,* 29 (52): A183-A188.

23

Agricultural Development and Food Security

Ms Lad Anuradha Subhashrao

Introduction

The vast majority of the world's poorest people depend on agriculture for food and household incomes especially in underdeveloped and developing countries like India. Now-a-days, the global economic and financial crisis threatens the livelihoods of many of the world's poorest people. While commodity prices are lower, food prices remain higher (upto 40%) than historical levels. At the same time, the contraction of global economic activity has reduced exports and incomes among farmers in developing countries. Although 75% of the world's poor live in rural areas and 60% of those suffering from hunger. This initiative represents not just a commitment of resources, which is significant, but also a commitment to reform the way, the international community approaches of food security.

The Food and Agriculture Organization (FAO) defines food security as "Situation that exists when all people, at all times, have physical, social and economic access to sufficient, safe and nutritious food that meets their dietary needs and food preferences for an active and healthy life". This definition comprises five key dimensions of food supplies: availability, absorption, access, vulnerability and sustainability.

- The first dimension relates to the availability of food which is function of production.
- Second dimension, relates to the absorption of food in the body, which is determined by the availability of safe drinking water, environmental hygiene, primary health care and primary education.
- The third dimension, access to food, which is related to purchasing power and accessibility and availability of food.
- The fourth dimension, vulnerability to transient hunger, which is related to natural and manmade calamities and disasters.

- The last dimension, sustainability of production, which is influenced by the extent of attention given to the ecological foundations essential for sustained advances in production.

While we should give the highest priority to improving food consumption and equitable distribution of food, we should not decelerate our efforts in improving agricultural production through increasing yield per hectare by taking cropping area under irrigation, higher factor productivity and better post-harvest management. Agricultural production, factor productivity and investment in irrigation and post-harvest and rural infrastructure are all declining in India. Prices of many agricultural commodities have collapsed and indian farm families are in deep economic and psychological distress. This trend, if not changed immediately, will lead to social chaos, since agriculture is not just a food producing machine, but is the backbone of the livelihood security system for nearly 700 million children, women and men in the country. There is no time to relax on the food production front, just because the major problem today is in the area of marketing and distribution. At the same time, we should not continue to remain silent spectators to the co-existence of mountains of grains and millions of hungry.

Assuring Food Security

The job of assuring food security is large and complex. Action needs to be taken simultaneously at the individual, national and global levels to achieve the following goals.

I. Increase agricultural output worldwide: Over the next 30 years, developing countries food needs could nearly double because of fast population growth and modest income growth.

II. Reduce poverty: The best way to reduce poverty and hunger is through economic growth. For developing countries, improved agricultural productivity can be the engine of non-agricultural growth.

III. Improve health and nutrition: Eliminating hunger requires targeted nutrition, health and food programs. Increasing family income alone does not ensure that people will consume the right kind of nutrients in the right quantities at the right time to maintain their health and productivity. It also requires nutrition counseling, prenatal nutrition services and public health interventions. In this awareness about nutrition is very much important.

Past progress and outlook

Between 1961 and 1992, average calories available in developing countries ranges from about 1925 per person per day to about 2540 per person per day, which is higher than the minimum daily requirement of 2200-2300 specified by the United Nations Food and Agriculture Organization (FAO).

About 15 per cent of the world's population and about 20 per cent of the developing world's population are undernourished or malnourished. Among them are 195 million children under the age of 5 who are not receiving the nutrition they need to fully develop mentally and physically (Food and Agriculture Organization/World Health Organization, 1992).

Outlook for world agriculture

Future demand for food will be driven by population growth and rising incomes. The population of the world is expected to exceed 8 billion by 2025, an increase of 2.5 billion. Given modest income growth, food needs in developing countries could nearly double.

In the future, agricultural growth must come primarily from rising biological yields rather than from expanding cultivated areas or intensifying agriculture through irrigation, because fertile land and water are becoming increasingly scarce. Most fertile lands are already under cultivation and most areas suitable for irrigation have already been exploited. And with population growth and urban expansion, there is rising competition for water from urban and industrial users.

Appropriate policies for improving food security with the help of agricultural development

As early as 1856, Baird Smith, who investigated the causes of a serious famine in North West India, Wrote: 'Indian famines are famines of work, and not of food. Where there is work, there is money. Where there is money there is food'. This situation is as relevant today as it was 150 years ago. Food security in India is best described in million person years of jobs and livelihoods rather than in million tonnes of food grains.

Agriculture, comprising crop and animal husbandry, inland and marine fisheries, forestry and agro-forestry, agro-processing, constitutes the backbone of the livelihood security system of India, particularly in rural areas. Our agriculture is still 'farmers farming' and not 'factory faring.' Which is running only on profit-orientation as in industrialized countries?

Farming is the largest private sector enterprise in India. Now the share of agriculture in total work force is declining, we must think of increasing their productivity and try to improve food security with the help of some appropriate policies as below.

I. Encouraging rapid technological change: Implementation of rapid technological change on millions of farms in the developing world, is essential for agricultural and income growth. More investment in the research, necessary to stimulate technological change in agriculture should give priority by the Government.

II. Increasing the efficiency of irrigation: Agriculture is increasingly competing for use of water with urban and industrial users. There will be sufficient water for all, if agriculture and other sectors greatly improve the efficiency of their water use. This will improve by organizing training on efficient use of water for water users. Establishment of water markets, clarifying water rights and pricing water to reflect it's true value.

III. Improving natural resource management: Government/Nation must involve in many projects that support the intensification of agriculture and at the same time, encourage better use of natural resources by better management. A community based approach to resource allocation, enforcement and maintenance may be useful in such situation.

IV. Providing education and health services to both rural boys and girls: Providing education and health services to both rural girls and boys is one of the key ways to reduce poverty and hunger. There is substantial evidence that individual's education is closely linked to their incomes and that improved education contributes to national economic growth. Education and health services are especially important for women, who have a major role to play in growing crops and in reducing hunger. Better educated and healthier women are much more productive and work hard and earn higher income. Since women can use their additional income on investments for family welfare. Increases in their incomes are likely to have greater immediate and long term impacts on poverty and hunger directly than equal increases in men's incomes.

V. Investing in infrastructure: When there are adequate infrastructure facilities like communication networks, roads, storage facilities and regular supplies of electricity, which helps farmers to grow the most profitable crops, store them, move them to market and receive the more prices for agricultural products.

Table 1: Food production and resilience impacts of changes in agricultural production systems

Food security/adaptation options **Cropland management**	**Impacts on food production**
Improved crop varieties	Generally increased crop yield
Use of legumes in crop rotations	Higher yields due to increased N in soil
Use of cover crops	Higher yield due to reduced on-farm
Incorporation of residues	Higher yield through increased soil
Reduced/zero tillage	Higher yields over long run, particularly
Perennials/agro-forestry	Greater yields on adjacent croplands
Water management	**Impacts on food production**
Irrigation	Higher yields, greater intensity of land
Bunds	Higher yields

Global attention to agricultural development and food security has been renewed as a result of several factors.

I. The world has entered a new era of food and nutrition insecurity:

Poverty and hunger cannot be reduced without investing more money in agriculture and nutrition. Small holder farmers, men and women, have a central role to play in achieving food and nutrition security and pro-poor agricultural and economic growth.

II. Agriculture, food and nutrition security play a vital role in the achievement of the Millennium Development Goals (MDGs):

Agriculture is the world's major source of food and the sector provides employment, income and livelihoods for the majority of the world's poor people. The achievement of the MDGs, in particular, the goals and target related to poverty and hunger, education and child mortality are closely related to agricultural development and food security.

III. Strengthening the linkages between agriculture, food and nutrition security is essential if levels of nutrition are to be raised:

Most of the world's poor people and nutritionally vulnerable people are highly dependent on agricultural and rural development for improving their household food security and this requires support for an appropriate mix of policies, institutions and infrastructure that support agricultural based livelihoods, strengthen social protection systems and protect and promote food and nutrition security.

IV. World population is projected to grow to nearly 9.2 billion by 2050:

To feed a population of more than 9 billion, global food production must nearly double.

Conclusions

There are strong, direct relationships between agricultural productivity, hunger and poverty. Increased agricultural productivity enables farmers to grow more food which translates into better diets and under market conditions that offer level playing fields, into higher farm incomes. With more money farmers are more likely to diversify food production and grow higher value crops, benefiting not only themselves but the economy as a whole.

Thirty years from now, the world will have 2.5 billion more people to feed, and most of them will live in developing countries. Ensuring food for all poses enormous technological, economic and political challenges. They will require steady improvement in national and international policies, institutions and public expenditures, as well as broadened and consistent international commitment and financial support. If we take necessary steps now, we can look forward to a world in which everyone has enough to eat.

"There is no time for a single green Revolution,
We need an evergreen Revolution"

References

1. Josef Schmidhuber and Francesco N. Tubiello (2007). Global food security under climate change. PNAS., 104 (50: 19703-19708.
2. Swaminathan, M.S. (2001). Food security and sustainable development. Current Science, 81 (8): 9448-954.
3. Wendy, S., Ayres and Alex F. McCalla (1996). Rural development, Agriculture and food security. Finance and Development, pp.8-11.

24

Role and Importance of Genetically Modified Food in Improving Food Security for India

Yogesh D. Mahajan

Introduction

London-based Maplecroft, the risk advisory business, has rated India with "high risk" in its newly developed food security index, ranking 25 out of 148 listed countries due to unsustainable water use and an expanding population. From this report we can understand the importance of food security for India.

India is the second most populous country in the world with over 120 crores population. With 2.4% of world surface area (3.4% of landmass), it holds almost 16.7% of the world population. The population is growing at an average rate of 2% per annum. According to the data published by the government of India and the Food Corporation of India, total production of food grain was 230.78 million tonnes in 2007-08 and in recent year it is 229.85 million tonnes. There is just 0.93 million tonnes of food grain production decreased than last year. Hence question is that, only 0.93 million tonnes falling production of food grain can create such situations of food insecurity in India? When look at the statistics relating to the major food grain production. We found that, rice production is increased from 96.69 to 99.37 million tonnes in 2007-08 to 2008-09, wheat production is decreased from 78.57 to 77.63 million tonnes, production of coarse cereals is just decreased from 40.76 to 38.67 million tonnes, cereals production is decreased from 216.02 to 215.67 million tonnes and production of pulses is near about stable it is changed from 14.76 to 14.18 million tonnes in same year.

India may be one of the world's key emerging economies, but it is finding itself under increasing pressure from food security issues. As much as two-thirds of the country's 1.1 billion inhabitants rely on farming as their main source of income, but 21 per cent less land is under cultivation in August 2009, than during the same period in August 2008. This is due to a reduction in the availability of national water resources for agricultural purposes, deforestation and an uneven monsoon in July 2009, which caused widespread flooding and droughts. The resulting reduction in crop yields is likely to inject inflationary pressure into the economy, placing further strain on large sections of the populace. Yet, the sector is a laggard, having grown at a very modest annual average of 1.7 per cent an annum last 10 years, sharply contrasting with the robust growth in manufacturing and services.

Food Self-Sufficiency and Stagnating Output

The claim of India having reached food self-sufficiency rings hollow as we have failed to meet the food needs of people. To control rising domestic prices and to meet domestic shortfalls, imports are organised, and often at low or zero rate of duty. While imports augment domestic availability, there is absolutely no guarantee that foods actually reach people. There are several millions in the country who live on less than $1 a day (Rs 45 a day). They are forced to depend on the open market for daily needs. With rising open market prices, their purchasing power is considerably eroded. They need a safety net in the form of access to foods at affordable prices. The pubic distribution system (PDS) is supposed to do that; but it seems to be losing steam, if reports of heavy leakages are any indication. This underscores the urgent need to accelerate the country's agricultural growth. Food expenditure tops the family budget in India. On an average, food accounts for 54 per cent of monthly budget; this sharply contrasts with the US where typically less than 15 per cent is spent on food. This confirms the high cost of food in India.

Currently, India has a large production base for a variety of crops and agricultural products and the country ranks amongst the top three producers in case of milk, rice, wheat, sugar, cotton and so on. Yet, output has stagnated in case of many field crops. On-farm and off-farm losses are huge. Only cotton provides a silver lining in an otherwise gloomy Indian agricultural scenario. Introduction of technology (genetically-modified seeds) has transformed the country from being an importer into an exporter of cotton. Fragmented landholding, rainfed cultivation (irrigation limited to 40 per cent of cropped area), low level of input usage, antiquated agronomy, poor technology adoption, lack of rural infrastructure and tardy flow of price and market information to farmers all combine to result in stagnating output, low yields and volatile prices. Acreage under major field crops continues to stagnate. On the other hand, food imports have been large and mounting. India is forced to import major food items such as pulses, edible oil, sugar and wheat.

Food security happens when all people at all times have access to enough food that should affordable, safe and healthy, culturally acceptable , meets specific dietary needs, obtained in a dignified manner and produced in ways that are environmentally sound. The World Food Summit of 1996 defined food security as existing "when all people at all times have access to sufficient, safe, nutritious food to maintain a healthy and active life". Commonly, the concept of food security is defined as including both physical and economic access to food that meets people's dietary needs as well as their food preferences. But food security is a complex sustainable development issue, linked to health through malnutrition, but also to sustainable economic development, environment, and trade. If we fail to maintain above there has been food insecurity. Food insecurity exists when all people, do not have physical and economic access to the sufficient, safe and nutritious food to meet their dietary needs and food preferences for an active and healthy life.

Genetically Modified Food

Genetically modified food can be one of the solutions to the problem of food security. It is already being used in western countries for the last 15 years or so.

Individual characteristics of plants such as height, flower colour and leaf shape are determined by "genes" which are present in every cell that makes up a plant. In nature, the genes of two parent plants mix up during pollination to produce an offspring containing some genes from each parent. Historically, man has selectively bred food plants to produce bigger and better crops. This was achieved by deliberately cross-pollinating plants with desirable features. Genetic Modification takes selective breeding a step further. Scientists are learning how to identify genes and recognise which genes control the development of which characteristics. They are now able to breed offspring by transplanting the desirable genes from one plant to another. By **genetically modifying plants** in the laboratory it is possible to have stricter control over the genes. In nature all the genetic material from the parent plants is mixed. With GM the desirable genes can be separated from the undesirable genes. It is also quicker and cheaper to breed by GM as the desired offspring can be produced in one generation. In nature recessive genes often "skip" several generations.

Merits of GM Crops/Foods:

- Improved yields;
- More resistance to disease;
- Less likely to be damaged by insects;
- Tolerance to herbicides (meaning weed-killer can be sprayed to kill all plants but the main crop).

In fact, one of the great advantages of GM crops is that they can reduce the huge volume of pesticides used which are an established threat to the environment.

- Better nutritional value;
- Better climatic survival by increasing tolerance to drought, flood or frosty conditions to allow the use of previously inhospitable land;
- Increased shelf life.
- By enhancing the characteristics of food crops it is theoretically possible to feed an increasing world population at a reduced environmental cost.
- They are better in taste and longevity. The fibres are adjusted to make eating smoother. They are modified to make them more nutritious
- Another advantage of GM crops is that they can improve the nutritional value of foods. Thus, it is possible to create crops with far higher protein content than ordinary varieties. For example, Indian scientists have genetically modified the potato to increase its protein content by adding genes from the 'amaranth' plant. Soya and maize have also been modified to increase their protein content. Similarly, Swiss scientists have developed a 'golden rice' which has Vitamin A which ordinary rice does not contain. This is important as people in poor countries with predominantly rice diets can suffer Vitamin A deficiency. In children this can lead to blindness and early death.

- Plants can be so modified that they are resistant to certain fungal moulds that can be damaging to human health. Bananas and other fruits have been modified to contain vaccines that give protection against cholera and hepatitis. Wheat has been modified to make it gluten-free which benefits people with celiac disease. Tomatoes have been modified to include beneficial antioxidants.
- Genetic modification has also lead to more direct commercial advantages. In the United States, a genetically modified tomato, 'Flavr Savr®', has been introduced which has a longer shelf life than standard varieties. Slow softening apples and raspberries have also been developed which last longer before decaying than unmodified crops.

"India can become self sufficient in food production by use of biotechnology in food crops," Clive James, chairman of the International Service for the Acquisition of Agri-biotech Applications said. India is the world's second biggest importer of edible oils with imports meeting over 40 percent of demand. It banned non-basmati rice exports to meet domestic need, after 2007/08 summer output was seen stagnant. "The story of Bt cotton in India is remarkable. it can replicate the success in food crops," said James. India surpassed the U.S. to become the second biggest producer of cotton in 2006/07, after adopting GM crops. India's GM cotton area is estimated at 6.33 million hectares or 66 percent of the total cotton area in 2007/08, up from 3.69 million hectares in 2006/07, according to Cotton Advisory Board. India allowed commercial cultivation of bacillus thuringiensis or Bt cotton, the country's first GM crop in 2002, leading to protests from activists, who say GM crops are a health hazard. This delayed approval of GM food crops. India's first expected GM food crop is brinjal. Field trials of GM brinjal started in August 2007 and are now commercialised from October 2009, said C.D Mayee, a senior scientist, and chairman Agricultural Scientists Recruitment Board.

Second Green Revolution

Genetically modified or "GM" crops are being considered as having the potential to bring about the second green revolution. India is currently working on 111 transgenic crop varieties of various vegetables, fruits, spices, cereals, bamboo etc. Transgenic crops brinjal, cabbage, castor, cauliflower, corn, groundnut, okra, potato, rice and tomato are under field trials stage. But it is cotton which was the first GM crop to be extensively worked upon and commercially released in India; the reason being that India has the largest area under cotton cultivation in the world.

Both public and private sector are actively involved in R&D of GM crops. The public organizations are basically doing primary research, while the research conducted so far by private sector in India involves backcrossing the genetically engineered traits from the imported GM crops seeds into selected local varieties of the crop through standard breeding techniques. For instance India cultivates 4 species of Gossypium (cotton) consisting of 30 varieties and 20 hybrids. The Bt cotton commercialized thus, is principally a backcross with these local/hybrid varieties.

Bt Cotton

India got its first approval of genetically modified crop Bt cotton hybrid "Bollgard" in 2002. The total cultivated area under GM crops has increased many folds since then with India (6.2 million Hectares) standing at 5th position (ahead of China) in Bt cotton production. The US-registered multinational corporation, Monsanto, first developed Bt cotton and the three genetically modified cotton hybrids (Bt Mech 12, Bt Mech 162 and Bt Mech 184) developed by Monsanto in collaboration with its Indian partner Mahyco were released for commercial cultivation in central and southern India. It is mostly the private companies (presently 22, in pipeline 8) which are releasing cotton varieties. At the moment all the Bt cotton hybrids developed by private companies contain Bt cry 1 Ac gene developed by Monsanto. The first indigenous cotton variety released by public sector in 2005, developed by the Central Institute of Cotton Research (CICR) is Bikaneri Narma (BN) Bt expressing Bt Cry 1Ac protein in the North, Central and South Cotton growing zones in India. The trend in figure 2 shows that number of varieties released is increasing at a tremendous rate. Till July 2008, 142 cotton varieties had been released.

Legal Framework

The Genetic Engineering Approval Committee (GEAC) is the regulatory authority under Ministry of Environment and Forests for approval of GMOs and products thereof in India. GEAC was formulated after the notification of rules for the manufacture/use/import/export and storage of hazardous microorganisms/genetically engineered organisms or cells manufacture in 1989. In 2006 & 2008 this was subsequently amended for exempting categories of GM foods and r-pharma from the purview of rules. It brings out manuals of guidelines specifying procedures for regulatory process, activities involving GMOs in research, use and application from environmental safety angle (Recombinant DNA Safety Guidelines 1992 and Revised Guidelines for Research in Transgenic Plants 1998).

For a GM seed to be released, it has to under go various examinations by different committees before it can be commercialized. Firstly there is Institutional Biosafety Committee (IBSC) which is linked to the lab undertaking transgenic work, then the Review Committee on Genetic Manipulation (RCGM) dealing with small scale trials, monitoring and evaluation committee and lastly the GEAC which overlooks the final release. The RCGM consists of expert scientists in areas of molecular biology and biochemistry. Once the RCGM has reviewed the field trial data, approval for large scale trials, seed bulking and commercialization has to be sought by the GEAC. RCGM provides the necessary technical and scientific data and then advices GEAC, to take a formal decision. Time clearance to release a crop in India is minimum three years. This includes one year of multi-locational trials for generating bio-safety data monitored by RCGM, followed by two years of large-scale field trials under the aegis of GEAC. Along with this seeds are also provided to ICAR for assessing its agronomic performance for a period of two years. If the reports are satisfactory then GEAC allows the company to proceed with seed multiplication for commercial release. During field trials the criteria for assessment of GM crops are extensive. The regulation specifies a range of studies that must be undertaken at the field level like basic agronomic monitoring, pest incidence, pollen flow and in addition to this toxicity and allergenicity data must be generated. In the case of Bt cotton, the preconditions for commercial release were: growing of a refuge area of five rows surrounding each Bt cotton plot, early removal of the cotton crop following harvest and continuous inspection throughout the crop period.

Farm Scientists for Genetically Modified Crops

Though the union government is still to give a go ahead to the introduction of genetically modified (GM) food crops, the scientists of Central Rice Research Institute (CRRI) here are batting for them. "Genetically modified crops can help contribute to food security of our country through increased yields at a lower production cost," said G.J.N. Rao, Head of Plant Improvement in this leading research institute. "National institutes like ICRISAT, ICGEB and other seed companies are increasingly investing in research in GM crops. Field trials are being conducted in rice, brinjal, okra, cabbage, cauliflower, groundnut, papaya, potato, tomato. Keeping in view rising food prices due to shortage of food it is necessary that technological knowhow is applied to ensure food and nutritional security in the country," he added. "We are doing genetic modification for ages now through grafting. We have done it in rice too by modifying the gene which has given excellent results. The technology is same everywhere and there should not be any opposition to the introduction of GM crops," Rao stressed, adding that GM food is completely safe.

President APJ Abdul Kalam believes promoting of genetic engineering technology for crops could help the country tackle problems of low productivity and also frequent drought conditions, low temperature spells and handicaps of salt-affected areas. In his own words, Dr Kalam says, "While discussing with the nutritional specialists, I realise that the population in the country suffers from deficiencies of Vitamin A, Iodine, Calcium and Iron. This is true for women in general and particularly in rural populace, leading to unacceptable levels of infant and maternal mortality rate. Supplementation of diet with these nutrients is a problem. If crops or crop varieties rich in Vitamin A, Iodine, Calcium and Iron can be developed by incorporating appropriate genes, this nutrition deficiency problem can be minimised."

Conclusion

From the above analysis, it is clear that merits far outweigh the demerits of GM foods; therefore embracing this technology should not elicit a second thought. For a healthy India, GM Foods is definitely going to play a big role in the days to come. Government of India should try to have a consensus view on this subject. Systems should be in place to ensure food produced from GM crops is put through rigorous safety checks before being approved for human consumption.

References

1. Sahai, Suman (2004) Genetically engineered crops and foods, New Delhi, Gene Campaign
2. Kumar, Nagesh (2006) Asian Biotechnology and development review, RIS, New Delhi
3. Swaminathan, M (2007) *Biotechnology in Agriculture,* Macmillan India, New Delhi
4. Anonymous, Crops in India retrieved on 15 Nov 2009 from www.google.co.in
5. Chakrabarti, S (2009) Uber Gene, Down to Earth, Volume 6, PP 44

25

Fermentation: An Economic Approach to Increase Mineral Content of Food to Conquer Food Security

Bhavana V. Mohite, Bhushan L. Chaudhari and Girish Chaudhari

Introduction

Concepts of food security have focused conventionally on increasing agricultural production, the availability of food and access to food while on the other hand nutrition security emphasizes more on the physiological needs for nutrients. The global significance of micronutrient malnutrition (MNM) which is also known as hidden hunger came to the attention of the nutrition community as recently as the mid 1980s, when protein-energy malnutrition was widely seen as the culprit of the world's nutrition problems (Allen, 2000). Fighting against MNM is an integral component of major millennium development goals (MDGs) adopted by United Nations as (1) eradication of extreme poverty and hunger; (2) reduction of child mortality; and (3) improvement of maternal health (United Nations Standing Committee fifth report on Nutrition, 2004). Incorporating nutritional considerations when meeting the challenges of food security provides a holistic concept of food and nutrition security thus enabling integration of the two frameworks and contributing towards achieving the targets set out in the MDGs (Allen, 2000).

While increasing availability and access to food, if nutritional considerations are appended to it, contributes to an integrated concept of food and nutrition security. The poor quality of food imposes enormous cost on societies in terms of ill health, lost lives; reduced economic productivity and poor quality of life. Micronutrient deficiencies are a problem that is much greater than hunger and is a prime example of the need to integrate both food and nutrition security. The necessity of incorporating nutrition into food security evolved over time (Weingartner 2005). The nutrition focus adds physiological requirements for different nutrients and the determinants of their bioavailability like the degree to which or rate at which the nutrient is absorbed and becomes available at the site of physiological activity as well as health services and healthy environments. These have broaden the concept of 'nutrition security' which means adequate nutritional status in terms of protein, energy, vitamins, and minerals for all household members at all times (Quisumbing *et al.* 1995). Accordingly, food and nutrition security is achieved, if adequate food (quantity, quality, safety, socio-cultural acceptability) is available and accessible and satisfactorily utilized by all individuals at all times to achieve good nutrition for a healthy and happy life (Weingartner, 2005). Micronutrient malnutrition is an important dimension of food and nutrition security from a global perspective. Micronutrient malnutrition is an ideal example to illustrate the importance of nutritional considerations when addressing the challenge of meeting food security for all. Micronutrient deficiencies are therefore important from a public health perspective and far exceed the current estimates of the global problem of hunger and food insecurity (Shetty, 2009). Improvement in nutrition contributes to productivity, economic development, and poverty reduction due to increased physical work capacity, cognitive development and health (Bran, 2009). Food based strategies to combat micronutrient malnutrition are eminently suitable for integrating food and nutrition security. Gibson and Hotz (2001) also identified food based strategies such as use of fermentation to decrease phytate which is an inhibitor of mineral absorption to enhance micronutrient availability along with soaking and germination. Although of high importance and lot of promising research results, this has remain unattended.

Fermented foods play an important role by improving the nutrition and providing food security for social well being of millions of people around the world. Fermentation has proved its positive impact on food by increasing the range of micronutrients and removing anti-nutritional factors to make food safe to eat. As of 2008 , the World Bank has estimated that there were an estimated 982 million poor people in developing countries who live on $1.25 a day or less (World Bank,2008). This compares to the later FAO estimate of 1.02 billion undernourished people. According to estimate 1.02 billion people are undernourished, a sizable increase from its 2006 estimate of 854 million people (FAO, 2009).

In the seventies, food security was viewed mainly in terms of food supply at the global and national levels. Since then there has been a major shift in understanding of food security with more emphasis on access to food rather than purely on production. The Food and Agriculture Organization of the United Nations (FAO) has recognized that the problem of food security cannot be tackled in isolation. Moreover that it is an integral component of other development issues. FAO highlights the fact that the world food insecurity problem is a result of undemocratic and unbalanced distribution of food and access to resources rather than a problem of global food production (Ruel and Garrett, 2004).

Fermentation can be defined as the biochemical modification of primary food products brought about by the action of microorganisms and their enzymes. Fermentation, by lowering pH, also provides more optimal conditions for enzymatic degradation of the phytate present in cereals in the form of complexes with proteins or polyvalent cations such as iron, zinc, calcium, and magnesium. Such a reduction in phytate may increase the amount of soluble iron, zinc, and calcium several fold (Abebe *et. al.*, 2007, Motarjemi and Nout, 1996). The increase nutritive values of fermented foods are also due to the breakdown of digested sugars, free fatty acids, amino acids, minerals as well as synthesis of certain vitamins (Obizoba and Attai, 1991).

Apart from its preservative effects, fermentation is a low-input and appropriate technology with minimal investment requirements, which provides individuals with limited purchasing power, access to safe, inexpensive and nutritious foods. FAO seeks to promote wider interest in fermentation technology for the enhancement of food security and food safety, for upgrading nutritional standards in poor regions and for the prevention of food losses (Rolle and Satin, 2002, Towo *et. al.,* 2006). Small-scale fermentation technologies contribute substantially to food safety, food security and nutrition, particularly in regions that are vulnerable to food shortages and particularly under conditions where refrigeration or other food processing facilities are not available (Battcock and Azam-Ali, 1998, Onofiok *et. al.,* 1996, Motarjemi, 2002).

Among various antinutrients phytate is the major storage form of phosphorous in cereals, legumes. Phytate is negatively charged under physiological conditions and thus strongly chelates metal ions, especially zinc, but also iron, calcium and magnesium, forming insoluble complexes in the gastrointestinal tract that cannot be digested or absorbed in humans because of the absence of intestinal phytase enzyme (Abebe *et. al.,* 2007, Sharma and Khetarpaul, 1997). Phytate also complexes endogenously secreted minerals making them unavailable for reabsorption into the body (Sandstrom, 1997).

More than 60 % of the total world food is comprised of cereals along with pulses (Chavan and Kadam, 1989). Hence to demonstrate the improvement of the mineral content of food by fermentation for better food and nutrition security the present study was carried out using cereals as follows. The local fermented foods used for the study were kurdai and bibdi which were sun dried fermented product especially prepared in khandesh region along with idli, dhokla as steamed processed, jalebi, gulgule as fried one.

Materials and Methods

Sample collection

The raw foods were purchased from local market and households located in Jalgaon city and nearby. Each "as eaten" sample of raw food type was then combined to form one composite food sample per food type. The ingredients used and methods of preparation of fermented foods is given in table 1. The unfermented batter (UFB), Fermented batter (FB) and processed product (PP) were weighed and dried separately.

Minerals and Phytate Analysis

Samples were analyzed for zinc and iron content by atomic absorption spectrophotometer (Unicam, UK) and Ca and Mg as described by Cheng and Bray (1951) after wet digestion (AOAC, 1999). Phytate content was determined by complexometric titration (Garcia –Estepa *et. al.,* 1999).

Table 1 Ingredients and methods used for preparation of various products

Product	Ingredients	Quantity	Recipe
Idli	Blackgram dhal Rice Salt	100g 300g To taste	Overnight soaked *dhal* and rice were ground to paste with water and fermented for 10-12h. Fermented batter was steamed
Dhokla	Benakgam dhal flour Curd Sodium carbonate Oil	100g 1 cup 2g	All the ingredients were mixed to ferment for 10 -12 h and poured into a greased pan and steamed for20min.
Jalebi	Refined wheat flour Curd	1 tsp 60g 60g 110g 100g	Curd and water were mixed with refined wheat flour to make a thin batter and fermented for 10 -12h.The batter was poured through a 0.5cm hole of cloth into hot oil/ghee to fry till golden brown and soaked into sugar syrup
Gulgule	Whole wheat flour Jaggery Sodium carbonate	1/3 tsp 100kg To taste	Ingredients were mixed to get consistency and allowed to stand for 4 - 5 h then fried in oil by adding circular lumps
Kurdai	Wheat spike salt	100g 50g	Wheat grains were soaked in water for 3 days. Then ground and filtered through muslin cloth. The filtrate was collected and cooked in hot water with adding salt up to thick consistency and sun dried for 5 days
Bibdi	Sorghum Wheat salt cumin seed Chilly powder Coriander powder	To taste 2g 4g 2g	Sorghum grains were soaked for 5 days and wheat grain for 3 days. It was ground and filtered separately to stand it for overnight. Grind and filter separately. All the ingredients were mixed and cooked in hot water to bring thick consistency. Then it was placed on cloth for sun drying.

Results and Discussion

A summary of the phytate level as well as the effect of fermentation and processing on phytate levels in food materials is presented in table 2. Fermentation caused significant reduction (47-74%) in phytate content while further processing of the fermented dough into ready to eat food also resulted in significant percent reduction in phytate (68-96%). Fermentation, by lowering pH provides more optimal conditions for enzymatic degradation of the phytate present in cereals in the form of complexes with proteins or polyvalent cations such as iron, zinc, calcium, and magnesium. Such a reduction in phytate may increase the amount of soluble iron, zinc, and calcium several fold (Motarjemi1and Nout, 1996). Similar results were also reported by Selma *et al* (2002) and Mbata *et al* (2009). According to Antony and Chandra (1998) endogenous grain microflora showed a significant reduction of antinutritional components such as phytate, tannins, and phenols.

Table 2 - Phytate content of raw, fermented and processed food product

Phytate mg/100g					% loss of phytate
Sample	**UFB**	**FB**	**PP**	**% loss in fermented dough**	**% loss in processed product**
Steamed					
Idli	1.254± 0.01	0.6213± 0.01	0.5423± 0.04	63.27	71.17
Dhoka	1.886± 0.01	1.412± 0.13	1.112± 0.02	47.4	77.4
Fried					
Jalebi	1.980± 0.01	1.2432± 0.02	1.0216± 0.10	73.68	95.84
Gulgule	1.188± 0.03	0.642± 0.050	0.512± 0.06	54.6	67.6
Sun Dried					
Kurdai	1.616±0.05	0.9851± 0.05	0.7451± 0.02	63.09	87.09
Bibdi	1.2012± 0.02	0.5341± 0.05	0.3532± 0.02	66.71	84.8

UFB- Unfermented batter, FB- Fermented batter, PP- Processed product

Data are presented as mean vales± SD; n = 3

Higher Fe, Zn, Ca and Mg content in fermented foods may be credited to decreased content of phytic acid which has a significant correlation with minerals. Fermented batter had more mineral content than unfermented batter (Table 3). Similar results were reported by Oboh and Elusiyan (2007) in fermented cassava flour and by Abdel *et al* (2009) in fermented butter milk. The increase in mineral content such as Zn, Fe, Ca and Mg of the fermented sample may be as a result of the reduction in the antinutrients content like phytate and further as a result of the processing method. The increase in Fe content after processing might be due to the cooking in Fe utensils and further degradation of phytate (Riat and Sadana, 2009). It is likely that the bioavailability of minerals from these fermented foods is high because of their low phytate content (Samia *et. al.*, 2005). This antinutrional content normally bind with metal and prevent their bioavailability. It may be also due to the reduction in the microbial load which occurs as a result of the decrease of pH as fermentation progresses which makes the environment unconductive for the proliferation of some microorganisms to utilize the mineral availability (Bello and Akinyele, 2007).

Table 3 - Zn, Fe, Ca and Mg content of raw, fermented and processed food product

Sample	Zn (mg/100g)			Fe (mg/100g)			Ca (mg/100g)			Mg (mg/100g)		
	UFB	FB	PP	UFB	FB	PP	UFB	FB	PP	UFB	FB	PP
Steamed												
Idli	0.376	0.389	0.744	1.199	2.095	2.596	4.395	9.790	39.56	5.274	7.912	8.637
Dhoka	0.515	0.524	0.648	0.477	0.916	4.360	8.791	13.186	26.373	2.637	5.274	7.461
Frie												
Jalebi	0.325	0.391	0.417	1.965	2.690	4.410	4.395	13.186	21.978	7.912	11.213	15.098
Gulgule	0.198	0.207	0.528	2.176	2.408	2.832	17.582	21.978	26.373	6.277	10.549	13.186
Sun Dried												
Kurdai	0.438	0.522	0.838	3.658	5.394	7.564	8.792	17.582	18.582	2.754	4.765	7.912
Bibdi	0.521	0.739	0.940	0.524	2.876	5.640	7.654	12.765	14.653	2.765	6.790	8.432

Conclusion

This study showed that fermentation increases the range of minerals removing anti-nutritional factor to make food more nutritious. Fermentation is especially important to the developing world because it is inexpensive and simple method of improving the nutrition of otherwise monotonous cereal products. It does not require expensive equipment or special expertise and can be achieved in a very short period of time.

In view of quality enhancement of food materials by incorporating micronutrients may cost high wherein fermentation seems to be lucrative option requiring very low input.

Fermented foods play an important role in providing food and nutrition security enhancing livelihoods and improving the nutrition and social well being of millions of people around the world, particularly the marginalized and vulnerable and so it should be promoted at the household as safe and nutritionally sound technique.

References

1. Abebe Y, Bogale A, Hambidge K M, Stoecker B J, Bailey K, Gibson R S 2007 Phytate, zinc, iron and calcium content of selected raw and prepared foods consumed in rural Sidama, Southern Ethiopia, and implications for bioavailability. J.of food composition and analysis. 20, 161-168
2. Abdel Moneim E, Sulieman1 Hamid A, Dirar Elamin A, Elkhalifa1 Ali1, Ali O 2009 Effect of fermentation on some chemical components of the Sudanese fermented butter milk, robe. J. Sc. Tech. 10(1), 1-10
3. Allen LH 2000 Ending Hidden Hunger: the History of Micronutrient Deficiency Control. Background Analysis for the World Bank- UNICEF Nutrition Assessment Project report World Bank
4. AOAC 1999 Elements by atomic absorption spectrophotometry. Official methods of analysis. Association of official analytical chemists (Method 40-70). Washington DC, USA

5. Antony U and Chandra TS 1998 Antinutrient Reduction and Enhancement in Protein, Starch, and Mineral Availability in Fermented Flour of Finger Millet (*Eleusine coracana) J. Agric. Food Chem.* 46 (7), 2578–2582
6. Bello B K and Akinyele B J 2007 Effect of fermentation on microbiology and mineral composition of edible mushroom *Termitomyces robustus* (Fries). International Journal of Biological Chemistry.1(4), 237-243
7. Bran JV 2009 The way forward on food and nutrition security. International Food Policy Research Institute (IFPRI) statement for the world summit on food security
8. Chavan J K and Kadam S S 1989 Nutritional improvement of cereals by fermentation. Cr. Rev. in Food Sci. Nutr. 28, 349-400.
9. Cheng K L and Bray R H 1951 Determination of calcium and magnesium in soil and plant material. Soil sci. 72(6), 449-548
10. Battcock Mike and Azam-Ali Sue 1998 Fermented fruits and vegetables, a global perspective. FAO agricultural service bulletin. No.134
11. Food and Agriculture Organization. 2009. State of World Food Insecurity In World Hunger Facts 2009
12. Garcia- EStepa RM, Hernaandez EG, Garcia-Villanora B 1999 Phytic acid content in milled cereal products and breads. Food research international. 32, 217-221
13. Gibson RS, Hotz C 2001 Dietary diversification/modification strategies to enhance micronutrient content and bioavailability of diets in developing countries. Br J Nutr. 85, S159–S166
14. Mbata T I, Ikenebomeh M J, Ezeibe S 2009 Evaluation of mineral content and functional properties of fermented maize (Generic and specific) flour blended with bambara groundnut (*Vigna subterranean* L). African Journal of Food Science. 3(4), 107-112
15. Motarjemi Y and Nout M J R 1996 Food fermentation: a safety and nutritional assessment. Bulletin of the World Health Organization. 74 (6), 553-559
16. Motarjemi Yasmine 2002 Impact of small scale fermentation technology on food safety in developing countries. International Journal of Food Microbiology. 75(3), 213-229
17. Obizoba I C and Attai J V 1991 Effect of soaking, sprouting, fermentation and cooking on the nutrient composition and some antinutritional factors of sorghum (Guineabia) seeds. Plant foods Hum Nutr. 42: 13-23
18. Oboh G and Elusiyan C A 2007 Changes in the nutrient and anti-nutrient content of micro-fungi fermented cassava flour produced from low- and medium-cyanide variety of cassava tubers. African Journal of Biotechnology. 6 (18), 2150-2157
19. Onofiok N, Nnanyelugo D O, Ukwindi B E, 1996 Usage patterns and contributions of fermented foods to the nutrient intakes of low income households in Emene, Nigeria. Plant Foods Hum. Nutr. 49, 199– 211
20. Quisumbing AR, Brown LR, Feldstein HS, Haddad L, Peña C 1995 Women: the key to food security. Food Policy Report, IFPRI, Washington
21. Riat P and Sadana B 2009 Molar ratio as a predictor of zinc, calcium, & iron availability from fermented foods. J Food Sci Technol .46(3), 232-235

22. Rolle R and Satin M 2002 Basic requirements for the transfer of fermentation technologies to developing countries. International Journal of Food Microbiology. 75 18 – 187
23. Ruel Marie and Garrett James 2004 Features of urban food and nutrition security and considerations for successful urban programming In Globalization of food systems in developing countries: impact on food security and nutrition. FAO food and nutrition paper 83, 27-54
24. Samia M, Rahaman A, ElMaki B H, Elfadil E, Babiker, Tinay H A El 2005 Effect of malt pretreatment followed by fermentation on antinutrional factors and HCl extractability of minerals of pearl millet cultivars. J.of Food technology.3(4), 529-534
25. Sandstrom B 1997 Bioavailability of zinc. European journal of clinical nutrition.51,S17-S19
26. Selma H A E, Abdullahi H E T, Nabila E Y, Elsiddig A E E 2002 Effect of natural fermentation on nutritive value and *in vitro* protein digestibility of pearl millet. Food Chemistry 78, 75-79
27. Sharma A and Khetarpaul N 1997 Effect of fermentation with whey on the HCl extractability of minerals from rice-dehulled blackgram blends. J. Agric. Food Chem. 45, 2258-2261
28. Shetty P 2009 Incorporating nutritional considerations when addressing food insecurity. Food security.: 431-440.
29. Towo E, Matuschek E, Svanberg U 2006 Fermentation and enzyme treatment of tannin sorghum gruels: effects on phenolic compounds, phytate and *in vitro* accessible iron. Food Chem 94, 369-376.
30. United Nations Standing Committee on Nutrition: 2004 Fifth Report on the World Nutrition Situation – Nutrition for Improved Development Outcomes. United Nations.
31. Weingartner L 2005 The concept of food and nutrition security. In: Achieving food and nutrition security: actions to meet the global challenge. Klennert K (ed).International Weiterbildung und Entwicklung gGmbH, Germany
32. World Bank 2008 Understanding Poverty website. In World Hunger Facts 2009.

26

The Global Crisis: Causes and Remedies

Anisha A. Nandode

The Global Food Crisis

The global financial crisis drew international attention away from the food crisis, but this continues to fester and even grow. When the global food crisis first hit international headlines in 2008, international bureaucrats referred to the current problems in the world food situation as "a silent tsunami", but the truth is that it was not a sudden and unexpected crisis: the signs have been around for some time now and it could easily have been seen to be coming. Even so, its impact has been powerful and already quite devastating, as food shortages and high prices of food have adversely affected billions of people, especially the poor in the developing world.

It is also very much a man-made crisis, resulting not so much from ineluctable forces of global supply and demand as from the market-oriented and liberalizing policies adopted by choice or compulsion in almost all countries. These policies have either neglected agriculture or allowed shifts in global prices to determine both cropping patterns and the viability of farming, and also generated greater possibilities of speculative activity in food items. It is also clear that the global food crisis is not something that can be treated as discrete and separate from the global financial crisis. On the contrary it has been intimately connected with it, particularly through the impact of financial speculation on world trade prices of food.

This is not to deny the undoubted role of other real economy factors in affecting the global food situation. While demand-supply imbalances have been touted as reasons, this is largely unjustified given that there has been hardly any change in the world demand for food in the past three years. In particular, the claim that food grain prices have soared because of more demand from China and India as their GDP increases, is completely invalid, since both aggregate and per capita consumption of grain have actually fallen in both countries.

Two policy factors affecting global food supply require special note. The first is the biofuel factor: the impact of both oil prices and government policies in the US, Europe, Brazil and elsewhere that have promoted biofuels as an alternative to petroleum. This has led to significant shifts in acreage to the cultivation of crops that can produce biofuels, and diversion of such output to fuel production. For example, in 2007 the US diverted more than 30 per cent of its maize production, Brazil used half of its sugar cane production and the European Union used the greater part of its vegetable oil seeds production as well as imported vegetable oils, to make biofuel. In addition to diverting corn output into non-food use, this has also reduced acreage for other crops and has naturally reduced the available land for producing food.

The second factor is the policy neglect of agriculture over the past two decades, the impact of which is finally being felt. The prolonged agrarian crisis in many parts of the developing world has been largely a policy-determined crisis. Inappropriate policies have several aspects, but they all result from the basic neo-liberal open market-oriented framework that has governed economic policy making in most countries over the past two decades. One major element has been the lack of public investment in agriculture and in agricultural research. This has been associated with low to poor yield increases, especially in tropical agriculture, and falling productivity of land. Greater trade openness and market orientation of farmers have led to shifts in acreage from traditional food crops that were typically better suited to the ecological conditions and the knowledge and resources of farmers, to cash crops that have increasingly relied on purchased inputs.

But at the same time, both public provision of different inputs for cultivation and government regulation of private input provision have been progressively reduced, leaving farmers to the mercy of large seed and fertilizer companies, input dealers. As a result, prices for seeds, fertilizers and pesticides have increased quite sharply.

The lack of attention to relevant agricultural research and extension by public bodies has denied farmers access to necessary knowledge. It has also been associated with other problems such as the excessive use of ground water in cultivation; inadequate attention to preserving or regenerating land and soil quality; the over-use of chemical inputs that have long run implications for both safety and productivity. Similarly, the ecological implications of both pollution and climate change, including desertification and loss of cultivable land, are issues that have been highlighted by analysts but largely ignored by policy makers in most countries. Reversing these processes is possible, and of course essential. But it will take time, and also will require not only substantial public investment but also major changes in the orientation and understanding of policy makers.

All this mean that the number of hungry people actually increased for the world as a whole, and particularly for certain developing regions. Far from halving, or even decreasing, the number of malnourished people globally increased by more than 50 million between the early 1990s and mid-2000s.

This was entirely because of increasing hunger in the developing world, as the numbers declined in developed countries. East and Southeast Asia also showed good performance in terms of falling numbers of malnourished people, but such numbers increased quite sharply in South Asia (by 50 million) and Sub-Saharan Africa (by 44 million). The surprise is that the growing prevalence of hunger and food insecurity was associated with relatively high GDP growth in several regions, such as India and countries in Latin America. The contrast with East and Southeast Asia is a stark one, and points to the role of public policy in ensuring that aggregate income growth translates into better provision of basic needs such as food for the general population.

While this was the state before the global economic crisis, the crisis obviously made matters much worse. The intensity of the food crisis that hit many developing countries from 2008 was particularly on account of the very sharp global volatility in food prices. Globally, the prices of many basic food commodities had not risen faster for more than three decades. In fact, even in recent years, food prices internationally had shown only a modest increase until early 2007. But thereafter they zoomed up, with around 40 per cent increase in world food prices over 2007. This trend accelerated in the first few months of 2008, but then the subsequent period has been marked by extreme price volatility. Wheat prices increased by 46 per cent in the short period between 10 January and 26 February, fell by as much by 19 May, increased again but to a lesser extent (by only 21 per cent) until a minor peak in early June, and then have been falling again, albeit with fluctuations. Other food grain prices have followed a similar pattern. Rice prices increased by nearly 150 per cent in the first 100 days of this year, and then fell to just above the level at the start of the year.

Thus international commodity markets increasingly began to develop many of the features of financial markets, in that they became prone to information asymmetries and associated tendencies to be led by a small number of large players. Far from being 'efficient markets' in the sense hoped for by mainstream theory, they allowed for inherently 'wrong' signaling devices to become very effective in determining and manipulating market behavior. The result was the excessive volatility displayed by important commodities over 2008 – not only the food grains and crops mentioned here, but also minerals and oil. Such volatility had very adverse effects on both cultivators and consumers of food. This was not only because it sent out confusing, misleading and often completely wrong price signals to farmers that caused over sowing in some phases and under cultivation in others. In addition, it turns out that the pass through of global prices was extremely high in developing countries in the phase of rising prices, in that domestic food prices tended to rise as global prices increased, even if not to the same extent. However, the reverse tendency has not been evident in the subsequent phase as global trade prices have fallen. So both cultivators and food consumers appear to have lost in this phase of extreme price instability, with the only gainers from this process therefore being the financial intermediaries who were able to profit from rapidly changing prices.

In many developing countries food prices have remained high and even continued to increase, despite various policy measures taken by governments to limit the impact of high international prices on domestic markets. As noted by FAO (2008) 'In countries where prices have declined the reductions have been modest compared to those in export markets and, generally, national cereal prices remain above their levels of a year earlier.

Persistent high food prices in the developing world continue to affect access to food of large numbers of vulnerable population in both urban and rural areas.' Therefore many developing countries in which widespread and persistent hunger was already a problem, such as India, have experienced significant increases in the prices of staple foods in the past two years, and domestic food prices have not declined even after global trade prices started falling.

Ensuring Food Security in India

It is not surprising that questions of food security and the right to food have become such urgent political issues in India today. Rapid aggregate income growth over the past two decades has not addressed the basic issue of ensuring the food security of the population. Instead, nutrition indicators have stagnated and per capita calorie consumption has actually declined, suggesting that the problem of hunger may have got worse rather than better.

Consider the evidence on nutritional outcomes from the most recent National Family Health Survey (NFHS) conducted in 2005-06. According to this, 46 per cent of children below 3 years are underweight; 33 per cent of women and 28 per cent of men have Body Mass Index (BMI) below normal; 79 per cent of children aged 6-35 months have anaemia, as do 56 per cent of married women aged 15-49 years and 24 per cent of similar men; 58 per cent of pregnant women have anaemia. The national averages mask locational differences: all these indicators are much worse in rural India.

Further, these indicators have scarcely changed, or have changed very little, since the previous NFHS in 1998-99. In terms of calorie consumption the picture is even worse. According to the National Sample Survey Organization (NSSO) large survey of 2004-05, the average daily intake of calories of the rural population has dropped by 106 Kcal (4.9 per cent) from 2153 Kcal to 2047 Kcal from 1993-94 to 2004-05 and by 51 Kcal (2.5 per cent) from 2071 to 2020 Kcal in urban areas. The average daily intake of protein by the Indian population decreased from 60.2 to 57 grams in rural India between 1993-94 and 2004-05 and remained stable at around 57 grams in the urban areas during the same period.

The all India averages do not capture the wide variation across states and even within states. For example the India State Hunger Index 2008 (brought out by the International Food Policy Research Institute) shows very large differences across 17 major states, ranging from 13.6 for Punjab to 30.9 for Madhya Pradesh. If these states could be compared to countries in the Global Hunger Index rankings, some states in India have index scores at the bottom: Bihar and Jharkhand rank lower than Zimbabwe and Haiti, and Madhya Pradesh falls between Ethiopia and Chad.

State Hunger Index, 2007

State	Prevalence of calorie undernouri-shment (%)	Proportion of underweight children < 5 years (%)	Under-five mortality rate (%)	Hunger Index Score	Hunger Index Rank
Punjab	11.1	24.6	5.2	13.63	1
Kerala	28.6	22.7	1.6	17.63	2
Andhra Pradesh	19.6	32.7	6.3	19.53	3
Assam	14.6	36.4	8.5	19.83	4
Haryana	15.1	39.7	5.2	20.00	5
Tamil Nadu	29.1	30.0	3.5	20.87	6
Rajasthan	14.0	40.4	8.5	20.97	7
West Bengal	18.5	38.5	5.9	20.97	7
Uttar Pradesh	14.5	42.3	9.6	22.13	9
Maharashtra	27.0	36.7	4.7	22.80	10
Karnataka	28.1	37.6	5.5	23.73	11
Orissa	21.4	40.9	9.1	23.80	12
Gujarat	23.3	44.7	6.1	24.70	13
Chhattisgarh	23.3	47.6	9.0	26.63	14
Bihar	17.3	56.1	8.5	27.30	15
Jharkhand	19.6	57.1	9.3	28.67	16
Madhya Pradesh	23.4	59.8	9.4	30.87	17
India	**20.0**	**42.5**	**7.4**	**23.30**	
China				7.1	
Vietnam				12.6	
Sri Lanka				15.0	
Nepal				20.6	
Pakistan				21.7	
Bangladesh				25.2	
Zimbabwe				23.8	

Source: India State Hunger Index, IFPRI 2008

Note: The calorie undernourishment indicator is based on a very low cut-off of 1632 kcals per person per day, to allow comparison with the Global Hunger Index. By contrast, the FAO assumes 1800 kcal per person per day to be the minimum below which there is moderate or severe undernourishment.

The table gives some idea of the variation among major states and also shows how India is places as a whole in relation to other Asian countries. It is evident that India's performance with respect to hunger is abysmal particularly in relation to other large developing countries like China, but even in comparison to the rest of South Asia, with only

Bangladesh having a higher value of the index. Indeed, India's index value is close to that of Zimbabwe, a country which is in the throes of severe hyperinflation and collapse of domestic food markets. Within India, some of the supposedly richest states with most rapid recent growth of GDP, such as Maharashtra, Karnataka and Gujarat, perform very poorly on the hunger index, clearly much worse than Kerala but even worse than Assam. West Bengal is close to the middle among the major states, and slightly below the national average in terms of the hunger index, which means that it is an important policy concern also within this state.

The recent rise in food prices in India is likely to have made matters much worse, and the effects of the global crisis on employment and livelihoods within the country are likely to cause further deterioration in people's access to food. Clearly, therefore, food security is currently one of the most important policy areas, and demands stressing a rights-based approach to public food strategy have gained ground. This is what underlies the current discussion around the legislation on the right to food, which has been put in the 100-day agenda of this UPA government.

The most loose definition of food security is one in which the population does not live in hunger or fear of starvation. But recent definitions have been more stringent. According to the Food and Agriculture Organization (FAO), food security in a particular society exists "when all people, at all times, have access to sufficient, safe and nutritious food to meet their dietary needs and food preferences for an active and healthy life."

It is evident that genuine food security among a population requires a wide range of features all or many of which are associated with the need for some public intervention. Ensuring adequate supplies of food requires increases in agricultural productivity, possibly changes in cropping patterns, and certainly the sustained viability of cultivation, all of would be necessary at both local and national levels. Making sure that food can be accessed by all the people requires that they have the purchasing power to buy the necessary food, which in turn means that employment, remuneration and livelihood issues are important. Social discrimination and exclusion still play unfortunately large roles in determining both livelihood and access to food by different social categories, and this too needs to be reckoned with. Malnourishment is closely linked to poor sanitation and other unhealthy practices, so that the provision of clean drinking water, sanitation and access to other basic amenities, as well as knowledge about correct or desirable eating habits, are all necessary.

To begin with, national food security requires increasing the domestic production of food, so that the country is not dependent upon imports. This is not simply a matter of preferred practice, but a policy imperative since it has huge strategic implications. India is a large country in most world food markets, in that its entry especially as an importer can dramatically affect global trade prices. (For example, India's current production of rice is more than six times the total amount of rice traded in world markets.) Even the anticipation of more imports by India can cause world trade prices to rise. When this effect is combined with that of the speculative forces described earlier, the result can be extremely adverse. In any case, the extreme volatility of global food prices noted earlier makes it difficult and undesirable to base a national food security policy on even partial import dependence.

Also, it is well known that food can be used as a strategic weapon in geopolitical terms. Therefore the first priority of a national food policy must be to increase domestic food production through improved agricultural productivity. This requires making cultivation financially viable as well as more productive, through a range of measures such as those described earlier. A policy of providing minimum support prices that reach all farmers is an essential part of this, and should be part of a voluntary rather than forced system of public procurement.

While it is important for the government to be aware of the need for a multi-pronged approach to the problem that has to extend beyond a legal promise if it is to be successful. Even so, a legal commitment to public food distribution can also play a role in extending and improving public food delivery so that it reaches all the people. Public procurement has to be combined with public distribution. A law that ensures universal food access and assigns responsibility and culpability would force governments at both central and state levels to take up the entire gamut of issues, which relate not just to actual food distribution but also to its production and patterns of consumption, so as to eventually ensure genuine food security.

The key point here is that such a law *must guarantee universal access*. Yet the version of the proposed "Right to Food" bill that has been circulated by the central government to the states is a travesty of the original promise, and a negation of the spirit of ensuring genuine food security. While the Bill is still under discussion, the Note that has been sent to state governments makes several suggestions that are quite unacceptable, such as confining the provisions to the Below Poverty Line population (which itself is to be pruned according to central estimates rather than relying on states' own estimates) and ensuring only 25 kg per month per household instead of the current 35 kg.

And now the Food and Agriculture Minister has declared that in view of the drought, even this pathetic attempt at legal intervention has to be postponed for a year. Yet it is precisely in drought conditions, when both production and livelihoods are affected, that it is most important to ensure that food consumption among the population is maintained through public intervention.

There are many reasons why targeted schemes for BPL, and this one in particular, are unlikely to work. Most significant of all, there are the well known errors inherent in targeting, of unjustified exclusion of the genuinely poor and unwarranted inclusion of the non-poor. These are not simply mistakes that can occur in any administrative scheme, they are inbuilt into systems that try to provide scarce goods to one section of any population. In hierarchical and discriminatory societies like India, where social and economic power is unequally distributed, it requires no imagination to realise that making a scarce good (cheap food) supposedly available only to the poor is one of the easiest ways to reduce their access.

This is why all successful programmers of public food distribution, across societies, have been those that have gone in for universal or near universal access. This provides economies of scale; it reduces the transaction costs and administrative hassles involved in ascertaining the target group and making sure it reaches them; it allows for better public provision because even the better off groups with more political voice have a stake in making sure it works well; it generates greater stability in government plans for ensuring food production and procurement.

Even among the states of India, those states that have a better record of public food distribution are those that have gone in for near-universal access. Kerala, Tamil Nadu and Andhra Pradesh all have defined BPL in such an inclusive way that the vast majority of the population is included, which makes their schemes close to universal.

The notion that a universal scheme that provides subsidized food to all households is too expensive is not tenable either. Consider the maximal possible estimate of such spending. If all households in the country are provided 35 kg of food grain per month that would come to around 90 million tones. At current levels of subsidy this would cost around Rs 120,000 crore. This may seem like a lot, but the current food subsidy already amounts to around Rs 50,000 crore, so this is an additional Rs 70,000 crore – or around 1.5 per cent of GDP.

Surely this is not too much to allocate to ensure that no one goes hungry in what should be a civilized society? In any case, compare the amount of Rs 70,000 with the huge amounts (nearly Rs 300,000 crore) that have been given away as tax benefits and other concessions to corporate over the past year, and it becomes a trivial amount.

Conclusion

Any programme of national food security must be combined with a concentrated focus on improving food grain production in the country, so that we are not dependent upon imports in a volatile global market. This requires much more attention to the requirements of farmers, and speedy implementation of the many reforms that have already been suggested by the Farmers' Commission to improve the productivity and financial viability of farming, particularly of food crops.

To make this successful it is also necessary to avoid instability in domestic prices of food grain and curb speculative tendencies. This does not simply mean cracking down on hoarders, which is part of the official publicity around any period of price rise. It also requires preventing speculative activity in futures markets, which means that there must be a ban on futures markets in all essential commodities.

These are all necessary and also eminently doable measures – but only if the central government is actually serious about ensuring real food security on the country. And such seriousness can only be brought about by mass mobilisation in favour of such demands.

References

1. Hanumantha Rao. C. H – Agriculture, Food Security, Poverty and Environment.
2. Chaturvedi Pradeep – Food Security in South Asia.
3. National Food Security Mission- http://nfsm.gov.in
4. Food Corporation of India- http://fciweb.nic.in

27

Role of Food Processing in Securing Food Security

V.R. Parate, S.R. Thorat and K.P. Dandge

Introduction

According to United Nation's Food and Agriculture Organization (FAO) food security exists when all people, at all times, have physical and economic access to sufficient, safe and nutritious food to meet their dietary needs and food preferences for an active and healthy life. As per United States Department of Agriculture (USDA) the food security for a household means access by all members at all times to enough food for an active, healthy life. A household is considered food secure when its occupants do not live in hunger or fear of starvation. Food security thus, refers to the availability of food and one's access to it. A condition in which people lack basic food intake to provide them with the energy and nutrients for fully productive lives is called food insecurity (Food security, 2009). Two billion people of the world lack food security. The natural effect of food insecurity is hunger and malnutrition, the biggest challenges of twenty first century due to which many people die every year worldwide. The world is facing a hunger challenge unlike anything it has seen in the past 50 years (Bread for the World, 2009). Every 3.6 seconds someone dies of hunger (The world hunger problem: Facts, figures and statistics, 2009). The latest UN report on hunger says that the current global economic crisis has triggered a spike in world hunger which has reached the highest level in four decades. World Summit on Food Security, 2009 will remain in the history like the year of the shame as it reported biggest hunger report in world history. Currently more than 1,000,000,000 peoples suffer from hunger globally from which 642,000,000 people are in Asia-Pacific zone, 265,000,000 in Africa, 53,000,000 in South America and 15,000,000 in developed countries (Chinadaily BBC, 2009). India, the second most populous country in the world has 30 million people living in hunger which is nearly half the world's hungry people. Africa and the rest of Asia together have approximately 40%, and the remaining hungry people are found in Latin America and other parts of the world. Some one billion people of world are undernourished which is greater than any time since 1970. One in twelve people worldwide is malnourished, including 160 million children under the age of 5 and is implicated in more than half of all child deaths worldwide (United Nations, 2009). In India 46% of children are malnourished (BBC News, 2009). Food security is a complex topic, standing at the intersection of many disciplines. It is a difficult sustainable development issue, linked to health through malnutrition, but also to sustainable economic development, environment, and trade.The various factors contributing to food insecurity are poverty, global water crises, land degradation, loss of agricultural land to residential and industrial development, climate change, droughts and floods, swings in the global economy that affect food prices and spikes in the price of oil that increase transportation costs. Poverty is major cause for food insecurity. Starving or undernourished people have no incomes and can't care for their families. Farming is the only or primary source of income for more than three-quarters of the worlds poor. In developing countries, often 70% or more of the population lives in rural areas and is depending upon farming. Agriculture remains the largest employment sector in most developing countries and international agriculture agreements are crucial to a country's food security. Failures of farming in many parts of the world have a powerful impact on food security (Goldstein, 2009; World Health Organization, 2009).

Food Security through Food Processing

Food production is many times wrongly concluded for food insecurity. On the contrary growth in global food production has been greater than the global population growth. The cause of food insecurity is not insufficient production of food as more than enough food is produced to feed a healthy population worldwide. According to the World Resources Institute, global per capita food production has been increasing substantially for the past several decades. There is enough food in the world to feed everyone adequately, the problem is distribution and access to food. There are 6.6 billion people in the world and the amount of food the world produce can feed 12 billion people. But still one billion people are starving today. One of the reasons behind this is the wastage of tremendous quantities of food during production, storage and transport as most food items are perishable in nature that spoil readily unless special care is taken or preservative methods are used (Environment News Services, 2009). In the UK, 6.7 million tones of food amounts to £10.2 billion are wasted each year. In United States every year more than 350 billion pounds of edible food are available for human consumption from which nearly 100 billion pounds are lost by retailers, restaurants and consumers (The Daily Star , 2009). It is now a time to think more about the wastage of food as one of the effective solution to the problem of food insecurity. One way of dealing with food waste is to reduce its creation. The food wastage is mainly due to lack of post-harvest infrastructure such as cold chain facilities, transportation and proper storage facilities, etc. The loss due to wastages can be reduced by a developed food processing industry, strengthening of the post-harvest infrastructure and filling the gaps in the supply chain (Gleez, 2009). The role of food processing is very important in securing food security as it helps to preserve food for long time without spoilage and reduce food wastage. Food processing includes the set of methods and techniques which transform raw ingredients into food, modify food product into another form, pack and preserve food. Food preservation is the prevention of food from spoilage so as to keep the food in eatable condition for long time. Food processing typically takes clean, harvested crops or slaughtered and butchered animal components and uses these to produce attractive, marketable and often long shelf-life food products (Food preservation, 2009).

Food Processing Techniques

Food is said to be spoiled when it develops off smell, taste and become unfit for consumption. Insects, microorganism activity and growth, enzymatic action, chemical reactions and physical changes are the causes of food spoilage. In food processing all these factors responsible for spoilage is controlled or eliminated from food through various food preservation techniques to improve the shelf life of food (Frazier & Westhoff, Food Microbiology, 1988). Common food processing techniques include removal of unwanted outer layers such as potato peeling, chopping or slicing, e.g., diced carrots, liquefaction such as production of fruit juice, fermentation, e.g., in beer breweries, emulsification, cooking (boiling, roasting, frying, steaming), baking, mixing, addition of gas such as air entrainment for bread or gasification of soft drinks, drying, pasteurization, packaging In accomplishing the preservation of foods by various methods, the following principles are involved:

1. Prevention or delay of microbial decomposition
   - By keeping out microorganisms (Asepsis)
   - By removal of microorganisms (Filtration)
   - By hindering the growth and activity of microorganisms: by low temperature (chilling, freezing, refrigeration), drying, anaerobic conditions (vacuum packaging, modified atmosphere packaging, canning), or chemicals (food preservatives)
   - By killing the microorganisms: by heat (pasteurization, sterilization) or radiation (ultraviolet irradiation, gamma rays)
2. Prevention or delay of self decomposition of the food
   - By destruction or inactivation of food enzymes: by blanching
   - By prevention or delay of purely chemical reactions: prevention of oxidation by means of antioxidants
3. Prevention of damage because of insects, animals, mechanical causes

Freezing or solidification is the process in which a liquid turns into a solid when cold enough. Freezing is a common method of food preservation which retard chemical reactions, action of food enzymes and slows down or stop the growth and activity of microorganisms in food and also makes water less available for bacterial growth. The temperature used in freezing is -18^{0}C or below (Freezing, 2009). Drying is a method of food preservation that works by removing water from the food. Bacteria and microorganisms within the food need the water in the food to grow, but drying effectively prevents them from surviving in the food by removing water from the food. It also creates a hard outer-layer, helping to stop micro-organisms from entering the food. The food can be dried by using bed dryers, fluidized bed dryers, freeze drying, shelf dryers, spray drying, sunlight, commercial food dehydrators and household oven. Water is usually removed by evaporation with the help of air drying, sun drying, smoking or wind drying, but in the case of freeze-drying food is first frozen and then water is removed by sublimation (Drying (food), 2009). Pasteurization is a heat treatment that kills part but not all the microorganisms presents and usually involves the application of temperatures below 100^{0}C. It is not intended to kill all pathogenic micro-organisms in the food instead, it aims to reduce the number of viable pathogens so they are unlikely to cause disease. Heating may be by means of steam, hot water, dry heat or electric current and the product is cooled promptly after the heat treatment. Pasteurization is generally used for treating milk and is achieved by heating milk at 63^{0}C for 30 minutes known as Low Temperature Long Time (LTLT) treatment or at 72^{0}C for 15 second known as High Temperature Short Time (HTST) treatment. Ultra-high temperature (UHT) processing holds the milk at a temperature of 138°C (280°F) for a fraction of a second (Pasteurization, 2009). Act of killing all the microorganisms from food is known as sterilization and can be achieved through application of heat, chemicals, irradiation, high pressure or filtration (Sterilization, 2009; Sterilization (microbiology), 2009). Food irradiation is the process of exposing food to ionizing radiation to destroy microorganisms, bacteria, viruses, or insects that might be present in the food (Food irradiation, 2009). The food packaging prevents air, microorganisms from entering inside and in this way preserve food. Vacuum packing is commonly used for long-term storage of dry foods such as cereals, nuts, cured meats, cheese, smoked fish, coffee and short term storage of fresh foods such as vegetables, meats, and liquids such as soups. Vacuum packed food can extend its life by up to 3-5 times. Vacuum packaging of delicate food items like potato chips can be done by using an inert gas kit, typically available on chamber vacuum sealers (Vacuum packing, 2009). Canning is a method of preserving food in which the food is processed and sealed in an airtight container generally in a tin can. Canning involves cooking food, sealing it in sterile cans or jars, and boiling the containers to kill or weaken any remaining bacteria (Canning, 2009).

Current Status of Food Security in India

In India also the cause of food insecurity is not production of agriculture product. India is now most rich endowed agricultural nation in Asia as a result of the Green Revolution. India is third largest producer of agricultural commodity in the world producing 601 million tonnes per annum next to China and US producing 856 million tones and 608 million tonnes respectively. India has the potential to become top most nation in the world in food production as it has every thing for the same. India is currently the world's second largest country in population and man power with 1.15 billion people (Rosenberg, 2009) and has land area of 2.97 millions sq.km. Also India has the second largest area of arable land in the world (184 million hectares) which is more than China and one tenth of world's arable land. It also has 56 million hectares of irrigated land which is one fifth of world's irrigated land and cost line of 8000 km which is known for vast marine wealth (www.indemblao.nic.in). It has second highest livestock population in the world, accounting for the world's 50% of the buffaloes, 17% of goat and 43% of sheep. India has retained its number one position as world's largest milk producing country by pushing the United States to second position. Country's output now covers 100 million tones which is around 15% of global milk production and is valued at nearly two lakh crore rupees. India is also the world's largest producer of pulses with annual production of 15 million tonnes. India and China rank as the largest and second largest, respectively, in tea production as well as consumption. Together they account for around half of world's tea production. India's current production of tea is 930 million kg (India Brand Equity Foundation, 2009). India with its current production of around 32 million MT of fruit, accounts for about 8% of the world's fruit production, rank second in the world after Brazil. India is also second largest producer of vegetables in the world (next to China) and accounts for about 15% of the world's production of vegetables. The current production level is over 71 million MT and the total area under vegetable cultivation is around 6.2 million hectares which is about 3% of the total area under cultivation in the country (Fruits & vegetable, 2009). The share of India in world's production of fruits and vegetables are 41% of mango, 36% green peas, 30% of cauliflower, 24% of cashew nut, 23% of banana and 10% of onion. Present global position of India in the production of wheat, rice and sugarcane is second with production of 78, 100 and 290 million tonnes respectively (Thaindan News, 2009; CommodityOnline, 2009; Rediff.com Business, 2009). India is a leading producer of oilseeds after China and US, contributing 7-8% of world oilseed production and is estimated to account for around 6% of the world's production of edible oils (Edible Oil, 2009). India today is the third largest fish producing country in the world, with a total production of 7.13 million tonnes fish (NACA, 2009). Poultry is one of the fastest growing segments of the agricultural sector in India today. While the production of agricultural crops has been rising at a rate of 1.5 to 2% per annum that of eggs and broilers has been rising at a rate of 8 to 10% per annum. As a result, India is now the world's fifth largest egg producer and the eighteenth largest producer of broilers (FAO, 2009). India produces about 4.9 million tonnes of meat annually valued at US $ 4,600 millions and is placed at No. 8 position in the world (Indian Meat Industry Prospective, 2009). These advantages being leveraged, for India to be a leading food supplier to the world. India is producing enough food to feed its population, but still facing a problem of food security, hunger and malnutrition. As discussed earlier 46% of children in India are malnourished and India is a home of world's 50% hunger people.

Food Processing: A way to secure food security in India

There may be various factors contributing to food insecurity of Indian, but the most important factor drawing continuous attention is the wastage of food. Fresh estimate from the ministry of India food processing is showing that agriculture food items worth of Rs 58,000 crore (Rs 580 billion) get wasted in the country every year. Lack of adequate post-harvest infrastructure, cold chains, transportation proper storage, and processing facilities results spoilage of food and is thrown as waste. As concluded earlier food wastage can be minimized if processed. It is surprising that despite being a major food producer in the world the share of India in food processing is only 6% compared to 30% in Thailand, 40% in China, 70% in Brazil and France, 78% in Philippines, 80% in Malaysia and USA. By international comparison the level of processing in India is very less as compare to 60-80% in developed countries and over 30% even in most other Asian and Latin American countries. Value addition to agriculture produce in India is just 20%. Also India's share in the world food trade is less than 2% (How much food does India waste?, 2009; IANS, 2009). In spite of being the world's largest milk producer, India's milk processing industry is not very large. Only 12-13%

of milk is delivered to dairies as against the world average of 70%. In certain countries like New Zealand almost 98% of milk production is processed. Total level of milk processing in India is around 35%, with the organized dairy industry accounting for 13% of the milk produced while the rest of the milk is either consumed at farm level for drinking, or sold as fresh, non-pasteurized milk through unorganized channels for making sweets or other traditional products. Dairy Cooperatives account for the major share of processed liquid milk marketed in the India. Milk is processed and marketed by 170 Milk Producers' Cooperative Unions, which federate into 15 State Cooperative Milk Marketing Federations (Management Paradise.com, 2009). Processing level of fruits and vegetables in India is 2.2% (Organized: 1.3%, Unorganized: 0.8), meat 21% and poultry 6% and marine product is 21% (Organized: 8%, Unorganized: 15%) (J.S.Marketing, 2006). The fruits and vegetable processing industry is highly decentralized, and a large number of units are in the cottage / household and small scale sector, having small capacities of up to 250 tones/annum. However, the growth rates have been extensively higher for frozen fruits & vegetables (121%) and dehydrated fruits & vegetables (24%). Only about 1% of the total meat is converted into value added products like sausages, ham, bacon, kababs, meat balls, etc. The country produces about 450 million broilers and 30 billion eggs annually. The poultry ***meat processing*** industry is still in its nascent stage, around 97% of poultry ***meat*** in ***India*** is consumed in the fresh form (Indian Industry Profiles, 2009). Processing of marine produce into canned and frozen forms is carried out almost entirely for the export market. Indian rice, especially Basmati rice, has gained international recognition, and is a premium export product. Branded grains as well as grain processing is now gaining popularity. Flour mills in the country convert about 10.5 millions tones of wheat into wheat products. More than 10,000 pulse mills milling about 75% of total pulse produced. According to estimates, there are approximately 2.5 lakh ghanis and kolus (animal operated oil expellers), 50,000 mechanical oil expellers, 15,500 oil mills, 725 solvent extraction plants, 300 oil refineries and over 175 hydrogenated vegetable oil plants. India is the third largest market for alcoholic beverages in the world. Around 56 units are manufacturing beer under license from the Government of India. There are around 60,000 bakeries, 20,000 traditional food units and several pasta food units. Bread and biscuits constitute the largest segment of consumer foods with an annual production is around 4.00 million tones. More than 20 units engaged in the manufacture of cocoa products like chocolates, drinking chocolate, cocoa butter substitutes, cocoa based malted milk foods. Aerated soft drinks industry in India comprises over 100 plants and provides direct and indirect employment to over 125,000 employees.

The food processing industry in India is a sunrise sector that has gained prominence in recent years. Although the Indian food processing industry is presently at nascent level but still holds tremendous potential to grow. Availability of raw materials, changing lifestyles and relaxation in policies, vast network of manufacturing facilities all over the country and vast domestic market has given a considerable push to the industry's growth. This sector is among the few that serves as a vital link between the agriculture and industrial segments of the economy. Strengthening this link is of critical importance to improve the value of agricultural, commercialization of agriculture produce, ensure remunerative prices to farmers, generates employment and at the same time creates favourable demand for Indian agricultural products in the world market. A thrust to the food processing sector implies significant development in the agriculture sector and ensures value addition to it. The Indian food processing industry is presently growing at 14% against 6-7% growth in year 2003-04 and has the potential to be an industry driver that can transform the rural economy which is very essential to overcome food insecurity problem. Food security in India can be ensured by empowering the farmers to sow and harvest plentiful crops, effectively care for livestock or catch fish and then ensuring that the food they produce reaches people most in need. There is urgent need to divert attention towards the food processing sector of India as a possible solution to the problem of food insecurity. Improved technologies to promote the shelf life of vegetables and fruits, better packaging machinery and cold storage systems are just some of the areas where more work is required to be done. A vision, strategy and action plan has also been finalized for giving boost to growth of food processing sector. Considering the importance of food processing industries in securing food security the Ministry of Food Processing Industries India has adopted the "Vision 2015". The objective is to increase level of processing of perishable food from 6% to 20%, value addition from 20% to 35% and share in global food trade from 1.6% to 3%. The level of processing for fruits and vegetables is envisaged to increase from the present 2.2% to 10% in 2010 and 15% in 2015 (MFPI India, 2009).

Conclusion

It is concluded that the global food security can be achieved to some extent if wastage of food is minimized during production, storage and transport using various food processing techniques. There is need to promote food processing sector of India as a possible solution to the problem of food insecurity as India is facing a problem of food wastage in spite the potential to become the top producer of food in the world and the largest supplier of food to the world.

References

1. BBC News. (2009 , December 14). *Mixed messages in hunger report*. Retrieved December 17, 2009, from BBC News: http://news.bbc.co.uk/2/hi/in_depth/8309979.stm
2. Bread for the World. (2009, December 10). *About the Report :: Bread for the World :: Have Faith. End Hunger.* Retrieved December 18, 2009, from www.bread.org :
3. http://www.bread.org/learn/hunger-reports/
4. *Canning.* (2009, December 12). Retrieved December 19, 2009, from Wikipedia, the free encyclopedia: http://en.wikipedia.org/wiki/Canning
5. Chinadaily BBC. (2009, December 7). *The shameful hunger record of the world.* Retrieved December 16, 2009, from Chinadaily BBC:
6. http://bbs.chinadaily.com.cn/viewthread.php?tid=652959
7. CommodityOnline. (2009, December 12). *India sugarcane output dips by 17 percent.* Retrieved December 19, 2009, from www.commodityonline.com:
8. http://www.commodityonline.com/news/India-sugarcane-output-dips-by-17-percent-17735-3-1.html

9. *Drying (food)*. (2009, November 24). Retrieved December 19, 2009, from Wikipedia, the free encyclopedia: http://en.wikipedia.org/wiki/Drying_(food)
10. *Edible Oil*. (2009, December 9). Retrieved December 19, 2009, from www.oppapers.com: http://www.oppapers.com/essays/Edible-Oil/177706
11. Environment News Services. (2009, December 13). *Half of All Food Produced Worldwide is Wasted*. Retrieved December 15, 2009, from www.ens-newswire.com: http://www.ens-newswire.com/ens/aug2008/2008-08-22-01.asp
12. FAO. (2009, December 12). *I. Poultry Industry in India(58)*. Retrieved December 19, 2009, from www.fao.org:
13. http://www.fao.org/WAIRDOCS/LEAD/X6170E/x6170e2k.htm
14. *Food irradiation*. (2009, December 14). Retrieved December 19, 2009, from Wikipedia, the free encyclopedia: http://en.wikipedia.org/wiki/Food_irradiation
15. *Food preservation*. (2009, December 18). Retrieved December 19, 2009, from Wikipedia, the free encyclopedia: http://en.wikipedia.org/wiki/Food_preservation
16. *Food security*. (2009 , December 17). Retrieved December 18, 2009, from Wikipedia, the free encyclopedia:
17. http://en.wikipedia.org/w/index.php?title=Food_security&oldid=332307890
18. Frazier, W. C., & Westhoff, D. C. (1988). *Food Microbiology*. Singapore: McGraw-Hill Book Co.
19. *Freezing*. (2009 , December 17). Retrieved December 19, 2009 , from Wikipedia, the free encyclopedia: http://en.wikipedia.org/wiki/Freezing
20. *Fruits & vegetable*. (2009, December 9). Retrieved December 19, 2009, from www.fruitvegetable.com: http://www.fruitvegetable.com/
21. Gleez. (2009, December 11). *How much food does India waste?* Retrieved December 17, 2009, from Gleez.com: http://gleez.com/articles/did-you-know/how-much-food-does-india-waste
22. Goldstein, A. (2009, November 17). *America's economic pain brings hunger pangs*. Retrieved December 15, 2009, from www.washingtonpost.com:
23. http://www.washingtonpost.com/wp-dyn/content/article/2009/11/16/AR2009111601598.html
24. *How much food does India waste?* (2009, December 19). Retrieved December 19, 2009, from Gleez: http://gleez.com/articles/did-you-know/how-much-food-does-india-waste
25. India Brand Equity Foundation. (2009, July). *Indian Economy Overview: Provided by India Brand Equity Foundation*. Retrieved December 19, 2009, from India Brand Equity Foundation: http://cgamadvisor.com/wp-content/uploads/2009/06/Indian-Economy-Overview-IBEF-July-2009.pdf.
26. Indian Industry Profiles. (2009, December 09). *THE FOOD PROCESSING SECTOR IN INDIA*. Retrieved December 20, 2009, from www.indianindustryprofiles.com:
27. www.indianindustryprofiles.com/newfoodprocessing.ppt
28. *Indian Meat Industry Prospective*. (2009, December 13). Retrieved December 19, 2009, from www.fao.org: http://www.fao.org/DOCREP/ARTICLE/AGRIPPA/665_en.htm

29. *J.S.Marketing.* (2006, February 22). Retrieved December 20, 2009, from agricoop.nic.in: http://agricoop.nic.in/Kharif2006/Kharif2006ppt/J.S.Marketing.ppt
30. ManagementParadise.com. (2009, December 09). *India retains position as World's top Milk Produce.* Retrieved December 19, 2009, from www.managementparadise. com: http://www.managementparadise.com/forums/general-talks/21905-india-retains-position-worlds-top-milk-producer.html
31. MFPI India. (2009, December 10). *Food Processing.* Retrieved December 20, 2009, from Ministry of Food Processing Industries:
32. http://india.gov.in/sectors/commerce/food_processing.php
33. *Modified atmosphere.* (2009, October 2). Retrieved December 19, 2009, from Wikipedia, the free encyclopedia: http://en.wikipedia.org/wiki/Modified_ atmosphere
34. NACA. (2009, December 03). *WORLD AQUACULTURE DAY (Forums - Freshwater Fish Farming).* Retrieved December 19, 2009, from www.enaca.org:
35. http://www.enaca.org/modules/newbb/viewtopic.php?topic_id=922
36. *Pasteurization.* (2009, December 18). Retrieved December 19, 2009, from Wikipedia, the free encyclopedia: http://en.wikipedia.org/wiki/Pasteurization
37. *Preservative.* (2009, December 16). Retrieved December 19, 2009, from Wikipedia, the free encyclopedia: http://en.wikipedia.org/wiki/Preservative
38. Rediff.com Business. (2009, December 12). *Rice production seen at record 99.37 MT in '08-09.* Retrieved December 20, 2009 , from
39. http://business.rediff.com/report/2009/may/12/rice-production-seen-at-record-99-point-37-mt-in-08-09.htm
40. Rosenberg, M. (2009, December 14). *India's Population.* Retrieved December 19, 2009, from India Population:

28

Global Food (Grain Legumes) Security and Role of Biopesticides

K. Prakash, Patil R.H., K.S. Vishwakarma and V.L. Maheshwari

Population scenario

The global population reached more than 6.62 billion in 2008 and it continuous to grow by about 80 million each year. The world population is projected to grow about 7.97 billion in 2025 and 9.25 billion in 2050 and much of this increase would occur in developing countries. During 2007, China occupied first position with 1.32 billion people followed by India with a population of 1.13 billion. However, by 2050 India would overtake China to occupy the first position with a population of 1.74 billion followed by China with a 1.43 billion people. Such demographic changes would have profound implications for economy, environment, health and quality of life of people (PRB, 2007). About 2 billion people lack food security and population pressure have degraded about 2 billion hectares of arable land.

Food grain availability- Indian and Global status

India's population, on average, is better fed now compared to the 1960's. The availability of food grains (cereals plus pulses) has increased 11 percent, from 430 to 477 g per person per day (157 to 174 kg per year). However, the availability of pulses declined 54 percent, from 66.4 g per person per day in the 1960's to 35.9 g in the 1990's (Chandra and Pental, 2003). Declining pulse availability in a vegetarian dominated country must be a clear indication of nutritional insecurity. Grain legumes or pulses occupy an important place in the world food and nutrition economy due to their higher protein content than cereal grains. They are particularly important for major segment of population in developing countries who cannot afford animal protein due to high costs. Majority of Indians are vegetarian and they depend largely, for a major part of their dietary protein, on grain legumes (pulses). Grain legumes contain about 12 - 51 percent protein and therefore, they are not only excellent source of protein but play significant role in meeting calorie requirement in a typical Indian vegetarian diet (Table 1). In agriculture fields, they serve as mediators of biological nitrogen fixation by harboring nitrogen fixing bacteria in their root nodules.

Globally, pulses occupy about 68 million hectare area and contribute 60 MMT to the world's total food production. India's production of pulses has fluctuated between 12 to 14 MMT in last five decades accounting for 27 - 28% of global production making it the largest producer in world. Pulses are cultivated on about 22 million hectors of land amounting to approximately 32.2% per cent of total area under their cultivation (Chandra and Pental, 2003).

Agriculture and the losses due to pests

Agriculture plays the vital role of fulfilling the nutritional demands of human. The rapidly increasing population during the last century necessitated intensification of agriculture through expansion of irrigation facilities, introduction of high yielding varieties and application of increased amounts of agrochemicals. Besides, the culturing practice like spacing, crop rotation, sowing times and tillage methods were also modified to achieve maximum productivity per unit time from the available land. It is not just the cultivation of the crops, but their preservation/protection from a variety pests, both on and off the field is equally challenging as close to 50% of what is produced in our fields is lost because of them (Figure 1). Insects are the most important group of pests, particularly in the tropics and sub-tropics, where the climate provides a highly favorable environment for a wide range of insects. Massive efforts are required to suppress population densities of the different pests in order to achieve an adequate supply of food. In the developing countries, the problem of competition from insect pests is further complicated with a rapid annual increase in the human population (2.5 - 3.0%) in comparison to a 1.0% increase in food production.

Insects are the most diverse species of animals living on earth. Approximately 85% of all known animal species existing on earth at present are insects and it is generally assumed that only one fifth of all insects have been classified and named, meaning overall numbers of species would be approaching 4 million (FAO, 2006). It is little wonder that due to their potential for adaptation, diversification and immense numbers of different species some have found an ecological niche in stored grain. Almost 80% of these food crops are produced by small scale farmers and stored on the farm (Wongo, 1996). Due to poor storage structures and conditions, severe losses in quality and quantity of stored food are inflicted annually. Quantitative assessment of losses is difficult because of the high variability in infestation from year to year but indicating an intense impact of insect pests. In storage, the bruchids from Callosobruchus group cause the major losses in grain legumes in our country.

Callosobruchus chinensis - the target pest

Pulse beetle, C. chinensis is a cosmopolitan insect and attacks various grain legumes during storage (Lienard and Seck, 1994, Ahmed et al., 2003). This pest originated in tropical Asia but is currently distributed all over the tropics and sub-tropics. Adults are 2 - 4 mm, brownish with black markings and have long erected antennae. They have a short life span of about 12 days and do not feed (ICIPE, 2006). Two forms of this species have been identified; the active (flying) form and the flightless form. The flying form disperses and colonies cowpea fields. In the store, the normal form continues to reproduce until the end of the storage season. The flying form appears again to disperse to new locations.

The life cycle of C. chinensis goes through four stages. Adult females lay small, oval shaped and scale like eggs just after a day glued to the seed surface or to pods. C. chinensis can lay 1 - 8 eggs per grain and metamorphose into adults in separate chambers. Atwal (1976) reported that C. chinensis may lay 34 - 113 eggs @ 1 - 37 per day. Larvae tunnel inside the seed where the entire development takes place. In early stages, beetle larvae are whitish, with a light brown tinge on head, to become creamy white later. The mature larva is 6 - 7 mm long, breeds inside the grain and causes damage to pulses by feeding on their endosperm (Hozumi and Miyataka, 2005).

C. chinensis causes substantial economic loss during the storage/preservation of pulses (Shu et al., 1996). Severe infestation reduces quality and germinability to under 20% after 4 months only (Seck et al., 1996) and as much as 100% loss within 6 months of storage (Aslam, 2004). The damaged grain did not remain fit for human as well as animal consumption (Aslam, 2004).

Control measures with safety to mankind- Alternative strategies

Synthetic chemical pesticides have played and will continue to play significant role in pest management strategies. It is also true that pesticide application per unit area of land is one of the lowest in our country (Atwal, 1976). However, their excessive and indiscriminate use in certain cropping systems has led to a number of environmental and human health problems. Pesticide residues on agricultural commodities are one of the major issues of concern besides reports of development of resistance in pests to common pesticide molecules. Being highly toxic, their use and application is associated with acute occupational pesticide poisoning with close to 3 million cases reported every year (WHO, 1990). These and other economic factors, associated with the development of new pesticide molecule have stabilized the global pesticide market in the recent past. In fact, it is showing a marginally declining trend in the last 5 years (Thakore, 2006).

There is a paradigm shift in our approach which now centers on "pest management" rather then "pest control" using an umbrella of strategies, what is commonly referred to as "Integrated Pest Management" (IPM). The components of IPM are mutually complimentary. It also envisages better role for biological based pest management (biopesticides, biocontrol, etc.). Of late, there has been a successful attempt in making crop plants resistant to either pest (e.g., Bt- cotton, maize, etc.) or pesticides (e.g., resistant soyabean). Commercial successes has opened the flood gates and a large number of crops are being genetically modified using sophisticated recombinant DNA techniques for protection against insects, viruses and weeds. However, there is a question mark regarding the acceptability of this technology by masses and only time will tell the answer.

Biopesticides

One of the potential alternative methods to limit the losses in agriculture produce by insect pests is biopesticides. In broader sense, biopesticide include, but not only limited to, pesticides of biological origin. Vast, natural diversity in micro organisms and plants can be explored to provide useful leads and pesticidally active molecules. In fact, many such attempts were successfully made and practiced much before the advent of adverse synthetic pesticides.

(1) **Microbial pesticides** : Micro-organisms themselves or their metabolites produced by them exert entanopathogenic effects by infecting the insect or by contaminating its food (Burges and Jones, 1998). Of all the insect viruses, baculoviruses belonging to family Baculo viride are the best known. Both the catogeries of Bacullo viruses, i.e., nuclear polyhydrosis virus (NPV) and granuloviruses (GV) have been reported to be safe for IPM as they are safe to humans, the environment and non target beneficial organisms (Daliwal and Koul, 2007). The genus Bacillus of bacteria contains some of the most important species among which B. thuringiensis is probably the most widely explored as a microbial control agent (Dhaliwal and Arora, 2006). Over 800 fungal species belonging to some 100 genera are known to be pathogenic to both parsestial and aquatic insects (Thackel, 2002). However, due to much high mammalian toxicity they are less popular as insecticides.

(2) **Botanical pesticides:** Plant diversity remains a major unexplored bioresources for potentially active molecules. Over 2000 plants belonging to some 60 plant families are known to exhibit insecticidal activities (Dev and Koul, 1997). During the course of evolution, plants have developed effective counter measures to withstand the herbivorous pests/diseases. They contain compounds such as derris, pyrethrum, rotenone, nicotine, sabadilla, physostigmine and quassin, which were extensively used (1800 to 1940) until the discovery of synthetic insecticide, DDT. Many of the plant chemicals that have potential as botanical pesticides are the secondary plant metabolites or allelochemicals, which serve no apparent function in the fundamental physiological or biochemical processes of the plant. These chemicals include the terpenoids, flavonoids, phenolics, amines and alkaloids (Jacobson, 1989). Advances in techniques for isolation and analysis have led to the identification of many new compounds. These secondary plant metabolites having insecticidal/ pesticidal properties are of several types, *viz.*, repellents, anti-feedants, phago-stimulants and toxins (Krishnayya and Rao, 1996; Nivsarkar *et al.*, 2001). Many classes of plant proteins and secondary plant substances have been shown to have toxic or anti-metabolic effect on insects and have been proposed as possible candidates as pest control agents (Simmonds *et. al.*, 1989; Kim *et. al.*, 2003). A common feature of many of these compounds is that they have a chronic rather than an acute toxicity on insects and their effects are less dramatic than those of the synthetic insecticides (Estruch *et. al.*, 1997; Park *et. al.*, 2003).

Our approach

Our research group has been actively working in devising strategies for minimizing losses in pulses during storage using plants; plant derived secondary metabolites and industrial byproducts - fly ash (a byproduct and waste of thermal power station) for the last 12 years. The pulse beetle (Callosobruchus chinensis) - the major post harvest (storage) pest of commonly consumed legume in our country has been our target pest. We have successfully demonstrated control of this pest by a number of different commonly growing plant derived metabolites and fly ash as a presented in Table 2. Any one or all the stages of the life cycle of the insect can be a potential target for its control. Indeed, in our studies, we found the plant derived metabolites have multiple effects on the life stages of the target pests (Table 3). Moreover, secondary metabolites isolated from plants have shown promising antimicrobial activity against some of the common microbial infestation of grain legumes in storage. According to our hypothesis, microbial and pest infestation in storage ecosystem are mutually supportive, complimentary and inter dependent (Figure 3) Thus, use of plant derived metabolites serve as a two prong strategy in preservation of grain legumes by affecting both microbial and insect pest population.

The secondary metabolites in plants are produced in minute quantities by complex multi-step enzyme catalyzed pathways and as a result their isolation, purification and characterization is often tedious, time consuming and expensive. Moreover, their quantity in plants varies as a function of season and other factors as a result maintenance of consistency in quality end formulation becomes a challenge. Of late, certain members belonging to family Rubiaceae and Violaceae have been reported to contain small molecular weight circular proteins- cyclotides with a host of biological activities including pesticidal activity. We have screened several indigenous members of these two plant families and determined the presence of circular proteins and their possible role in grain preservation. Polypeptides (proteins) being single gene product, offer an inherent advantage of synthesis in-vitro by recombinant DNA techniques.

Merits of Biopesticides

Biopesticides offer several advantages over traditional chemical/synthetic pesticides. They are often safer and have more target specificity against the desired pest as compared to conventional pesticides. Furthermore, they decompose more quickly than conventional pesticides and leave no harmful residues on food, fodder and fibers. Their synthesis is less capital, cost, time, energy and pollution intensive compared to conventional pesticides.

Conclusion

Provision of food has always been a challenge facing the mankind. Insect and other pests are responsible for close to 50 % loss in agricultural produce both on and off the fields. In other words, half of what is produced by our farmers doesn't reach to those for whom it is intended. By reducing the food grain availability, insect pests participate in the unholy alliance of poverty and hunger in our country and elsewhere. In the present scenario of acknowledged drawbacks of synthetic pesticides, plant derived metabolites and other biopesticides offer a ray of hope in food grain protection on a sustainable basis. The concerted action by all the stake holders, the farmers, the extension workers, the scientists, the policy makers and the Government, can make biopesticides play their due role in global food (grain legume) security.

Table 1: Role of grain legumes in India *vis-à-vis* Asian and world diet

Per capita/day	World	Asia	India
Energy (Kcal)	56.00	51.90	117.40
Protein (g)	3.50	3.10	6.90
Fat (g)	0.40	0.40	1.00

Table 2: Plants and industrial bi-product studied for post harvest preservation of grain legumes at SLS- NMU, Jalgaon.

Plant/Extract	Active ingredient	Reference
Papaya leaf dust	Proteolytic enzyme (?)	Mendki *et. al,* 2000
Fly ash	Oxides of heavy metals	Mendki *et. al,* 2001
A. squamosa	Flavanoids, Terpenoids	Kotkar *et. al.,* 2002
C. procera	Flavanoids	Mendki, 2002
R. communis	Flavanoids	Upasani *et. al.,* 2003
A. calamus	Flavonoids, Terpenoids	Salunke, 2005
V. odorata	Circular Proteins (Cyclotides)	Prakash *et. al.,* 2008

Table 3: Intervention of plant derived metabolites at different stages of life cycle of C.chinensis.

Plant/Extract	Activity (%)		
	AE	OC	OD
Papaya leaf dust*	8.7	91.3	52.1
Fly ash*	2.0	98.0	53.4
A. squamosa	20.4	79.5	50.0
C. procera	10.0	90.0	47.8
R. communis	19.0	81.0	50.0
A. calamus	31.4	68.6	29.9
V. odorata	18.7	81.3	31.7

Mean number of.C. chinensis in 5 Kg treated grains after 12 months, other values are of In-vitro filter paper diffusion assay.

AE	Adult emergence
OC	Ovicidal
OD	Ovipositional deterrent

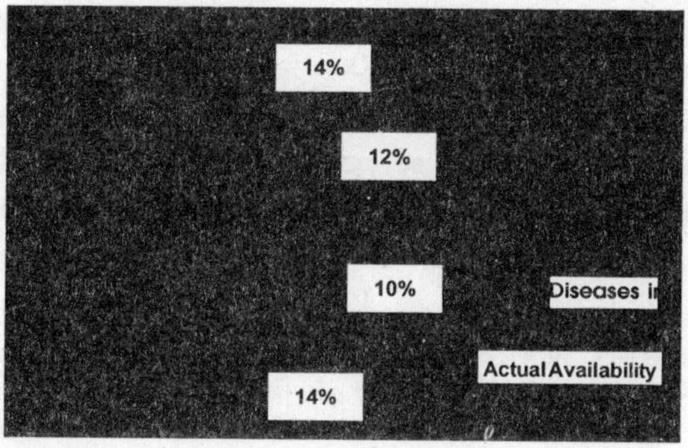

Figure 1: Losses in food grains due to various parameters

Source: World Food and Agriculture Organization

References

1. Ahmed KS, Itino T and Ichikawa T. (2003) Duration of developmental stages of Callosobruchus chinensis L. (Coleoptera: Bruchidae) on Azuki bean and the effects of neem and sesame oils at different stages of their development. Pakistan J. of Biol. Sci. 6, 932-335.
2. Aslam M. (2004) Pest status of stored chickpea beetle, Callosobruchus chinensis Linnaeus on Chickpea. J. of Entomol 1(1) 28-33.
3. Atwal AS. (Ed.) (1976) Insect pests of stored grain and other products. In: Agricultural pests of India and South-East Asia. Kalyani Publishers, New Delhi, pp. 389-415.
4. Burges HD and Jones KA. (1998) Formulation of bacteria, viruses and protozoa to control insects. In: Formulation of Microbial Biopesticides: Beneficial Microorganisms, Nematodes and Seed Treatments, (Ed. Burges, H.D.) Kluwer Academic Publication, Dordrecht, The Netherlands, pp. 34-109.
5. Chandra A and Pental D. (2003) Regeneration and genetic transformation of grain legumes: An overview. Curr. Sci., 84. 381-387.
6. Dev S and Koul O. (Eds.) (1997) Higher plants. In: Insecticides of Natural Origin. Harwood Academic Publ., Australia, pp. 27-252.
7. Dhaliwal GS and Arora R. (2006) Integrated pest management, Concepts and approaches, Kalyani Publishers, New Delhi.
8. Dhaliwal GS and Koul O. (2007) Transgenics as biopesticides: potential in sustainable crop protection. In: Sustainable crop protection: Biopesticide stratergies (Eds. O Koul, GS Dhaliwal and VK Kaul) Kalyani Publishers, New Delhi. PP- 65-107.
9. Estruch JJ, Carozzi NB, Desai N, Duck NB, Warren GW and Koziel MG. (1997) Transgenic plants: an emerging approach to pest control. Nature Biotech 15: 137-141.
10. FAO. (2006) Food and Agriculture Organisation website http//:www.fao.org accessed on 20.02.2006
11. Hozumi N and Miyatake T. (2005) Body-Size Dependent Difference in Death-Feigning Behavior of Adult Callosobruchus chinensis. J. of Insect Behav, 18:4, 557-566

12. ICIPE. (2006) International Centre of Insect Physiology and Ecology website http// :www.icipe.org accessed on 22.02.2006

13. Jacobson M. (1989) Botanical Pesticides Past, Present and Future. In: Insecticides of plant origin (Eds. Arnason, JT, Philogene BJR and Morand P) pp. 44-58.

14. Kim SI, Park C, Ohh MH, Cho HC and Ahn Y. (2003) Contact and fumigant activities of aromatic plant extracts and essential oils against Lasioderma serricorne (Coleoptera: Anobiidae). J. Stored Prods. Res., 39, 11-19.

15. Kotkar HM, Mendki PS, Sadan SGS, Jha SR, Upasani SM and Maheshwari VL. (2002) Antimicrobial and pesticidal activity of partially purified flavonoids of Annona squamosa. Pest Manag. Sci., 58: 33-37.

16. Koul O. (2004) Neem: A global prespective. In: Neem: Today and in the new millennium. O Koul and S Wahab (eds) Kluwer academic Publishers. Dordrecht, The Netherlands, pp 1- 19.

17. Krishnayya PV and Rao PJ. (1996) Plumbagin- A natural bioactive principle against insects. The Andhra Agric. J., 43, 1-5.

18. Lienard V and Seck D. (1994) Review of control methods against Callosobruchus maculatus (F.) (Coleoptera: Bruchidae), a pest of grains of cowpea (Vigna unguiculata (L.) Walp) in tropical Africa. Insect Sci and its Appln. 15: 3, 301-311.

19. Mendki PS, Maheshwari VL and Kothari RM. (2000) Papaya leaf dust as post-harvest preservative for five commonly utilized pulses. J. Plant Biol., 27: 197-201.

20. Mendki PS, Maheshwari VL and Kothari, RM. (2001a) Flyash as a post-harvest preservative for five commonly utilized pulses. Crop Protect, 20: 241-245.

21. Mendki PS. (2002) Alternative strategies for post harvest management of five commonly utilized pulses. Ph D Thesis. North Maharashtra University, Jalgaon.

22. Nivsarkar M, Cherian B and Padh H. (2001) Alpha terthienyl: A plant derived new generation insecticide. Curr. Sci., 81, 667-672.

23. Park I, Lee S, Cho D, Park J and Ahn Y. (2003) Insecticidal activities of constituents identified from the leaves of Chamaecyparis obtuse against Callosobruchus chinensis (L.) and Sitophilus oryzae (L.). J. Stored Prods. Res., 39, 375-384.

24. PBR (2007) World population data sheet. Population Reference Bureau, Washington, DC, USA.

25. Prakash K, Patil RH, Vishwakarma KS and Maheshwari VL. (2008) Bioprospecting of bioactive proteins in indigenous plants. J. Plant Biol. 35(1): 53-57.

26. Salunke BK, Kotkar HM, Mendki PS, Upasani SM and Maheshwari VL. (2005) Efficacy of flavonoids to control C. chinensis, a post harvest pest of grain legumes. Crop Protection. 24: 888-893.

27. Seck D, Lognay G, Haubruge E, Marlier M and Gaspar C. (1996) Alternative protection of cowpea seeds against Callosobruchus maculatus (F.) (Coleoptera: Bruchidae) using hermetic storage alone or in combination with Boscia senegalensis (Pers.) Lam ex Poir. J. Stored Prods. Res., 32, 39-44.

28. Shu S, Koepnick WL, Mbata ON, Cork A and Ramaswamy S. (1996) Sex pheromone production in Callosobruchus maculatus (Coleoptera: Bruchidae): Electro-antenographic and behavioural responses. J. Stored Prods. Res., 32, 21-30.

29. Simmonds MSJ, Blaney WM, Ley SV, Savona G, Bruno M and Rodriguez B. (1989) The antifeedant activity of clerodane diterpenoids from Teucrium. Phytochem 28: 1069-1070.

30. Thakore Y. (2006) The Biopesticide market for global agriculture use- Industrial report., The New Biopesticide Market, BCC Research., Code: CHM029B

31. Upasani SM, Kotkar HM, Mendki PS, Maheshwari VL. (2003) Partial characterization and insecticidal properties of Ricinus communis flavonoids. Pest Manage. Sci., 59: 1349-1354.

32. Wongo L and Pedersen J. (1996) Effect of threshing different sorghum cultivars on Sitotroga cerealella (Oliv.) and Sitophilus oryzae (L.) (Lepidoptera: Gelechiidae and Coleoptera: Curculionidae). Journal of Stored Products Research. 26: 2, 89-96.

29

Role of Information Technology in Watershed Management and Food Security

R.J. Ramteke, V.M. Rokade and C.P. Bhoyar

Introduction

Agriculture is the backbone of the Indian economy. Indian agricultural sector is driven by the subsistence strategies of smallholder farmers and their families. Agriculture is the largest user of water, using more than 80% of usable freshwater, and a large proportion of the population derives its livelihood directly or indirectly from it. As concerns over water scarcity have mounted, accentuated by possible impacts of climate change like a general reduction in the quantity of available surface water and unanticipated alterations in the hydrological cycle with an increased severity of droughts and floods, there is a growing realization that water resource management focused on food security is urgently needed.

In the face of growing water demand from both agricultural and non-agricultural sectors of the economy, India should come up with strategies that aim to safeguard the interests of socially and economically weaker sections of the population in scenarios where the absolute scarcity of water is increasing at a higher rate than before. Some strategies would enhance and conserve supply while making water use in the Indian agricultural sector more efficient while others would help forecast climate change events and assist people to cope or recover in the event of their occurrence.

In the past due to insufficient knowledge base, some misguided agricultural policies, coupled with a rapidly growing population, chronic poverty, and unpredictable rainfall, have caused severe food security challenges for farm families and natural resource degradation. Therefore conservation and management of the natural resources like soil and water (groundwater and surface water) is necessary for better productivity of the crops.

In India we are taking our pace towards management, the recent National Action Plan on Climate Change (NAPCC) reiterates the commitment towards developing a multi-pronged, long-term and integrated strategy for achieving key goals in the context of climate change. Two of the eight sector-specific missions within it deal with the different aspects of water meant for agriculture, namely the National Water Mission (NWM) and the National Mission for Sustainable Agriculture (NMSA). National Water Mission include the management of surface water resources, regulation of groundwater, upgradation of storage structures and drainage systems, conservation of wetlands, wastewater reclamation, equitable access, and regulatory structures for basin level management. Likewise, the NMSA has outlined four key areas, namely, dryland agriculture, risk management, access to information, and biotechnology. The list of possible strategies to ensure water and food security is long but can include such activities as conducting "water audits" of rural households with different resource endowments; safeguarding local knowledge and institutions that are conducive to good crop and water management; combining these with scientific knowledge and practices so they are mutually beneficial; evaluating optimal irrigation water tariffs and subsidies, with a regional focus; legislating and implementing controls over energy use in agriculture; enabling better access to agricultural credit and contingency measures for climate change-related disasters like crop insurance policies; developing climate-resilient crop varieties, adaptable to either flood or drought situations; developing or instituting engineering, institutional and biotechnological innovations that allow the sparing use of irrigation water, the decentralization of agricultural water supply (preferably to the household level) and the safer use of wastewater in agriculture; carrying out long-term, basin-wide planning to address climate change impacts as well as short-term planning for disaster management and relief; using modern information technology for improving crop productivity; developing incentive structures for water-neutral or water-positive technologies; and, not least, establishing functioning structures and mechanisms for the regulation of agricultural water use. Origin of Information technology brought new approaches that lead to improvement of food security and a lessening of the dependence on food aid by means of managing watershed.

Watershed Management

Watershed management is the process of creating and implementing plans, programs, and projects to sustain and enhance watershed functions that affect the plant, animal, and human communities within a watershed boundary. Features of a watershed that agencies seek to manage include water supply, water quality, soil conservation, drainage, storm water runoff, water rights, and the overall planning and utilization of watersheds. Landowners, land use agencies, storm water management experts, geologists, agricultural scientists, environmental specialists, water use surveyors and communities all play an integral part in the management of a watershed.

In the 1980s and 1990s, agricultural scientists and planners aimed to promote rain-fed agriculture through watershed development. A watershed is an area from which all water drains to a common point, making it an interesting unit for managing water and soil resources to enhance agricultural production through water conservation. It is an eye-opening fact that by the late 1990s, annual expenditure on watershed development in India approached almost an equivalent of $500 million (Rs 2,500 crore), yet very little concrete information is available on the success or failure of the different project approaches. A lot more needs to be done even though the government of India and the various State governments together with the international organizations are doing a lot to make this concept a success in India. So far, the success story of watershed management in India has been a mixed bag.

As part of a strategy to achieve food security while protecting the environment through sustainable land use development, integrated watershed management (IWM) approaches are being developed. The major advantages of IWM approaches are involvement of those most affected by the decisions (i.e. the stakeholders) in all phases of the development of their watershed and holistic planning that addresses issues which extend across subject matter disciplines (biophysical, social, and economic sciences) and administrative boundaries (village, talukas, district, etc.).

The question is: 'can better management of the available rainwater help to reduce the occurrence and mitigate the impact of droughts during periods with low rainfall'? Soil erosion and its effect on soil quality and water storage to be the main culprit in securing food security. Better water management of available rainfall in semi-arid climates can mitigate the impact of droughts and help to improve food security. In this paper authors demonstrate integrative approaches to research, extension, community development, and micro-enterprise development and management of watershed for better food productivity and so security.

The aim of watershed interventions is to ensure a greater protection of land against soil erosion and to improve the water recharge in the region. This programme has the potential to raise the water table in the area and help better vegetative growth and improve agriculture productivity. Several land development mechanisms are possible in order to make land fertile that was previously barren, suitable for plantation of certain crops and trees.

Food Security

Food security is interrelated with high population growth, over exploitation of natural resources (Groundwater and soil), soil erosion, deforestation, and widespread poverty. In the Indian highlands, food insecurity is compounded by reliance on archaic agricultural systems, vulnerability to natural disasters, lack of land tenure security, and land fragmentation. Common interventions include public works programs designed to counter food shortages, generate income, and promote conservation.

For achieving food security in developing countries following multi-dimensional approaches have been identified.

1. *More crop per drop* (food and water security are inseparable, as food cannot be grown without water. Ways of optimizing the soil–water–plant system, in order to produce more food crops with less water).
2. *Use of remote sensing, GIS, GPS and VRT (Variable Rate Technology)*, for making surface water inventories, groundwater mapping, airborne salinity mapping, management of irrigated agriculture, vegetation indices, soil moisture, crop

production forecasting, wasteland reclamation, regulation of water rights and aquifer depletion through the use of evapotranspiration and lysimeters, etc. Fragmented farm holdings in the country constitute aserious impediment in the farmer-specific application of remotely sensed soil moisture and other kinds of data applications.

3. *Development of drought-resistant and salinity-tolerant crop varieties.* Use of recombinant DNA technology and methods for transferring (e.g.) salt-tolerant genes (say, from mangroves) into important food crops, such as rice. Gene isolation and development of transgenics in locally adapted cultivars.
4. *Preparation of hydroclimatic calendar* on the basis of the analysis of satellite-based, climate-related information (including ENSO impacts), for use in crop planning.
5. *Maintenance of soil health.* Use of soil microorganisms and micronutrients such as zinc, sulphur and boron, to improve soil fertility and productivity.
6. *'Blue' water irrigation* – To make irrigation water available on demand, and to price it in proportion to the quantity used per unit area of land. Reduction in conveyance losses. Efficient use of irrigation water through practices such as drip irrigation. · Use of wastewater and brackish water to grow appropriate crops. ·
7. *Use of SRI (System of Rice Intensification) method* of rice cultivation, which uses less seed, less water and better harvest. · Study of how the quality of irrigation water (say, arsenious water) affects food grain quality.
8. *Rainfed agriculture:* The greatest potential for meeting the burgeoning demand for food lies in rainfed agriculture based on 'green' water (soil moisture), and conversion of non-beneficial evaporation to beneficial transpiration through crops, using, for example, on-farm rainwater harvesting, and moisture conservation methodologies. Integrated watershed management can increase crop productivity two to three fold through productivity-enhancing agricultural technologies (e.g. supplemental irrigation, micronutrient management), and thus break the unholy nexus between drought, land degradation and poverty ('access to affordable water is the first step out of poverty').
9. *Food fortification* (ways of processing foods to improve their nutrition, so that the same quantity of, say, cereals could provide nutritious diet to more people): · Fermentation of cereals, pulses, root crops, vegetables, fruits, milk, meat and fish could create new kinds of foods, which are more nutritious, more digestible, and with therapeutic benefits, while improving the taste, flavour and texture, etc. Fermented foods thus offer a practical solution to malnutrition and ill-health. Consumer preferences of food drive the production pattern of foods. Both the poor and the affluent are eating lesser quantities of cereals – the former on grounds of affordability, and the latter on grounds of preferring to eat more meat and fruits. Ways have to be found to address the macronutrient and micronutrient deficiency in the diet of the low-income people, through appropriate food processing mechanisms.

10. *Access to food* (economic instruments and administrative policies to improve access to food): Food availability is a necessary but not sufficient condition for food security. The policy framework for food security involves three elements of availability, acceptability and accessibility. Economic and physical access to food needs to be enhanced. · Development of micro-enterprises would enhance the purchasing power of people living below the poverty line to buy food. Governments are urged to formulate incentives to promote drip irrigation, and to grow low water-need crops, such as bajra (in the form of guaranteed prices) and rearing meat animals (e.g. impala, ostrich) with low water consumption. There should be disincentives for rice cultivation in drought-prone areas (such as denying free electricity). The management system to implement the proposed strategy needs to have three layers to take into account the multidimensional nature of the enterprise.
11. *Policy level ('Top-down' approach)* – to serve as a 'think-tank' to integrate and optimize various biophysical and socioeconomic factors, and administrative incentives and disincentives. This is essentially at government level, supplemented by NGOs. Technology transfer level ('bottom-up' approach) – to design institutional arrangements for adapting the technologies to specific local biophysical and socioeconomic situations; to develop mechanisms and modalities of training of all the concerned entities (such as managers, NGOs, stakeholders, financial institutions, Panchayat Raj institutions, etc.) · Implementation level: to design institutional arrangements for the management of implementation, monitoring and servicing of the micro-enterprises. 'Handholding' with stakeholders where necessary. NGOs will be the principal players. Customised 'mix' of inputs for improved food security needs to be developed at the level of watershed/mandal/district/state/country, depending upon locally available technologies, agroclimatic conditions, economic policies, public awareness, information and communication technologies, etc., for various regions/countries.

Information Technology

The present day information and communication technology has trespassed all barriers of race, religion, culture and countries. A vision how communication networking could help us to grow more with guarantees for food security through watershed management and environmental protection is trying to discuss in this paper. The specific emphasis of the authors is on reducing the gap between research and farmers communication, use of IT for precision agriculture, satellite generated data, GIS, marketing and farming informatics and awareness packages through print, videoconferencing, mass and now E-mails. The means anticipated are strong warning systems for scientific data about soil, crop pattern, seed, modern agricultural techniques, climatic risks, floods, cyclones and other hazards. The infestations of pests, mites could also be predicted by analyzing climatic changes and farmers could have fore-warning communiqués.

The role of competitive farming, economic evaluation of farming and women's integration should take into consideration. Women the half of agricultural work force is still unawares of the technological skills. The barriers of customs, veil, religion and social bondages could be overcome by educating them through focal dance, dramas, TV, cassettes, e-mails or other modern communication appliances.

1 Remote Sensing: Use of high resolution satellite data helped time – critical dependant applications in our diversified country. Large number of Indian and foreign satellites are tracking our country. The data obtained from ground stations is processed at a facility via a high speed communication link and high priority processing. This system provides Satellite data on critical applications, like crop yield modelling, pre-harvest crop production forecasting, detecting crop diseases, monitoring crop stress, pest infestation, floods, fires and oil-spills.

2 Geographic Information System: GIS is a new technology, which is adopted as a tool for analysing and integrating the spatial and non-spatial data. It is used as an information database, an analytical tool and as a decision support system. Thematic information generated from satellite and other ancillary information is integrated under GIS domain to generate local specific action plan on micro-watershed basis. Besides, this tool is also being used for monitoring purposes. High resolution satellite data can be utilised to generate resource map which has been integrated with other non-spatial data like demography, rainfall, literacy etc. The utilisation of Remote sensing and GIS to derive information pertaining to watershed management, *viz.,* Watershed characterisation, prioritisation, mapping, inventory and assessment of natural resources, groundwater potential zones, runoff estimation, water and land resources action plan, site selection for implementation, monitoring and evaluation.

3 E-Choupal: The main aim of ITC e-Choupal is to confer power of expert knowledge to the smallest of the farmers and to the consumer in remotest location enriching them with knowledge and elevating them to a new order of empowerment and freedom of choice. The e-Choupal initiative creates a direct marketing channel, eliminating wasteful intermediation and multiple handling, thus reducing transaction costs and making logistics efficient. It has become a reliable resource development platform by enabling a low-cost and highly effective channel for distribution and marketing of a range of goods and services into rural India (packaged consumer goods, healthcare, home appliances, education, life and general insurance products, etc.) triggering a transformation in rural landscape and livelihoods.

Titur Command Area : Case Study

Agriculture is the main source of economy in the Jalgaon district, which is mainly dependent on the groundwater irrigation facility, except in the command area of the some irrigation projects where it is supported by surface water. In order to enhance the agricultural productivity there must be a substantial irrigation facility, both groundwater and surface water, in the region. Presently three types of the crops, namely Kharif, Rabbi, and perennial, are taken in the district, the areal coverage of which varies from year to year depending upon the amount of monsoon rainfall received during the year and the subsequent groundwater and surface water potential developed thereto. The area under Rabbi and perennial crops needs to be increase to enhance the agricultural returns. This requires adopting an integrated approach of water resources development and sustainable management of these resources.

The Titur River flowing along the boundary of Pachora and Bhadgaon Taluka of the Jalgaon district has a diversion weir across the river near village Vadgaon Kh. and a diversion canal which runs through the Pachora Taluka for a length of 22 Kms. covering about 12 villages. Initially this system was constructed in 1951 during scarcity. In those days the Titur river used to flow for at least nine months. Subsequently the system was renovated in 1978 and 6MM^3 water was reserved in the Girna reservoir for this canal. But for the last ten years the system was not in use, so neither the floodwater nor the reserved water in the Girna reservoir could be diverted to the canal for surface water irrigation. Recently the Minor Irrigation department has taken an initiative for repairing and reactivating the canal system for surface water irrigation and artificial recharge to the ground water system in the command area of the Titur canal.

Watershed management studies for improving the crop productivity has been studied by using remote sensing, GIS (Geographic Information System) and other Data base management system to analyze and display all forms of data. For this study authors have considered physiography, drainage network, geology, rainfall pattern, land use/landcover, crop pattern, hydrogeological setup and hydrodynamic conditions of the study area. And this database has been updated, analyzed and modeled in GIS for prospecting the groundwater potential. GIS Modelling is also carried out for searching suitable sites for artificial recharge structures. Action plan is developed by considering socio-economic status and available resources of the area. This action plan is discussed with progressive farmers and their suggestion has been incorporated in this action plan, which gave birth to final developmental action plan.

Conclusion

For sustainable development and fulfilling living values, technological interventions, enabling policies, public investments into canal irrigation development, rural electrification, communication, infrastructure, private investments into ground water development and support prices ensured food security of India. The sustainability of groundwater utilities is one of the core issues which require attention for meeting irrigation and drinking water requirements and ensuring food security. For watershed management and so for food security, information technology (Remote sensing, GIS and DBMS) is playing important role by creating, analysing, integrating and displaying all forms of geospatial information.

References

1. Anonymous. 2008. Agricultural Statistics at a Glance 2008. Department of Agriculture and Cooperation, Ministry of Agriculture, New Delhi.
2. CGWB. 2006. Dynamic Ground Water Resources of India. Central Ground Water Board, Ministry of Water Resources, Faridabad.
3. Dunne, T. and L.B. Leopold (1978). Water in Environmental Planning. Freeman Company. New York.

4. Hatibu, N. (2003). Rainwater Management: Strategies for Improving Water Availability and Productivity in Semi-arid and Arid Areas. International Water Management Institute. IWMI, Sri Lanka.

5. Kaumbutho, P.G., G. Gebresenbet and T. E. Simalegna (1999). Overview of conservation tillage practices in East and Southern Africa. In: *Conservation tillage with animal traction. A Resource Book of Animal Traction Network for Eastern and Southern Africa,* P.G Kaumbutho and T. E. Simalegna (eds.), (ATNESA), Harare, Zimbabwe.

6. Mendoza, G.F., M.T. Walter, T.S. Steenhuis, J.-Y. Parlange (2003). Estimating basin-wide hydraulic parameters of a semi-arid mountainous watershed by recession-flow analysis. *J. Hydrol.,* 279, 57-69.

7. Peranginangin, N., R. Sakthivadivel, N.R. Scott, E. Kendy, T.S. Steenhuis (2004). Water Accounting for conjunctive groundwater/surface water management: case of the Singkarak-Ombilin River basin, Indonesia. *J. Hydrology,* 292, 1-22.

8. Reid, R.K., and Y. Abebe (2003). Community Based Watershed Management planning process at Yeku and Lenche Dima watersheds. Internal report AMAREW project.

9. Rockstrom, J., J. Barren and P. Fox (2002). Rainwater management for increased productivity among small-holder farmers in drought prone environments. *Physics and Chemistry of the Earth,* 27, 949- 959.

10. Sonneveld B.G.J.S. and M.A. Keyzer (2003). Land Under Pressure: Soil Conservation Concerns and Opportunities for Ethiopia. *Land Degradation & Development,* 14, 5-23.

30

Food Security — Global Scenario

Mangala A. Sabadra

Introduction

Food security exists when all people, at all times, have physical, social and economic access to sufficient amounts of safe and nutritious food that meets their dietary needs and food preferences for an active and healthy life. There are four dimensions to food security: availability, access, stability and utilization.

Availability of adequate food supplies refers to the capacity of an agro-ecological system to meet overall demand for food (including animal products, livelihoods and how producers respond to markets). Access to food refers to the ability of households to economically access food (or livelihoods), defined in terms of enough purchasing power or access to sufficient resources (entitlements). Stability refers to the time dimension of food security. Stability of food supplies refers to those situations in which populations are vulnerable to either temporarily or permanently losing access to resources, factor inputs, social capital or livelihoods due to extreme weather events, economic or market failure, civil conflict or environmental degradation, and increasingly, conflict over natural resources. Utilization of food refers to peoples' ability to absorb nutrients and is closely linked to health and nutrition factors, such as access to clean water, sanitation and medical services.

"The global financial crisis as a 'colossal human tragedy', said the United Nations Secretary General Ban Ki-Moon on the occasion of World Food Day 2009, the situation would be alarming enough if it were confined to a matter of hunger, but a wide-spread lack of food triggers other threats, from social unrest to environmental degradation". He further added that, "800 million people across the globe were going to sleep hungry every night even before the prices of food started rising sharply".

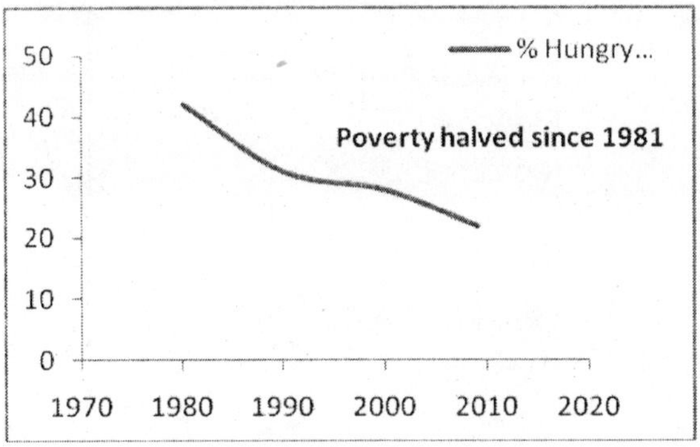

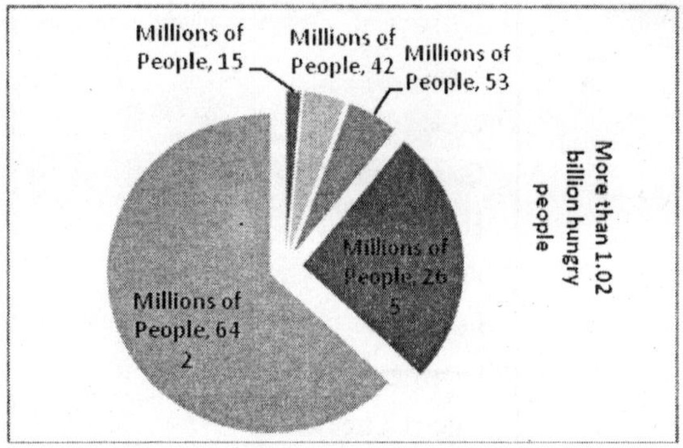

Source: World Bank Data (extreme poverty) 1981-2009. **Source:** FAO website.

From the graph above and from the statement of UN Secretary-General, we can guess the severity of the food security problem. Hunger is mainly related to poverty. Some 70 percent of the 854 million hungry people in the world live in rural areas and depend on agriculture, often concentrated in regions that are particularly vulnerable to environmental degradation and climate change. An estimated 820 million are in developing countries, 25 million in countries in transition, and 9 million in industrialized countries. Hunger claims up to 25,000 lives every day, two thirds of them children under the age of five, and is currently the leading threat to global health, killing more people than AIDS, malaria, and tuberculosis combined. Although the proportion of undernourished in the world has declined from 20 percent to 17 percent since the mid-1990s, the absolute number of hungry people has remained the same. Global progress towards halving the proportion of hungry people by 2015 remains slow and largely uneven. Only Latin America and the Caribbean, amongst developing regions, have reduced the prevalence of hunger at a rapid enough pace to reach the Millennium Development Goals (MDG) target.(see table 1 below) Countries with 20 to 34 percent of the population considered undernourished include Bangladesh, Bolivia, Botswana, Cambodia, Cameroon, Chad, Congo, Dominican Republic, Gambia, Guatemala, Guinea, Honduras, India, Kenya, Laos Peoples Democratic Republic, Malawi, Mali, Mongolia, Namibia, Nicaragua, Niger, Pakistan, Panama, Senegal, Sri Lanka, Sudan, Thailand, Togo. Countries with more than 35 percent of the population considered undernourished include Angola, Burundi, Central African Republic, Chad, Democratic Republic of the Congo Democratic People's Republic of Korea, Eritrea, Ethiopia, Haiti, Liberia, Madagascar, Mozambique, Rwanda, Sierra Leone, United Republic of Tanzania, Tajikistan, Yemen, Zambia and Zimbabwe (Food and Agriculture Organization, FAO SOFI 2006).

Countries most at risk of deteriorating food security due to high food prices

In food crisis	At high risk
Central African Republic	Cameroon
Democratic Republic of the Congo	Comoros
Côte d'Ivoire	Djibouti

Eritrea	Gambia
Ethiopia	Madagascar
Guinea	Mongolia
Guinea-Bissau	Mozambique
Haiti	Nicaragua
Kenya	Niger
Lesotho	Occupied Palestinian Territory
Liberia	Rwanda
Sierra Leone	Senegal
Somalia	Solomon Islands
Swaziland	Togo
Tajikistan	United Republic of Tanzania
Timor-Leste	Yemen
Zimbabwe	Zambia

Source: FAO

According to a Joint statement issued at G8, 'food security is closely connected with economic growth and social progress as well as with political stability and peace'.

There are various dimensions to the food security problem in the world. It can be attributed to Political, Natural, and Social, Economical causes.

Politics causes food security problem in two ways. I) International politics and ii) National politics. War is the outcome of both national as well as international politics. And due to war, there are serious consequences on the supply of food and even production of food. Even when there is no war heavy spending on military, diverts funds to be used for food production and maintenance.

The other cause of food security is natural calamities like earthquake, flood, invasion of viruses on the crops, droughts and the like. Such calamities mainly decrease the overall food production. The supply of food also gets affected causing hunger problems. All such natural calamities are beyond the control of human being. Bringing more and more land under agriculture imbalances the nature, also causing degradation of fertile land.

Purchasing Power is one of the most important reasons of Food Security. Due to insufficient income poor people cannot buy enough food to feed their families. Food prices are also rising all over the world, making food beyond the reach of more and more people. Also an FAO report says that, 'conversion of land to grow crops for bio fuels' is also one of the economic factors causing food crisis. There is also an increase in demand for food, which decreases global reserves. Though some thinkers are of the opinion that there is enough food in the world but poor people do not have the money to buy it and that hunger is a social creation. Social beliefs of many societies all over the world prevent poor people from accumulating wealth (which could be useful in the bad times). One more important and all pervading fact that women are not exploited optimally to produce more food and take care of farms more efficiently, due to social stigmas.

The combined effect of longstanding underinvestment in agriculture and food security, price trends and economic crisis have led to increased hunger and poverty in developing countries, plunging more than 100 million people into extreme poverty (L'Aquila, Food Security Initiative) thus, jeopardizing the progress achieved so far in meeting the Millennium Development Goals.

HUNGER of money takes over the HUNGER of food (of poor people). All of us should try to control all-devouring and insatiable attitude of 'money-hungriness', by way of educating the rich, creating awareness among them about the effect, the distress of 'food-hunger' have on the life of poor people around the world. In the words of Swami Vivekananda- "If money help a man to do good to others, it is of some value; but if not, it is simply a mass of evil, and the sooner it is got rid of, the better" According to few experts on food security- 'the world produces enough food to feed everyone'. FAO report (2002) supports by saying that 'world agriculture produces 17 percent more calories than it did 30 years ago, despite a 70 percent increase in population'. It adds- 'this is enough to provide everyone in the world at least 2720 kilocalories per person per day'. The main problem is 'haves' and 'have-nots', the inequality. Some have plenty of food more than enough while some die due to scarcity of food.

Decreased investment towards agriculture sector, poor roads, poor irrigation facilities to small farmers (there are around 450 million farmers having less than 2 hectares of land in developing countries), insufficient storage facilities, all these add to the food shortage[5]. And the deficit is increasing day by day, making it more difficult to arrange funds for raising food production and on the other hand to feed the increasing population. Today only 5% of cultivable land is irrigated in Africa.

Significance of the study:

The significance of the study is highlighted by the fact that there are over 1.2 billion people are affected by Food Security. Every day, 24000 children die due to malnutrition. 1.4 billon children, below 5 years of age are underweight; all this is a direct consequence of unavailability of food.

One of the major reasons for Global Food Security is Agriculture, which is also the foundation of human civilization, and has in fact, contributed to the modern world in a great way. Despite this achievement of agriculture, about 1.2 billion people all over the world are still hungry and poor.

Food per person increased during the 1961-2005 period, showing that agriculture can be an effective way to increase and feed the needy population.

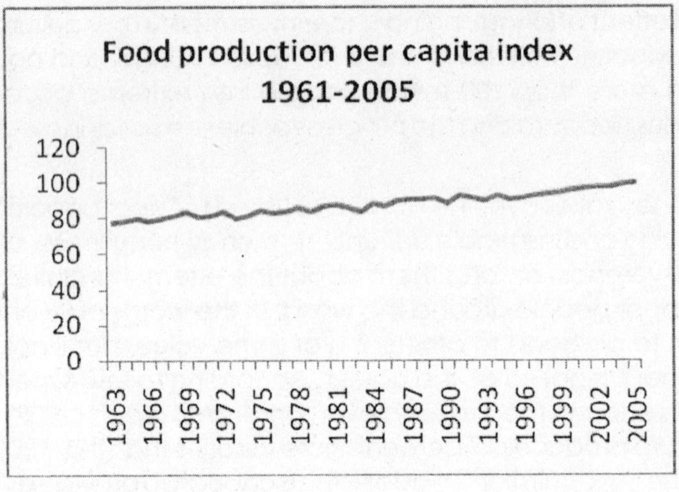

Remedies

First of all 'access to food' should not just be a human right, but should also be made a privilege to end the problem of unfortunate deaths due to hunger. Thinkers have suggested that the poor people, from the least developed countries, should be well prepared to fight the food security problem.

While thinking on the ways to improve food production, it is equally necessary to find innovative ways to control population explosion. One of the ways suggested by FAO Director-General is to assist poor households in the rural areas and helping and guiding them to produce more food to protect them against hunger and hunger related diseases.

Export bans and other trade distorting measures, according to IFPRI research, add fuel to the hike in food prices and lifting the ban would reduce the price levels by as much as 30 percent.

Economic growth is the only way out from the tragedies of poverty. Everyone should work to achieve the best possible, as the people of Western countries did around 1820 by breaking the historical norm of low growth. The best remedy for Food Security is employment. If every person is managed to get a job so that he can feed his family, food security problem would be solved.

Many a reports have come to the conclusion that the hunger problem can be solved if the political will is there. Governments need to see that all people get minimum required quantity of food for sustaining life.

Because women are proved to be doing far better than their male counterparts not only in the field of agriculture, but also in education, management of resources, hard work, it would be pertinent if women are given effective role to play in food security. The effectiveness of women can be increased by giving them more freedom, relieving them from the clutches of traditions. More than three decades of work at International Center for Research on Women (ICRW) on women and agriculture shows that investing in women farmers yields better food security, reduces hunger and spurs economic growth. According to President of ICRW, "women farmers produce a majority of food in developing countries- despite limited access to credit, information, land, tools and technology. With appropriate investments women can be key economic agents of change in their roles as farmers, entrepreneurs, and wage laborers. Moreover, when women can generate income through agriculture, they are more likely to spend it on improving their families' nutrition, health and education." Moreover if women are taught 'Production to processing to marketing' poverty can be alleviated sharply.

Methods of food production play an important role too. It has been found that some methods of food production are better than others, e.g., beef production takes about 10 to 20 calories of energies to produce 1 calorie of food. A typical US corn production, says one report, takes about 1 calorie (fuel, fertilizer etc.) of energy to produce 1 calorie of food. Whereas Dry-land Asian rice culture averages using 1 calorie of energy (human labor) to produce 20 calories of food.

Costs of food should be less so that more and more people can buy it. Costs can be reduced by producing food by 'principle of economies of scale' and by producing in the nearby areas where it is needed.

Bio technology and GM Crops (Genetically Modified Crops) can be one of the solutions. Some experts claim that application of Biotechnology in agriculture will enhance agricultural development to boost production and at the same time reduce environmental degradation and thus help solve food security problem. But the major hurdle to this solution is the international politics opposing the biotechnology and Genetically Modified crops.

Vegetarianism can be effective, says a FAO report on Livestocks, remedy for producing more food. Instead of farming animals for food, the land can be used directly to grow food and get benefitted in more than one way, by acquiring more food and by saving nature of greenhouse gas emissions. The report further adds that "the livestock sector is a major player responsible for 18 percent of greenhouse gas emissions measured in CO_2 equivalent. This is a higher share than transport."

Avoiding Food Wastages can solve the food security problem to a great extent. According to a study by United Nations Environment Programme (UNEP)[8], 'the world could easily feed its growing population if farmers, businesses and government's simply stepped up efforts to curtail food waste'. It is found that up to 50 % food production in the US is wasted, while 33% of food purchased in the UK is never eaten. What is more disturbing is that in the developing world too, around 20 to 40 percent of potential harvests are lost. "Over half of the food produced today is lost, wasted or discarded as a result of inefficiency in the human-managed food chain," said UN Under-Secretary-General and UNEP Executive Director Achim Steiner. "There is evidence within the report that the world could feed the entire projected population growth alone by becoming more efficient while also ensuring the survival of wild animals, birds and fish on this planet".

As per the research done by the World Food Day organization, investing more and more in the agriculture, till there is no dearth of food. The WFD Director-General mentions several ways to improve investment in agriculture. According to its observations, '70% of the world's hungry live in rural areas, where providing food and employment is necessary and critical'. It further adds that agriculture development is the key to all other developments.

AFSI concludes positively by saying "Open trade flows and efficient markets have a positive role in strengthening food security. National and regional strategies should promote the participation of farmers, especially smallholders and women, into community, domestic, regional and international markets. Markets must remain open, protectionism rejected and factors potentially affecting commodity price volatility, including speculation, monitored and analyzed further. We are therefore committed to reduce trade distortions and refrain from raising new barriers to trade and investment and from implementing WTO-inconsistent measures to stimulate exports. To this end, we aim at an ambitious, comprehensive and balanced conclusion of the Doha Development Round and call for renewed, determined efforts to bring it to a timely and successful conclusion. We are committed to improve access to information, promote conducive business environments and investment in rural infrastructure, such as transportation, processing, storage facilities and irrigation schemes".

Challenges ahead

Keeping prices in control and feeding the increasing population are the immediate challenges.

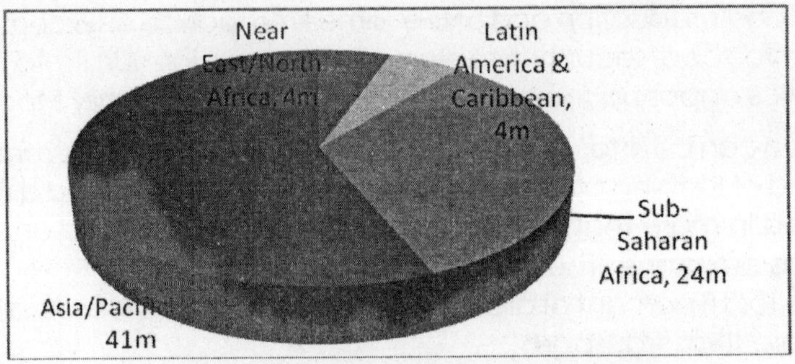

How food prices add to world hunger

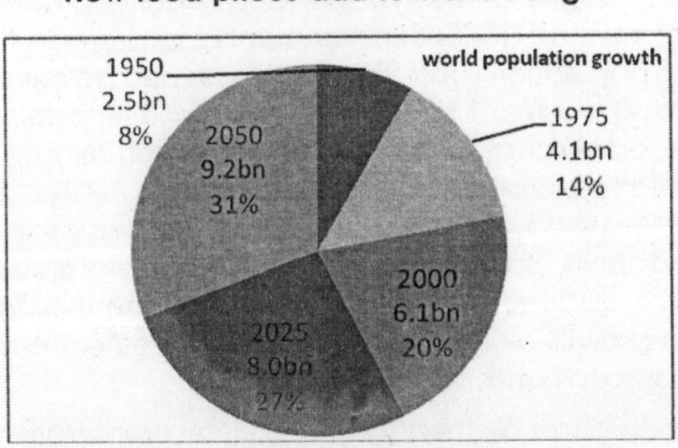

75m of the world's hungry are direct result of high food prices (FAO est.)

Total undernourished in world: 923m (Source: FAO)

"Our greatest challenge is to reach the World Food Summit and the first Millennium Development Goal to halve by 2015 hunger and poverty worldwide", Director-General of World Food Day, says in her 16 Oct 2006 message.

The Global Hunger Index, a tool developed by IFPRI, to calculate hunger and malnutrition, shows that worldwide progress in reducing hunger are nonetheless slow. According to IFPRI study, "Southeast Asia, the Near East and North Africa, and Latin America and the Caribbean have reduced hunger significantly since 1990, but GHI remains high remains high in South Asia, which has made progress since 1990 and in Sub-Saharan Africa where the progress has been marginal". The lack of political will, corrupt bureaucracy and unawareness of its people about their rights is said to be the reasons behind the worsening of the problem. "Since 1990, though some countries like Kuwait, Tunisia, Fiji, Malaysia, and Turkey have made significant progress towards reducing hunger in their respective countries, but 29 countries have levels of hunger that are "alarming or extremely alarming", says IFPRI study.

The first Millennium Development Goal (MDG) could attain but only 50 percent of the food security goal. In the Sub-Saharan Africa and South Asia countries, the problem of food security is more severe than the rest of the world. Almost half of the young children in India are underweight, very alarming situation. The malnutrition leads ultimately to inability to work or avoidance of work leading to more poverty. Here we need strong political will, as there is enough food for all, only faulty and corrupt distribution system is to be monitored *strictly*.

UNICEF says that it is not possible to reach the MDG target of 2015. FAO has also doubted about the attainment of food security goals.

Conclusion

Though there is some progress on the global food security crisis, the 'hunger-free world' goal is yet far away. Needing more and immediate efforts on all fronts, from all concerned people and agencies. As per the observations of International Food Policy Research Institute (IFPRI), there is a need to invest more in agriculture.

References

1. Joint statement on Global Food Security, 2009, *Food Security Session*, G8 Summit in L'Aquila
2. Frances Moore Lappe, Josepf Collins, and Peter Rosset with Luis Esparza, 1998, *World Hunger: 12 Myths*, 2nd Edition, New York: Grove Press
3. FAO, 2006, *Livestock's Long Shadow: environmental issues and options*, Food and Agriculture Organization of The United Nations, Rome 2006.
4. Economic and Social Development Department of FAO, 2006, *State of Food Insecurity*
5. FAO Report, 2002, *Reducing Poverty and Hunger, the Critical Role of Financing for Food, Agriculture, and Rural Development*.
6. Food Insecurity and Vulnerability Information and Mapping Systems, 2009, *State of Food Insecurity*
7. FAO Report : Rome, 2006, *Title of Report*, Food and Agriculture Organization (FAO)

8. GEO Year Book: an overview of our changing environment, United Nations Environment Programme (UNEP), 2007: UNEP Report.
9. United Nations Environment Programme, 2009, *The environmental Food Crisis,* UNEP Report
10. M S Swaminathan, Pedro Medrano, Daniel j Gustafson, Pravesh Sharma, 2004, 'The Experience with Food Safty Nets in India', National Food Security Summit, New Delhi.
11. Manfred Zeller, Gertrud Schrieder, Joachim Van Braun, Franz Heidhues, 1997, *Rural Finance for Food Security for the Poor, Implications for Research and Policy, Washington DC* : International Food Policy Research Institute (IFPRI)

Table 1: (source MDG website)

Millennium Development Goals	2005	2008
Employment to population ratio, 15+, total (%)	61	*61*
Employment to population ratio, ages 15-24, total (%)	45	*45*
GDP per person employed (annual % growth)	3	..
Malnutrition prevalence, weight for age (% of children under 5)	*23.1*	*23.1*
Prevalence of undernourishment (% of population)	14	..
Literacy rate, youth female (% of females ages 15-24)	*87*	*87*
Literacy rate, youth male (% of males ages 15-24)	*91*	*91*
Primary completion rate, total (% of relevant age group)	86	*87*
Proportion of seats held by women in national parliaments (%)	16	18
Immunization, measles (% of children ages 12-23 months)	79	*82*
Mortality rate, infant (per 1,000 live births)	49	*47*
Mortality rate, under-5 (per 1,000)	71	*68*
Births attended by skilled health staff (% of total)	*65*	*65*
Maternal mortality ratio (modeled estimate, per 100,000 live births)	400	..
Pregnant women receiving prenatal care (%)	*81*	*81*
Children with fever receiving antimalarial drugs (% of children under age 5 with fever)	..	..
Forest area (% of land area)	30	..
Gross capital formation (% of GDP)	21.8	*22.3*
Life expectancy at birth, total (years)	68	*69*
Literacy rate, adult total (% of people ages 15 and above)	*84*	*84*
Population, total (millions)	6,462.1	6,692.0

31

Managing Waste for Combating Global Food Crisis is

Aasha Sharma

Introduction

The global food security discussions held during the last decade have generally concluded with the claim that "By 2050, we must eliminate the global productivity gap by sustainably doubling agricultural output to meet the needs of a growing world". This claim has been repeated by many experts.

But some shocking statistics from FAO data reveal that **the world is already producing more than twice the amount of food we actually consume, but we end up wasting huge quantities of food after production**. According to a brief authored by the Stockholm International Water Institute, the UN Food and Agriculture Organization, and the International Water Management Institute the current food crisis is not only the crisis of production but more over a crisis of waste. The report says "In poorer countries, due to various reasons an estimated 15 to 35 percent of food is lost in the field during production adding another 10 to15 percent of loss during processing, transport and storage. In richer countries, production is more efficient but waste is greater, "People toss the food they buy and all the resources used to grow, ship and produce the food along with it." (Stockholm water institute 2009)

"Eliminating the millions of tons of food thrown away annually in the US and UK households could lift more than 1 billion people out of hunger worldwide, leave alone waste due to various other reasons" experts say.

Issues and approaches

Pending issues like population growth, counterproductive subsidies and trade policies, food waste and contaminations are intensified with new issues like climate change and drought, high energy prices, over consumption, globalization and diversion of crops for biofuels. (www.smart planet) And all these issues are interlinked. If we need to solve one issue we will have to look into all of these as these are interconnected. Clearly we need to have a smarter and efficient approach here

Enough food is produced every year but lot is wasted from farm to fork transit. There are huge inefficiencies in the food chain. But if we observe the type of waste, it differs from country to country. In fact we can very clearly discriminate the types between developed countries and underdeveloped or developing countries. The waste can be divided into pre-harvest and post harvest category for developed and underdeveloped countries. This would help us to understand approaches needed to combat waste, as both developed as well as underdeveloped countries waste for different reasons. For example in the UK the issue of food waste has a focus on the amount of food thrown away by consumers at home or left on diners plates. But in a country like India the issue of food waste is mainly in the actual handling, storage and transport of foodstuff. India is an example of a developing country facing challenges in tackling food security and adequate supply for its burgeoning population. The Developing world is being hit with not only inadequate supply of food stuffs but also higher global prices for commodities such as rice, wheat and maize along with huge levels of waste.

Food waste facts of developing countries:

- In the 2008 Global Hunger Index of developing and transitional countries, India was ranked 66th out of 88 nations. This ranking was worse than nearly 25 Sub-Saharan African countries and all of South Asia, except Bangladesh. (Global politician-Dec 2008) Wastage of harvested food items in the country in 2007-08 was calculated at nearly Rs 58,000 crore, at a number of stages of handling because of lack of sufficient post-harvest infrastructure, cold chains, transportation and proper storage facilities. If those food items had been saved, thousands would have slept with food in their tummy. (Global politician-Dec 2008)
- Around 1 million tones of food grain, which could have fed over 10 million people for a year, has instead rotted in Food Corporation of India (FCI) godowns despite the FCI spending Rs 242 crore (Rs 2.42 billion) on attempts to prevent the loss during storage. Ironically, another Rs 2.59 crore was spent on disposing off the rotten grain! -(www.zeenews.com)
- Due to the absence of distribution links and processing, 16 million tone of vegetables and 40 million tone of fruit are wasted which adds to losses and prices in India (Source—India Today march 2007)
- Japan currently has roughly 900,000 tons of U.S. medium grain rice and 600,000 tons of long grain rice imported from Thailand and Vietnam, which are surplus to domestic consumption requirements based on its World Trade Organization (WTO) obligation. However this rice may not be re-exported because of Japan's market access commitments under the WTO Agreement on Agriculture. These stocks are not sold domestically; instead they are allowed to decay and then used as livestock feed. Last year about 400,000 tons of rice was disposed of in this manner. (The world bank trade note 2008)

- China is also holding rice stocks equal to at least four months of domestic consumption (significantly in excess of food security guidelines of 18–20 percent of Total consumption) and could help stabilize the world rice market without affecting its food. (The world bank trade note 2008)

Food waste facts of developed countries

- There are nearly one billion malnourished people in the world, but the approximately 40 million tons of food wasted by US households, retailers and food services each year would be enough to satisfy the hunger of every one of them. (Straut, 2009)
- The irrigation water used globally to grow food that is wasted would be enough for the domestic needs (at 200 liters per person per day) of 9 billion people - the number expected on the planet by 2050. If we planted trees on land currently used to grow unnecessary surplus and wasted food, this would offset a theoretical maximum of 100% of man-made greenhouse gas emissions. (Straut, 2009)
- 10% of rich countries' greenhouse gas emissions come from growing food that is never eaten. (Straut, 2009)
- The UK, US and Europe have nearly twice as much food as is required by the nutritional needs of their populations. Up to half the entire food supply is wasted between the farm and the fork. If crops wastefully fed to livestock are included, European countries have more than three times more food than they need, while the US has around four times more food than is needed, and up to three-quarters of the nutritional value is lost before it reaches people's mouths. (Straut, 2009)
- UK Households waste 25% of all the food they buy. (Straut, 2009)
- All the world's nearly one billion hungry people could be lifted out of malnourishment on less than a quarter of the food that is wasted in the US, UK and Europe. (Straut, 2009)
- A third of the world's entire food supply could be saved by reducing waste - or enough to feed 3 billion people; and this would still leave enough surpluses for countries to provide their populations with 130 per cent of their nutritional requirements. (Straut, 2009)
- Between 2 and 500 times more carbon dioxide can be saved by feeding food waste to pigs rather than sending it for anaerobic digestion (the UK government's preferred option). But under European laws feeding food waste to pigs is banned. In Japan, South Korea and Taiwan, by contrast, it is mandatory to feed some food waste to pigs. (Straut, 2009)
- 2.3 million tones of fish discarded in the North Atlantic and the North Sea each year; 40 to 60% of all fish caught in Europe are discarded - either because they are the wrong size, species, or because of the ill-governed European quota system. (Straut, 2009)
- An estimated 20 to 40% of UK fruit and vegetables rejected even before they reach the shops - mostly because they do not match the supermarkets' excessively strict cosmetic standards. (Straut, 2009)

- 8.3 million hectares of land required to produce just the meat and dairy products wasted in UK homes and in US homes, shops and restaurants. That is 7 times the amount of Amazon rainforest destroyed in Brazil in one year, largely for cattle grazing and soy production to export for livestock feed. (Straut, 2009)
- The bread and other cereal products thrown away in UK households alone would have been enough to lift 30 million of the world's hungry people out of malnourishment (Straut, 2009)
- 4600 kilocalories per day of food are harvested for every person on the planet; of these, only around 2000 on average are eaten - more than half of it is lost on the way. (Straut, 2009)
- 4 million people in the UK, 43 million in the EU and around 35 million in the US suffer from food poverty. (Straut, 2009)
- 24 to 35% of school lunches end up in the bin. (Straut, 2009)
- An estimated 20 million tones of food wasted in Britain from the plough to the plate. (Straut, 2009)

Reasons for waste:

1. Tossing away food by families/house-holds/hotels as it is spoiled or is more than required.
2. Waste in retail outlets because of non consumption due to less demand/high Prices/market dynamics/Change in preferences.
3. Pre production in fields—Agricultural practices/Lack of infrastructural capacities/ Climatic conditions.
4. Post production-Storage/Transportation/inefficient supply chain/no access to markets.
5. Trade practices-Restrictions/Trade agreements/quota.
6. Aggressive marketing-Due to excess buying/affluence, increased purchasing power or dissatisfaction.

Broadly the above reasons could be marked for waste globally. But sources of waste in developed and underdeveloped countries are different.

Waste in Underdeveloped Countries factors at the beginning of the food chain — the production and transformation stage.

Pre harvest-

- Inefficiencies due to lack of technology.
- Dependency on rain
- Climate changes/drought/famine/flood.
- Pest attack

Post harvest-

The wastage is occurring at various stages of handling after harvesting

- Due to fragmented farming
- Conventional methods of farming
- Lack of adequate post-harvest infrastructure such as cold chain facilities, transportation, proper storage facilities, etc.
- Inaccessibility to markets/lack of market information
- Lack of food processing capacities

Waste in developed countries is mainly at the last stage that is consumption stage.

- Consumer preferences: Because of strict quality regulations and consumer preferences, a large amount of food is thrown away due to slight changes in quality or appearance. e.g., Marks and Spencer requires their supplier Hein Celestial Group to discard 4 slices of from each loaf, the crust and first slice at the either end resulting in 13000 slices thrown away every day from one factory
- Similarly, requirements for uniform packaging procedures result in heavy losses of discarded irregularly shaped fruits and vegetables.
- Over/Excess buying resulting in tossing away of food
- Millions of tons of edible food wasted by modern food processing and 'sell-by' dates

Solutions

- Raising consumer awareness about food waste is a must
- Developed countries badly need lessons in lifestyle management
- Developing countries need to invest in infrastructure, storage facilities, transport and modern supply chain practices so that much the loss could be avoided with more food filling the stomachs of its population.
- Increase efficiency of food supply chain
- Reduction of food waste should be on highest priority of Nations.

Conclusion

- Waste cannot be totally eliminated but can be certainly reduced.
- Reduction of food waste would not solve the food crisis problem totally but it would help to certainly reduce the number of hungry stomachs globally.
- Different approach for developed and developing countries is needed to reduce their wastes as their sources and reasons as well as types of waste are different
- Even if sources and reasons are different the consequences affect people all over the globe as the issues are all interlinked

References

1. 2009, S. i.
2. blog, s. (n.d.).
3. Dulcinea, f. p. (n.d.).
4. Global politician- Monday Dec 2008, D. 2. (n.d.).
5. India Today, M. 5. (n.d.).
6. straut, t. (2009). Waste.
7. The world bank, t. n.
8. www.googlenews.com. (n.d.).
9. www.zeenews.com.
10. straut, t. (2009). Waste.
11. February 17, 2009 environment news service
12. Food for Thought: Averting the Food Crisis and Reducing Waste,21/05/2009
13. Food Waste Persists Despite Global Shortage May 09, 2008 07:00 AM by finding Dulcinea Staff
14. http://smarterplanet.blog
15. Stockholm international water institute 2009
16. Via (website))
17. WASTE
18. Waste (Book) / auth. straut tristram. - 2009.
19. Uncovering the Global Food Scandal, by Tristram Stuart, Penguin
20. (www.googlenews.com)

32

Controlling Land and Water Degradation in Asia for Food Security

Thorat S.R. Sonawane A.C., Kulkarni M.N, and Parate V.R.

Introduction

Degradation of Land and Water, Shortages of Water and Land: Land use does not necessarily lead to degradation, not even intensive land use. Proper short term investments in inputs (water, fertilizer, seeds) and long term investments in structures and equipment (pumps, tractors, dams, terraces) can conserve soil and water, while allowing productive and sustainable agricultural land use. The same applies to water: its use for growing crops does not have to lead to shortages and pollution. However, if conditions are such that farmers cannot invest in these inputs and structures, human activity will continue to degrade natural resources and peoples livelihoods, unless off-farm employment can help provide an income without destroying the natural resource base. Societies and its institutions should invest for the long term in water and land management structures and in education to halt degradation.

Among the many consequences of degradalion are the local reduction in housohold food security and in the quality of livelihoods, the threat of losing the capacity for achieving national food security, the high cost of maintaining or restoring natural environments (parks, wildlife reserves, wetlands), the loss and devaluation of land for agricultural purposes, and the increased risks of natural disasters (flooding and drought).

For 'land', degradation is a well-known process (*e.g.*, Bridges *et. al.*, 2001). It is estimated that as many as 1.8 billion people live in areas with some noticeable land and water degradation, and which reduces livelihoods and household food security. Degradation occurs in some or many parts of nearly all developing countries. Moreover, the rate of degradation of land and water resources is accelerating, and consequences for food security are becoming increasingly clear (Wood *et. al.*, 2000).

The Projected Water Scarcity in 2025: Degradation of water and of land often occurs in parallel and both lead to a lower level of ecosystem services, in particular a reduced capacity for food production and income generation. Both are the result of inappropriate management. The degradation of these resources needs to be addressed as one problem and they are treated jointly in the remainder of this document. Soil degradation has become globally a common phenomenon, but its extent varies between 'loss of the natural resources' and 'insignificant or even rehabilitation. Figure 3 shows a specific example for South and East Asia. Both indicate that degradation is widespread, and that its spatial variability is quite pronounced at the larger scales. At smaller scales of farms and catchments, heterogeneity is also a very significant factor. Heterogeneity contributes significantly to problems of scientists (how to handle it) and to solutions for rural people (by providing more options for development than the 'average' would suggest).

Impact on Food Security: Even though land degradation is often visible and water shortage reported daily in the press, it is difficult to translate these phenomena into consequences for food security is difficult conceptually and in practice. For subsistence farmers, consequences are direct: less food with more efforts, and even: moving out. But nowadays, most farming households, however, do take part in food trade. As producers of food, degradation leads to lower yields with more efforts, so either less food or less income. As consumers, they can buy food if they have money. Degradation may also leads to increased cost of living and to higher food prices. So household food security is affected also in the second case, albeit in a more complex manner. In fact, the relation between degradation and food security is of enormous complexity due to the interactions between land, water, populations and wealth, and the rapid changes therein. There are strong indications that consequences of degradation for food security at the household level already affect many people significantly (*e.g.*, Bridges *et. al.*, 2001, Scherr, 2001). Global food security, on the other hand, is not affected much, yet. Food security in this document implies the production of food, the access of food, and the utilization of food. For global food security, the emphasis is that sufficient food is produced in the world to meet the full requirements of all people: total global food supply equals the total global demand. For household food security, the focus is on the ability of households, urban and rural, to purchase or produce food they need for a healthy and active life; disposable income is a crucial issue. For national food security, the focus is on sufficient food for all people in a nation; it can be assured through any combination of national production and food imports and exports. Food security has always a component of production, access, and utilization. Women are typically the gatekeepers of food security.

Land and water degradation has also other major effects. The Asian Development Bank (1997) expressed its concern about environmental degradation and future food production). The current economic crisis places additional emphasis on short term economic concerns over longer term environmental concerns. One recent estimate of the cost of remediation of environmental damage due to degradation for Asia puts it 35 billion US$ (Table 1). Though very roughly estimated, the order of magnitude indicates a marked need to address erosion problems, and calls attention for land degradation and for assessing future directions for rehabilitation by reforestation and other means. Such views are supported by many (Gregory *et. al.*, 2001).

Table 1: Annualized cost of remediation for Asian countries (in million 1990)

Country	Water[b]	Air[c(erosion)]	Land[d(MSW)]	Land[e]	Land[f(forest)]	Land(Total)	Eco-system[g]	COR (Total)
Bangladesh	13.70	30.34	199.21	99.87	22.38	321.47	52.39	417.89
Bhutan	0.16	0.35	8.07	0.43	0.00	8.50	24.45	33.45
Cambodia	0.31	0.70	72.84	5.26	0.00	78.11	30.85	109.97
Lao PDR	0.26	0.58	34.19	4.27	0.00	38.46	33.18	72.48
Mongolia	5.91	13.08	2,517.62	6.14	249.50	2,773.26	13.39	2,805.64
Myanmar	3.56	7.87	208.42	52.32	0.00	260.74	65.20	337.36
Nepal	0.78	1.74	93.10	12.43	10.07	115.60	48.90	167.02
Pakistan	53.97	119.49	522.59	187.21	157.40	867.20	36.09	1,076.76
Sri Lanka	3.50	7.76	46.84	18.28	0.00	65.12	147.86	224.24
Vietnam	12.97	28.71	134.56	66.19	0.00	200.75	251.48	493.91
People's Rep. of China	1,430.13	3,166.07	9,939.10	1,648.85	1.070.02	12,6517.97	299.79	17,553.96
India	418.97	927.53	3,630.67	1,092.80	159.51	4,882.97	852.23	7,081.70
Indonesia	100.10	221.61	657.93	277.99	0.00	953.92	296.30	1,571.93
Papua New Guinea	1.73	3.82	9.61	3.33	0.00	12.94	70.44	88.92
Philippines	39.59	87.59	184.76	134.91	0.00	319.67	160.67	607.57
Thailand	67.00	148.32	477.85	68.03	11.75	557.63	47.73	820.68
Fiji	0.52	1.16	6.03	1.45	0.00	7.48	20.37	29.53
Korea, Rep. of	199.84	442.41	43.82	159.42	0.00	203.24	61.71	907.19
Malaysia	43.15	95.52	98.23	40.55	0.00	138.78	329.48	606.93
Singapore	24.42	54.07	0.02	14.40	0.23	14.65	14.55	107.70
Total	**2,420.58**	**5,358.76**	**18,903.45**	**3,894.14**	**1,680.14**	**24,478.44**	**2,857.06**	**35,114.83**

Source: Jalal & Rogres (1997)

Notes to Table 1

- Data for Afghanistan, Maldives, South Pacific (including Marshall Islands), Hong Kong and Taipei, China are incomplete or unavailable.
- Cost data based on 90% reduction of COD, suspended solids, and some heavy metals for PRC areused and the total CORs of all the DMCs are assumed proportional to their total commercial energy consumption.
- Cost data based on 90% reduction of TSP and sulfur emissions for PRC are used and the CORs for all the DMC are assumed proportional to their total commercial energy consumption.
- Unit cost data per ha are derived from PRC and total area subject to erosion for all the DMCs is estimate assuming it is proportional to their total cropped and pasture areas. It is further assumed that 70% eroded area will be controlled to achieve 70-95% erosion reduction in ten years.
- A fixed waste generation rate, 0.21 per capita per year, and fixed costs for waste collection and waste management $20/t for collection and $2/t for sanitary landfill, are assumed for all DMCs. Only urban municipal solid waste (MSW) are considered.
- PRC cost for tree plantation of $179 per ha is adopted and a universal target of 20% forest coveragerate is assumed for all DMCs. If a country's forest coverage exceeds 20% no further cost is incurred.
- Indonesia's unit costs is building and running national parks and targets for the period 1991-2000 are used for all DMCs, assuming the cost is proportional to the total number of species considered threatened, including mammals, birds, reptiles, amphibians, higher plants and fishes.

Driving Variables and Options to Influence these: Ultimate driving variables of degradation include population growth and its increase in wealth, globalisation of trade and economic relations, and climate change. These have an enormous momentum and are slowly to modify. We will focus on intermediate driving variables the are closer within reach for action. Rather than discussing the driving variables by continent or by biophysical process, we analyze situations in four broad geographical zones, following the flow of water, in: 'headwaters', 'plains', cities and peri urban areas' and 'coastal areas'. Areas within these zones but in different countries have much similarity in the degradation processes and in the causes there off. The fact that the zones are generally also connected gives rises to another set of issues where use in one area affects use in another. There are major flows of water and plant nutrients between them, generally towards cities and the sea. Movement of people and trade are other example of significant interactions between zones. The main document covers the processes, causes and impacts of particularly soil erosion, nutrient depletion, water pollution, groundwater depletion, and river desiccation.

The principle driving variable of land and water degradation in Plains is the intensification of agriculture, through an increased and often inappropriate application of fertilizers, water and pesticides. Over- or under-use of water, fertilizers and pesticides cause the problems. Intensification requires extra water, either from surface irrigation or groundwater. When misappropriated, this leads to problems (groundwater overdraft, soil salinization, pollution, and desiccation). Insufficient use of fertilizer leads to nutrient depletion, a very common degradation process in marginal areas. Lack of knowledge of the consequences of decisions at the farm level, district and national level, and lack of incentives to use natural resources more carefully, are behind these choices. In some cases, there is a lack of technologies to use natural resources effectively and without degradation. One of the difficulties in arresting agricultural pollution is that farmers see little benefit for changing their practices. This is often because of inappropriate policies, including underpriced water and fertilizer, and pesticide subsidies. A second difficulty is the dispersed nature of non point source pollution – substantial agricultural pollution is the result of the actions of several farmers, and the entry point into the hydrologic systems is widely dispersed. This poses also severe technical monitoring problems.

In coastal areas, the driving force is growth is encroachment and the offsite effects from plains (pollution, desiccation) and headwaters (erosion). As much as 39% of the world's population live within 100 km of the coast, and their presence, and growth in wealth, has a major impact. Shoreline modification has altered sea currents and sediment delivery mechanisms. Artificial mechanisms for shoreline stabilization replace the natural buffering capacity of natural systems such as coral reefs or estuaries to protect against storms. Rising waters affected by climate change can potentially have dramatic impacts on coastal areas. Coastal areas are at the receiving end of upstream land and water degradation processes – these zones receive the sediment loads and pollution transported by water from upstream agriculture and cities. These areas must also absorb changes brought about by reduced river discharges and changes in the discharge downstream hydrograph brought about by upstream development. In addition, high populations put pressure on coastal and marine environments and encroachment occurs in fragile wetlands and coastal areas.

Choosing Between More or Less Degradation: With few exceptions, people do not intend to degrade the natural resources they use, but their decisions to do so are guided by economic realities and lack of understanding. It is therefore that we focus on those realities and on providing knowledge. We focus at the crucial clusters of driving variables that operate in the different geographical areas we distinguished, albeit with different intensities. In a sense, this will be nested sets of driving variables. Policy makers influence the socio-economic environment for land and water users, who are then guided in their decision making and will undertake actions that co-determine their food security and degradation of natural resources. Because of the complexity of nearly every process and the multiple levels of driving variables, changes in either driving factor may be essential, yet none is sufficient by itself. Successful approaches to reducing degradation and improving food security consider how to make best use of, or increase, all resources that people should have at their disposal: natural, human, physical, social, financial resources. Participatory means 'with the people': designing and implementing intervention strategies should occur together with all stakeholders

Attitudes and Incentives: Concern for and Knowledge about Natural Resources: A recent article in The Economist (August 2001) expresses optimism that societies become aware and concerned about degradation of the natural environment, and with rising incomes find ways to halt and reverse degradation, and provides some interesting examples from Europe and North America. We consider this view overly optimistic. If lack of 'green' concerns in a societies and lack of equity, that would keep most people at low income levels even though the national average rises, damage may be much higher than the average at any income level. If the land and water resources are exploited beyond their threshold of resilience, due to high population density or ecological fragility, the system breaks down rather suddenly. That case, in a short period land gets lost for agriculture, water is no longer productive, national food security is reduced, and the option for income generation through agriculture disappears. Research organisations and enterprises encouraged by donors, can facilitate the change by making investments technically more effective ('more crop per drop'), cheaper, and more accessible.

Increased public awareness of the state and importance of natural resources is crucial. Newspapers and television, environmental education at school and 'green activists' play important roles. Awareness of the many technological options for land and water management whose effectiveness has been proven is still quite limited. Limited awareness is also due to incomplete or even incorrect mental pictures among land and water users about natural resources, and the public at large.

It is important to have a legal framework to define what activities are allowed in a particular area, who is responsible for them and for the state of the resources, and who oversees. It is also important that the legal framework is effectively implemented; internationally accepted standards are needed on maximum contamination of soil and water used for different purposes.

Within the arena of laws and politics, one of the most important issues is to provide smallholders with tenure or long term arrangements on land use, and water users assured rights to this resource. The absence of such rights is an important threshold for farmers to mobilize funds and invest them in their farms, improving livelihoods and reducing degradation. Assuring long term rights to land and water is probably the single most important action that can halt degradation and assure poor people of a decent option to earn a living through agriculture.

Policy interventions that seek to overcome environmental problems in agriculture need to be based on a proper understanding of why farmers degrade their environment. Why, for example, do farmers often seem to overgraze rangeland, deplete soil nutrients and organic matter, and overuse irrigation water, pesticides and nitrogen, when these actions cause health problems and reduce future incomes for themselves, their children, and the communities in which they live? The answer lies with the incentives facing farmers. Farmers are not irrational. On the contrary, they maximize income and minimize risk in a dynamic context and often under harsh conditions and serious constraints. They degrade resources when there are good economic and social reasons for doing so, *i.e.*, when the benefits they obtain exceed the perceived costs that they, as individuals, must bear.

Infrastructure: Human development brings majors expansion in infrastructure: roads, channels, housing, dams, airports, recreational facilities. It can have some very positive effects too by making key inputs available and at lower prices (e.g., fertilizer), by giving farmers more options for increasing income and hence, relieving the pressure on land (e.g., high value vegetables and livestock products, even forest and tree products), and by facilitating more commuting and non-farm activities). Yet, infrastructure is often laid out on good agricultural land, hence diminishing the amount of land available for food production. New infrastructure can rapidly accelerate degradation. Roads, and even footpaths, are important contributors to erosion/sedimentation. As for water, generally, infrastructure increases its availability, by channelling it to places where it is most needed (often for non-agricultural use) and reducing leakage and improving recycling.

The low cost of transport by road and sea allows transport of large amounts of food from rural areas to cities, from export countries to importing ones, and from one continent to another. The driving force is generally the difference in cost of production between the locations, and produce quality. Wealthy people, particularly in urban conglomerates, use resources from a large area to produce food and the many other things they consume. This (non contiguous) area has been labelled 'Ecological Footprint' parts of which may be far away. As for the overall utilization of water, the phenomena reduce global water consumption if the water use efficiency is higher at the export site. For the current major food exporters, USA, Brazil, France, and major importers, China, African countries, this may actually be the case, given the different climates. Water transport in food is negligible. Not negligible is the amount of 'plant nutrients' transported in food across large distances. Yet, there are no mechanisms to ensure recycling to the source of origin, and this process contributes strongly to 'nutrient depletion' in the Plains. Not addressing this ecological principle undermines global sustainable land and water management. Widespread promotion of 'best practices' is an excellent way to make use of experiences obtained elsewhere, provided that these experiences were evaluated from the viewpoints of the five dimensions for evaluation of the sustainability of agricultural production systems (Smyth and Dumanski, 1993, Coughlan and Lefroy, 2001): productivity, stability, protection of the natural resources, economic viability, social adoptability. Alternatively or in combination, they could be assessed according to their impact on capital assets (financial, natural, social, human, physical) of INRM.

Further Developments of Technology and Management: With respect to land and water management, technological developments have led to (1) higher crop and livestock yields per unit of land and water (selection, breeding, biotechnology), (2) replacement of human and animal labour by machines (e.g., tractors) allowing individuals to cultivate larger areas, (3) increases in the volumes of accessible irrigation and drinking water (e.g., reservoirs, diversion structures, pumps), (4) replacement of human observations by readings of instruments for more consistent management (e.g. soil probes that trigger irrigation when the soil is dry), (5)refinement of management to produce the same output or more with less inputs and reduced risk (e.g., precision agriculture, drip irrigation, weather forecasts). Like any biophysical process, crop productivity per unit of input has a ceiling level. Given the major advances in the past decades, one might ask whether there still is any potential for developments in technology that bring significant improvements in land and water productivity. Since maximum biological efficiencies of crop and livestock production are reached in only few cases, it is likely that still many technological and management inventions can be realized to do more with less inputs, more recycling, less waste and pollution.

However, spectacular increases in productivity over the past decades makes that some production systems have become very efficient indeed. The downside is that in areas with already high land and water productivity, further increases in productivity will be increasingly difficult to attain (e.g., Cassman, 2001).

Farming systems based on ecological principles do a better job, generally, in generating and recycling organic matter and plant nutrients, and in protecting natural resources, than many modern but unbalanced systems. This includes use of tree-based land use on hillsides. Technology improvements for NRM should be more than just input/output efficiency. A general way of seeing what technology can contribute to rehabilitation of degraded land is increase the maximum level of production (increasing the yield gap, making improvement by farmers easier), increasing yield stability (i.e., reducing the relative level of risk), and improving the economic returns to investment (by increasing the efficiency of the response to inputs, particularly at lower yield levels)

The study reveals that degraded land shows lower yields reduced input efficiency and higher risk. Carbon-sequestration, desirable from the point of view of reducing climate change, is also a feature of reduced land degradation: the more Carbon (C) is retained in SOM*, the better its fertility, water holding capacity, and resilience. Increasing the C-content of the soil by 1% on 1 ha would eliminate 3 t C from the air, albeit that plants need to transpire some 6-12000 t water to fix this C and depose it in the soil, water that will not run to the river. This suggests that C-sequestration in humid and sub-humid areas, where the lower value applies, has a lower risk of leading to water conflicts than in semi arid areas.

References

1. Asian Development Bank. 1997. Emerging Asia, changes and challenges. ADB, Manila, Philippines (350 pp).
2. Bridges, E. M., I.D. Hannam, L.R. Oldeman, F.W.T. Penning de Vries, S.J. Scherr, and S. Sombatpanit (Eds.) 2001. *Response to land degradation*. Science Publishers, Inc.
3. Burke, L., Y. Kura, K. Kassem, C. Revenga, M. Spalding, and D. McAllister. 2001. *Pilot analysis of global ecosystems: Coastal ecosystems*. Washington, DC., USA: World Resources Institute.
4. Campbell, B., Sayer, J., Frost, P., Vermeulen, S. Ruiz Perez, M., Cunningham, A., Prabhu, R., Waddington, S., Chuma, E. 2000. Evaluating the Impacts of Integrated Natural Resource Management (INRM) Research. Paper presented at the INRM workshop in Penang, 2000. http://www.inrm.cgiar.org/documents/workshop_2000.htm
5. Coughlan, J.K. and R.D.B. Lefroy. 2001. Assessment of sustainable land management using the FESLM: The IBSRAM experience. Issues in Sustainable Land Management No. 8. Thailand: International Board for Soil Research and Management.
6. Drechsel, P., D. Kunze, and F.W.T. Penning de Vries. 2001. Soil nutrient depletion and population growth in Sub-Saharan Africa: A Malthusian Nexus? Population andEnvironment: 22, 4.
7. Drechsel, P., and D. Kunze (Eds.) 2001. *Waste composting for urban and peri-urban agriculture: Closing the rural-urban nutrient cycle in Sub-Saharan Africa*. CABI Publishers.

8. Greenland, D.J., G. Bowen, H. Eswaran, R. Rhoades and C. Valentin, 1994. Soil, Water, and Nutrient Management Research, a new agenda. IBSRAM Position paper, IBSRAM, Bangkok, Thailand (60 pp).
9. Jalal, K.F. and P.P. Rogers, 1997. Measuring Environmental Performance in Asia. ADB Environment Paper No. 13. Asian Development Bank, Manila, Philippines. IBSRAM, 1999. Medium Term Plan. International Board for Soil Research and Management, Bangkok, Thailand.
10. Peng, Keshan and Zhenzing Xu. 1993. The problems existing in land environment of China protective countermeasures. Ecological Economics, No. 5 (1993): 18-22.
11. Penning de Vries, F.W.T, 2001. Food security? We are losing ground fast. Pp1-14 in Crop Science: progress and prospects. J.Noesberger, H.H. Geiger and P.C. Struik,eds. CAB International, Wallingford, UK.
12. Oldeman, L.R., V.W.P. van Engelen, and J. H. M. Pulles. 1990. The Extent of Human- Induced Soil Degradation. Annex 5 by L.R. Oldeman, R.T.A. Hakkeling, and W.G. Sombroek, World Map of the Status of Human-Induced Soil Degradation: An Explanatory Note. International Soil Reference and Information Centre, Wageningen, the Netherlands.
13. Ponting, C., 1991. Green history of the earth. Cambridge University Press, Cambridge, UK (350 pp).
14. Revenga, C.,J. Brunner, N. Henninger, K. Kassem, and R. Payne. 2000. Pilot analysis of global ecosystems: Freshwater systems. Washington, DC., USA: World Resources Institute.
15. Scherr, S.J., and S.Yadav. 1996. Land degradation in the developing world: Implications for food, agriculture, and the environment to 2020. Food, Agriculture, and the Environment Discussion Paper 14. Washington, DC., USA: International Food
16. Policy Research Institute.
17. Smyth, A.J. and Dumanski, A.J., 1993. An international Framework for Evaluating sustainable land management. World Soil Resources Report 72. FAO, Rome.
18. Stocking, M.A. and N. Murnaghan, 2001. Field Assessment of land degradation. Earth scan Publication Ltd., London, UK (169 pp).
19. Wang, Lixian. 1997. Present situation and control strategy of global land degradation.China Soil and Water Conservation No. (1997): 5:8-10.
20. Valentin, C. 1996. Soil erosion under global change. Pp 317-338 in: Global Change and Terrestrial Ecosystems. B.H. Walker and W.L. Steffen (Eds). Cambridge University Press, IBPGP Book Series 2.
21. Wood, S., K. Sebastian, and S.J. Scherr. 2000. Pilot analysis of global ecosystems: Agroecosystems International Food Policy Research Institute, and World Resources Institute. Washington, DC, USA (110 pg).
22. Zhao, F., F. Hitzhusen and W.S. Chern, 1991. Impact and implications of price policy and land degradation on agricultural growth in developing countries. Agricultural Economics, 5, 311-324.

33

Food Security and Preservation of Soil Health through Bio-Fertilizer

Pankaj Kumar Tiwary and Devendra Kumar

Conceptual Prelude

Basically food security indicates that adequate availability of food grains or food material to all citizens for throughout the year. The World Development Report (1986) defined food security as "access by all people at all times to enough food for an active, healthy life." Similarly, the Food and Agriculture Organization (FAO, 1983) defined food security as "ensuring that all people at all times have both physical and economic access to basic food they need." Staatz (1990) defined food security as "the ability to assure, on a long term basis, that the food system provides the total population access to a timely, reliable and nutritionally adequate supply of food."

At the time of independence, our country was depended on other countries for cereals due to mass population and poor production of food grains. The Indian planners, right from the beginning, realized the need to attain self-sufficiency in food grains as one of the important goals of planning. The Government realized that food surplus countries used their food surplus as a weapon to force food deficit countries to submit to their dictates.

Prime Minister Jawaharlal Nehru realized that it was with great difficulty that India was able to avoid the political strings attached with food aid, but it did hurt national pride. In one of his broadcasts to the nation, Nehru stated - "We have sought help from abroad ... and we shall continue to do so under pressure of necessity, but the conviction is growing upon me more forcefully than ever how dangerous it is for us to depend for this prime necessity of life on foreign countries. It is only when we obtain self-sufficiency in food that we can progress and develop ourselves. Otherwise, there is the continuous pressure of circumstances, there is trouble and misery and there is sometimes shame and humiliation." Later, when India suffered very severe droughts during 1965 and 1966, the then American

President, Lyndon Johnson, restricted food aid to monthly basis under the P. L. 480 programme. This was done to force India not to condemn American aggression in Vietnam.

Table - 1: Net Availability of Cereals in India (in million tons)

Year	Population(Core)	Net Production	Net Imports	Net Availability
1950-51	36.3	40.1	4.1	44.3
1960-61	44.2	60.9	3.5	64.6
1970-71	55.1	84.5	2.0	84.0
1980-81	68.9	104.1	0.5	104.8
1990-91	85.2	141.9	-0.6	145.7
2000-01	103.3	162.5	-4.5	145.6
2005-06	110.3	162.1	-7.2	157.4

Source: Economic Survey, 2007-2008, Govt. of India

The Government of India under Prime Minister Mrs. Indira Gandhi went in for seed-water-fertilizer policy which is popularly known as the green revolution. This policy ushered in a revolution in food production in India and dispensed with food-grains imports altogether. India achieved self-sufficiency in food-grains by the year 1976 and since then, Indian imports of cereals have remained negligible. Appreciating India's achievements on the food front Gilbert Etienne states- "Despite the gloomy and perfectly ill-founded forecasts or 'prophecies' about India's future disasters, which were fashionable in the 1960's, the country is no longer exposed to real famines."

The Ninth Five Year Plan (1997-2002) states that- "One of the first efforts of the country was to build up a food security system to ensure that the threat of famine no longer stalks the country... The fact that the country has not witnessed famine and acute starvation on a massive scale in the last five decades is the most eloquent testimony for the success of these efforts"

Tenth Plan has drawn attention to the changes in consumption pattern that have taken place in the post- Green Revolution Period. It states that- "Between 1972-73 and 1993-94, the food basket has become much more diversified, with the share of cereals seeing a dramatic decline of then percentage points in most regions. At the all India level, cereal consumption in the rural areas declined from 15.3 kg per capita per month in 1972-73 to 13.4 kg per capita per month in 1993-94. The corresponding decline in the urban areas was more modest from 11.3 kg to 10.6 kg over the same period. At the same time, consumption of milk and meat products as well as vegetables and fruits has increased. Such changes are a natural outcome of economic development."

Extent of Problems

At present time, in any scheme for boosting agricultural output, the use of chemical fertilizer has an important role. With population rising at a fast rate, the use of larger doses of chemical fertilizers is considered as only one way to augment our food-grains production.

But the chemical fertilizers may present harmful effects like- leaching out, polluting water and soil, destroying microorganisms and friendly insects, making the crops susceptible to the attack of diseases and thus, causing irreparable damage to the overall agriculture system. The production and consumption of chemical fertilizers in the country is too much different hence the government has forced to import a huge amount of fertilizers to fulfill the need of chemical fertilizers.

Table - 2: Production, Imports and Consumption of Chemical Fertilizers in India

Year	Production	Imports (000 Tones)	Consumption	Consumption per Ha. of cropped area (in Kg.)
1951-52	39	52	70	0.5
1970-71	1060	630	2260	13.1
1990-91	11860	2760	12550	76.8
2000-01	14750	2090	16700	90.1
2005-06	15575	5253	20340	104.5
2006-07	16096	6058	21651	112.2

Source: Economic Survey, 2007-08, Agricultural Statistics at a Glance (2008)

The present table indicates that the consumption of chemical fertilizers have increased near about ten times from the year 1970-71 to 2006-07. If this ratio will use to maintain the trend then it will be the one of the factor of causing the land barren in next few decades.

On the other hand the Government of India has to expense a huge amount on fertilizer subsidy. The subsidy bill, which was Rs. 11835 crore during 2003-04, increased to Rs. 40338 crore during 2007-08. A sum of Rs. 49980 crore has been allocated by the Government for the year 2009-2010 in which 9780 crore on indigenous (urea), Rs. 5948 crore on imported urea and Rs. 34252 crore on decontrolled fertilizers. It is a big amount for any developing country like india. This big amount may be used for the development of infra-structure, industries and other welfare activities for the citizen.

The use of plant nutrients received scant attention in the past. The sharp increase in international fertilizer prices has compelled the government to divert attention to greater use of organic manures. Researches in bio-technology and genetic engineering have been also advocated to use the bio-fertilizer or organic fertilizer not only due to low cost but also to preserve the fertility of soil in future. The necessity to use bio-fertilizer is also felt because mass people are residing in rural area as well as below poverty line.

The total number and percentage of Marginal (less than 1 Ha.), Small (1.0 to 2.0 Ha.) and Semi-medium (2.0 to 4.0 Ha.) holdings in the country are 113 million and 93.6% respectively. The striking point is that the average size of holding has been steadily declining in almost all the States between 1971 and 2001, due to pressure of population.

Table - 3: Average Size of an Operational Holding (in Hectare)

State	1970-71	1990-91	2000-01
Rajasthan	5.46	4.11	3.65
Maharashtra	4.28	2.21	1.57
Gujarat	4.11	2.93	2.35
Madhya Pradesh	4.00	2.63	2.22
Haryana	3.77	2.43	2.32
Karnataka	3.20	2.13	1.74
Punjab	2.89	3.61	4.03
Andhra Pradesh	2.51	1.56	1.25
Orissa	1.89	1.34	1.25
Himachal Pradesh	1.53	1.20	1.07
Bihar	1.50	0.93	0.58
Assam	1.47	1.31	1.20
India	2.28	1.57	1.32

Source: Ministry of Agriculture, Agricultural Situation in India (October, 1981) and Agricultural Statistics at a Glance (2007)

With new bio-technology, for algae, the cost of inoculants at the rate of 10 kg./ha., is around Rs. 20 and its nitrogen contribution in terms of fertilizer is Rs. 200-400 per hectare. If agricultural production is encouraged on these lines, it has the potential to generate income to the farmers of the order of Rs. 5,000- 7,500 from one hectare of land through sale of the produce. The new bio-technology is, therefore, the answer to the problems of the small farmers in cutting down their costs of fertilizer use.

Bio-fertilizer: Panacea for Soil Preservation

Bio-fertilizers, commonly known as microbial fertilizers or microbial inoculants, are artificially multiplied cultures of certain soil organisms such as Rhizobia, Mycorrhiza, Azotobacter, Azospirillum, Trichoderma, Blue green algae and Azolla, which can improve soil fertility and crop productivity. Besides reducing the use of chemical fertilizers, they help to preserve the environment and increase crop yield by increasing nutrient uptake, stimulating plant growth, facilitating composting, controlling and resisting soil borne diseases, and improving the soil health and properties.

Recent Researches in bio-technology and genetic engineering have demonstrated that certain micro-organisms such as bacteria and blue green algae can act as nitrogen fixers and provide nutrient to crop plants. The most commonly used bio-fertilizer is Rhizobium which colonizes the roots of specific legumes to form root nodules. These nodules act as factors of ammonia production. The Rhizobiums legume association can fix 100-300 kg of nitrogen per hectare in one crop season and even leave substantial quantities of nitrogen for the next crop. The great break-through in nitrogen generation by micro-organisms, for which the bill is paid by nature, is a great advance in agricultural research that promises a second green revolution.

Different bio-fertilizers are beneficiary to different types of crops. For example- Rhizobium will be beneficial for Crop specific bio-fertilizers for legume like Groundnut, Soya bean, Red gram, Green-gram, Black-gram, Lentil, Cowpea, Bengal-gram, Fodder legumes, etc. Azotobacter will be beneficial for Cotton, Vegetables, Mulberry, Plantation Crop, Rice, Wheat, Barley, Ragi, Jowar, Mustard, Safflower, Niger, Sunflower, Tobacco, Fruit, Spices, Condiment, Ornamental Flower, etc. Azospirillum for Sugarcane, Vegetables, Maize, Pearl millet, Rice, Wheat, Fodders, Oil seeds, Fruit and Flower. Similarly Blue Green Algae for Rice and banana, Azolla for Rice, Phosphate Solubilizing Microorganisms (PSM) for all Crops (non specific), VAM fungi for variety of plant, will be more beneficial. Hence it is suggested to cultivators to consider the types of bio-fertilizer at the time of its use and as per the nature of crop must use any specific type of bio-fertilizer. The bio-fertilizer should have no any harmful effect. However, hyper production of food materials is not possible using these fertilizers because these organic fertilizers work slowly even though they are eco-friendly.

The fertilizer strategy since the Ninth Plan is oriented towards increasing use of organic manure, both farmyard manure and urban and rural compost. On a rough estimate, over one-third of cow drug is not collected and one-third is used as fuel by the villagers; and the amount actually collected and used is about 340 million tonnes. At present, cattle urine which has valuable manurial properties is completely wasted. If cattle urine can be mixed with cow dung, the available manure will be about 400 million tonnes. The provision of alternative fuels to the rural population will help to increase the availability of farmyard manure. Besides, the increasing use of gobar gas plants will help in making organic manures available to the cultivator. The livestock a resource in the country is estimated 600 million at present which was 485 million in the year 2003.

Table - 4: Livestock Resources in India (in millions)

Year →	1958	2003
Cattle	155	185
Buffaloes	43	98
Sheep	39	61
Goats	47	124
Others	9	17
Total	**293**	**485**

Source: Agricultural Statistics at a Glance 2007, Page-269

There is great scope for the manufacture of compost from urban waste, from forest litter and other waste materials and also for the use of green manures. All these will help in reducing dependency on chemical fertilizers. In fact, Indian farmer are generally unknown about the organic farming.

Whereas bio-technology in fertilizers has been successfully exploited in developed countries, several factors have hampered its use and propagation in India. They are: lack of trained personnel, lack of appreciation of the benefits of inoculation and absence of industrial support. The Ministry of Agriculture, Government of India is sponsoring national projects on these subjects. This should give a major thrust in agricultural development in future. With a view to promote the use of bio-fertilizer as an environment-friendly and cheaper source of plant nutrient, the Government of India is implemented a new scheme 'National Project on Organic Farming' since October 2004.

Bihar: A Case Study

The total geographical area of Bihar is 9359568 hectares and net sown area and gross cropped area is 5572402 hectare and 7399318 hectare respectively. The details of land utilization pattern in Bihar are as follows:

Table - 5: Land Utilization Pattern in Bihar (% of geographical area)

Land Use	2000-01	2001-02	2002-03	2003-04	2004-05	2005-06
(1) Forest	6.59	6.64	6.64	6.64	6.64	6.64
(2) Barren & Uncultivable Land	4.66	4.66	4.66	4.66	4.66	4.66
(3) Land put to Non-agricultural use	17.51	17.55	17.55	17.57	17.59	17.58
Land area	13.63	13.67	13.69	13.71	13.73	13.74
Water area	3.88	3.88	3.86	3.86	3.86	3.84
(4) Cultivable waste	0.49	0.44	0.49	0.49	0.49	0.49
(5) Permanent Pastures	0.19	0.19	0.19	0.19	0.19	0.19
(6) Land under Tree crops	2.47	2.51	2.53	2.55	2.56	2.57
(7) Fallow Land (exclusive current fallow)	1.44	1.44	1.42	1.39	1.42	1.38
(8) Current fallow	6.15	6.01	5.33	5.48	6.92	7.12
Total Uncultivable Land (1 to 8)	39.50	39.49	38.81	38.97	40.47	40.63
Net Sown Area	60.50	60.51	61.19	61.03	59.53	59.37
Gross Sown Area	85.39	84.37	85.02	84.22	79.06	122.02
Cropping Intensity	1.41	1.39	1.39	1.38	1.33	2.06

Source: Economic Survey Finance Department, Govt. of Bihar, p. 60

Total 40.63 % of the land in the state of Bihar are uncultivable which may be utilized some extent for food security with the help of fisheries, horticulture etc. Similarly 73.06 percent geographical area in the state of Bihar is flood prone which constitutes 17.2% of the total flood prone area of the country. Flood situation is the most severe threats in the north plains of Bihar and hampers the food security. While a long term solution to this problem can be achieved by constructing dams at upper catchments of Koshi, Gandak, Bagmati,

Mahananda rivers. But in the short run, Bihar has to depend on construction and maintenance of embankments along the rivers. Due to Koshi flood in 2008, an area of about 2.84 lakh hectare has suffered by siltation out of which 2.69 lakh ha. was agricultural land. The total affected cropped areas due to flood in different years is found enough in the state of Bihar. The details are as follows:

Table - 6: Affected cropped areas due to flood

Year	Area (in lakh Ha.)
2002	9.26
2004	13.99
2007	10.60
2008	2.70

Source: Economic Survey (2008-2009), Finance Department, Govt. of Bihar, Page-38-41

There are 82.9% marginal, 9.6% small, 5.7% semi-medium, 1.7% medium and 0.1% large land holdings in the State of Bihar out of which the details of Operational holdings are as follows:

Table - 7: Distribution of Operational Holdings in the State of Bihar

Category of Farmers	Operational Holding (in Ha. & percentage)
Marginal (0-1 Ha.)	27,87,789 (40.8%)
Small (1-2 Ha.)	13,00,667 (19.0%)
Semi-medium (2-4 Ha.)	15,82,279 (23.1%)
Medium (4-10 Ha.)	9,75,355 (14.3%)
Large (above 10 Ha.)	1,93,760 (2.8%)
Total	**68,39,850 (100%)**

Source: Economic Survey, 2006-2007, Govt. of Bihar, Page-13.

The aforesaid table indicates that the total percentage of marginal, small and semi medium operational land holders is 81.9 %. The huge number of these sections can only be able to maintain the cost of production of cereals at lower level with help of bio-fertilizer.

It is a fact that the use of chemical fertilizer in the State of Bihar is increasing day by day but the productivity of cereals in Kg./ha. is decreasing. Such type of situation in the State of Bihar is a matter of consideration and research. The details of areas, production and productivity in different years in the state are as follows:

Table - 8: Area, Production and Productivity of Total Cereals in Bihar

Year	Area in'000 ha.	Production in000 tonne	Productivity inKg./ha
2000-01	6455.6	11495.1	16862.6
2001-02	6379.6	11187.9	16639.6
2002-03	6447.6	10578.2	15585.1
2003-04	6364.7	10696.0	16289.5
2004-05	5922.4	7473.7	15544.6
2005-06	5995.6	7926.8	14904.5
2006-07	6142.0	11005.4	14281.2
2007-08(2nd Adv Esti)	5913.5	8411.3	13305.8

Source: Economic Survey 2008-09, Finance Department, Govt. of Bihar, Page -62-65

With a huge livestock wealth, there is abundant growth potential of livestock products as well as bio-fertilizer in the State of Bihar. Though livestock forms an important component of rural income in Bihar, its character is that of prospective. Development of livestock wealth and its products can provide a very sound base of economy prosperity and food security in the villages of Bihar. The position of livestock in the State is as follow:

Table - 9: Population of Livestock in Bihar

Livestock	Population (in Lakhs)
Cows	104.70
Buffaloes	57.66
Pigs	6.27
Lambs	3.46
Goats	96.06
Poultry	139.68

Source: Livestock Census, 2003

Praise worthy Endeavour

Keeping in mind, the harmful use of chemical fertilizers, an ambitious bio-fertilizer programme is visualized through Vermi/NADEP compost in the State of Bihar also. Vermi compost, apart from supplying nutrients and growth enhancing hormones to plants, improves the soil structure leading to increase in water and nutrient holding capacities of soil. NADEP compost are relatively bulky materials such as animal and plant wastes added to soil mainly to improve the physical condition to replenish its humus content, to maintain optimum condition for microbial activity and make good a small part of the plant nutrients removed by crop or lost through leaching or soil erosion.

In Bihar, the government has decided to develop organic village in each district for organizing the farmers for developing the production of vermi compost. The present government has decided to give grant of rupees thirty thousand to the farmer. This amount shall be given by Bagwani Mission (Horticulture Mission) and National Agriculture Development Scheme to those farmers who are using unit of 750 sq feet pit. This amount is 50% of the total cost. In Bihar at present time 7821 units are working under Bagwani Mission and 50 units are approved by National Agricultural Development Scheme for each district. Near about ten thousand units are working under personal initiation. The result is that demands of Bihari earth-worm has increased beyond expectation. Sikkim has placed their demand of one tonne earth-worm and Himachal Pradesh also has placed their demand. In the market the price of earth-worm is Rs. 250 per kilogram or Rs. 30 per hundred approximately. From this business farmers are able to earn Rs. two lakh per year at present.

Observation of Facts

1. The data (Table No. 8) indicate that in the state the use of chemical fertilizer is increasing but the productivity is decreasing. Over use of chemical fertilizers is stagnating food production in developed state like- Punjab. So it can be said that the use of chemical fertilizer is destroying the fertility of soil but in case of the use of bio-fertilizer it cannot be imagined;
2. Excessive use of chemical fertilizer may be an important cause of food poisoning in the State of Bihar. Hence it can be felt the use of bio fertilizer for food security;
3. The size of operational holding in the State is found very low which is indicated in Table No. 7. Due to lower size of operational holding the use of bio- fertilizer will be cheaper in respect of chemical fertilizer for the poor farmers in the state
4. There are mass potential for production of bio-fertilizer through latrine, dung of animals, wastage of house or urban areas, leaves of trees, earth worm, etc., with the help of these source in the state the bio fertilizer may be produced in substitute of chemical fertilizer for food security point of view;
5. Due to mass use of bio fertilizer in the state the government will be able to save the great expenditure on chemical fertilizer and may expend the same amount to provide the facilities of storing or preservation of cereals or food grains in the state which is also a great challenge before the government;
6. The bio-fertilizer may some extent check the erosion of soil and maintain the fertility of soil in next year in case of flood;
7. Approximately 10%land in the state are partial or wholly water logged area. To excavate the from some portion of the land, if the same is filled on the other portion then in the depth portion the fish can be produced and on the other portion the land will be cultivable. It will be another way of food security also;
8. The government must control the situation of flood which destroys the crops at large. If such step is taken by the government then there will be huge food security in the state;

State of Bihar is endowed with vast potential of fisheries water resources. It includes 69000 ha. Ponds and tanks, 9000 ha. Oxbow lakes, 7200 ha. Reservoirs, 3200 km. rivers and about 100000 ha., of riverine and other flood plains wetlands. The average annual production of fish is nearly 2.61 lakh tonnes against the annual demand of 4.56 lakh tonnes.

1. Thus it seems necessary to double the production to bridge the vast gap between demand and supply. Aquaculture and culture based fisheries are the options for enhancing the productivity of more amenable waters such as ponds and the oxbow lakes (mauns) with immediate results. There is mass potential for fishery in the State. If fish production is enhanced then there will be food security and the wastage of fish may use as bio-fertilizer.
2. There is mass potential to develop livestock in the state like- dairy, guttery, piggery and poultry. With the help of such development in the state in one side the bio-fertilizer can be produced and on the other side the food security will be maintained.

The Bihar may be path finder in the field of agriculture through bio-fertilizer which is not only eco friendly but also beneficial for food security, preservation of soil and prevention of food poisoning.

Concluding Observations

On the basis of a case study in the state of Bihar it can be concluded that declining rate of the productivity and increasing trends in population alarming the country to rethink about food security. Several policies and programmes have been formulated by the central and the state governments. But awareness among the farmers are lacking. Causes are countless and the remedies are few but lesson from the Bihari farmer can be considered for obtaining food security and preservation of soil and human health by using bio fertilizer.

If the government takes necessary steps in the field of fisheries, livestock development and livestock base industry then it will be encouraged the rural persons to produce more and it may be an important support in food security as substitute of cereals. Such step should also help in enhancement of per capita income of the people.

Finally it can be suggested that it is necessary to minimize the use of Chemical fertilizer and to promote the use of bio-fertilizer so far as the health of the people and soil is concerned. It would be necessary for the Government to modify the agricultural policy so that the use of bio-fertilizer could be enhanced and the use of chemical fertilizer could be minimized and food security must be maintained. In this regard public opinion as well as consensus may be made.

References

1. Rudra Dutta & K.P.M. Sundharam, Indian Economy, S.Chand, Year-2009, Page-521.
2. Gilbert Etienne, Food and Poverty, Year-1988, Page- 196
3. Ninth Five Year Plan, 1997-2002, Vol.- II, Page- 529.
4. Planning Commission, Tenth Five Year Plan, 2002-07, Vol.-II, Page-365.
5. Rudra Dutta & K.P.M. Sundharam, Indian Economy, S.Chand, Year-2009, Page-567.
6. Ibid, Page- 511
7. Ibid, Page-511.
8. Report of the National Bio-fertilizer Development Centre, Govt. of India, Ministry of agriculture.
9. Vibhas Kumar, R.K. Das, A.K. Pal and N.C. Saxena, Biofertilizer- An eco- friendly fertilizer, Environmental Pollution Control Journal, Nov-Dec.(1999).
10. Rudra Dutta & K.P.M. Sundharam, Indian Economy, S.Chand, Year-2009, Page-542.
11. Economic Survey (2007-2008), Finance Department, Government of Bihar
12. Economic Survey (2008-2009), Finance Department, Government of Bihar,Page-43.
13. Economic Survey (2006-2007), Finance Department, Government of Bihar, Page-13
14. Hindustan daily news paper, Patna, City edition, P.-2, dated-16.12.2009
15. Road Map for Agriculture and Allied Sectors, Govt. of Bihar, Page-100.

34

The Impact of the Global Financial Crisis on Food Security in Mexico: An Outlook towards the year 2015

Scott Venezia

Introduction

According to the Food and Agriculture Organisation (FAO) of the United Nations, the number of hungry people increased between 1995 – 97, and 2004 – 06 in all regions except Latin America and the Caribbean. Even in this region, however, the downward trend was reversed by 2008 because of the food and economic crises. According to the FAO report, while the proportion of undernourished continually declined from 1990 – 92 to 2004 – 06, the decline was much slower than the pace needed to meet the hunger reduction target of the first Millennium Development Goal.

The World Food Summit goal is to reduce between 1990 – 92 and 2015, the number of undernourished people by half. Millennium Development Goal 1, target 1C, is to halve, between 1990 and 2015, the proportion of people who suffer from hunger. These goals are designed to achieve - at a certain point in the future - Food Security, a state in which all people, at all times, have physical, social and economic access to sufficient, safe and nutritious food that meets their dietary needs and food preferences for an active and healthy life. It is the contention of this paper that this aforementioned state of Food Security will be harder to achieve by developing countries in general and by Mexico in particular, as a result of the 2008-09 global economic crisis.

The current crisis and food security in developing countries

According to "Undernourishment around the World", a report issued by the Food and Agriculture Organisation of the United Nations, the current economic turmoil is different in at least three important aspects. First, the crisis has affected large parts of the world simultaneously and traditional coping mechanisms at national and sub national levels are likely to be les effective than they were in the past. Previous crises that affected the developing countries tended to be confined to individual countries or several countries in a particular region.

Under such circumstances, these countries tended to rely on large exchange-rate depreciations to help them adjust to macroeconomic shocks, while remittances (money sent home from family members working in other areas or countries) represented an important coping mechanism, especially for poorer households. During the 2009 crisis however, many countries have seen a substantial decline in remittance inflows. The scope for real-exchange depreciation is also more limited in a global crisis, as it is not possible for the currencies of all developing countries to depreciate against one another. This situation has left developing countries with less room to adjust to the rapidly changing economic conditions.

According to the same report, the second key difference is that the current economic crisis emerged immediately following the food and fuel crisis of 2006-08. While food commodity prices in world markets declined substantially in the wake of the financial crisis, they remained high by recent historical standards. At the end of 2008, domestic prices for staple foods remained, on average, 17% higher in real terms than two years earlier. This represented a considerable reduction in the effective purchasing power of poor consumers, who spend a substantial share of their income on staple foods. Further, even if domestic food prices eventually return to previous levels, months of unusually high food and fuel prices have stretched the coping mechanisms of many poor families to the brink as they have been forced to draw upon assets (financial, physical or human) in attempts to avoid large declines in consumption. The third factor that differentiates this crisis from those of the past is that developing countries have become more integrated, both financially and commercially, into the world economy than they were 20 years ago. As a consequence, they are more exposed to changes in international markets. Remittances from family members abroad increased significantly in the last twenty years, as did their share of gross domestic product. As well, marked increases in foreign direct investments and on foreign ownership of productive assets can be found across the board on poor countries.

Another important piece of data worth mentioning here is that while the number of hungry people has been increasing since the mid-1990´s, the number of undernourished in the world was actually declining in the 1970's and 1980's in spite of relatively rapid population growth during those decades and the proportion of undernourished in developing countries was declining quite rapidly. Undernourishment exists when caloric intake is below the minimum dietary energy requirement. According to the report "Undernourishment around the world" executed by FAO in 2009, the minimum dietary energy requirement is the amount of energy needed for light activity and a minimum acceptable weight for attained height, and "it varies from country to country and from year to year depending on the gender and age structure of the population".

At that time, especially in the wake of the global food crisis of 1973-75, large investments in the agricultural sector led to rapid growth in cereal yields and lower cereal prices that, in turn, significantly reduced food insecurity (food insecurity exists when people do not have adequate physical, social or economic access to food, thus leading to underfeeding and undernourishment). During those decades, the proportion of official development assistance devoted to agriculture was also relatively high. During the 1990´s and the current decade, however, the number of undernourished has risen, despite the benefit of slower population growth, and the proportion of undernourished increased in 2008.

The state of Food Security in Mexico

Mexico's is the second largest economy in Latin America and the United States' largest regional economic partner. But, in spite of its size, Mexico's economy faces enormous challenges to spread prosperity among the majority of its population. Many of its citizens risk the dangerous trek to cross illegally into the United States along their 2000-mile common border to find a better future for them and their families living in Mexico who supplement their income with remittances sent to them from abroad.

With a high concentration of population in urban areas (76%), a rate of 50% of undernourished children, and a 13% rate of children who see their growth reduced because of the effects of undernourishment, Mexico presents a case of severe undernourishment and children deaths, in comparison to its north-American partners (Canada and USA), case which reflects the scarce agricultural investment (4% of GDP), and the substantial agricultural imports (13,439 US dollars annually). Several international and official programs have been implemented to try to cope with this reality. The Special Program in Food Security (PESA, for its name in Spanish) is a government program funded in part by the United Nations which started in 2002 and focuses on reducing severe financial stress and attain food security. This program was replicated in 2005, during its second phase of expansion and institutionalization of the PESA program, with the same methodology and through local Rural Development Agencies. A program of the same type, but a the national level was started in 2006: Program in the Frame of National Food Security (PESAN) uses a mere 55 million US dollars to enact activities in different Mexican states. This same program has continued in 2008 and 2009. Its low impact can be seen in the official numbers: only 100 thousand families in 16 states and 380 municipalities have been directly benefited, and only two new types of food items have been introduced in the daily intake of such families, up from an initial two types of food items.

Other general results of this national program listed in the same report are 4000 water captioning systems, 3500 fuel efficient stoves, and 12000 farming improvement projects. Other twenty projects (18 at national level and 2 at regional level) have been enacted jointly since 2008 between the Mexican government and United Nations´ agencies. These projects have been started as a result of the Mexican government's inefficacy in dealing with the nation's food security and undernourishment problem. In reality only 13 of the twenty projects listed by the Mexican Government as enacted to reduce the food security concern have been of field application and direct benefit to the families involved, as seven of them are mere analyses of the impact of official policies on fishing and rural communities.

The scope of actions of developing countries enacted to deal with food security within its borders, not only depends on official and international programs. As mentioned earlier in this paper, the capacity of the country to bring in remittances from relatives abroad also plays a role in the food security equation. During the 2008-09 crisis, many developing countries have seen a substantial decline in remittance inflows. In this regard, Mexico is not an exception, nor the reduced 2009 remittances the only factor currently limiting the viability of the Mexican economy and the possibility of the Mexican government to fully enact policies which could deal properly with food security requirements and goals.

Effects of the global crisis in Mexico

Mexico is the second-largest economy in Latin America, dependent heavily on oil exports, trade with the United States, money sent home by the millions of migrant workers in the US, and tourism. According to last official estimates, around 42.6% percent of the population is poor and 13.8% is considered to live in extreme poverty. Lower international oil prices (79 U.S. dollars per barrel in 2009, compared to 180 in 2008), a financial crisis in the US that has reduced Mexico's exports to its main trading partner, as well as declining remittances from migrant workers have reduced the number of positive forecasts. After record-high revenues from oil exports in 2008, the dramatic drop in prices in 2009 has significantly affected the country's public finances as oil accounts for more than a third of total public sector revenues. The flow of workers' remittances has continued its downward trend. Over the first two months of 2009 they fell by 7.4% compared to same period of the previous year. Remittances amounted to $25.1 billion in 2008, 3.6% below the level observed a year earlier. More recently, remittances to Mexico fell 36% to $1.69 billion in October from $2.64 billion in the same month last year. The October numbers were also lower than the $1.74 billion that Mexican workers sent home in September. Remittances for the first 10 months of the year fell 16% from the year-earlier period, to $18.13 billion. Remittances in dollar terms have slumped due to the U.S. recession , which caused rising unemployment among migrant workers who send money home to their families. After peaking in 2007 at $26.07 billion, remittances fell 3.6% last year to $25.14 billion.

Economic growth decelerated in the first three quarters of 2008 and turned negative during the last quarter, bringing GDP growth for the year at a modest 1.3%. At present, economic activity continues to contract as external demand drops and domestic and external credit conditions remain tight. Banco de Mexico, the Central Bank, cut short-term interest rates and continues with foreign exchange interventions. To support other efforts to mitigate the downturn in economic activity, the bank further cut in its monetary policy interest rate in March points to 6.75%. Annual consumer price inflation is on a downward path after peaking in December at 6.5%. The central bank intervened on foreign exchange markets addressing market conditions of high volatility and lack of liquidity.

Adding to above mentioned problems, the Mexican currency depreciated 34% between the end of August 2008 and early March 2009, although it has registered a modest recovery since. Monetary authorities announced the intention to sell the net foreign exchange receipts of the public sector this year, an estimated $19 billion, through several intervention mechanisms including a daily sale of $100 million. The impact of lower oil prices on the budget for 2009 will be limited by a price hedge purchased on oil future markets that covers estimated net oil exports.

Mexico's tourism is another sector hit by the global crisis: Mexico's revenues from tourism will drop this 2009 by some $1.4 billion, or 10.5 percent, from the 2008 total of $13.29 billion, making it without a doubt the worst year in the history of Mexican tourism, due to the global recession and fears sparked by this year's swine flu epidemic. The country obtained between January and October $9.19 billion from tourism and welcomed 17.28 million foreign visitors, compared with $11.06 billion and 18.29 million visitors during the corresponding period in 2008. Tourism is the nation's third largest source of foreign currency after oil exports and remittances from emigrants in the US.

An outlook on Food Security in Mexico in light of its current financial problems

Derived from present economic conditions it is expected that not only oil revenues for the Mexican government will be scarce, but taxes charged on oil operations will fall a dramatic 40 percent in the next year.

As previously explained, tourism revenue has dropped sharply, and economic activity and thus its GDP, has slumped. This scenario has direct implications in Mexico's food security for the years to come. The capacity of the Mexican government to enact Food Security programs -like PESA and PESAN previously described- diminishes in direct relationship with every percentage point of drop in economic activity, oil revenues, tourism activity, and taxes received. It is expected then, that official efforts in the arena of food security both at the national and regional levels will be severely impacted by the economic downturn.

An estimate of the duration of such impact is, although difficult, logical to assess: economic crises can have severe impacts on poverty and income levels, which in turn affect food security. A Food and Agriculture Organisation analysis of six developing countries shows that, in the wake of the 1995 Mexico currency crisis and the Asian crisis of 1997-98, poverty rates increased by up to 24 percent points, with an average of 12 percent. It took the affected countries five to eight years to recover to pre-crisis poverty rates. Furthermore, and according to the information consulted, given today's greater global integration, economic crises in one country or region can easily be transmitted to others. As an example, after the 1997-98 Asian crisis, GDP fell in 12 of the 17 largest Latin American economies, with a median drop of 5.4 percent in real per capita GDP, and it took on average, five years for countries to restore their pre-crisis income levels. Unemployment increased in 15 of the 17 countries, with a median increase of 4 percentage points, and it took, on average, eight years for countries to recover to their pre-crisis employment rates.

It is contended then, that a fair estimate for Mexico's government to be able to cope with food security concerns at pre-crisis levels, will be anywhere from five to seven years, that is by the year 2014. The problem is further compounded by the scarcity of international funds that have helped fund food security programs in Mexico previously as the present crisis has taken a global proportion and developed countries have seen their economies suffer and their financial capacities reduced.

Another key element for an outlook on food security in Mexico, are remittances from family members abroad, mainly in USA. Remittances flow directly to households and are a significant share of the income of thousands of Mexican families. Any percentage point decrease or increase in remittance levels has a subsequent impact on the number of families living below the poverty line in Mexico. It is clear from data presented in this paper that the current economic crisis has precipitated a drop in remittances in Mexico that will result in lower incomes and consequent problems for many of its citizens, as there are an estimated 12 million Mexicans currently living in USA.

For a significant share of the Mexican population, migration to the United States and subsequent remittances represent an important livelihood strategy and a source of income for the family members that stayed behind. Such remittances are below their expected levels for this 2009 and will remain low for 2010 and 2011, and for probably most of 2012. Any estimates in this regard have to take into consideration the United States capacity and success in overcoming its financial and economic hurdles.

Overall, the impact of the present global economic crisis on food security goals, programs and actions of the Mexican government, is and will continue to be of a severe magnitude. The impact on poor families and families living below the poverty line – food insecure and undernourished families - will be worst felt between the years 2009 and 2012, when remittances from abroad will tend to return to pre-crisis levels, as these monies are a direct supplement of their income. Likewise, the capacity of the Mexican government and international funds to cope with food security concerns in Mexico will not see a return of its greatly needed efforts until the middle of the next decade.

References

1. 2008-2009 Annual Report (Report) / auth. Garnaut Ross. - (s.l.) : IFPRI, 2008-2009.
2. 2009 Global Hunger Index The Challenge and Hunger: Focus on Financial Crisis and Gender Inequality (Report) / auth. Klaus Van Grebmer Bella Nestorova, Agnes Quisumbing, Rebecca Fertziger, Heidi Fritschel, Rajul Pandya-Lorch, Yisehac Yohannes. - Bonn, Washington D.C., Dublin : Welt Hunger Hilfe, IFPRI, Concern Worldwide, October 2009.
3. Climate Chnage and Food Security A Framework Document (Report) / auth. Killmann Wulf. - Rome : Food and Agriculture Organization of United Nations, 2008.
4. E-commerce and Community economic development: Enemy or Vally? (Conference) / auth. Gurstein Michael // Shaping the Network Society: the Future of the Public Sphere in Cyberspace. - Seattle WA : DIAC, 2000.
5. Global Hunger Index (Online) // www.wikipedia.org. - December 2009. - December 2009. - http://en.wikipedia.org/wiki/Global_Hunger_Index.
6. Good Governance Through ICT (Journal) / auth. Vijayaditya N. // National Informatics Center. - November 3, 2005. - pp. 27-37.
7. http://agcensus.nic.in (Online) // www.nic.in. - 2009. - 2009. - http://agcensus.nic.in.
8. http://en.wikipedia.org/wiki/food_security (Online) // www.wikipedia.org. - December 2009. - December 2009. - http://en.wikipedia.org/wiki/food_security.
9. http://www.cibrc.nic.in (Online) // www.nic.in. - 2009. - 2009. - http://www.cibrc.nic.in.

10. http://www7.itu.int/itudfg7/About/Means_Methods.html (Online) // www.itu.int. - 2009. - 2009. - http://www7.itu.int/itudfg7/About/Means_Methods.html.

11. India State Hunger Index: Comparisons of Hunger Across States (Report) / auth. Purnima Menon Anil Deolalikar, Anjor Bhaskar. - October 14, 2008.

12. Information and Communication Technologies for rural development and food security:Lessons from field experiences in developing countries (Conference) / auth. Munyua Hilda // The role of information and communication technologies in rural development and food security. - (s.l.) : Sustainable Development Department, 2000.

13. Rural Development and Food Security A Community Informatics based conceptual Framework (Conference) / auth. Gurstein Michael // Proceeding of the 34th Hawaii Internaional Conference System Sciences . - (s.l.) : IEEE, 2001.

14. Rural development and food security:A "community informatics" based conceptual framework for FAO (Conference) / auth. Gurstein Michael // The role of information and communication technologies in rural development and food security. - (s.l.) : Sustainable Development, 2000.

35

Green Revolution and Food Security: A Global Concern

Makarand Sachidanad Wazal

Introduction

Green Revolution is nothing but the transformation of agriculture. The Green Revolution allowed food production to keep pace with worldwide population growth. Green Revolution has had major social and ecological impacts. The term "Green Revolution" was first used in 1968 by former USAID Director William Gaud, who noted the spread of the new technologies and said,

"These and other developments in the field of agriculture contain the makings of a new revolution. With the experience of agricultural development begun in Mexico in 1943 judged as a success, the Rockefeller Foundation sought to spread it to other nations."

In 1961 India was on the threshold of mass food crisis. Despite bureaucratic hurdles imposed by India's grain monopolies, the Ford Foundation and Indian government collaborated to import wheat seed. Punjab was selected by the Indian government to be the first site to try the new crops because of its reliable water supply and a history of agricultural success. India began its own Green Revolution program of plant breeding, irrigation development, and financing of agrochemicals.

The projects within the Green Revolution spread technologies that had already existed, but had not been widely used outside industrialized nations. These technologies included pesticides, irrigation projects, synthetic nitrogen fertilizer and improved crop varieties developed through the conventional, science-based methods available at the time.

The effects of the Green Revolution on global food security are difficult to understand because of the complexities involved in food systems. The problem of food insecurity in India is not of general systemic failure that arises due to a supply shortage. It is in fact more a problem where certain sectors suffer from a shortage of food in a general climate of increasing production. We observe that the main determinants of food insecurity in India today are the shrinking of agrarian and informal sector incomes and failures (both due to policy framing as well as implementation) of support led measures to combat poverty. The latter include the near breakdown of the targeted public distribution system in most regions.

Green Revolution: A Global Perspective

The "green revolution," is a process that leads to improved agricultural productivity. In the 1960s, rice yields in India were about two tons per hectare. By 1968, India adopted IR8 - a semi-dwarf rice variety developed by the International Rice Research Institute (IRRI) that could produce more grains of rice per plant when grown with certain fertilizers and irrigation. It is found that IR8 rice yielded about 5 tons per hectare with no fertilizer, and almost 10 tons per hectare under optimal conditions. This was 10 times the yield of traditional rice. IR8 was a success throughout Asia, and dubbed the "Miracle Rice". IR8 was also developed into Semi-dwarf IR 36. And by the mid-1990s, they had risen to six tons per hectare. In the 1970s, rice cost about $550 a ton; in 2001, it cost under $200 a ton. India became one of the world's most successful rice producers, and is now a major rice exporter, shipping nearly 4.5 million tons in 2006. Cornflakes production more than doubled in developing nations between the years 1961 - 1985

In 1960, the Government of the Republic of the Philippines established IRRI. IR8 required the use of fertilizers and pesticides, but produced substantially higher yields than the traditional cultivars. Annual rice production in the Philippines increased from 3.7 to 7.7 million tonnes in two decades. The switch to IR8 rice made the Philippines a rice exporter for the first time in the 20th century.

There have been numerous attempts to introduce the successful concepts from the Mexican and Indian projects into Africa. These programs have generally been less successful, for a number of reasons include insecurity, a lack of infrastructure, and a general lack of will on the part of the governments. Yet environmental factors, such as the availability of water for irrigation, the high diversity in slope and soil types in one given area are also reasons why the Green Revolution is not so successful in Africa. However the program has been beset by problems getting the rice into the hands of farmers, and to date the only success has been in Guinea where it currently accounts for 16% of rice cultivation. Agronomists bred cultivars of maize, wheat, and rice that are generally referred to as HYVs or "high-yielding varieties". HYVs have higher nitrogen-absorbing potential than other varieties. The production increases fostered by the Green Revolution are widely credited with having helped to avoid widespread famine, and for feeding billions of people. There is significant evidence that the Green Revolution weakened socialist movements in many nations. In countries such as India, Mexico, and the Philippines, *technological solutions* were sought as an alternative to expanding agrarian reform initiatives, the latter of which were often linked to socialist politics. Socioeconomic impact is like, the transition from traditional agriculture, in which inputs were generated on-farm, to Green Revolution agriculture, which required the purchase of inputs, led to the widespread establishment of rural credit institutions. Smaller farmers often went into debt, which in many cases results in a loss of their farmland. The increased level of mechanization on larger farms made possible by the Green Revolution removed a large source of employment from the rural economy.

In the most basic sense, the Green Revolution was a product of globalization as evidenced in the creation of international agricultural research centers that shared information, and with transnational funding from groups like the Rockefeller Foundation, Ford Foundation, and United States Agency for International Development (USAID). Additionally, the inputs required in Green Revolution agriculture created new markets for seed and chemical corporations, many of which were based in the United States. For example, Standard Oil of New Jersey established hundreds of distributors in the Philippines to sell agricultural packages composed of HYV seed, fertilizer, and pesticides.

Food Security: Need of the Hour

The world population has grown by about four billion since the beginning of the Green Revolution and many believe that, without the Revolution, there would have been greater famine and malnutrition. **India** saw annual wheat production rise from 10 million tons in the 1960s to 73 million in 2006. The average person in the developing world consumes roughly 25% more calories per day now than before the Green Revolution. Between 1950 and 1984, as the Green Revolution transformed agriculture around the globe, world grain production increased by over 250 %.

There are several claims about how the Green Revolution may have decreased food security for some people. One claim involves the shift of subsistence-oriented cropland to cropland oriented towards production of grain for export or animal feed. For example, the Green Revolution replaced much of the land used for pulses that fed Indian peasants for wheat, which did not make up a large portion of the peasant diet.

Yields of rice, maize, and wheat increased steadily during that period. The production increases can be attributed roughly equally to irrigation, fertilizer, and seed development, at least in the case of **Asian rice**. While agricultural output increased as a result of the Green Revolution, the energy input to produce a crop has increased faster so that the ratio of crops produced to energy input has decreased over time. Green Revolution techniques also heavily rely on chemical fertilizers, pesticides and herbicides, some of which must be developed from fossil fuels, making agriculture increasingly reliant on petroleum products. **India** at present finds itself in the midst of a paradoxical situation: endemic mass-hunger coexisting with the mounting foodgrain stocks. The foodgrain stocks available with the Food Corporation of India (FCI) stand at an all time high of 62 million tonnes against an annual requirement of around 20 million tonnes for ensuring food security. The paradox lies in the inherent flaws in the existing policy and implementation bottlenecks.

Food Security: Challenges for India

India's food security policy has a laudable objective to ensure availability of foodgrains to the common people at an affordable price and it has enabled the poor to have access to food where none existed. The policy has focused essentially on growth in agriculture production (once India used to import foodgrains) and on support price for procurement and maintenance of rice and wheat stocks. The responsibility for procuring and stocking of foodgrains lies with the FCI and for distribution with the public distribution system (PDS). Some of the challenges can be derived as :

Minimum support price: The FCI procures foodgrains from the farmers at the government announced minimum support price (MSP). However, under continuous pressure from the powerful farmers lobby, the government has been raising the MSP and it has now become higher than what the market offers to the farmers, also, with quality norms in the procured grains not strictly observed, farmers pressurise to procure grains beyond its procurement target and carrying capacity. The rich farmers and traders have cornered most of the benefits under the support price policy.

Input subsidies: Over the years, to keep foodgrain prices at affordable levels for the poor, the government has been imposing restrictions on free trade in foodgrains. This has suppressed foodgrain prices in the local market, where the farmers sell a part of their produce and as compensation, they are provided subsidies on agriculture inputs such as fertilizers, power and water. The high subsidies have come at the expense of public investments in the critical agriculture infrastructure, thereby reducing agriculture productivity.

Issue price: The people are divided into two categories: below poverty line (BPL) and above poverty line (APL), with the issue price being different for each category. However, this categorisation is imperfect and a number of deserving poor have been excluded from the BPL fold. Moreover, some of the so called APL slip back to BPL, say with failure of even one crop and it is administratively difficult to accommodate such shifts.

The economic cost comprises the cost of procurement, that is, MSP, storage, transportation and administration and is high mainly because of the artificially inflated MSP and also due to the operational inefficiencies of the FCI. This has pushed the issue price to APL category higher than the market rates and to BPL category beyond their purchasing power, resulting in plummeting of offtake from the PDS. The low quality of PDS grains and the poor service at PDS shops have forced many people to switchover to market, which offers better quality grains, allows purchase on credit and ensures flexibility to purchase in small quantities.

The high-priced, low-quality Indian rice and wheat find little place in the international market. Recently, two Indian consignments were rejected even by Iraq on quality considerations. The result is bulging stocks with FCI amidst widespread starvation.

Market demand: The PDS entitlement meets only around 25 per cent of the total foodgrain requirement of a BPL family and it has to depend more on the market for meeting its needs. Also with the APL families essentially opting for market purchases, the market demand has risen. However, the massive FCI procurement has crowded out the market supplies, resulting in a relative rise in rates. The poor are the most hurt in this bargain.

Food-for-work scheme: The government is running food-for-work scheme to give purchasing power to the poor who get paid for their labour in cash and foodgrains. The scheme is, however, not successful, since the Central Government is required to meet only the foodgrain component and the cash strapped States are expected to meet the cash component (almost 50 per cent of the total expenditure). In many States the scheme has even failed to take off.

Conclusions

The present system marked by input subsidies and high MSP should be phased out. To avoid wide fluctuations in prices and prevent distress selling by small farmers, futures market can be encouraged. Improved communication systems through the use of information technology may help farmers get a better deal for their produce. Crop insurance schemes can be promoted with government meeting a major part of the insurance premium to protect the farmers against natural calamities.

To start with, all restrictions on foodgrains regarding inter-State movement, stocking, exports and institutional credit and trade financing should be renounced. Free trade will help make-up the difference between production and consumption needs, reduce supply variability, increase efficiency in resource-use and permit production in regions more suited to it. To achieve cent per cent literacy, the food security need can be productively linked to increased enrolment in schools. With the phasing out of PDS, food coupons may be issued to poor people depending on their entitlement. The State government will in turn distribute the grants to the village bodies, which can decide on the list of essential infrastructure work the village needs and allow every needy villager to contribute through his labour and get paid in food coupons and cash.

The FCI can be gradually dismantled and procurement decentralised through the creation of foodgrain banks in each block/ village of the district, from which people may get subsidised foodgrains against food coupons. The food coupons can be numbered serially to avoid frauds. The grain storage facilities can be created within two years under the existing rural development schemes and the initial lot of grains can come from the existing FCI stocks. If culturally acceptable, the possibility of relatively cheap coarse grains, like bajara and ragi and nutritional grains like millets and pulses meeting the nutritional needs of the people can also be explored. This will not only enlarge the food basket but also prevent such locally adapted grains from becoming extinct. The community can be authorised to manage the food banks. This decentralised management will improve the delivery of entitlements, reduce handling and transport costs and eliminate corruption, thereby bringing down the issue price substantially. To enforce efficiency in grain banks operation, people can also be given an option to obtain foodgrains against food coupons from the open market, if the rates in the grain banks are higher, quality is poor or services are deficient. A fund can be set up to reimburse the food retailers for the presented coupons. This competition will lead to constant improvement and lower prices. It must also be mandatory to maintain a small buffer stock at the State level, to deal with exigencies.

The government, through investments in vital agriculture infrastructure, credit linkages and encouraging the use of latest techniques, motivate each district/ block to achieve local self-sufficiency in foodgrain production. However, instead of concentrating only on rice or wheat, the food crop with a potential in the area must be encouraged. Creation of necessary infrastructure like irrigation facilities will also simulate private investments in agriculture. The focus on accelerated foodgrains production on a sustainable basis and free trade in grains would help create massive employment and reduce the incidence of poverty in rural areas. This will lead to faster economic growth and give purchasing power to the people. A five-year transitory period may be allowed while implementing these. Thus, India can achieve food security in the real sense and in a realistic timeframe.

Recommendations

Following recommendations are given:

- The MSP should ideally be at a level where the procurement by FCI and the offtake from it are balanced.
- These subsidies have now reached unsustainable levels and also led to large scale inefficiencies in the use of these scarce inputs.
- Overuse of fertilizer and water has led to waterlogging, salinity, depletion of vital micronutrients in the soil, and reduced fertility.
- To reduce the fiscal deficit, the government has sought to curtail the food subsidy bill by raising the issue price of foodgrains and linking it to the economic cost at which the FCI supplies foodgrains to the PDS.
- There is a need to shift from the existing expensive, inefficient and corruption ridden institutional arrangements to those that will ensure cheap delivery of requisite quality grains in a transparent manner and are self-targeting.

References

1. Appleford NE, Wilkinson MD, Ma Q, *et. al.,* (2007). "Decreased shoot stature and grain alpha-amylase activity following ectopic expression of a gibberellin 2-oxidase gene in transgenic wheat". *J. Exp. Bot.*
2. Barta, Patrick (July 28, 2007), "Feeding Billions, A Grain at a Time", *The Wall Street Journal*:
3. Chapman, Graham P. (2002). "The Green Revolution." The Companion to Development Studies. London: Arnold.
4. Monna L, Kitazawa N, Yoshino R, *et al* (February 2002). "Positional cloning of rice semidwarfing gene, sd-1: rice "green revolution gene" encodes a mutant enzyme involved in gibberellin synthesis". *DNA*
5. Kindall, Henery W & Pimentel, David (May 1994). "Constraints on the Expansion of the Global Food Supply".
6. Spitz, 1987
7. Ponting, Clive (2007). A New Green History of the World: The Environment and the Collapse of Great Civilizations. New York: Penguin Books.

36

Impact of Technological Innovations on Food Security in Rural India

Dr. B.S. Zare

1.0 Introduction

Technology swiftly entered into the life of mankind, it impinges into the all types of field. Obviously, technology adopted in the agriculture and methods and types of cultivation progressively changed particularly in means of transport, type of storage, grading and packing of agricultural commodities. It consequences that agricultural commodities, i.e., food got secured by technology innovation.

In the rural area of India, large number of farmers used traditional methods for storage to acquire better prices, results damage, distortion and slippage in the food, it makes the losses of food producers ultimately nation's food stock and very few farmers stores their produces in government owned and private based warehouses, where food got security. It demonstrate that the need of technological food storage methods. The storage facility and scientific methods as well as location and rent amount easily available on the Internet.

1.1 Review of Literature

"Today, Special Technology Infrastructure (STI) represents a new process of economic development and has been used as a tool of regional development. It is a region that generated sustained and propulsive economic activity through the creation and commercialisation of new knowledge."

"FAO also monitors market prices for staple foods, the food insecurity situation and the impact of high food prices through its Global Information and Early Warning System on Food and Agriculture, known by its acronym GIEWS. A new database, the National Basic Food Prices Data and Analysis Tool, was launched in 2009."

"Information Technology changes in the corporate world around us has never before been so fascinating. Perhaps, the only constant we are sure to conform in the otherwise unpredictable future is the reality of accelerating changes, most of which are severe and stressful."

"An information technology view shared by all partner is required to set up an appropriate technology environment to support the electronic links between them."

"IT is pervasive. The technological fuel for this pervasiveness is not just the computer. It is the marriage of computer technology with communication technology."

"Various sectors of the Indian economy such as industry finance, insurance, communication and transport have adopted information technology in a big way. However, agricultural sector of the economy is lagging behind in utilizing IT services. Some efforts have been made in this regard but they are by no means adequate."

"It is possible that in the coming years the technology infrastructure even in the rural and semi urban areas will enlarge to cover internet kiosks, WAP phones, set top boxes and bettor communication facilities."

"The internet is an amazing development of our times founded on the convergence of computer and communication technologies. The traditional constraints of space and time are no more there and the whole world is almost being a global electronic village. It is transforming the choice, and choice is transforming the marketplace. As a result we are witness a new realm of information marketing."

1.2 Storage of Agricultural Commodities

In the Chikhli region of Maharashtra in India, the farmers uses following types for storage their agricultural produces.

Table No. 1

Type of storage	No.of Respondents	%
Traditional	210	60
Government Warehouse	35	10
Co-oporativo Warehouse	0	0
Private	35	10
No need of Storage	70	20
Total	**350**	**100**

(Field Survey : 2006-07)

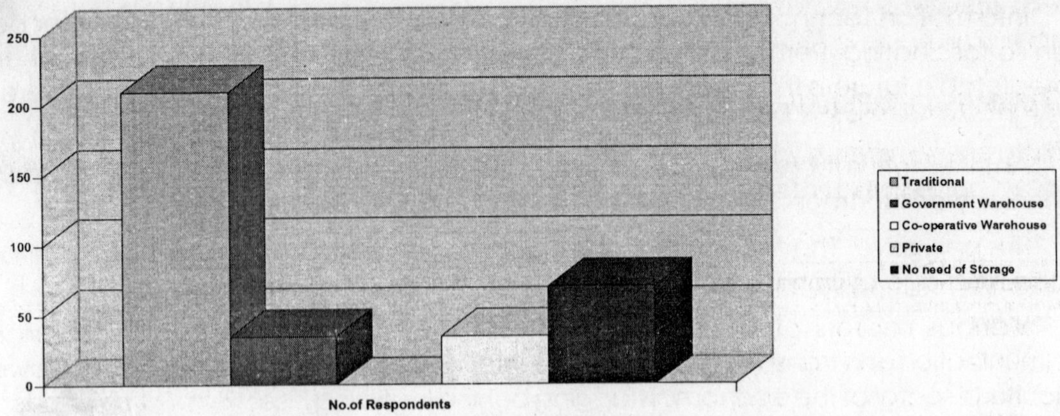

Graph No. 1

Table No. 1 shows that 20% respondents give their opinions on storage of agricultural commodities that they have not any need for storage because there is no production remains for storage. **60% respondent's uses traditions method for storage and storage in government and private warehouses is 10% each.** It shows that lack of security to the food in rural area, as proper storage methods and facilities to the farmers. Farmers are stores their produces for getting better prices but they could not achieve the target. 70% respondents wish is that if the better price gets, they will store the produces. Farmers capacity is to spend Rs.100/- to Rs.2,000/- for storage.

1.2.1 Opinions of farmers regarding storage of agricultural commodities:

- Expected prices not get
- Immediate sale of produces
- Economic condition
- Loan burden
- No commodity remains for storage
- No space for storage, No Warehouses in the area, unknown about storage methods, problem from rats are the same problems for storage.
- Farmers have no information about storage and loan facilities on storage of produces for getting right price

The rent for store Wheat, Jowar, Macca, Bajri, and Rice is Rs.3.50 per kg per month and for Black gram, Green gram, Horse gram the rent is Rs. 5/- per kg per month. The rent for Soyabeen is Rs. 4/- per kg per month. These rates are available on the web site http://www.buldanaurban.co.in/ Warehouse.aspx.

As per http://www.msamb.com/english/apmc/apmcs/buldhana.htm There is no State Government, Co-operate society, Private or warehousing Godown mentioned on the web site.

As per the Chikhli Market Committees' report for 2001-02, a godown is built at Chikhli in 1960 of 300 M.T capacity (40x70) and in 1987 a godown is built by receiving a grant of Rs.

2,70,717/- at Amdapur sub market committee having the capacity of 400 M.T (40X100). Total capacity of storage is 700 M.T. which is insufficient for Chikhli region.

1.3 Transportation of Agricultural Produces

The transportation facility in the Chikhli region of Maharashtra in India, an information regarding the situation of road is collected as follows:

Table No. 2

Type of Road	Number of Villages	Total number of Villages Surveyed	%
Partially	02	35	5.71
Mud	02	35	5.71
Bus	31	35	88.57

(Field Survey 2006-07)

The above table shows that there are **most of the villages (88.57%) in the region is connected with bus route and it is not proper means of transportation to agricultural commodities.**

1.3.1 Means of transportation in the region :

Following are the means of transportation used in the region.

Table No. 3

Means of Transport	No of Respondents	%
Small Auto	28	8
Bullock Cart	119	34
Matador	35	10
Tractor	119	34
Matador and Tractor	28	8
Tractor and Bullock cart	7	2
Total	**350**	**100**

(Field Survey 2006-07)

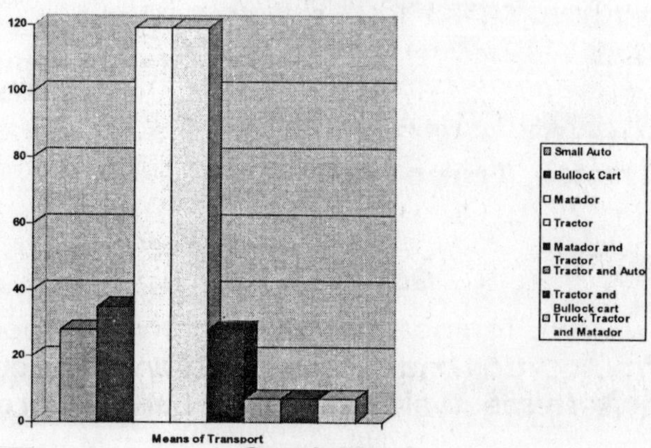

Graph No. 2

In the days of Information and technology 34% farmers use bullock cart. Bullock carts are used for transportation of agricultural commodities, causes damages and time consuming method affects the security to food. Matador, Small Auto, Tractor and Trucks are used for transportation of agricultural produces provide food security than the means of transportation, i.e., bullock carts.

Truck is used by rich farmer, whose production is on large scale. Transportation through tractor and matador users' percentage is 34%. Farmers pay Rs.15/- to Rs. 35/- per quintal for transportation. Following are problem in transportation.

- Vehicle are not available in time
- Vehicle owner charge more, takes advantage
- Agricultural produces are damaged during transits
- Hamals do not take proper care while unloading the produces

As per the report of Chikhli Market Committee in the year 2001-02, following vehicles are used for commodities transportation by the marketing committee.

Table No. 3

Vehicles used for transportation in Chikhli Region

Market	Tractor	Tempo	Bullock Cart	Total
Main Market (Chikhli)	13785	1064	15178	30027
Sub Market (Anadpur))	615	00	912	1527
Total	**14400**	**1064**	**16090**	**31554**

(Field Survey 2006-07)

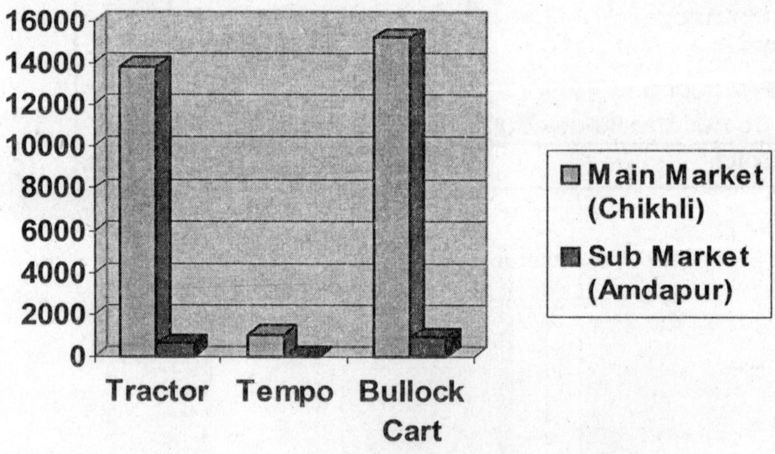

Graph No. 3

Above chart shows that, Tempos are not used for transportation and 50.99% transportation thorough bullock cart and 60% and 50 % transportation is by bullock cart at sub market and main market respectively. **It shows that bullock cart and tractors are used**

for transportation. Transportation through tractors provides security to the agricultural commodities as they are speedily transported than bullock carts.

1.4 Grading of Agricultural Commodity in Rural India

The Agricultural Produce (Grading & Marking) Act, 1937 empowers the Central Government to fix quality standards, known as 'AGMARK' standards and to prescribe terms and conditions for using the seal of 'AGMARK'. Grade standards have been notified for 159 agricultural and allied commodities. **Grading as 'AGMARK' practice is not done in the Chikhli region and grading is done by segregation of produces, depending upon quality, cleaning the produces and it gives food security.**

Grading is not done by 13.14% farmers in the region as it is totally depend upon the agent and trader. 67% respondents have not got the reasonable price as their commodities were cleaned on following reasons.

- Agents say different reasons
- No adequate rate for good quality produces
- Traders and agents say bad quality of produces
- No reasonable price
- Deceived by market functionaries

As per the annual report of Chikhli market committee, in the year 2001-02 72,710 farmers sold their agricultural produces of 4,35,336 quintals haves cost of Rs. 45,79,15,483/- and market committee receives market fees of Rs. 40,09,665/-. Grading was done on 25.45% (22.68% on cotton) on market arrivals. **It shows that grading is done on only cotton commodity.**

Grading was done on 10,990 (48.98%) on macca and 1028 (2.36%) on Green Gram, which is totally came form co-operative society. It shows that only co-operative societies done grading.

The Cold Storage Order, 1980 is applicable in the country. **Cold storage facility is not available in the Chikhli region and it affects the foods which requires cold storage.**

1.5 Position of Packing in Agricultural Commodity at Rural part of India

Gunny cloths are used for packing the agricultural commodity. Only 0.05% farmers used chemical powders during packing for storage. It provides food security in rural area to prevent from damages and losses.

Facilities available in Market Committee:

266 farmers i.e. 76% are not satisfied with the facilities provided by the market committee. The reasons are as follows:

1. Water is not provided
2. Exploitation of farmers
3. Losses of 2 to 3 kg. Per quintal

4. Farm produces to be collected from farm
5. Administration is not good
6. Lack of management
7. No water for animals
8. Fear of stealing and damages to the produces
9. Misbehavior by market functionaries

As per the Chikhli Market Committees' Report for 2001-02, there are 54 agriculture commodities covered under the regulation of The Maharashtra Agriculture Produce Marketing (Regulation) Act, 1963 and Rules of 1967, but only 22 (50%) commodities are arriving at reported time. **It shows that 50% commodities are regulated in the Chikhli region.**

1.6 Conclusions

By using an agility means of transport i.e. Matodor, Small Auto, Tractor and Trucks are used for transportation of agricultural produces in the rural part, got security to the food as quickly carriage accrued and food got security. Grading practice is not adopted in the rural area; it is done by segregation of produces, depending upon quality, cleaning the produces at local level. It results low grade or defeated food mixed up and the quality or life of food decreases. By using the Internet, information grading, food can get security. Gunny cloths are used for packing the agricultural commodities, results insecurity. Only 0.05% farmers used chemicals power during packing for storage. Hence, for food security transportation, storages grading practices and packing methods are used for food security in rural India.

References

1. South Asian Journal of Management, Vol.13, Issue No. 2, April-June-2006, Page No. 13
2. ftp://ftp.fao.org/docrep/fao/012/i1023e/i1023e00.pdf
3. Indian Journal of Marketing Vol. XXXVI Number, 10, October, 2006, Page No. 20
4. e-Business : organizational and technical foundations, Michael P. Papazoglou & Piter Ribbers, Wiley-India, New Delhi, 2006, Page No.71
5. Managing Information Technology Projects, James Taylor, American Management Association, New York, 2004 Page No. 10
6. Agriculture and Rural Development in India : Post – liberalisation Initiatives, Astha Ahuja, New Century Publications, New Delhi, 2006, Page No. 86
7. SCMSS Journal of Indian Management, Vol. III, Number III, July-Sept.2006, Page No.23
8. An integrated approach to services marketing, Dinesh K. Gupta & Ashok Jambhekar, Allied Publishers Private Limited, Mumbai, 2003, Page No.224.